Constructing America's Freedom Agenda for the Middle East

'Skillfully navigating ideologically infested waters, Hassan arrives at valuable insights and persuasive, dispassionate conclusions about US policy under both Bush and Obama relating to Arab political change. A fine example of rigorous, reflective scholarship applied to current policy issues of considerable importance and controversy.'

Thomas Carothers, Carnegie Endowment for International Peace

This book explores how George W. Bush's Freedom Agenda for the Middle East and North Africa was conceived and implemented as an American national interest, from the Bush era right through to the initial stages of the Obama administration. It highlights how the crisis presented by September 11, 2001, led to regime change in Afghanistan and Iraq, but more broadly how the American policy towards the region had a softer imperial side, which drew on broader economic theories of democratisation and modernisation. The Freedom Agenda contained within it a prescribed method of combating terrorism, but also a method of engaging with and reforming the entire Middle East region more broadly, with many institutions seeking to use the opportunity to implement neoliberal market logics in the region. *Constructing America's Freedom Agenda for the Middle East* highlights the particular understanding of 'freedom' that underpins America's imperial project in the region; a project trapped between a policy of democratisation and domination. This book analyses the Freedom Agenda in significantly more depth than in available current literature and will be of interest to students and researchers of global politics and international foreign policy of recent years.

Oz Hassan is an Assistant Professor in US National Security at the University of Warwick, UK.

Routledge studies in US foreign policy

Edited by: *Inderjeet Parmar, University of Manchester and John Dumbrell, University of Durham*

This new series sets out to publish high quality works by leading and emerging scholars critically engaging with US Foreign Policy. The series welcomes a variety of approaches to the subject and draws on scholarship from international relations, security studies, international political economy, foreign policy analysis and contemporary international history.

Subjects covered include the role of administrations and institutions, the media, think tanks, ideologues and intellectuals, elites, transnational corporations, public opinion and pressure groups in shaping foreign policy, US relations with individual nations, with global regions and with global institutions, and America's evolving strategic and military policies.

The series aims to provide a range of books – from individual research monographs and edited collections to textbooks and supplemental reading for scholars, researchers, policy analysts and students.

United States Foreign Policy and National Identity in the 21st Century
Edited by Kenneth Christie

New Directions in US Foreign Policy
Edited by Inderjeet Parmar, Linda B. Miller and Mark Ledwidge

America's 'Special Relationships'
Foreign and domestic aspects of the politics of alliance
Edited by John Dumbrell and Axel R Schäfer

US Foreign Policy in Context
National ideology from the founders to the Bush Doctrine
Adam Quinn

The United States and NATO since 9/11
The transatlantic alliance renewed
Ellen Hallams

Soft Power and US Foreign Policy
Theoretical, historical and contemporary perspectives
Edited by Inderjeet Parmar and Michael Cox

The US Public and American Foreign Policy
Edited by Andrew Johnstone and Helen Laville

American Foreign Policy and Postwar Reconstruction
Comparing Japan and Iraq
Jeff Bridoux

Neoconservatism and American Foreign Policy
A critical analysis
Danny Cooper

US Policy towards Cuba
Since the Cold War
Jessica F. Gibbs

Constructing US Foreign Policy
The curious case of Cuba
David Bernell

Race and US Foreign Policy
The African-American foreign affairs network
Mark Ledwidge

Gender Ideologies and Military Labor Markets in the U. S.
Saskia Stachowitsch

Prevention, Pre-Emption and the Nuclear Option
From Bush to Obama
Aiden Warren

Corporate Power and Globalization in US Foreign Policy
Edited by Ronald W. Cox

West Africa and the US War on Terror
Edited by George Klay Kieh and Kelechi Kalu

Constructing America's Freedom Agenda for the Middle East
Democracy and domination
Oz Hassan

Constructing America's Freedom Agenda for the Middle East

Democracy and domination

Oz Hassan

LONDON AND NEW YORK

First published 2013
by Routledge
2 Park Square, Milton Park, Abingdon, Oxfordshire OX14 4RN

Simultaneously published in the USA and Canada
by Routledge
711 Third Avenue, New York, NY 10017

First issued in paperback 2014

Routledge is an imprint of the Taylor & Francis Group, an informa business

© 2013 Oz Hassan

The right of Oz Hassan to be identified as author of this work has been asserted by him in accordance with the Copyright, Designs and Patent Act 1988.

All rights reserved. No part of this book may be reprinted or reproduced or utilised in any form or by any electronic, mechanical, or other means, now known or hereafter invented, including photocopying and recording, or in any information storage or retrieval system, without permission in writing from the publishers.

Trademark notice: Product or corporate names may be trademarks or registered trademarks, and are used only for identification and explanation without intent to infringe.

British Library Cataloguing in Publication Data
A catalogue record for this book is available from the British Library

Library of Congress Cataloging in Publication Data
Hassan, Oz.
Constructing America's freedom agenda for the Middle East : democracy and domination / Oz Hassan.
p. cm. — (Routledge studies in US foreign policy)
Includes bibliographical references and index.
ISBN 978-0-415-60310-2 (hbk.) — ISBN 978-0-203-10254-1 (ebk.) 1. United States—Foreign relations—Middle East. 2. Middle East—Foreign relations—United States. 3. United States—Foreign relations—2001– 4. Democratization—Government policy—United States. 5. National interest—United States—History—21st century. I. Title.
DS63.2.U5H38 2012
327.73056—dc23
2012006269

ISBN 978-0-415-60310-2 (hbk)
ISBN 978-1-138-81128-7 (pbk)
ISBN 978-0-203-10254-1 (ebk)

Typeset in Times New Roman
by Prepress Projects Ltd, Perth, UK

This work is dedicated to the people whom I met fighting for their freedom in Tahrir Square and throughout the Middle East. Their resistance showed courage and character that is an inspiration to all who believe in freedom and democracy around the world.

Contents

Acknowledgements		x
Abbreviations		xii
	Introduction	1
1	American interests and a history of promoting the status quo	11
2	A constructivist institutionalist methodology	31
3	From candidate to crisis	56
4	September to December 2001	82
5	Constructing the Freedom Agenda for the Middle East	104
6	Institutionalising the Freedom Agenda	126
7	Obama's Freedom Agenda	157
	Conclusion	181
Notes		186
Selected bibliography		195
Index		225

Acknowledgements

I started at university just weeks after the events of September 11, 2001, and spent much of much of my time there contemplating what these events meant and how I could understand them, as I watched two wars from the comfort of my television set. It was not until people I knew, serving in the UK forces, were reported killed in action that the effects of September 11, 2001, had an authentic impact on my life. Yet, subsequently, the events of September 11, 2001, have come to permeate features of my everyday life in a very real and concrete way, whether it is disproportionately 'random' searches at airports, being made to go though 'secondary processing' whilst the people I am travelling with are waved through, having to wait a lot longer than others for visas or facing racist slurs on the public transport system. In effect the research that this volume presents is not merely an academic exercise, but rather my attempt to understand how, in my formative years, the world has changed and why it has done so in a particular manner.

As you can imagine, on such a journey one accrues a lot of people who touch one's life. This has certainly been the case with the journey undertaken to complete this research, which has been enriched by both personal and professional relationships I have forged along the way. These people have supported me when I was ill, helped me stand after falls, and encouraged my enthusiasm for learning. They have shared words of wisdom, support and friendship and for this I owe them all my eternal gratitude. First and foremost I must thank my family. To my parents, Meyrem and Mustafa Hassan: without your support and the lessons you taught me growing up this would not have been possible. I would also like to extend a special mention to my brothers and sister, who are my best friends and provide lively debate and a competitive spirit, which has seen me through my darkest hours: Erol, Altan, Ali, Perihan and Isa – thank you. And a special mention to Clare Fairchild, who has endured reading this research on countless occasions; you are one in a billion.

I also owe many friends boundless thanks for everything they have done over the years, but would like to make a special mention of those who have become more like an extended family. In particular Michael Lister and Andrew Futter; I cannot think of any better people to share wine, whiskey, off-colour jokes and card games with. To all of you, thanks for enduring sleepless nights with the Beatles on loop, the consistent supply of winnings, and being there when I needed your sage-like advice and boundless generosity. You have taught me the meaning of friendship and bring meaning to 'With a Little Help from my Friends'.

At the University of Warwick, a special mention goes to Stuart Croft, without whom this book would never have been written. Your advice has been invaluable, and even the occasional interrogation about why I think Gadamer is important in IR whilst waiting for a 05.00 a.m. flight is greatly appreciated. Moreover, to George Christou, my partner in crime, thank you for all the support. To my other colleagues, I cannot imagine a better bunch of people to work with in my early career. Your willingness to share ideas, tolerate my jokes and toast over a lusty golden brew is appreciated; for enriching this journey I thank you.

I would also like to thank Inderjeet Parmar and John Dumbrell for allowing me to contribute to the USFP series, and to Nicola Parkin at Routledge for being so patient with this development of this book. I would also like to thank all of the people in Washington DC, Egypt and Morocco who gave up their time to talk to me. Moreover, I would like to thank the ESRC and the European Commission (FP7) for funding much of the research. And last but certainly not least, to the *John W. Kluge Center* at the Library of Congress. You have been kind hosts on multiple occasions, and supported this research in so may ways there is not enough space to list them. I have the fondest memories of my time there and would like to thank Mary Lou Reker and Carolyn T. Brown for making me so welcome. I only hope that you can see the rewards of that labour in this research.

I hope I have done you all proud.

Abbreviations

ABM	Anti-Ballistic Missile
ACDP	Advisory Committee on Democracy Promotion
ADA	ADVANCE Democracy Act
BIT	bilateral investment treaty
BMD	Ballistic Missile Defense
BMENA	Broader Middle East and North Africa Initiative
CAQDAS	computer-assisted qualitative data analysis
DLO	Democracy Liaison Office
DOS	United States Department of State
DRL	US Department of State Bureau of Democracy, Human Rights and Labor
ESF	Economic Support Funds
FIS	Islamic Salvation Front
FLN	Front de Liberation Nationale
FPA	Foreign Policy Analysis
FSFME	Forward Strategy of Freedom in the Middle East
FTA	free trade agreement
FY	fiscal year
GMEI	Greater Middle East Initiative
GSP	Generalised System of Preferences
Hamas	Harakat al-Muqawama al-Islamiya
IDF	ideological-discursive formation
INC	Iraqi National Congress
IR	International Relations
JSP	Joint Strategic Plan
MEFTA	Middle East Free Trade Area
MENA	Middle East and North Africa
MEPI	Middle East Partnership Initiative
NDS	National Defense Strategy
NEA	Bureau of Near East Affairs
NED	National Endowment for Democracy
NGO	non-governmental organisation
NSC	National Security Council

NSPD	National Security Presidential Directive
NSS	National Security Strategy
OEF	Operation Enduring Freedom
QDDR	Quadrennial Diplomacy and Development Review
TIFA	trade and investment framework agreement
UAE	United Arab Emirates
UN	United Nations
USAID	United States Agency for International Development
USTR	U.S. Trade Representative
WTO	World Trade Organization

Introduction

On December 17, 2010, Mohammed Bouazizi, a 26-year-old Tunisian, set himself alight with paint thinner outside the Sidi Bouzid regional council house. He died of his wounds nearly three weeks later on January 5, 2011. This self-immolation was a direct protest against the injustice of the Tunisian political system and a lack of economic opportunities. Indeed, Bouazizi was responding to being beaten and humiliated and having his property confiscated by Tunisian police officers for selling fruit and vegetables from a street stool without a licence. The following day hundreds of youths gathered in Sidi Bouzid to protest about the way Bouazizi had been treated, only to be met with police firing tear gas at the crowds. Further suicides followed, with Lahseen Naji electrocuting himself in despair at 'hunger and joblessness', and Ramzi Al-Abboudi killing himself because of the business debt accrued under the 'country's micro-credit solidarity programme' (Sadiki 2010; Andoni 2010). Throughout late December 2010, what started as an isolated incident had sparked the 'Sidi Bouzid Revolt', or so-called 'jasmine revolution', in which 'solidarity' uprisings rapidly began spreading throughout Tunisia.

By December 26, 2010, social protests against unemployment broke out in the capital Tunis. With state media limiting its coverage of events, protesters increasingly turned to both new methods of mobilisation, such as text messaging, Facebook, Twitter and BlackBerry Messenger, in combination with older institutions such as labour unions. President Zine al-Abidine Ben Ali's regime responded with increasingly violent strategies on the street combined with nighttime raids, leading to the detention of lawyers, journalists, students and bloggers. Yet, as popular pressure began to mount, the regime began to increasingly concede ground to the protesters, offering to create 300,000 jobs, reshuffling the cabinet, releasing many of the people who had been detained during the riots and creating a committee to investigate corruption, and on January 13, 2011, Ben Ali declared that he would not be standing for 're-election' in the presidential 'campaign' due in 2014. This, however, was all too little too late. President Ben Ali had begun to lose the support of the army that had brought him to power in 1987. By January 14, thousands took to the streets calling for the President's immediate resignation, leading to the Ben Ali family fleeing to Saudi Arabia, and Prime Minister Mohammed Ghannouchi becoming interim President.

The removal of President Ben Ali marked a significant turning point for the Middle East and North Africa (MENA). Within 28 days, popular protest had managed to end President Ben Ali's 23 years of power. The Tunisian people had succeeded in overthrowing their authoritarian regime and opened up a new realm of political possibility. Tunisian's had accomplished something that the 2006 'Arab Spring' and the 2009 Iranian 'green revolution' had failed to deliver. Tunisia had demonstrated to the world, and more specifically to the peoples of the wider MENA region, that change is possible and that autocrats can be overthrown through popular protest. Thus, the Sidi Bouzid revolt fundamentally altered the prevailing narratives about the MENA and inspired much wider revolts against autocratic regimes throughout the entire region.

In Egypt, January 25, 2011, became the 'Day of Rage', sparking anti-government demonstrations across the country, and Tahrir Square in Cairo became a central locale for youth movements to call for President Hosni Mubarak to leave. On January 27, the Mubarak regime blocked Facebook and Twitter, in an attempt to prevent the following day turning into a 'Friday of Anger'. This failed, and, as Tahrir Square was occupied by protestors, army tanks moved into the city and mobile phones and internet services were shut down. The police met protestors with violence, driving vehicles into crowds, throwing tear gas and firing shotguns filled with metal pellets at random. In return protestors began setting fire to buildings, targeting the police and defying the imposed curfew. February 2 turned into the 'Battle of the Camel', with Mubarak supporters storming Tahrir Square on camels and horseback, starting fierce street battles and intensifying the mêlée. Yet, in spite of this, hundreds of thousands of Egyptians continued to march to Tahrir Square and protests continued throughout the country. February 8 saw the largest demonstrations in Tahrir Square yet, as Egyptians responded to Wael Ghoneim's television appearance, following his release from nearly two weeks of interrogation by state security services. Ghoneim was a marketing manager at Google Middle East and North Africa, who set up a Facebook page called *We Are All Khaled Said*, in response to a the murder of a young man outside an internet café in Alexandria in June 2010. Khaled Said was beaten by police officers before being arrested and dying in custody. His brother took photos of his nearly unrecognisably disfigured corpse, which was then shown to the world as an example of the routine manner in which Mubarak's police violated human rights with impunity. By February 11, as protestors began marching towards the presidential palace in Heliopolis, a highly distinguished suburb of Cairo, Mubarak finally heeded to calls to step down.

Within 18 days, protests had ended nearly 30 years of Mubarak's autocratic rule, and six months later the former President, his sons, and seven other officials would have their trials televised. Within less than two months, two autocrats had been removed, and popular protests in Algeria, Bahrain, Iran, Iraq, Jordan, Kuwait, Lebanon, Morocco, Oman, Pakistan, Saudi Arabia, Syria and Yemen had broken out to greater and lesser degrees. In Libya a civil war against Colonel Gaddafi's regime was initiated, with the United Nations Security Council coming together to pass Resolution 1973 backing NATO intervention to secure a no-fly zone and protect civilians. Given such circumstances, it is clear that the MENA kaleidoscope was shaken and that the pieces placed in flux. Events throughout the end of 2010 and 2011 occurred at such a rapid pace that it remains far from certain where the pieces will eventually land, and what sort of geopolitical landscape will emerge in the MENA in the decades to come. Will the fall of autocratic regimes lead to turbulent transitions to democracy or simply the emergence of renewed autocratic rule? Needless to say, the 'crisis' introduced a considerable amount of uncertainty. Nonetheless, before anything resembling democracy can emerge, generations of transformatory consolidation work will need to be conducted throughout the region. This is perhaps the only certainty the revolutions in the MENA brought with them.

In spite of this uncertainty, however, 2011 also brought with it a considerable level of premature triumphalism from within the United States. Overlooking the uncertainty that these events have brought to the international system, former members of the George W. Bush administration attempted to seize the crisis, and imbue it with a very particular meaning: one that attempted to rescue the legacy of George W. Bush's so-called Freedom Agenda, and justify the history of American intervention in the region. On the day that President Mubarak stepped down, Paul Wolfowitz appeared on BBC *Newsnight*, asserting the triumph of the Freedom Agenda and comparing the events to the fall of the Berlin Wall. Wolfowitz argued that the Bush administration had played an important role 'leaning hard' on Mubarak and challenging the regime 'on the record'. The Fox news network equally attempted to highlight the role of the Freedom Agenda, with *Fox and Friends* asking Donald Rumsfeld 'Does the George W. Bush Freedom Agenda deserve credit for some of this change?' and ramping up the rhetoric of the Freedom Agenda being 'vindicated' (Kilmeade 2011; Wolfowitz 2011, February 11 and Wolfowitz 2011). Further still, Elliott Abrams, former national security adviser to President G. W. Bush, declared in *Foreign Policy* that 'it is neither perfect nor pretty, but the Arab Spring proves that neoconservatives were right all along' (Abrams 2012). This built on his earlier assertions that 'in the streets of Cairo, proof Bush was right . . . it turns out . . . that supporting freedom is the best policy of all' (Abrams 2011). Similarly, the George W. Bush Presidential Center in Texas held a conference, on May 23, 2011, entitled *The Wave of Freedom: The Early Lessons for the Middle East.* Condoleezza Rice once again argued that there are 'moral' and 'practical reasons for the United States to spread human freedom', and the former President G. W. Bush himself added that:

> I'm not surprised that freedom continues to march forward . . . I have read a lot of history in my sixty-four years. It's clear that it takes time for freedom to take root, so whilst these are exciting times these times also require a degree of patience . . . one of the dangers for the freedom movement around the world is that the United States grows weary, and becomes isolated from the inevitable march of freedom.
>
> (Bush 2011, May 23)

4 Introduction

Clearly the G. W. Bush administration considers the Freedom Agenda to be the greatest foreign policy legacy of its time, and in part has attributed the events in the MENA to its actions when in office. Members of the administration have attempted to appropriate these events in their official narrative in an attempt to vindicate, and rescue, their record. Equally, attempts to do this have been undertaken by parts of the Washington commentariat, with Charles Krauthammer writing in the *Washington Post* that:

> Today, everyone and his cousin supports the 'freedom agenda'. Of course, yesterday it was just George W. Bush, Tony Blair and a band of neocons with unusual hypnotic powers who dared to challenge the received wisdom of Arab exceptionalism – the notion that Arabs, as opposed to East Asians, Latin Americans Europeans and Africans, were uniquely allergic to democracy. Indeed, the left spent the better part of the Bush years excoriating the freedom agenda as either fantasy or yet another sordid example of US imperialism.
>
> (Krauthammer 2011a)

Krauthammer would later add that 'revolutions are sweeping the Middle East and everyone is a convert to George W. Bush's Freedom Agenda . . . Facebook and Twitter have surely mediated this pan-Arab (and Iranian) reach for dignity and freedom. But the Bush Doctrine set the premise' (Krauthammer 2011b).

What is notable about these prematurely triumphant statements is that the official representation of the Freedom Agenda suggests that it was more concrete than the policy in fact was. The policy is being articulated into contemporary discourses and misrepresented for political advantage, rather than being analysed and reflected upon with due care and attention. Indeed, many of the arguments currently presented in the mythology of the Freedom Agenda narrow, distort and essentially misrepresent the policy. Furthermore, when it is credited with causing the events of 2011 it is clear that such arguments are premised on the *post hoc, ergo propter hoc* fallacy. This is clearly problematic at best and dangerous at worst.

The narrative presented by members of the former administration, its supporters and those who have bought into the mythology risks obscuring what important lessons can be drawn from the Freedom Agenda, and how these can better inform democracy promotion policy. The mythology surrounding the Freedom Agenda also creates a perverse logic, attributing revolutions to policy in Washington, whilst writing out the extent to which Washington had continued to support autocratic regimes throughout the twentieth century and continued to do so during President Bush and President Obama's time in office. This is a strategic discursive move designed to remove democratic ownership of the regions struggles from those fighting throughout the MENA region, and attribute revolutions to a foreign polity. Yet, more fundamentally, the official narrative of the Freedom Agenda attempts to promote itself as both successful and causally attributable, when in fact the events of 2011 are the ultimate expression of the policy's failure.

In light of the events of 2011, the notion that the Freedom Agenda was a failure will be highly contested. Yet the conclusion presented in this volume draws together nearly a decade's worth of research, and is based on the analysis of over 2,500 texts, interviews with officials in Washington and throughout parts of the MENA, extensive interviews with recipients of aid from Freedom Agenda institutions, including civil society groups and international organisations, interviews with protesters and political groups throughout the MENA, and ethnographic research with youth movements and organisation leaders protesting in Tahrir Square. The findings in this volume clearly problematise and challenge the 'official' representation of the Freedom Agenda.

To elucidate this position, this book goes beyond the superficial nature of the official Freedom Agenda narrative, and returns to first-order questions, such as 'how and why was the Freedom Agenda constructed by the Bush administration?' and 'how was the Freedom Agenda constituted by the Bush administration and why was it done in this way?' This allows the volume to demonstrate the Bush administration's prioritisation of a particular understanding of democracy promotion, elevating it to the level of grand strategy in US–MENA relations, whilst also providing a broader commentary on US foreign and security policy relating to the MENA in the aftermath of September 11, 2001. This is important because all too often the analysis of the Freedom Agenda has been based on the assumption that what is meant by democracy promotion is unitary and widely understood. This is a factor that proponents of the Freedom Agenda's success now rely upon. Yet it is imperative to look beyond this, and ask what definitions the Bush administration was using, and how these were operationalised. Answering these questions reveals the highly ideological manner in which the Bush administration articulated particular discourses to legitimise its Freedom Agenda policy.

This volume proceeds on the premise that interrogating the deeper meanings and narratives underpinning the construction of the Freedom Agenda, is simply fundamental to understanding it fully. Consequently, this volume provides an assessment of the policy through an analysis of the ideological-discursive formation (IDF) underpinning its construction. Such an approach requires an empirically rich, but theoretically driven, methodology as a guide. Consequently, this book mixes theoretical innovation, which builds on the 'constructivist turn' in the social sciences, with empirical research, adding value to the current debate on the Freedom Agenda at both a theoretical and empirical level. As a result this volume looks at the Freedom Agenda through a constructivist institutionalist lens. Adopting this interdisciplinary approach strengthens the arguments being made, and provides a heuristic tool to demonstrate how the Freedom Agenda was constructed in a particular manner after discursive tracks were laid in the aftermath of September 11, 2001. The Freedom Agenda was designed to *gradually* reform the region over a period of generations working with *friends* and *partners*. The objective was to incrementally transform the region in a stable manner compatible with the pursuit of American interests, such as the free flow of oil and gas, the movement of military and commercial traffic through the Suez Canal, contracts for infrastructure construction projects, the security of regional allies such as Israel and Saudi Arabia, and cooperation on military, counter-terrorism and counter-proliferation issues. Accordingly, the findings of this volume are important on multiple levels. First, they provide a deeper understanding of the Bush administration's policy towards the MENA, explicating the level of continuity and change that the Freedom Agenda presents within a *longue durée*. Second, they problematise and critique the policy by illustrating how essentially contested concepts such as 'freedom' and 'democracy' were sedimented into a particular IDF, consequently constructing and propagating particular power relations and rule structures. Third, they illustrate problems with democracy promotion both philosophically and in practice, therefore signalling wider problems with the modality of the Freedom Agenda.

To undertake this task, Chapter 1 provides a historical context to the Freedom Agenda, and illustrates how America's traditional interests have historically led to the USA promoting a status quo policy in the region. Since the end of the Second World War successive administrations have propagated the notion that American national interests in the region were satisfied by preventing the spread of communism, securing the free flow of oil and protecting the security and integrity of Israel's borders. By advocating the democratisation of the region, however, the Bush administration was seen by many to challenge this status quo. Instead the Bush administration argued that American national interests lay in promoting democracy, as this would be a method of eradicating terrorism, promoting regional stability, creating regional economic growth and ending tyranny. This added to the 'conflict of interests' problem at the heart of US–MENA relations, which the Bush and Obama administrations have attempted to navigate and resolve throughout their times in office.

By constructing the Freedom Agenda, the Bush administration invited a considerable amount of discord concerning US–MENA relations. A series of critiques emerged that challenged the Freedom Agenda by arguing that it would empower Islamist movements, would cause regional instability, was based on a misunderstanding of movements such as al-Qaeda, and ultimately that the Freedom Agenda would harm indigenous groups promoting democratic reform. Conversely, a wide-ranging consensus emerged to support the Freedom Agenda and argued that promoting democracy in the region was a necessity and the only method of combating the form of terrorism that demonstrated itself on September 11, 2001. Yet the level of this debate has been overly concerned with strategic questions, rather than exploring what exactly the Bush administration believed the Freedom Agenda was supposed to be promoting. To redress this issue it is argued that an analysis is needed, which returns to first-order questions, before critiques of praxis are conducted. It is only by doing this that it is possible to reactivate the sedimentary logics that underpinned the Freedom Agenda.

Before proceeding with this analysis, however, Chapter 2 of this volume sets out the ontological and epistemological foundations of the constructivist institutionalist methodology. It is argued that such a methodology is theoretically robust, and better equipped to answer the questions of how and why the Freedom agenda was constructed, and why it evolved in its particular institutional formation. It is not vital that the reader engage with this methodology to understand the empirical case set out in the following chapters; however, this methodology does set out the worldview that underpins this volume. It provides a highly theoretical account of why we should ask different questions of the Freedom Agenda than typically has been the case, and outlines how constructivist institutionalism is capable of theoretically and historically (re)constructing the context from which the Freedom Agenda developed whilst being sensitive to institutional changes. The constructivist institutionalist methodology is able to guide this research because it builds on an insight by Michael Barnett (1999), who argues that traditional constructivist literature in International Relations has failed to incorporate a core insight of institutionalism, namely that actors strategise in institutional settings. Conversely, institutionalism fails to incorporate a core insight of constructivism, namely that actors are embedded in and circumscribed by a normative structure that demarcates the limits of legitimate and possible policy options.

With this guiding mantra in place, it is argued that the constructivist institutionalist methodology is able to surmount this problem by explicitly developing a stance on ontological and epistemological debates, namely the role of structure and agency, and ideas and material in political action. By virtue of engaging with these debates, it is argued that political time can be understood as a process of punctuated evolution, whereby 'normal' policy making is disrupted by crises and consequently evolves along an alternative path. Whereas this describes the shape of political time, it is argued that how crises are narrated provides the content of political change. Consequently, it is necessary to elucidate the IDF and rule structures that underpin post-crisis narration to understand policy development and institutional evolution. Deploying the constructivist institutionalist methodology in this research has a direct impact on the methods used for data analysis, and, at the end of this chapter, the qualitative methods used in this research are outlined along with specific details of how a process-tracing narrative discourse analysis was conducted using computer-assisted qualitative data analysis software.

With the methodological premises of constructivist institutionalism established, Chapter 3 elucidates the empirically rich but theoretically driven findings. It presents an analysis, embedded within a narrative of its own, that sets out the post-Cold War context in which the 2000 presidential campaign was contested. It argues that, although the presidential campaign between Al Gore and George W. Bush was unexceptional, the importance of the campaign for the Freedom Agenda was that Bush set out a distinctive IDF. Notably, Bush's vision for US foreign policy, under the banner of a 'Distinctly American Internationalism', combined US primacy with hegemonic stability theory as a proposed means of preventing American decline. Furthermore, this was articulated with an understanding of how 'freedom' could be promoted through neoliberal methods, based on a particular understanding of modernisation thesis, to create a utopian organisation of democratic, prosperous, peaceful, secure interdependent states. Notably, this guiding philosophy was *not* applied to US–MENA relations prior to September 11, 2001. However, the importance of this IDF was that it provided the foundations for the initial response to September 11, 2001, and evolved throughout the end of 2001 to early 2009, culminating in the Freedom Agenda being institutionalised.

Furthermore, the chapter details how the events of September 11, 2001, constituted a moment of punctuation in political time, which allowed the Bush administration to construct a strategic narrative that would underpin any policy innovation. Accordingly, it is possible to understand the events themselves as critical to the structuring of political time, in that they introduced an uncertainty condition that strategically selective actors in the state bureaucracy sought to overcome. Initially, this was done by narrating the events as a tragedy. However, the Bush administration radically began to assimilate the events into a large historical understanding, constructing them as part of a morality play that required a 'war on terrorism'. By seamlessly transforming this morality play into a moral crusade, the Bush administration foregrounded moral realism and American exceptionalism in an attempt to legitimise its response. As this IDF grasped multiple concepts together, the Bush administration provided a distinctive understanding of terms such as 'freedom', 'democracy', 'peace' and 'security', which were then institutionalised into the Freedom Agenda.

Chapter 4 continues this analysis by tracing how discursive tracks were laid in the immediate aftermath of the September 11, 2001, attacks through to December 2001. It argues that the Bush administration was strategic in the construction of its war on terror narrative, and turned the war in Afghanistan into a moralistic crusade. Crucial to this were multiple definitions of 'justice' articulated with the concept of 'security', which helped construct a policy that was focused on counter-terrorism and disembedding the USA from legal norms. Such a strategy was adverse to the notion of nation-building and democracy promotion, and ran counter to the strategy being pursued by the UN. However, by consistently evoking the concept of freedom, and articulating it with security, the Bush administration invited contestation within the foreign policy bureaucracy. This shaped the content of change in the post-crisis context, and opened up a political space for contestation within the administration over what exactly had gone wrong and what should be done. This established a milieu conducive to construction and evolution of the Freedom Agenda throughout 2002 and 2003.

Chapter 5 takes this analysis forwards, detailing how the perceived success of the war in Afghanistan emboldened the Bush administration to construct a vindicationalist strategy for the Middle East. It characterises the manner in which policy-makers puzzled under conditions of uncertainty, to construct the Iraq war and the Freedom Agenda. These are analytically separate, but were conceived to be part of the same strategic plan derived at a secret 'Bletchley II' meeting held in late November 2001, whereby pushing Iraq would create a domino effect throughout the region. By late 2002, Freedom Agenda institutions were being constructed to aid in this process, but, as the Iraq war became a growing problem, these institutions would evolve a distinctiveness of their own. They would be underpinned by an IDF that articulated multiple ideas together to justify an imperial policy. This formed the basis of a new policy paradigm.

Chapter 6 explicitly deals with the institutionalisation of the Freedom Agenda and the manner in which it evolved from 2002 until President Bush left office. It argues that, in spite of the Bush administration's bold assertions that democracy promotion was in the national interest, the Freedom Agenda can be described as a policy of conservative radicalism. The approach is *radical* to the extent that it insists on political democracy, yet *conservative* in its desire to safeguard the socio-economic privileges and power of the established order to secure regional stability. Such a strategy was caught between democracy promotion and free trade as the positive route to liberty, and domination to the extent that negative liberty was undermined in favour of stability. As the Bush administration oscillated between emphasising both of these elements it enabled a double standard in the Freedom Agenda to emerge. This was characterised by a slow gradualist policy guided by an understanding of freedom in economic terms for regional allies. However, for regimes that challenged American policy in the region, a strategy of regime change was pursued. This approach highlights the central contradictions in the Bush stratagem, which ultimately led to a retreat from the agenda in 2006 through to leaving office in January 2009. The Bush administration was ultimately unable to convert vision into action, because the zeal with which the strategy had been constructed contained ideological blind-spots. Because of the shallow understanding of freedom, based on neoliberalism, and the modernisation thesis being a dominant part of the Bush administration's IDF, it became evident that the administration was promoting a policy of low-intensity democracy in an inhospitable strategically selective context. Indeed, the Freedom Agenda contains within its very construction and institutionalisation a supposed imperial right to rule over the region informally.

Chapter 7 details how Obama inherited the Freedom Agenda and silently carried on the policy. What emerged from the Obama administration was a policy of conservative pragmatism, whereby the administration attempted to reach out and engage regimes such as Iran and Syria, downplaying the radical dimension of the Freedom Agenda, but continued with attempts to gradually reform the region in partnership with autocratic regimes. What it reveals is a high level of continuity between the Bush administration and the Obama administration, but also areas in which the Obama administration's policy evolved to include a greater focus on civil society, development and the use of digital technology. Nonetheless, with these elements proving to be somewhat marginal, in the aftermath of the 2011 revolutions the administration increasingly relied on a mixture of pragmatic moves underpinned by the same neoliberal doctrine espoused by the Bush administration.

The Conclusion provides an overview of the analysis and demonstrates the importance of challenging the representation of the Freedom Agenda. There is value in highlighting the imperial pitfalls of the approach the Bush administration constructed, the limitations of the approaches institutionalisation, and ultimately the conservative manner in which the policy was pursued. The importance of this cannot be overstated given that the Obama administration not only inherited these problems but has largely embraced them in its response to regional unrest. This highlights the unfortunate manner in which the Bush and Obama administrations clearly recognised the symptoms of the 2011 revolutions long before they happened, but ultimately failed to prescribe the correct policy. What is needed is a post-colonial approach to democracy support for the twenty-first century, which embraces dialogue, empowerment and respect, rather than seeking to socially engineer the peoples of the Middle East towards some externally inspired utopian end state.

1 American interests and a history of promoting the status quo

The ambition of promoting democracy in the Middle East is not new to the American people or their foreign policy. Since the early nineteenth century, American missionaries have sought to take American values and plant them in the region. Inspired by the Second Great Awakening of the nineteenth century and a desire for adventure on a new frontier, missionaries went to the Middle East to set up schools, clinics, churches and colonies, all with the aim of 'letting in the light' and spreading the 'American Eagle of freedom' (Oren 2007: 210–27; Mead 2001: 158–62; Hahn 2005: 2). Moreover, after the First World War, whilst Britain and France were fighting over 'the great loot of the war',[1] it was President Wilson who was arguing for 'self-determination' and 'autonomous development' for all 'nationalities . . . under Turkish Rule' (Oren 2007: 377).[2] Subsequent American presidents have claimed that they support democratic governance for the Middle East, and at the birth of the Eisenhower Doctrine the President argued that 'Our country supports without reservation the full sovereignty and independence of each and every nation of the Middle East' (Eisenhower 1957).

Contrastingly, in the same period, the political rhetoric did not match policy, with American idealist notions of self-determination and anti-colonialism giving way to imperial counter-revolutionary policies (Hahn 2005: 35–46; Yaqub 2004: 87–121; Gaddis 1997: 172–6). Thus, as Steve Smith (2002: 65) has noted, 'the debate about US democracy promotion seems to assume that the US has had a clear long-standing commitment to such a policy, I see the record as far more complex'.[3] What can, however, be asserted is that throughout the twentieth century, as the United States increasingly became involved in Middle Eastern affairs, and concerned with the region's geopolitical orientation, the notion of promoting democracy in the Middle East was always at least a stated goal of US foreign policy.

Yet it was under the George W. Bush administration, and in the aftermath of the September 11, 2001, attacks, that promoting democracy in the Middle East was elevated and believed to be central to American national security interests. Thus, as Jessica Mathews (2005: vii) notes:

> Of all the tectonic shifts in US foreign policy emerging from the aftermath of 9/11, none is more potentially transformative than the widespread conviction

in the US policy community that America must reverse its long time support for friendly tyrants in the Middle East and push hard for a democratic transformation of that troubled region.

At a surface level President Bush provided a succinct answer to explain why this shift was necessary. He agued that:

> Sixty years of Western nations excusing and accommodating the lack of freedom in the Middle East did nothing to make us safe ... As long as the Middle East remains a place where freedom does not flourish, it will remain a place of stagnation, resentment, and violence ready for export. And with the spread of weapons that can bring catastrophic harm to our country and to our friends, it would be reckless to accept the status quo.
> (Bush 2003, November 6)

Accordingly, the intention behind the Freedom Agenda was to use the full spectrum of means available to the United States for the 'advancement of human freedom and human dignity through effective democracy' (NSCT 2006: 9). The objectives were to 'eradicate terrorism', 'promote regional stability', 'promote regional economic growth', 'end tyranny' and 'create peace' (see NSCT 2006).

Undoubtedly, these objectives were dominated by liberal ideals, and the Freedom Agenda was the quintessential expression of a liberal grand strategy, whereby it was the 'policy of the United States to seek and support democratic movements and institutions in every nation and culture, with the ultimate goal of ending tyranny in our world'. Not only was the Bush administration concerned with the 'fundamental character of regimes', but changing the nature of these regimes was portrayed as 'the best way to provide enduring security for the American people' (NSC 2006: 1). Within this context, America's self-interest and values align and assist one another whist enhancing American global influence (see Smith 2000).

The Bush administration was not the first to assert this symbiotic synergy of principles and interests, as the origins of this approach date back as far as the eighteenth and nineteenth centuries. Yet the innovation of the Freedom Agenda was the manner in which the Bush administration sought to spread democracy through coercive regime change, and to institutionalise a *Forward Strategy of Freedom in the Middle East* (FSFME). Whereas the former was most obviously expressed in the form of the 2003 Iraq war, the latter culminated in the Bush administration reinforcing and expanding the bureaucratic organisations in the US government that promote democracy. Indeed, just as the Iraq war is part of the President Bush's democracy promotion legacy, so too is the institutional construction of the Middle East Partnership Initiative (MEPI), the Middle East Free Trade Area (MEFTA) and the Broader Middle East and North Africa initiative (BMENA). Furthermore, it was President Bush who codified his democracy promotion strategy in *National Security Presidential Directive 58*, entitled *Institutionalising the Freedom Agenda*, and who signed the ADVANCE Democracy Act of 2007 into law.[4] Thus, it is important to note that the Freedom Agenda was far more than simply the war in Iraq. By the time President Bush left office, hundreds of millions of dollars had been channelled through these institutions and spent on promoting democracy in the MENA, and the USA had declared with the force of law that it would prioritise, along with other foreign policy goals, the promotion of democracy and human rights around the world.

Accordingly, the decision to advocate freedom and democracy in the MENA challenged decades of US foreign policy. That President Bush challenged the historical conduct of past policy was in and of itself a rare admission of failure, which reflected a serious conceptual change concerning US–MENA relations. President Bush accepted a consistent pattern of American foreign policy towards the region, whereby in the name of stability the US backed autocratic regimes with diplomatic, military and economic assistance. To point out the obvious implications of the President's admission, since the steady growth of American involvement in the MENA from 1945, the USA has tried to control events in the region. To this extent, it is widely acknowledged that the USA slowly took over Britain's historical 'oversight role' and the 'security management services' of the region (Boot 2004: 47; Murden 2002: 43). That this role began during the Second World War is not a coincidence. It coincided not only with the decline of the British and French imperial moments in the Middle East, but also with the rise of the USA as a global superpower and the onset of the Cold War.[5]

It was during the Second World War itself that the geopolitical orientation of the MENA was for the first time seen as vital to US interests, both through the need to maintain a supply corridor to the Soviet Union through Iran, and as a staging ground to invade Italy from North Africa. Yet it was in the war's aftermath and the accompanying new international order that subsequent US administrations increasingly began to define US interests as intrinsically linked to the fate of the MENA region. In the immediate post-war milieu, containment became the dominant US strategic doctrine in US–MENA relations, and as the USA sought to contain Soviet expansion it began filling the power vacuum left by the withdrawal of old colonial powers (Taylor 1991: 49). The first sign of this creeping insurrection occurred over the issue of post-war Soviet retention of troops in Northern Iran (see Truman 1956: 98, 100–1).[6] This subsequently expanded into concerns over the Turkish–Iranian border, Turkish sovereignty and ultimately the geopolitical orientation of the entire Middle East. Reacting to the July 1946 note from Moscow to Turkey, proposing a new Turkish–Russian defence structure to control the Dardanelles, President Truman (1956: 102) argued:

> The Russians, in addition to their efforts to outflank Turkey through Iran, were beginning to exert pressure on Turkey for territorial concessions . . . This was indeed an open bid to obtain control of Turkey . . . To allow Russia to set up bases in the Dardanelles or to bring troops into Turkey, ostensibly for the defense of the straits, would, in the natural course of events, result in Greece and the whole Near and Middle East falling under Soviet control.

In response to these events a 'patience and firmness' strategy was adopted, which ultimately transformed itself into the Truman doctrine (Gaddis 1982: 22–3). This established for the first time, and albeit focused on the 'northern tier', a situation in which the USA would actively endeavour to strengthen its own position in the MENA whilst containing Soviet advances.[7] To this end, the USA increasingly asserted the need for stability and the maintenance of the established political order in the region throughout the Cold War. The regional status quo was favoured to the extent that it was perceived to benefit US interests, even if this meant challenging the internal dynamics emerging from the region. This was certainly the case with the 1953 CIA-engineered coup of Mohammed Mossadegh and the reinstatement of Mohammad Reza Shah in Iran (see Kinzer 2003; Pollack 2004: 40–80). In a similar vein, the Eisenhower doctrine led to the interventions in Jordan, Syria, Lebanon and Iraq through the 1957–8 period, with the aim of maintaining the regional status quo and winning American influence in the region. This status quo policy was pursued by successive administrations throughout the Cold War; culminating in President Carter advising the Shah of Iran to use force to crush the 1979 Islamic revolution to maintain 'an island of stability', and President Reagan asserting that 'I will not permit [Saudi Arabia] to be an Iran' after US-trained Saudi Arabian National Guard forces crushed an anti-regime uprising in 1981 (see Hahn 2005: 42–43, 70–85; Zunes 2003: 15; Freedman 2008: 63–149). Accordingly, to fortify this counter-revolutionary policy in the early stages of the Cold War, the USA demonstrated willingness to condone and participate in both coercion and subversion in an effort to dominate the region.

In addition to directly violent methods of securing stability and the maintenance of the established political order, the USA also sought to pursue a status quo policy through foreign and military assistance. The genealogical origins of this, in US–MENA relations, lay with the precedent set by the Truman doctrine's aid packages to Greece and Turkey. With this as a model, President Eisenhower declared his own doctrine to a joint session of Congress on January 5, 1957. Approving it in March the same year, Congress authorised the Eisenhower administration to use force if necessary to protect American interests in the Middle East. However, this was coupled with $200 million in economic aid to support any nation in the Middle East 'requesting assistance against armed aggression from any country controlled by international communism'. This was substantially less than the $400 million originally intended by Secretary of State John Foster Dulles, who retained the idea that economic aid would be used 'as a means of building our position in the Middle East' (Little 2004: 132–7; Yaqub 2004; Heiss 2006).[8] Commenting at the time, Milton Friedman observed:

> The President is empowered to make payments to certain countries, particularly in the Middle East, the purpose of which is to induce the recipient countries to support particular policies that are thought to be in our interest – these are, in essence, straight military or political subsides.
>
> (Friedman 1958 [1995]: 3)

As a method of securing stability and influence, economic and military aid to the MENA has waxed and waned but continues to the present day. From 1950 to 1970 both economic and military aid to the region totalled a sum of $7,845 million.[9] This figure takes into account the 80 per cent drop in foreign assistance between 1965 and 1970, which was the result of the June 1967 War and the impact of the war in Vietnam. Yet these sums are meagre in comparison with the dramatic rise in foreign assistance that accompanied the 1970s, and would continue into the 2000s. From 1971 to 2001 economic and military aid to the region totalled a sum of $144,969 million, and by the time President Bush left office, the region was receiving 16 per cent of all American global economic assistance, and 49 per cent of American global military assistance (see Sharp 2011; USAID 2011).[10]

During the Cold War, foreign assistance packages to the MENA were portrayed as necessary for containing communism. The assumption was that patronage could be bought and foreign aid used as a bargaining chip to stop key strategic countries such as Egypt, Jordan, Iran and Syria falling under Soviet influence. In effect, it provided a less direct means of confronting the Soviet Union than military intervention, which would have increased the risk of escalating the Cold War (see Banfield 1963). An added virtue of foreign assistance was that it was also perceived in terms of a development policy, which would strengthen the Western bloc. Indeed, a predominant assumption in America at the time was that 'communism flows from poverty' (Packenham 1973: 52). As a logical corollary of this, economic aid was portrayed as a method of combatting communism by helping raise the living standards in less developed areas and making communism less attractive. In turn, raising living standards would also bolster the Western powers, by laying the foundations of 'world prosperity, political freedom, and international cooperation' (Packenham 1973: 50–1). That foreign assistance to the MENA continued in the post-Cold War era is testimony to the fact that it also sought to guarantee longer-term interests in the region that have survived the collapse of the Soviet Union.

Although the USA has no other superpower challenging its hegemonic power over the region in the post-Cold War era, reasons for America to intervene in the region remain. Accordingly there are a set of interests that the USA consistently maintains, which could be jeopardised by regional instability. Notably geography has played a distinctive role. The reason for this was recognised as early as 1945 by the State Department, which described the Middle East as 'a stupendous source of strategic power, and one of the greatest material prizes in world history' (in Zunes 2003: 2). This was a far cry from earlier assertions by the State Department in 1923 that the region 'is of little commercial importance' (Oren 2007: 407). The fundamental distinction between these two quotes relates to the role of oil in the region and the manner in which it began transforming the world in the early twentieth century. Accelerated industrialisation combined with an increasing demand on oil-dependent consumer goods, such as automobiles and household electricity supplies in the United States, played an unprecedented role. Moreover, what became apparent from both world wars was that oil was a decisive factor in providing military personnel with the ability to travel further faster, consequently providing a strategic advantage in warfare. To quote the young Winston Churchill's enduring principle, which referred to the use of oil instead of coal on British warships: 'Mastery itself is the prize' (Yergin 1993).

16 *A history of promoting the status quo*

Notably, by 1947, oil-producing MENA states provided half of the oil consumed by the US armed forces, which led to the CIA deeming Middle Eastern oil 'essential to the security of the United States' (in Hahn 2005: 7). Yet oil from the region was playing a much more important strategic role by fuelling the revitalisation of Western European economies. As one US government report commented at the time, 'without petroleum the Marshall plan could not have functioned' (Yergin 1991: 424). This was because in the post-war era a fundamental transition in Europe took place, in which coal-based economies transitioned to importing oil.[11] This helped produce a symbiotic confluence of events in which European needs and the development of Middle Eastern oil combined. Thus, by 1955 approximately 90 per cent of oil consumed in Western Europe came from the Middle East (Hahn 2005: 7; see also Kapstein 1990; Yergin 1991: 425). From the American perspective, Middle Eastern oil was now fundamental to the material balance of the world, and its efforts to create an integrated transatlantic market system.

The twenty-first century still bears the marks of the post-war decision to move from coal power to oil. As Kenneth Pollack (2003: 3) has argued:

> The reason the United States has a legitimate and critical interest in seeing that Persian Gulf oil continues to flow copiously and relatively cheaply is simply that the global economy built over the last 50 years rests on a foundation of inexpensive, plentiful oil, and if that foundation were removed, the global economy would collapse.

Furthermore, in today's highly technological hydrocarbon society the demand for oil is increasing, and the Middle East contains around 66 per cent of the world's known oil reserves (Milton-Edwards 2006: 73). Of particular concern to the United States is that in the intermediate future 'oil supply is expected to continue to concentrate in the Persian Gulf, which holds the world's largest geologically attractive reserves' (CFR 2006: 22). The cause of America's concern is that the highly industrial US economy is becoming more dependent on oil for growth. The United States, with only 4.3 per cent of the world's population, uses 25 per cent of the world's oil, and significantly 60 per cent of this need is dependent on import and expected to rise in the coming decades (CFR 2006: 22). Yet, as consumption is increasing, America's domestic production is decreasing. This makes the USA significantly dependent on foreign oil from places such as Saudi Arabia, which provides 20 per cent of America's crude oil imports (Milton-Edwards 2006: 239). As Beverley Milton-Edwards (2006: 239) argues:

> The maintenance and future growth of the American economy owes much to the import of oil from the Middle East. In this way unimpeded access to that resource is vital to national interest. If there were any doubt that this were not the case, the Arab oil embargo during the 1973 Arab–Israeli conflict, although it occurred more than thirty years ago, remains fresh in the collective consciousness of American policy-makers.

In addition to American demand for oil, however, the region's resources are also increasingly being claimed by expanding global economic powers such as India and China. Indeed, the Chinese government is pursuing a strategy of 'locking up' particular supplies for the Chinese market, and is aligning its relationships with Saudi Arabia and Iran in order to secure these exclusive oil supplies. This is a direct challenge to American hegemony in the region and is impacting Middle Eastern politics more widely (see Salameh 2003; Jaffe and Lewis 2002; Xu 2000; Rubin 1999: 49–50). The effect of this is that US influence in the region was diminishing before the 2011 revolutions; this caused foreign policy analysts such as Henry Kissinger to predict international conflicts over hydrocarbon resources (see Leverett and Bader 2005: 187; Ikenberry 2008). This demonstrates that concerns over the material balance of the world and the geopolitical orientation of the Middle East are as strong in the twenty-first century as they were in the Cold War era. With oil being linked to the 'American way of life', economic growth and strategic military power, the consequences of instability or a loss of regional hegemony are intricately linked to America's global position.

The geographical location of the Middle East also plays a distinctive role in wider military-strategic concerns of the USA. Previous to the development of intercontinental ballistic missiles in the 1960s, the USA enjoyed a significant strategic advantage over the USSR by having allies that bordered the Soviet Union. This gave the USA the potential power to invade its rival from Turkey or Iran, whereas the Soviets had no comparable access to the United States (Sluglett 2005: 43). More widely, throughout the Cold War, military bases were seen as a strategic advantage essential to winning a direct conflict with the Soviet Union. Not only would they have provided the ability to launch aerial offensives, but they also allowed the build-up of troops for a ground invasion and the positioning of intelligence-gathering personnel and equipment for covert operations (see Cohen 1997: 1–94).

Significantly, although the threat of war with the Soviet Union passed, the Middle East remains an important strategic location for American defence interests. Military bases in the region could provide a method of projecting American military might in future conflicts with rising powers. With bases in the Middle East, the USA would be able to strike China from the west, as well as from eastern bases in the Pacific. Whereas this represents an 'external' dynamic to the projection of US military power from the region, there are also 'internal' and 'inter-regional' strategic concerns. With political unrest spreading throughout the region even before 2011, the dilemma represented by Iran's nuclear programme and the instability in Iraq, there is a perceived need to maintain a military presence in the region (see Pollack 2003, 2004; Sick *et al.* 2008; Cordesman 2008). Furthermore, the MENA has been considered part of an 'arc of instability' and a 'breeding ground for threats' to US interests (NMS 2004: 5). In the 2005 *National Defense Strategy* (NDS), the USA declared the objective of securing 'strategic access' and retaining 'global freedom of action'. The logic underlying this is simple: 'the United States cannot influence that which it cannot reach' (NDS 2005: 6; see also Posch 2006). That is to say that military bases are part of the US security governance architecture and linked to the notion that American interests are global in scope. The overall result of this is, as the highly influential Council on Foreign Relations has concluded:

> Even if the Persian Gulf did not have the bulk of the world's readily available oil reserves, there would be reasons to maintain a substantial military capability in the region . . . At least for the next two decades . . . the United States should expect and support a strong military posture that permits suitably rapid deployment to the region, if required.
>
> (CFR 2006: 29–30)

In addition to the region's oil supply and military strategic concerns, the USA has also held a historical interest in maintaining the security of Israel. At times the US–Israeli 'special relationship' has conflicted with the goal of securing the region's oil, by antagonising the populations of other regional allies. However, the extent of the relationship is visible in the vast quantity of foreign assistance that Israel has received. Notably since France withdrew its assistance to Israel, in protest at the pre-emptive launch of the June 1967 War, the USA has stepped into a patron role (Sharp 2011: 5; Mearsheimer and Walt 2007: 53; Bowen 2005: 55). From 1971 to 2010, the USA gave foreign assistance to Israel at an average rate of $2 billion per year, making it the 'largest annual recipient of US aid and the largest recipient of cumulative US assistance since World War II' (Mark 2006: 2–21; Sharp 2011: 5).[12]

A clear turning point in the US–Israeli relationship, and in the US–Egyptian relationship, was the signing of the Israel–Egypt Peace Treaty in 1979. This was the result of secret negotiations and the signing of the Camp David Accords, which ushered in an era of financial support for relative stability between Israel and its Arab neighbours (Milton-Edwards 2006: 247). As a consequence, Israel and Egypt became sequentially the highest recipients of US aid. Combined, these two countries receive almost 93 per cent of all annual funding to the region (Sharp 2011: 7). Since this period the USA has remained 'engaged' in the peace process as a 'peace broker', but remained committed to strengthening Israel.

America's interests in the MENA are large and expanding. The USA not only perceives its security interests ranging from oil and gas to military reach, cooperation on counter-terrorism and counter-proliferation issues and the security of Israel and Saudi Arabia, but also has more commercial interests in securing the movement of commercial traffic through the Suez Canal into the Mediterranean, and the procurement of lucrative contracts for business and infrastructure projects. Given this, US interests in the region cannot be parsimoniously reduced to economic and material factors. Rather they are a much more complex and multifaceted collection of perceived material and ideational interests that are intricately entwined and often conflicting. This is what makes the delineation between them often ad hoc, and perceived to be better served by the status quo in the region. Uncertainty, within this context, is highly problematic. Yet the Bush administration's addition of democracy promotion as a national interest added another

A history of promoting the status quo 19

layer of complexity within this ad hoc system. This contributed to what Tamara Coffman Wittes (2008a: 18) has termed the 'conflict-of-interests' problem at the heart of US–MENA relations. On one hand, the Bush administration asserted the need for regional reform through democratisation, and, on the other, the need to meet traditional long-term interests persisted. Although the Freedom Agenda was portrayed as 'challenging' past policy, these long-term historical interests remained, providing the strategically selective context in which the Freedom Agenda had to navigate. Accordingly, it was this conflict of interests that caused the greatest level of debate and discord within Washington through Bush's time in office, and led to considerable debate about the merits of promoting democracy versus maintaining the established stability approach to US–MENA relations; a debate that, in light of the 2011 revolutions, is worthy of much more attention than it received at the time.

The Freedom Agenda's critics: Islamists, instability, terrorists and credibility

The conflict of interests problem has been central to critiques of the Freedom Agenda, from even some who served within the Bush administration. Thus, as Flynt Leverett, Middle East expert on the Secretary of State's Policy Planning Staff from 2001 to 2002 and Senior Director for Middle East Affairs at the National Security Council (NSC) from 2002 to 2003, argued:

> Spreading democracy in the Middle East is a bad idea ... Of course US interests in the Middle East are complex and multifaceted, but ... our most important interests in this critical region ... [are] first, the free flow of oil from the Persian Gulf, second, the security and welfare of the state of Israel, and third, keeping the Middle East from providing a platform for further mass-casualty terrorist attacks of the sort that we suffered on 9-11 ... I believe that promoting democracy in the Middle East is not just not helpful for these interests, it is downright harmful to them.
>
> (IQ2 2007)

Beyond the administration itself, however, opposition to the Freedom Agenda has come from a wide and varied range of proponents, that cut-cross any party political and indeed ideological divides. However, many of the arguments presented overlap and can be broken down into a series of four core objections to democracy promotion in the Middle East:

1 The 'Islamist dilemma'.
2 Promoting democracy in the Middle East may cause regional instability.
3 Promoting democracy does not weaken terrorist organisations such as al-Qaeda, because they rely on ideological appeal and are not a product of political or economic marginalisation. They do not rely on a lack of democracy or poverty to recruit future terrorists.

4 The USA is a discredited actor and by promoting democracy may harm indigenous groups promoting democratic reform.

The 'Islamist dilemma' has been a dominant argument summoned in order to reject promoting democracy in the MENA. At its core lies an empirical observation: throughout the MENA, Islamists have established themselves as major political players and before the 2011 revolutions in the region it was widely believed that they represented the only viable opposition forces to undemocratic regimes (see Sharp 2006). Consequently, as many argued, 'should free and fair elections be held in the Middle East tomorrow, it would be likely that radical religious forces [sic] would win a sweeping victory in many countries' (Neep 2004: 82; see also Byman 2007: 143–4). This was seen as a problem because it could result in the 'one person, one vote, one time' scenario, in addition to helping the formation of 'Islamic' states. The creation of such states raises the spectre of the Iranian revolution in 1979 and the prospect of hostility towards American interests. It is still commonplace to ask the questions 'will country X be another Iran? Is so-and-so another Ayatollah Khomeini?' (Esposito and Voll 1996: 150). Accordingly, as many critics of the Freedom Agenda have illustrated:

> The problem with promoting democracy in the Arab world is not that Arabs do not like democracy; it is that Washington probably would not like the governments Arab democracy would produce . . . Assuming that democratic Arab governments would better represent the opinions of their people than do the current Arab regimes, democratisation of the Arab world should produce more anti-U. S. foreign policies.
>
> (Gause III 2005)

Proponents of this argument often cite the events of 1989–91 and its aftermath in Algeria, as evidence for their position. In response to outside pressure and the desire for internal stability the single ruling party in Algeria, the Front de Liberation Nationale (FLN), began making attempts at pluralism in 1989. Through constitutional changes the FLN monopoly on the state apparatus was to be ended and a competitive multiparty system established. However, as a direct result the Islamic Salvation Front (FIS) swept to victory in municipal and later parliamentary elections. As a result, an Islamic movement had come to power 'not through bullets but through ballots, not by violent revolution but by working within the system' (Esposito and Voll 1996: 150; see also Esposito and Voll 1996: 150–72; Burgat 2003: 102–21). In January 1992, the military decided that the Algerian people had 'voted unwisely' and that the FIS had 'hijacked democracy'. This led to military intervention, which amounted to a de facto coup, and a civil conflict that reversed the political openings made throughout 1989–91 (see Quandt 2003; Willis 1999).

For many proponents, the Islamist dilemma argument was vindicated throughout the 2005–6 period, with the electoral victory of Harakat al-Muqawama al-Islamiya (Hamas) in the 2006 Palestinian parliamentary elections.[13] This represented a pattern of Islamic groups, hostile to Washington and Israel, winning significant gains through elections in what the Bush administration termed the 'Arab Spring'. This included the Muslim Brotherhood in Egypt, Hezbollah in Lebanon and Shiites backed by militias in Iraq (Weisman 2006a). This was coupled with the 2006 Israel–Hezbollah war in Lebanon and increasing civil violence in Iraq despite hopes that the elections would calm the insurgency (Kurth 2006).

In addition to the Islamist dilemma argument being propagated by some of the US foreign policy commentariat, it has also been voiced within the MENA region. Within the region itself autocrats regularly depicted Islamists as the only viable alternative to their own autocratic rule. This served their interests by generating support and backing from Western governments, and created a 'stability bargain' between autocratic rulers and sections of their own societies that saw Islamists as a threat (Feldman 2004: 19–25; Deeb 2008). Accordingly, as Noah Feldman (2004: 23) has noted:

> The optimal strategy for the autocrats is [or was] therefore to eliminate secular democratic dissent, keeping just enough Islamist opposition alive to make Islamism the only alternative without enabling it to become strong enough to overthrow the government.

A second dominant argument summoned in order to reject promoting democracy in the MENA has been the assertion that promoting democracy may cause greater regional instability and conflict. This argument has been widely asserted and strongly influenced by Mansfield and Snyder's book *Electing to Fight: Why Emerging Democracies Go to War* (see Epstein *et al.* 2007: 8; Smith 2007: 159–61; Traub 2008: 7; Kaye *et al.* 2008: 25; Owen 2005). The thrust of the argument directly challenges the manner in which democratic peace theory was portrayed by the Bush administration. Although Mansfield and Snyder (2005: 1–2) acknowledge that 'no mature democracies have ever fought a war against each other', they argue that 'in the short run . . . the beginning stages of transitions to democracy often give rise to war rather than peace'. Moreover, in agreement with Fareed Zakaria's (2004) analysis in *The Future of Freedom* and Samuel Huntington's (1968) *Political Order in Changing Societies,* Mansfield and Snyder (2005: 13) argue that 'rising political participation leads to conflict and instability in states with weak political institutions'.

For those who opposed the war in Iraq, the implications of this study directly challenge the Bush administration. As Tony Smith (2007: 159) has pointed out:

> If Mansfield and Snyder are correct, their findings deliver a body blow to the facile assumption of the Bush Doctrine that terrorism is more likely to come under control in the Middle East as a result of the conquest of Iraq followed by its democratisation. Indeed, exactly the opposite seems likely.

Moreover, when Mansfield and Snyder's (2005: 278) findings are applied to the MENA, and vis-à-vis the Freedom Agenda, they argue that 'democratising the Arab states is a major political gamble in the war on terror'. The reasoning behind this is worth quoting at length.

> Although democratisation in the Islamic world might contribute to peace in the very long run, Islamic public opinion in the short run is, in most places, hostile to the United States, reluctant to condemn terrorism and supportive of forceful measures to achieve favourable results in Palestine, Kashmir and other disputed areas. Although much of the belligerence of the Islamic publics is fuelled by resentment of the U.S.-backed authoritarian regimes under which many of them live, simply renouncing these authoritarians and pressing for a quick democratic opening is unlikely to lead to peaceful democratic consolidations. On the contrary, unleashing Islamic mass opinion through sudden democratisation could only raise the likelihood of war. All the risk factors are there: the media and civil society groups are inflammatory, as old elites and rising oppositions try to claim the mantle of Islamic or nationalist militancy. The rule of law is weak, and existing corrupt bureaucracies cannot serve a democratic administration properly. The boundaries of states are mismatched with those of nations, making any push for national self-determination fraught with peril.
>
> (Mansfield and Snyder 2005: 13)

For those who oppose the Freedom Agenda the notion that emerging democracies in the Middle East may in fact have a destabilising effect on the region is highly problematic, and would jeopardise American security.[14] The events of 2011 certainly do not refute Mansfield and Snyder argument, with varying degrees of regional instability resulting from the revolutions in Tunisia, Egypt, Libya, Yemen, Syria and Bahrain.

The third argument put forward to reject the Freedom Agenda has been the assertion that promoting democracy and/or reducing poverty does not weaken terrorist organisations such as al-Qaeda. They rely on ideological appeal, and therefore a 'drain the swamp' approach fails to provide an effective counter-terrorism strategy. Notably, this challenges the core assumption of the Freedom Agenda: that political and economic marginalisation cause the sort of terrorism witnessed on September 11, 2001. One of the most prominent proponents arguing against this premise has been Gregory F. Gause III, who argues that al-Qaeda 'are fighting to impose their vision of an Islamic state', and that this is no evidence to support the notion that 'democracy in the Arab world would "drain the swamp", eliminating soft support for terrorist organisations among the Arab public and reducing the number of potential recruits for them' (Gause III 2005: 62). The implication of Gause's argument is that an absence of democracy is not an underlying causal factor leading to the sort of terrorist threat presented on September 11, 2001. This conclusion is seconded by Katerina Dalacoura's (2011: 180; see also Dalacoura 2006) extensive case study research, which concludes that:

> There is no necessary causal link between the lack of democracy in the Middle East and Islamist terrorism. Although in some cases a link does exist, it is not consistent enough to establish a regular (that is, theoretical) pattern.

Moreover, as Douglas Borer and Michael Freeman argue, al-Qaeda's goals are to stop the perceived foreign occupation of Islamic lands and to establish Sharia law as a guiding principle of an Islamic caliphate. Democracy promotion is unlikely to satisfy these grievances and may in fact create the perception that Islamic identity and culture are threatened (Borer and Freeman 2007; Freeman 2008; Kaye *et al.* 2008: 21). Further still, Scott Atran (2006: 144) argues that:

> Those who believe suicide terrorism can be explained by a single political root cause, such as the presence of foreign military forces or the absence of democracy, ignore psychological motivations.

Significantly, empirical evidence appears to raise serious questions concerning the 'democracy deficit–terrorism' and 'poverty–terrorism' links. It has been widely demonstrated that the MENA does not have a monopoly on terrorism, and that factors other than a democratic deficit and poverty play a role (see Hobson 2005: 43; Dalacoura 2006). As Flynt Leverett has argued:

> From Osama bin Laden on down, that claim that jihadist terrorists are products of economic and political marginalisation is simply false. The 9-11 hijackers were truly trust-fund terrorists, from economically and politically advantaged backgrounds.
>
> (IQ2 2007)

Moreover, there is the phenomenon of 'home grown' terrorists in democratic states, such as three of the individuals who carried out the July 7, 2005, bombings in London, or Rezwan Ferdaus, who was arrested in Boston after planning to fly remote-controlled aircraft with explosives into the Pentagon. Such cases clearly demonstrate the falsifiability of a causal link between a democracy deficit or poverty and terrorism, as presented by the Bush administration.

The impact of questioning these links has been pronounced. It has led Francis Fukuyama and Michael McFaul, long-term proponents of democracy promotion, to assert that:

> The deep sources of terrorism are much more complex than just the Middle East's democratic deficit. One can argue in fact that the modernisation process produces terrorism and that more democracy is likely to exacerbate the terrorism problem, at least in the short run.
>
> (Fukuyama and McFaul 2007: 30)

This builds on Francis Fukuyama's earlier assertion that attacked the Bush administration and the Freedom Agenda directly:

> The problem of jihadist terrorism will not be solved by bringing modernisation and democracy to the Middle East. The Bush administration's view that terrorism is driven by a lack of democracy overlooks the fact that so many

terrorists were radicalised in democratic European countries. It is highly naïve to think that radical Islamists hate the West because of ignorance of what the West is.

(Fukuyama 2006a: 12)

Notably, however, this has not stopped these authors asserting that democracy promotion is a moral good in and of itself, and that the USA should enhance the role of democracy promotion in its foreign policy (Fukuyama and McFaul 2007: 34–44).

The fourth argument put forward to reject the Freedom Agenda has been the assertion that the USA is a discredited actor. For some, this has been caused by US actions over the last few decades, in which it has 'allied itself with autocratic regimes and has supported Israel against the legitimate rights of the Palestinian people' (Dalacoura 2005: 973). Further still, some have argued that the invasion of Iraq has discredited US democracy promotion efforts. As Shibley Telhami has argued:

> In essence, we have given democracy a bad name. It is hard for people in the region, including people who badly and desperately are looking for democracy and freedom, to think of democracy and freedom the American way without thinking about the horrors of Iraq. We have paid a price by diverting attention from the important issue of human rights, which we often confuse with spreading democratic systems. That issue which we should trump and advocate has paid a price as a consequence of this policy.
>
> (IQ2 2007)

Notably, because the Iraq war was constructed by the Bush administration as a method for promoting democracy in the MENA region, many critics of the Freedom Agenda have argued that US democracy promotion is in disrepute. For example, Strobe Talbott (2008: xi–x) has argued that 'democracy' has become 'a controversial if not dirty word' caused by 'George W. Bush's invocation of that goal in Iraq and in the Greater Middle East'. This setback to democracy promotion as a cornerstone of American foreign policy was exacerbated by events in Abu Ghraib prison. Indeed, upon capturing Saddam Hussein, President Bush (2003, December 14) declared that 'this event brings further assurance that the torture chambers and the secret police are gone forever'. Yet, months earlier, the USA had taken over Abu Ghraib prison, which for over 40 years had been a notorious centre for torture under the Ba'ath Party regime in Iraq. Under the prison's new title, Baghdad Central Confinement Facility, torture did not stop (see Williams 2006: 7–49). Throughout 2003–4, American military personnel engaged in practices such as stripping prisoners naked, binding them, sexually abusing them, beating them, menacing and attacking them with dogs, and killing them (see Eisenman 2007: 7).

The visual documentation of these events has been widely broadcast throughout the world, and for many has severely damaged America's 'soft power' (see Nye 2004; Gardels 2005). Similarly, the use of extraordinary rendition and the role of detention facilities in Guantanamo Bay and beyond have raised serious credibility questions about the Freedom Agenda (Hassan 2008; Neep 2004: 79–80). Thus, as Thomas Carothers (2006: 64) argued, 'even as the president [Bush] has repeatedly asserted his commitment to a "Freedom Agenda," he has struck blow after self-inflicted blow against America's democratic principles and standards'. The effect of the Bush administration's policies has been to raise suspicion about US motives, which, combined with the MENA region's colonial legacy, has had a significant impact on the Freedom Agenda, leading many indigenous groups to distance themselves from Washington and from the democracy assistance offered (Dalacoura 2005: 969; Kubba 2008; Hassan 2011a). Indeed, as founding members of the April 6th movement in Egypt argued, 'We can't be seen anywhere near an American, could you imagine if we were photographed outside the American embassy what that would do [to our movement]?' (Rashed 2011). Such sentiments are constantly expressed by multiple groups and activists across the region, and hostility towards the USA was clearly evident in Tahrir Square with signs reading 'America, should support the people *not* the tyrant' and 'USA WHY YOU SUPPORT Dectatour [sic]' (Hassan 2011a).

The Freedom Agenda consensus and necessity

In spite of the Freedom Agenda's critics the Bush administration did receive considerable support within the US for promoting democracy in the MENA. The reasons for this are complex, but were well summarised by one of the architects of the Freedom Agenda, Elizabeth Cheney, who argued that:

> The truth is that spreading democracy in the Middle East is not a bad idea nor is it a failed idea. Nor is it an idea that would have been good except that George W. Bush adopted it. It is, by any objective measure, a good idea, the right idea and a necessary policy choice for America today . . . For too many years America perpetuated this status quo. We supported those authoritarian regimes; we ignored the aspirations of their people. This policy . . . brought only a false sense of security and stability.
>
> (IQ2 2007)

By many commentators the notion that the USA should democratise the MENA, coercively if necessary, has been attributed to the neoconservative movement. Since September 11, 2001, it has been widely asserted that a 'neoconservative revolution' or 'neoconservative coup' took place within the Bush administration (Lind 2003: 10; Hudson 2005: 298–301). Accordingly, President Bush was described as the 'callow instrument of the neoconservative ideologues' (Epstein 2003: 13). For some, this 'coup' was simply self-evident, leading to claims such as:

> Unless you lived at the bottom of a well, you've probably noticed that 9/11 and Iraq have had a transforming effect on the American Right. The short formulation is that so-called neoconservatism has triumphed.
>
> (Rauch 2003: 1607)

This is an assessment shared by both critics and advocates of neoconservatism. Richard Perle has argued that the Bush administration followed a neoconservative agenda on 'issue after issue', and William Kristol argued that President Bush's foreign policy was 'basically a neocon foreign policy' (in Hurst 2005: 75–6; see also Fukuyama 2006b). Moreover, by accepting the premise that the Bush foreign policy was neoconservative, some academics have even resorted to critiquing the Bush era vis-à-vis critiquing the neoconservative ideology (see Reus-Smit 2004; Hudson 2005).

That many neoconservatives have advocated democracy promotion in the MENA is unquestionable. Equally, that many neoconservatives advocated the removal of the Saddam Hussein regime in Iraq is unquestionable. Assertions of these positions are readily available within the records of the neoconservative magazine the *Weekly Standard* and past papers produced by the American Enterprise Institute. Relatedly, upon hearing President Bush's second inaugural address, which placed democracy promotion centre stage, Robert Kagan asserted that, 'This is real neoconservatism . . . It would be hard to express it more clearly' (in Mcmanus 2005). Throughout the 1990s, many neoconservatives openly disagreed with the Clinton administration's policy towards Iraq and the MENA more broadly. Paul Wolfowitz long opposed American policy in the region adopted after the 1991 Gulf war, claiming that 'containment is not a static policy: the political dynamics of the Middle East will tend to weaken sanctions over time' (Wolfowitz 1997: 111). By December 1997, this culminated in the conclusion:

> Overthrow Him . . . Military force is not enough . . . it must be part of an overall political strategy that sets as its goal not merely the containment of Saddam but the liberation of Iraq from his tyranny.
> (Khalilzad and Wolfowitz 1997: 14)

Similarly, the desire to overthrow Saddam Hussein was recorded as a wider neoconservative commitment in 1998, under the auspices of *The Project for a New American Century* letter to President Clinton, which argued that it was a 'necessity' to deal with Iraq (PNAC 1998; see Plesch 2005; Mann 2004).[15]

Simply put, the reason for many neoconservatives advocating democracy promotion as a strategy towards the MENA is ideological. It derives from the belief that the internal constitution of a state, and the nature of a regime, matters in international affairs, and that there is an imperative to liberate people (Fukuyama 2007: 114). This belief is supplemented by the notion that values such as 'freedom, democracy and free enterprise' are not culturally specific. Accordingly, they are prescribed a 'universal' appeal, in which all cultures desire them. As a logical corollary of this premise, these values can be applied to all cultures. Democracy constitutes the default condition all societies would adopt, if and only if tyrannical rule were removed (Reus-Smit 2004: 47; Fukuyama 2007: 114–54; Mead 2005: 117). These premises were certainly embedded within the Bush administration's discourse. However, the notion that the Freedom Agenda was the result of a 'neoconservative coup' is deeply problematic, both theoretically and empirically.

On a theoretical level, the 'neoconservative coup' thesis is problematic because it asserts an overtly intentionalist argument. This is done by removing agents from wider cultural and bureaucratic structures. As Tony Smith (2007: 43–4) has argued:

> If the neoconservatives did indeed pour a poison of unlimited expectations into the president's ear, along with those of Vice President Cheney and Secretary of Defense Rumsfeld, these men were more than ready to heed the tempters' message . . . The neoconservative appeal could not have been as great as it was without finding resonance in older and varied sources of American culture and belief.

The 'neoconservative coup' thesis writes out responsibility, and indeed culpability, attributable to a wider group of political actors. This is the case regarding the Iraq war and the Freedom Agenda more broadly. Accordingly, it is essential to note that there was a broad bipartisan consensus in Washington to invade Iraq in 2003, which was demonstrated by the overwhelming congressional approval for the war.[16] As commentators pointed out at the time:

> Not since Congress passed the 1964 Gulf of Tonkin resolution, which helped Lyndon B. Johnson to rapidly expand the Vietnam War, has a President won such broad authority to prosecute an undefined military operation and possible war.
>
> (Reid 2002: 20)

Similarly, calls for promoting democracy in the Middle East, to combat terrorism, have come from a wide spectrum of political actors who are not affiliated with the neoconservative movement, but who contributed to the debate before the 2011 revolutions (see Gause III 2005: 62–3). There are, of course, individuals associated with neoconservatism, such as Charles Krauthammer, who proposed a doctrine of 'democratic realism'. He has argued that 'there's nothing neo about Bush, and there's nothing neo about Blair', and regarding democracy promotion in the MENA claims that 'there is not a single, remotely plausible, alternative strategy for attacking the monster behind 9/11' (Krauthammer 2004a,b).

However, the need to promote democracy in the MENA has also come from neoliberal 'hawks' and political 'moderates'. This is evident in Madeline Albright's (2003) claim that:

> Although I was proud of the Clinton administration's foreign policy, and I understand that democracy cannot be imposed from the outside, I regret not having done more to push for liberalisation in the Arab world.

Further still, individuals such as Kenneth Pollack (2006), former director of Persian Gulf affairs at the NSC, have argued that

> The end state that America's grand strategy toward the Middle East must envision is a new liberal order to replace a status quo marked by political repression, economic stagnation, and cultural conflict... America must move aggressively and creatively to help reformers throughout the Arab world.

Similarly, Larry Diamond and Michael McFaul (Diamond and McFaul 2006: 49–50) have written for a think tank affiliated with the Democratic Party, the Progressive Policy Institute, claiming that:

> In this new embrace of democratic reform in the Middle East, Bush has been correct in intent, even if late to the cause ... Over time, expanding political freedom and accountability through democratising reforms would help to change the political and socio-economic conditions that have spawned terrorist groups and ideologies in the region.

This line of argument strongly resembles that put forward by a Council on Foreign Relations task force directed by Steven A. Cook and co-chaired by Madeline Albright and Vin Weber. One of the central conclusions of this report was that:

> The United States should support democracy consistently and in all regions of the world. Although democracy entails certain risks, the denial of freedom carries much more significant long-term dangers. If Arab citizens are able to express grievances freely and peacefully, they will be less likely to turn to more extreme measures. They will also be more likely to build open and prosperous societies with respect for human rights and the rule of law.
> (Cook *et al.* 2005: 3–4)

Further still, Tamara Cofman Wittes (2008b: 146), in the highly detailed analysis of the Freedom Agenda *Freedom's Unsteady March*, argues that promoting democracy in the Middle East is 'neither a luxury nor a pipe dream. It is a necessity'.

The emergence of a consensus among 'neoconservatives', 'neoliberal' hawks and parts of America's 'moderate' political commentariat has been widely discussed (see Smith 2007; Kaye *et al.* 2008). For Anatol Lieven and John Hulsman the emergence of this consensus represents the formation of a 'Democratist ideology' or 'Democratism' (Lieven and Hulsman 2006). Undoubtedly, there are risks in conflating proponents of democracy promotion into a single united ideology. Although such an approach can be used as a heuristic tool, it runs the risk of obscuring significant disagreements between actors. However, to the extent that there has been disagreement between proponents of democracy promotion it has largely concerned questions of means. The most serious example of this concern is the use of military force, which, in light of the Iraq war, has increasingly been condemned; either entirely as a method of promoting democracy, or through claims that the Bush administration's approach was an 'unsound application' of a 'sound doctrine' (see Traub 2008; Lynch and Singh 2008; Carothers 2007a; Diamond 2005; Fukuyama 2005; Asmus and Pollack 2003). This represents a tension between those who advocate a vindicationalist strategy and those who favour exemplarism. The distinction between the two positions is that those advocating the former view 'America as [a] crusader', whereas those advocating the latter see 'America as [a] beacon' (Kissinger 1994: 18).

A similar tension exists concerning the most fruitful methods of providing democratic assistance to bring about democratic change, in which many exponents of promoting democracy have debated the virtues of promoting economic growth, institutional reform and directly targeting civil society. This is unsurprising given that there is no consensus in the democratisation literature over how best to promote democracy through foreign assistance. Consequently this debate has been particularly pronounced over the question of 'sequencing' and issues concerning how to reshape America's democracy bureaucracy to better coordinate and deliver assistance (see Carothers 2007b). Accordingly, much of the academic and policy debate about the Freedom Agenda was persistently concerned with issues of tempo, between exponents who viewed democracy promotion as best delivered gradually through 'top-down' liberalisation of authoritarian regimes, those who saw the Freedom Agenda as acting slowly alongside already emerging regional trends, and those who saw a more urgent imperative to encourage challenges to autocratic regimes from below (Fukuyama and McFaul 2007; Wittes 2008b; Gerecht 2005).

Going beyond the debate

What is clear from an analysis of the debate surrounding the Freedom Agenda is not only how bifurcated the debate is, but also how the level of analysis underpinning the debate is operating at a purely policy level. It has been based around strategic questions, reviewing issues of whether the United States 'should' promote democracy in the MENA given other long-term interests, and issues of whether the USA 'can' promote democracy given problems such as the 'Islamist dilemma'. In light of the 2011 revolutions, these questions remain important for US policy, but, despite the extensive level of debate, the deeper and more analytical questions appear to have been overlooked almost in their entirety. The question of what exactly President Bush and members of his administration meant when they referred to 'democracy' and 'freedom' is shrouded in silence. Put differently, what exactly was it that the Bush administration believed the Freedom Agenda was supposed to be promoting? These are particularly pertinent questions given that both 'democracy' and 'freedom' are essentially contested concepts (see Whitehead 2003). Both terms are descriptive labels as well as values, which are highly contested between and within specific cultures. Such concepts have contingent meanings, with the 'democracy' of Ancient Greece not being equivalent to the 'democracy' of modern-day America. Similarly, what the Founding Fathers meant by the term 'freedom' is not the same as how the term 'freedom' is deployed in modern-day America. Carl Becker summed up this problem when he referred to 'freedom' as a 'magic but elusive word' (in Foner 1998: xiv). The obvious implication of this is that deploying essentially contested concepts is not a neutral act. Through deploying such terms dialogue emerges with other competing meanings.

This omission is significant as it demonstrates a failure to address first-order questions and a simultaneous obfuscation of a greater understanding of the Freedom Agenda. It excludes an explicitly hermeneutic dimension, and instead proceeds straight to critiques of praxis. On a superficial level, there has been some partial discussion of how and why the Freedom Agenda was developed. For many it is simply a result of the September 11, 2001, terrorist attacks, which led the Bush administration to move from a 'realist' to an 'idealist' foreign policy (see Mazarr 2003). Yet to posit this binary fails to explore the space between them and evaluate the importance of the 'crisis' itself. In turn, such a failure stymies an understanding of how the Freedom Agenda was constituted, and questions of why it was done in this way. Simply put, this has prevented deeper lessons about the Freedom Agenda being learnt at a philosophical level, through to the level of policy praxis. Such a void in our understanding is deeply problematic. Not only does it obscure the institutional legacy the Obama administration inherited, but it also keeps important lessons from being learnt that could inform America's response to the 2011 revolutions in the decades to come.

Accordingly, it is necessary to return to first-order questions and explicitly add a deeper hermeneutic dimension to the analysis of the Freedom Agenda. It is only by doing this that it is possible to reactivate the sedimentary logics that underpinned the Bush administration's approach to the region.[17] This Husserlian aim is of critical importance given the role of 'ideology' within the administration. Indeed President Bush advocated a 'foreign policy based on liberty' and a 'hopeful ideology called freedom' to defeat extremists and their 'hateful ideology' (Bush 2006, July 28). That the President described his strategy as 'ideological' raises questions about the assumptions upon which this ideology rested and how these affected the Freedom Agenda.

To add this hermeneutic dimension and create a greater understanding of the Freedom Agenda, it is necessary to elucidate the methodology and methods that underpinned this research. In the chapter that follows, a constructivist institutionalist methodology is elucidated in detail, demonstrating how such an approach is capable of theoretically and historically (re)constructing the context from which the Freedom Agenda developed. Whilst being sensitive to institutional change, the development of this methodology demonstrates how it is possible to analyse both the underpinning philosophy of the Freedom Agenda and the manner in which this was turned into praxis, adding value to the prevailing literature on the Freedom Agenda.

2 A constructivist institutionalist methodology

The most accurate term to label the methodology pursued in this research is *constructivist institutionalism*, designed explicitly to answer the questions:

- Why was the Freedom Agenda constructed?
- How was the Freedom Agenda constructed?
- Why did the Freedom Agenda develop in its particular institutional formation, rather than in other formations?
- How did the Freedom Agenda evolve over time?

Answering these questions required an approach that was explicitly concerned with political continuity and change within institutional settings. This is provided through the constructivist institutionalist methodology outlined below. Yet the term 'constructivist institutionalist' is highly problematic at one level, as there are a multitude of constructivist positions. Many authors have documented the plethora of positions that fall under the constructivist umbrella, and added many adjectives as a result. For John Gerard Ruggie (1998a: 35–6) there is 'neoclassical', 'postmodernist' and 'naturalistic'. For Katzenstein, Keohane and Krasner (1998: 675–8) there is 'conventional', 'critical' and 'postmodern'. For Christian Reus-Smit (2005) constructivism has evolved into 'systemic', 'unit-level' and 'holistic' variants. Moreover, Emanuel Adler (1997: 335–6) originally settled on cleavages between 'modernist', 'rule-based', 'narrative knowing' and 'postmodernist', but then altered the boundaries to 'modernist', 'modernist linguistic', 'Critical' and 'Radical' (Adler 2005: 95–8). Still some authors simply choose to distinguish between the constructivism espoused by various scholars, thus distinguishing 'Wendt-ian', 'Kratochwil-ian' and 'Onuf-ian' constructivism (Zehfuss 2002). The list of possible adjectives that could be applied to constructivist approaches does appear to be dizzyingly endless along a spectrum of 'thick' to 'thin'.

Evidently, adding 'institutionalist' to a constructivist framework would appear to be just another adjective. Yet the term does serve a function. First, the term 'constructivist institutionalism' has arisen from new institutionalist literature in comparative political analysis. Given this, it implies a distinctive analytical position for those who are familiar with authors such as Colin Hay and Vivien Schmitt.[1] Significantly, it should be recognised that constructivist institutionalism has affinities with constructivism in International Relations (IR), but the two 'are perhaps best seen as parallel if initially distinct developments' (Hay 2006: 64). However, whilst their origins are distinct, the methodology outlined below synthesises constructivist institutionalism with 'rule-based/modernist linguistic' constructivism. The intention of this synthesis is to stress the centrality of complex institutional change, and the specific ontology that this implies, whilst providing an account of social reality in which social facts are constituted by language and rules. This allows an interpretive account of the Freedom Agenda to materialise, which specifically addresses the questions set out above.

Unsurprisingly, such an interpretive account makes space for the role of agency, discourse and narratives, and writes out the need for systemic approaches to IR and the notion that we can legitimately attribute anthropomorphic qualities to the state. Thus, it should come as no surprise that this volume engages with the structure and agency debate, specifically, so a constructivist institutionalist conception of *social change* and *social action* is brought forward. One could easily add that it is agents that do the 'constructing' so central to social constructivism. This is of course not to say that the notion of the state is not important to the analysis, but rather that the constructivist institutionalist conception of the state is that of an institutional structure created by agents. This clearly concurs with Bob Jessop's assertion that 'it is not the state which acts: it is always specific sets of politicians and state officials located in specific parts of the state system' (Jessop 1990: 367).[2] Given this, foreign policy cannot be abstracted from the domestic context from which it arises, and it must be recognised that the construction of foreign policy takes place within institutional settings.

Notably the use of the term 'institutions' itself needs explaining. Much like constructivist literature in IR, a varied and incommensurable set of positions are espoused in new institutionalist literature, ranging from Rational Choice institutionalism to Discursive institutionalism (see Schmidt 2006).[3] Apparent in each is a different conception of not only what an institution is, but as a logical consequence the nature of the state and how to study it. The constructivist institutionalist approach outlined in this research arises from an initial engagement with this literature, and a desire to overcome its limitations. Its starting point is therefore with insights outlined by Colin Hay (2006: 57–60), who argues that:

> Constructivist institutionalists were motivated by the desire to capture, describe, and interrogate institutional disequilibrium. As such, rational choice and normative/sociological institutionalism, which rely albeit for rather different reasons on the assumption of equilibrium, were theoretical non-starters . . . most routes to constructivist institutionalism can trace their origins to historical institutionalism. Yet, if historical institutionalism has typically served as an initial source of inspiration for constructivist institutionalists, it has increasingly become a source of frustration and a point of departure.

The underlying logic of historical institutionalism is that of presumed equilibrium exemplified by the term 'path-dependent'. Fundamentally, this draws to different extents on calculus and cultural logics, both of which either presume equilibrium or are equilibrating (Hay 2006: 61; see also Hall and Taylor 1996). Such schemes could take this volume only so far in answering the questions it seeks to address. If carried forward they would desensitise the study of the Freedom Agenda to post-formative institutional change. Moreover, without a well-built conception of change it is particularly difficult, if not impossible, to develop an understanding of the Freedom Agenda, its formation and its subsequent evolution. What is needed, and what constructivist institutionalism provides, is an account of political agency that does not see actors as 'driven' in the same way as other forms of institutionalism. Whereas rational choice institutionalism is dominated by accounts of actors being driven by utility maximisation, sociological institutionalism simply replaces the drivers with norms and cultural conventions, and historical institutionalism appeals to both (see Hay 2006: 61). If policy is 'driven' in such a manner it is difficult to account for social change, and more fundamentally it brings into question notions of what role there is for agency in policy making.

If agency is to be understood as a concept which expresses the free will that actors exercise in social action, then, to the extent that actors are 'driven', this is reduced. This fails to identify the fact that individual agents create and remain at the centre of these very 'drivers'. In this context, assertions that the Freedom Agenda is simply driven by 'America's democracy promotion tradition' or 'American exceptionalism', as if 'tradition' and 'exceptionalism' are driving factors of behaviour, are deeply problematic. Such factors cannot be treated as if they are inbuilt logics fated to be reproduced irrespective of which agents hold power over the American foreign policy making apparatus. Without addressing issues of interpretation and strategic action, agents become characterised as cultural dupes destined to perform rigid acts of social (re)construction without any reflexivity or possibility of societal change. Avoiding such a parsimonious fallacy is at the heart of the constructivist institutionalist approach, and demonstrates the added value it brings to the analysis of the Freedom Agenda. Moreover, it is this refusal to substitute actors in the name of analytical parsimony that has allowed constructivist institutionalism to develop a distinct ontology and a distinctive approach to the structure and agency debate.

Structure and agency: the strategic-relational approach

The basic crux of the structure and agency debate revolves around how these two factors relate to one another (Adler 2005: 104). Notably, in IR literature, it is difficult to discover a position that refers to the structure and agency debate in such stark terms as to exclude the other entirely. It is therefore more useful to think of positions in IR as degrees between two extreme poles of structuralism and intentionalism.[4] Within such a context, it is more fruitful to consider how structure and agency interact, and how a vernacular can be constructed that resonates with existential human experience. This will provide an account of the relationship between structure and agency that can be carried through this volume and help describe the construction and institutionalisation of the Freedom Agenda.

Central to the constructivist institutionalist position is a focus on understanding complex institutional change, and it is through its account of structure and agency that this is made possible. As Colin Hay (2006: 63) argues:

> Actors are strategic, seeking to realise certain complex, contingent, and constantly changing goals. They do so in a context which favours certain strategies over others and must rely upon perceptions of that context which are at best incomplete and which may very often prove to have been inaccurate after the event.[5]

Whilst this may appear to be a deceptively obvious statement it is worth deconstructing and developing further. Notably the 'actor' is seen as an analytically distinct entity that engages with and within social structures. As a result, it is worth making a further analytical distinction between Dasein and agency.[6] The former is literally an entity 'being-there', and as a term is 'purely an expression of its being' (Heidegger 1967: 33). Dasein is 'thrown' into the world and has agency when it engages with its social condition (see Gadamer 1994; 2004: 244–53). The term 'agency' refers to such action and social conduct; its etymological roots lie in the term *agere*, meaning 'to do'.[7] This distinction implies *intentionality*, which is an intrinsic property of Dasein and provides the capacity to act consciously with free will and at least deliberate between choices and potential routes of action.[8] However, Dasein by definition is a 'being-in-the-world' and consequently is constrained/bound by the context that world provides. The importance of this is that the mind and the body become intricately linked to the world, removing the Cartesian anxiety whilst making the distinction between structure and agency a purely analytical construction. Accordingly, structure and agency are in practice completely interwoven; a premise that provides a pragmatic starting point for an existentialist analysis.

A similar dialectical position is adopted by Nicolas Onuf and the Miami International Relations Group. Central to this group's thinking is that the distinction between agency and structure is an analytical one, as one implies the other. In such circumstances to remove either removes the ontological status of the other. Both are mutually constitutive. Thus:

> Fundamental to constructivism is the proposition that . . . social relations *make* or *construct* people – *ourselves* – into the kind of beings that we are. Conversely, *we make* the world what it is, from the raw materials that nature provides, by doing what we do with each other and saying what we say to each other . . . *people make society, and society makes people. This is a continuous, two-way process.*
>
> (Onuf 1998: 59, emphasis added)

To assert this ontological dualism[9] between structure and agency creates analytical problems. It implies a need for what Anthony Giddens calls a 'third ontology' beyond both structuralism and intentionalism (Giddens 1976, 1979, 1984). Indeed both constructivist institutionalism and rule-orientated constructivism owe a great deal to Giddens's structuration theory. The similarities clearly lie in the rejection of ontological individualism and pure ontological structuralism. Yet both constructivist institutionalism and rule-orientated constructivism have departed from structuration theory in significant ways. Notably, the reason in both cases is that structuration theory fails to provide a mechanism capable of merging structure and agency at a methodological level. Both point to an irony in Giddens's work, in which he 'appeals to an ontological duality (interlinking) of structure and agency, [whilst] he delivers an analytical dualism (separation)' (Hay 2002: 120; see also Layder 1998: 100; Gould 1998: 79–81).

The attempt to transcend the structure–agency dualism is, however, made in different ways. The most established approach in constructivist institutionalism draws on Bob Jessop's 'strategic-relational approach', the focus of which is 'upon the dialectical interplay of structure and agency in real contexts of social and political interaction' (Hay 2002: 127). As a result, the focus is shifted to focusing on the *strategic actor* and the *strategically selective context*; not on the inseparable ontological factors of structure and agency. Thus, the terms inscribe the dualism within them (see Jessop 2005; Hay 2002: 126–34). By focusing on the strategic content of action, it is accepted that:

> agents both internalise perceptions of their context and consciously orient themselves towards that context in choosing between potential courses of action . . . Yet for that action to have any chance of realising such intentions, it must be informed by a strategic assessment of the relevant context in which strategy occurs and upon which it subsequently impinges.
> (Hay 2002: 129)

The innovation behind this approach is that it provides a method of describing the dualism of structure–agency, but also recognises that Dasein orientates itself towards its environment and in doing so comes up against a strategically selective context. In such a schema, certain strategies are more likely to be rewarded than others and, whatever the context, outcomes are never determined structurally. Given this, an actor's preferences are never assumed to be fixed, or to be determined by the material circumstances in which the actor finds itself. Therefore, different actors in similar material circumstances will construct their interests and preferences differently. Moreover, the same actor will review, revise and reform his or her perceived interests and preferences over time (Hay 2002: 130). Once Dasein is recognised as possessing strategic ability, which is a capacity to devise and revise in order to realise its intentions, it is implied that Dasein engages with its environment by judgement. Dasein becomes an agent with agency, and that agent's knowledge of the world and strategic orientation towards that world is in a continuous process of pragmatic interpretation (see Sharpcott 1994: 71).

Once policy-makers are therefore seen as *strategic agents*, ideas assume a critical relevance because it is ideas that provide the point of mediation between policy-makers and their environment. The perceptions they hold are at best incomplete and may prove to be inaccurate after events. Thus they can be seen to be normatively orientated towards the *strategically selective context*. Such sentiments represent constructivist institutionalism's commitment to a 'turn to ideas'.

Ideas and the construction of interests

In opposition to rationalist theories, constructivist institutionalism takes interests as needing to be explained rather than to do the explaining with (Blyth 2003: 702). This directly challenges the distinction between ideas and interests. This lies in stark contradiction to the manner in which ideas are often treated in the analysis of foreign policy. For many scholars 'ideas' are frequently treated as objects that provide an explanatory variable that are persistently separated from interests. The seminal volume exemplifying this trend is Judith Goldstein and Robert Keohane's *Ideas and Foreign Policy* (Goldstein and Keohane 1993). Although 'ideas' are introduced as a variable this is not intended to 'challenge the premise that people behave in self-interested and broadly rational ways' (Goldstein and Keohane 1993: 5). As such 'variations of interests are not accounted for by variations in the character of the ideas that people have' (ibid.: 27). Within this scheme, consideration of where interests come from is avoided and ideas are reduced to post-hoc rationalisations that justify policies made on the grounds of already given material interests (see Laffey and Weldes 1997: 199–201).

For constructivist institutionalism, ideas are constitutive and define interests. Interests are seen as social constructions and therefore are not natural or independent of agents. Consequently, interests are produced, reproduced and transformed through the discursive practices of strategically selective actors, and emerge out of the representations they construct of the strategically selective context they face (see Weldes 1998: 218). Thus, it is out of descriptions of the situation, and definitions of the problem (representations), that state officials make sense of the world around them and construct interests (Weldes 1996: 280).[10] The implications of this are clearly applicable to the concept of the 'national interest'.[11] Thus:

> national interests ... are social constructions that emerge out of a ubiquitous and unavoidable process of representation through which meaning is created. In representing for themselves and others the situation in which the state finds itself, state officials have already constructed the national interest.
> (Weldes 1996: 283)[12]

This clearly demonstrates constructivism's desire to return to first-order questions and focus on interest formation, rather than a rationalist focus on interest satisfaction (Reus-Smit 2005: 203). Moreover, this all rests on the ontological nature of ideas and the distinctions made between modernist constructivism and constructivist institutionalism. Whereas the former, epitomised in *The Culture of National Security* (Katzenstein 1996), largely conceptualises norms and identities as constituted by culture and therefore as stagnant ideational structures, the latter rejects such naturalistic assumptions in favour of espousing narrative explanatory protocols that account for the dynamic nature of ideas (see Schmidt 2006: 112).[13] This creates a 'tipping-point' between modernist constructivism, which has a close affinity with sociological institutionalism (see Finnemore 1996a; Berman 2001), and constructivist institutionalism, which asserts the importance of how actors (re)conceptualise the world 'as a resource to promote change' (Schmidt 2006: 112). Thus the dividing line rests on how ideas and 'causation' are related to behaviour; whether ideas are 'causes of action' or provide 'reasons for action' (see Ruggie 1998b: 22).

Ideas: towards a conception of continuity and change

The turn to ideas is central in answering the questions about the Freedom Agenda. At the acme of the constructivist institutionalist position is a definition of institutions as 'codified systems of ideas and the practices they sustain' (Hay 2006: 58).[14] This is important because, if ideas provide the basis of institutional creation and perpetuation, then institutions are 'observer-dependent'. As John R. Searle (2007: 82) explains:

> A feature is observer-dependent if its very existence depends on the attitudes, thoughts and intentionality of observers, users, creators, designers, buyers, sellers and conscious intentional agents generally. Otherwise it is observer (or intentionality) independent. Examples of observer-dependent features include money, property, marriage and language. Examples of observer-independent features of the world include force, mass, gravitational attraction, the chemical bond, and photosynthesis.

This distinction has a significant impact on the study of politics and political change, not least because most of political reality is observer-dependent. Accordingly 'something is an election, a parliament, a president or a revolution only if people have certain attitudes toward the phenomena in question' (Searle 2007: 83). Political phenomena therefore require ontological subjectivity, which once acknowledged opens a subjunctive 'ontology of possibility'. Consequently, the notions of political continuity and change are inseparably linked representations of the world and how these help generate regulative and constitutive rules for strategic agents.

Without breaking them down in this way, constructivist institutionalists have reached similar conclusions about the role of ideas and agency in relation to political continuity and change. Such a position is highly indebted to Peter Hall's (1993) sustained, consistent and systematic attempt to accord a key role to ideas in institutional outcomes whilst synthesising it within a historical context. Notably, Hall draws an analogy between Thomas Kuhn's (1962) *Structure of Scientific Revolutions* and the policy making process. This allowed Hall to introduce the concept of paradigms into institutional analysis.

Kuhn argued that science develops in a succession of enduring paradigms that are punctuated by periods of 'revolutions'. Within the revolutionary period the existing paradigm is challenged and replaced. Subsequently, it is possible to distinguish a phase of 'normal science' in which the paradigm is ascendant and uncontested. Within the 'normal' period the paradigm provides an interpretive framework for 'routine puzzle-solving', which demarcates the boundaries and methods of scientific competence. By contrast, however, with an increase and accumulation of 'anomalies' a challenge to the paradigm can emerge because of a loss of confidence, and thus create a period of 'exceptional' science. Within such a period, the anomalies cause some scientists to reject the former paradigm's constraints in search of answers not provided by the old paradigm. This creates a period in which competing approaches emerge, until a consensus can be created and institutionalised. Thus, the space created by the failure of the old paradigm is replaced with a new paradigm, which emerged in the 'exceptional science' period, consequently establishing a new phase of normal science under the domination of a new paradigm (see Kuhn 1996; Hall 1993; Hay 2001: 196–7; Benton and Craib 2001: 58–63).

Hall extends this analogy to the policy making arena, by arguing that policy is made within context of a 'policy paradigm'. Thus Hall (1993: 279) asserts that:

> policy makers customarily work within a framework of ideas and standards that specifies not only the goals of policy and the kind of instruments that can be used to attain them, but also the very nature of the problems they are meant to be addressing . . . this framework is embedded in the very terminology through which policy makers communicate about their work, and it is influential precisely because so much is taken for granted and unnameable to scrutiny as a whole . . . this interpretive framework [is] a policy paradigm.

A policy paradigm is internalised by politicians and policy experts, and acts as a source of guidance for conducting and evaluating policies, which defines the range of legitimate methods available. This in turn demarcates the very intentions and objectives of policy itself. This in short 'comes to circumscribe the realm of the politically feasible, practical and desirable' (Hay 2001: 197). Ideas are therefore perceived not as static objects but rather as dynamic social products that can help maintain continuity and produce change. Such thinking has increasingly been incorporated into the study of foreign policy making by authors such as Jeffrey Legro, who has argued that:

> in addition to preferences and strategies, actors must also have ideas or beliefs, that is, some notion about which strategy . . . is best suited to achieving the preferred outcome. For example to know that states prefer security above all other goals tells us little about what behaviour they believe will achieve it.
> (Legro 2005: 24–5)

The importance of this insight, and Hall's appeals to Kuhn's theory, is that it informs the constructivist institutionalist approach to understanding political continuity and change between policy paradigms.

As Figure 2.1 demonstrates, there are distinct 'phases' to this conception of continuity and change. Notable is the manner in which it deals with the *form of change* and not the *content of change*. It provides an account of not *what* will change, but *how* change will occur.[15] This conception of social change is often characterised by the term 'punctuated equilibrium'. As such it draws a 'basic analytic distinction . . . between periods of institutional creation and periods of institutional stasis' whilst asserting that 'new structures originate during periods of crisis' (Krasner 1984: 240).

By representing the form of political change in this way, it is possible to ask *what preceding crisis led to the development and consolidation of the Freedom Agenda for MENA?* This question appears to have a resounding answer in the form of September 11, 2001. The events of that day are seen as path-shaping because of their ability to change American foreign policy-makers' conceptions of threat and the national interest, and therefore events shortly before and after September 11, 2001, provide a starting point for the empirical account of the Freedom Agenda developed in later chapters.

Understanding political change in this form provides a conceptual framework that has clear methodological implications. It links the events of September 11, 2001, to the adoption of the Freedom Agenda policy at a theoretical level, and therefore provides a framework on which to support empirical data. Moreover, by linking the process of change to strategically selected agents' representations of the world, this form of change is not epiphenomenal. The task is to identify the meanings strategically selected agents construct to understand events, and not look for hidden 'causes' 'driving' action. Thus, the context of post-crisis action cannot be divorced from an understanding of the crisis, and, consequently, understanding the Freedom Agenda requires tracing its genealogy back to the moment of crisis that shaped its birth. This point is all the more serious if it is accepted that 'policy responds less directly to social and economic conditions than it does to the consequences of past policy' (Hall 1993: 277). As a result, the moment of crisis and the manner in which it is understood are seen as pivotal, as the theoretical assertion being made is that a change in ideas precedes a change in policy. Consequently, defining and elucidating what is meant by the term 'crisis' is fundamental.

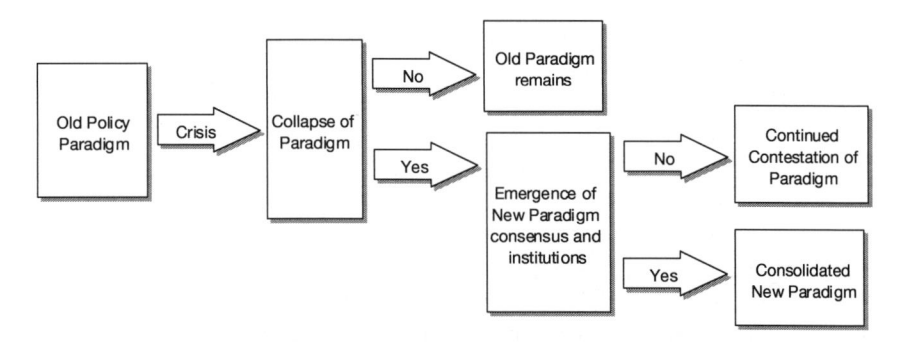

Figure 2.1 Process of continuity and change within the policy paradigms.

Crisis: a constructivist institutionalist approach

'Crisis' is an often invoked but ill-defined term. Significantly, the literature within International Relations, Foreign Policy Analysis and Crises Studies tends to converge on a definition that focuses on situations that have a high risk of war. Such approaches have taken considerable amounts of research down the route of identifying 'under what conditions do crises lead to war, and when are they resolved peacefully?' (Richardson 1994: 3). As such, the aim has been to treat crises as self-evident empirical challenges, and all too often what constitutes a crisis is received uncritically as 'a-problem-to-be-solved'. Once a crisis is defined by its referential descriptive elements, the next step is to go about 'setting a strategy' to resolve the 'problem'. Such accounts demonstrate little appreciation of or desire to analyse the observer-relative nature of 'crises'. They consequently fail to return to first-order questions about how threats are recognised, how enemies are labelled, how groups come to imagine danger and how these help constitute a 'crisis'. Such factors are paramount to this research's aim of understanding the formation of the Freedom Agenda.

An excellent example of this referential theory of crisis, which has understandably received considerable attention, is the Cuban Missile Crisis. According to the popular narrative the crisis was constituted by the Soviet Union strategically placing offensive weapons on Cuba (see Young and Kent 2004: 236–41).[16] Yet such a description is problematic, especially once it is considered that early on Secretary of Defense Robert McNamara identified that placing missiles on Cuba made no difference to the strategic balance (see Weldes 1999a: 84–6; Allison and Zelikow 1999: 89; Hudson 2007: 92).[17] This creates the need for a moment of reflection and for analytical distinctions to be made. What made the Cuban Missile Crisis a 'crisis' was not, to use John Searle's distinction, the 'brute facts'; it was not the ontologically real placement of the weapons on Cuba itself (see Searle 2005 [1969]: 50–3, 1995: 1–9). The intrinsic qualities of the weapons themselves were incapable of generating a 'high risk of war'; rather it was the *meaning* attached to the objects that was of critical importance, and what this meant for US credibility around the world (Weldes 1999a: 85). The importance of this is that it demonstrates a hermeneutic quality that underlies observer-dependent phenomena. This moves us closer to understanding how a particular situation becomes understood as a 'crisis' and therefore to answering the question 'what exactly is a crisis?' Accordingly, a closer inspection of the etymology of 'crisis' highlights this observer-relative quality.

The term was originally used in drama and medicine, to denote 'moments when the intensification of processes requires some resolution' (Sztompka 1994: 34). This etymology is reflected in Habermas's medical analogy. The thrust of the analogy asserts that a crisis is 'the phase of illness in which it is decided whether or not the organism's self healing powers are sufficient for recovery' (Hay 1996a: 86). The significance of such a proto-definition is, as Habermas (1975: 1) argues, that 'the crisis cannot be separated from the viewpoint of the one who is undergoing it . . . to conceive of a process as a crisis is tacitly to give it a normative meaning'. Thus, to term a situation a 'crisis' is to interpret and make a judgement about that situation. Moreover, as Colin Hay (1996a: 87; see also Bell 1971; Brecher, Wilkenfeld, and Moser 1988) argues:

> [I]f we trace the etymology of the term, we find that this fusion of subjective perceptions and objective considerations is in fact crucial to the origins of the term. 'Crisis' ... literally 'to decide' – is a moment of decisive intervention, a moment of rupture and a moment of transformation.

This implies abrupt systemic transformation, which highlights that a crisis is not just a moment of impending demolition evident in a policy's failure, but rather a catalyst for alteration and development, 'a moment in which a new trajectory is imposed upon the system *in* and *through* crisis'. To paraphrase Alexander Wendt, crises are 'what states make of them'; that is to say that crises are what the strategic foreign policy agents bound within a strategically selective context 'make of them'.

Any conception of crisis, when understood in these terms, requires both ontologically objective and subjective considerations; both brute and institutional facts. What constitutes a foreign policy crisis is not intrinsically self-apparent in the events themselves. The events themselves, to paraphrase Mark Blyth (2003), 'do not come with instruction sheets'. During crises, strategic actors are not only faced with the 'uncertainty condition', but also disagreement amongst actors across large bureaucracies. This culminates in a situation where

> agents must argue over, diagnose, proselytize, and impose on others their notion of what a crisis actually *is* before collective action to resolve the uncertainty facing them can take any meaningful institutional form.
> (Blyth 2002: 9)

Within this scheme, representations ascribed to a particular situation assume critical importance. No longer is a crisis definable by reference to the existence of objective conditions external to the actors themselves. Crises are part of the political process, wherein *strategic interpreters*, embedded in a *strategically selective context*, intervene. Crises are 'acts of intervention where sources of uncertainty are diagnosed and constructed' (Blyth 2002: 10).

Crisis narration: the content of political change

Once foreign policy actors are seen as *strategic interpreters,* the fact that they puzzle under conditions of general uncertainty should come as no surprise. Representations of September 11, 2001, become crucial not only to the initial creation of the war on terror, but additionally to post-formative policy development and institutional evolution. Herein lies the key relationship between September 11, 2001, the war on terror and the eventual formation and adoption of the Freedom Agenda. These events were placed within a narrative built in the aftermath of the initial crisis. This point is particularly salient because it fuses the espoused definition of crisis with one of the key practical insights of Narrative Policy Analysis, namely that:

> Stories commonly used in describing and analysing policy issues are a force in themselves, and must be considered explicitly in assessing policy options ... these stories often resist change or modification even in the presence of contradicting empirical data, because they continue to underwrite and stabilise the assumptions for decision making in the face of high uncertainty, complexity, and polarization.
>
> (Roe 1994: 2)

Narratives are therefore a means of suppressing uncertainty, because they embed representations of 'what has gone wrong' and of 'what is to be done'. Strategic foreign policy actors attempt to assimilate the meaning of new events in terms of past experience, and therefore confidently maintain beliefs. Part of the process of constructing a crisis is therefore explaining the failure of previous policy by narrating its causes and establishing a model for crisis resolution. Strategic policy makers are forced to fix a narrative of the past, as it is only by doing this that it is possible to create an understanding of how to proceed. Whereas 'punctuated evolution' describes the form of change, the content and directionality of change is derived from and tied to resulting 'crisis narratives'.

The critical importance of narratives is that they are by necessity distorted representations of events serving a social function, rather than simply mirroring 'reality'; thus deploying a narrative is not a neutral discursive act.[18] When narratives are articulated they consist of logically structured plots and configurative emplotment of events and actors into a storyline, pragmatically establishing order and meaning.[19] Moreover, they identify forces and attribute motivations and lessons for the future, giving rise to 'a collective understanding of how to understand the past, situate the present and act towards the future' (Barnett 1999: 8). Story-telling becomes a communicative method of 'securing and endorsing the assumptions needed to make decisions under conditions of uncertainty and complexity' (Roe 1994: 9).

The implication of this is that narratives are generated from, and help reconstruct, particular theoretical substructures that influence praxis. This is important because it has been a long accepted premise of many Foreign Policy Analysis (FPA) scholars that:

> *[P]rofessional analysts of foreign affairs and policy makers (as well as ordinary citizens) think about problems of foreign and military policy in terms of largely implicit conceptual models that have significant consequences for the content of their thought.*
>
> (Allison and Zelikow 1999: 3, italics in original)

It is narratives that embody these in the social world and make this content publicly accessible. This 'theoretical substructure' has been given many names ranging from 'heuristic content' to 'security imagery' to 'policy paradigm', but the point remains that it is ontologically subjective. It is inseparably tied to Dasein's existential intrinsic constitution, to being in a world that is constantly changing and vastly complex, requiring simplification by re-presentation.[20] However, in the same process:

> What the facts are, what kind of event has occurred, which interpretation of an event makes sense and can therefore become myth, and which facts are relevant to the understanding of an event are all in part determined by the narratives in which these facts and events are embedded and through which they take on meaning.
>
> (Weldes 1999a: 40)

Thus, to understand the transformation of US foreign policy that led to the rise of the Freedom Agenda, it is necessary to understand the mechanisms and processes by which perceptions of the September 11 crisis were mobilised and shaped. Consequently, the process of crisis 'narration' is fundamental to the empirical account of the Freedom Agenda, as this social act constructs how threats and identities are discursively constituted and born throughout a crisis. As Jutta Weldes (1999b: 37) argues, 'crises are social constructions that are forged by state officials in the course of producing and reproducing state identity'. Within this framework practices of representation assume a critical importance, and have vital implications on methodological analysis. Under such conditions, there is little choice but to accept the perceptual and discursive qualities of the moment of crisis in an analysis of subsequent institutional change. If it is narratives of crisis that represent events and are responded to, rather than the conditions that gave rise to the crisis, then the response to the crisis can only be studied by de-structuring the narrative.[21] This creates a separation between the conditions that gave rise to the crisis and the response, because the crisis narration need not be sophisticated or accurate in its understanding of the crisis context (Hay 2001: 204).[22] This has clear implications on the methods deployed in this research. A variety of narrative discourse analysis is required that allows for theoretically informed process-tracing, in addition to allowing the theoretical substructure of policy narratives to be rendered apparent.

Discourse and ideological effects

Crucial to the espoused constructivist institutionalist methodology is a concern with how ideas are sedimented in 'discourses' that are articulated through narratives. Under these circumstances, to identify a discourse is

> to point to the existence of structured sets of ideas, often in the form of implicit and sedimented assumptions, upon which actors might draw in formulating strategy and indeed, in legitimising strategy pursued for quite distinct ends.
>
> (Hay and Rosamond 2002: 151)

This highlights the importance of agents not only in the construction of institutions, but also in the maintenance of an institution in its post-formative period and transformation. In this schema it is discourses that become sedimented, and help to (re)produce institutional rules and practices. Consequently, by defining social institutions as codified systems of discourses and the discursive practices they sustain, the manner in which institutions are a product of and embedded in a tapestry of IDFs can be rendered apparent. This is of crucial importance because institutions are seen as 'an intermediate level of social structuring, which faces Janus-like "upwards" to the social formation, and "downwards" to social actions' (Fairclough 1995: 37).

An IDF can be understood as a system of signification that is complicit in producing the practice of domination and subjugation. This can be elucidated by looking at how discourse relates to ideology. In a general sense, 'discourse' commonly refers to language, yet it has come to mean something more specific. As a result of the influence of Michel Foucault on 'Discourse Theory', the term 'discourse' is often used to define various 'systems of representation' (see Hall 2001; Foucault 2002; Foucault and Gordon 1980). Thus, as Stuart Hall (1996: 201) explains, 'discourse' refers to

> a group of statements which provide a language for talking about – i.e. a way of representing – a particular kind of knowledge about a topic. When statements about a topic are made within a particular discourse, the discourse makes it possible to construct the topic in a certain way. It also limits the other ways in which the topic can be constructed.

Not only is the constructed and constitutive nature of knowledge recognised within such a definition, but so too is historical contingency.[23] Discourses provide a way of representing knowledge about a particular topic at a particular historical moment through symbols and language (Hall 2001: 72). Discourses are therefore complicit in the construction of social reality. Not only do they help (re)constitute systems of knowledge and beliefs, but in doing so they help constitute social subjects and social relations (Fairclough 1992: 36). The power of a discourse therefore culminates in its ability to constitute identities and perceived interests, and therefore to help to frame interpretations of behaviour (see Klotz and Lynch 2007: 11). Moreover, discourse when institutionalised has the ability to create a form of power that is qualitatively different to that of brute physical force (see Lincoln 1989: 3–12); discourse (re)constructs *deontic powers*. The internalisation of a discourse brings with it rights, duties, obligations, commitments, authorisations, requirements, permissions and privileges; all of which 'exist as long as they are acknowledged, recognised, or otherwise accepted' (see Searle 2007: 93). Given this it is discourses that help establish and constitute rules.

By emphasising the role of discourses in the construction of social reality, it is clear that 'speaking is doing' (Gould 1998: 81), and speech acts are both representative and performative. Speaking consists of prescriptive statements that establish rule(s) for action, which are constitutive and regulative. Moreover, as relatively stable sets of rules take shape and help form institutions, the ruling structure embodied in the institution always works to the advantage of some agents at the expense of others (Onuf 1997: 15). Moreover, rules provide a universal social experience that Dasein is thrown into and can never escape. Once understood in this way, discourses can be seen as constituting towards 'rule-making' and the 'naturalisation' of ideologies. This role is clear if it is accepted that, whereas discourses are complicit in processes of signification, once they are reified into prevailing systems of rule(s), the term 'ideology' can be used to represent 'effects'.

Although traditionally the term 'ideology' has had clear Marxist connotations towards the problematic dichotomy of 'true' and 'false' consciousness, if understood as the effects of discourse this need not be carried forward.[24] Whilst discourses define the rule(s), in doing so they seek to legitimise power relations that have 'directionality' and 'ideology effects' born from the rule structure they seek to maintain. Such effects are 'ideological' to the extent that they pertain to 'relations of domination/subordination, [and] facilitates their reproduction ... what makes some discourses ideological is their connection with systems of domination' (Purvis and Hunt 1993: 497).[25] The crucial point to note is the manner in which this 'operates systematically to reinforce and reproduce dominant social relations' (Purvis and Hunt 1993: 497; see also Eagleton 1991; Thompson 1984; Dijk 1998; Fairclough 2003). Indeed, as Nicolas Onuf emphasises, '*rules yield rule*' (Onuf 1998: 74), by being re-articulated to legitimise systems of rule and the hierarchies they help to maintain. This point is all the more pertinent if one takes the example of Edward Said's *Orientalism*. The discourse signifies to the extent that it deals with the Orient as a constructed object, but this process is not separate from ideological effects and systems of rule(s). As Said ([1978] 2003: 3) points out:

> Orientalism can be discussed and analysed as the corporate institution for dealing with the Orient – dealing with it by making statements about it, authorising views about it, describing it, by teaching it, settling it, ruling over it: in short, Orientalism as a Western Style for dominating, restructuring, and having authority over the Orient.

To understand IDFs therefore requires an understanding of the imbricated articulations that underpin them as well as the systems of rule(s) this helps (re)construct. It is only by doing this that the Husserlian aim of 'reactivating' the IDFs that underpin the war on terror and the Freedom Agenda's 'sedimentation' is possible. Moreover, such a move recognises that 'understanding a practice involves theoretically and historically (re-)constructing its context' (Grossberg 1992: 55). Therefore, at an empirical level it is necessary to diachronically investigate the processes of articulation and interpellation. These are the very processes in which ideas are drawn together to produce discursive representations that culminate into IDFs more generally and the war on terror crisis narrative in particular. Once 'articulation' and 'interpellation' are seen as mechanisms, they provide a route into analysing existing structured sets of ideas and the implicit and sedimented assumptions that discourses contain. These concepts go beyond the notion that all that is important to politics is representations, and raise first-order questions about 'how dominant constructions were produced and why alternatives, which were theoretically or logically possible, were easily marginalised' (Weldes 1999a: 119). Therefore, to understand the Freedom Agenda as a strategic policy pursued for quite distinct ends requires an understanding of articulation and interpellation.

Articulation

To utilise the concept of articulation, it clearly requires delicate unpacking.[26] Thus, as Stuart Hall argues:

> [T]he term has a nice double meaning because 'articulate' means to utter, to speak forth, to be articulate. It carries that sense of language-ing, of expressing, etc. But we also speak of an 'articulated' lorry (truck): a lorry where the front (cab) and back (trailer) can, but need not necessarily, be connected to one another. The two parts are connected to each other, but through a specific linkage that can be broken.
>
> (Hall and Grossberg 1996: 141)

The definition that Hall provides is instructive as it draws to attention the etymological roots the term has from the Latin *articulāre*, which means to divide (meats etc.) into single joints. An 'articulation' refers to 'a joint' and a 'setting of bones'. Once this is acknowledged, it provides Hall with a starting point to build upon:

> [A]n articulation is thus the form of the connection that *can* make a unity of two different elements, under certain conditions. It is a linkage which is not necessarily, determined, absolute and essential for all time . . . So the so-called 'unity' of a discourse is really the articulation of different, distinct elements which can be rearticulated in different ways because they have no necessary 'belongingness'. The 'unity' which matters is a linkage between that articulated discourse and the social forces with which it can, under certain historical conditions, but need not necessarily, be connected.
>
> (Hall and Grossberg 1996: 141)

Thus, to articulate is to generate a moment of speculative 'closure' or 'fixity'. It is to signify, which inevitably draws upon and works with discursive formations, and thus reconstitutes them (see Weldes 1999a: 98). This opens up a situation in which the existential nature of being-in-the-world determines that articulations must occur. However, the content of such articulations is neither random nor necessary, as they draw on a variety of historically contingent resources, such as tradition and language (see Weldes 1999a: 98–100). This introduces an element of the 'conventional' into the analysis, and, if articulations embed a history/genealogy, then they are not arbitrary but a 'specific product of the people who have developed the language in question' (Williams as cited in Weldes 1999a:

100). Moreover, it is through the process of articulation that speech acts are able to connote socially meaningful assumptions and logics, that is to say that they (re)present a propositional content that is larger than a strictly lexical interpretation of the content would allow; they carry a hermeneutic element that is not necessarily the same to all observers. In this manner articulations help reconstruct, represent and regulate a 'common sense' that acts as a 'background' for future articulations; contingent connections are therefore presented as 'inherently or necessarily connected, and the meanings they produce come to seem natural, come to seem an accurate description of reality' (Weldes 1999a: 99). Thus:

> Insofar as linguistic phenomena cannot represent the world, they constitute a world of their own, a world true only to itself. Words are performative, but only in a theatrical sense. By enacting the propositional content of what is spoken, any such performance simultaneously objectivizes the world it creates and hides behind its representational success.
>
> (Onuf 2001: 246)[27]

Onuf's theatrical metaphor is particularly fecund, as it echoes a wealth of constructivist literature that utilises the heuristic metaphor of 'game-play' (see Milliken 2001; Howard 2004). The use of this metaphor, however, differs greatly from that of Game Theory and Rational Choice approaches. Whereas the others indulge in the language of 'utility calculations' and notions of positivist objectivity, the constructivist institutionalist approach outlined above remains dedicated to a hermeneutic-understanding approach.[28] Such a position recognises that the social world is woven together by rules and meanings (see Hollis and Smith 1991: 5; 68–91).[29] This puts aside the behaviourist accounts of social action, and places rules and meaning as central for consideration.

The adoption of the game metaphor is significant because it challenges the notion that September 11, 2001, was 'epochal', yet allows the analysis to cut to the crisis moment when a decisive intervention in the form of a re-articulation of ideological discourses was being performed. Thus, out of the brute moment of destruction, brought by turning aircraft into kinetic weapons, US foreign policy agents were able to construct a crisis, and from the narrative that pursued develop an alternative policy paradigm.[30] Starting the analysis at this historical point in time, however, runs the risk of suggesting that September 11, 2001, provided an epochal moment. This is not what is being put forward, as it is rather more helpful to think of the events of September 11, 2001, as an escalation in an already ongoing round of interactions; a rearrangement and not a rupture with the past. At their heart, since the Second World War, US–MENA relations have been forged by a set of intermingled partnerships and conflicts. Yet the events of the war did provide the catalyst for a transformation in the rules of that game, and helped establish subsequent categorisational logics embedded in America's 'war on terrorism' discourse. This is important because the manner in which the war on terror and Freedom Agenda were constructed did not arbitrarily arise from a vacuum, but equally was not epiphenomenally determined. The construction of the crisis marks a period of 'bound innovation', in which path-shaping discourses were (re)articulated and framed by strategic agents to enact an elite project. That is to say, the construction of the crisis enabled strategically selective actors to take persistent discourses, and articulate them together to make a securitisation move, which was subsequently institutionalised within the body of the American foreign policy bureaucracy.

To enact such a project is not a simple task. Within highly complex societies such as the United States, foreign policy cannot simply be imposed from the top down; it must be articulated to the public at large and translated down the line to the level of policy implementation. In effect, policy change requires cooperation and acceptance if it is to be institutionalised (see Jackson 2005: 8). To understand the role of strategic foreign policy actors and the elite project they have termed the *Freedom Agenda*, the notion of articulation is invaluable, as it is through articulation that foreign policy actors were able to render intelligible their historical situation on September 11, 2001. Moreover, it is from this process of articulation that the crisis was constructed; as a particular phenomenon that was represented in a very specific way and given very particular meanings on which action was then based. To postulate the role of articulation in this process is to render apparent the power of the foreign policy elite. This was not confined to the power to *respond* to a crisis, but additionally located in *identifying, defining and constituting* a crisis discourse. This is instructive because it establishes that politics finds its sources not only in power relationships 'but also in uncertainty ... [g]overnments not only "power" ... they also puzzle. Policy making is a form of collective puzzlement on society's behalf' (Heclo as cited in Hall 1993: 275–6). Thus, strategic political agents do not just project their representations onto the world with a prescriptive will, but rather they *react* to phenomena as it happens; they *react* and *prescribe*.

Strategic policy-makers are forced to fix a narrative of the past as it is only by doing this that it is possible to create an understanding of how to proceed. The process of constructing a crisis discourse is therefore not imposed by outside actors, but rather constructed inside the state, by actors who are bound by the normative context in which they find themselves (see Fay 1996). In this manner narratives, and the discourses they articulate together, have cognitive and normative functions that attempt to produce perlocutionary effects. They assert a representation of the world that resonates with, and attempts to reconstruct, national identities as well as provide the foundations for conceptually sound policy programmes in the hope of producing a motivational force; they structure cognition and provide a model for future action.[31] The narratives embodied in the 'war on terrorism' discourse therefore provide a key locale for analysis because they embody the articulations that gave rise to, and are embedded in, the institutionalisation of the Freedom Agenda.

Interpellation and Identity

The concept of interpellation is analytically separable from articulation, yet is inseparably linked in the process of social construction. The term was first used by Louis Althusser (1971: 163) in *Ideology and Ideological State Apparatuses*, to suggest that ideology 'acts' or 'functions' in such a way that it 'recruits' subjects among the individuals (it recruits them all), or 'transforms' the individuals into subjects (it transforms them all) by that very precise operation which I have called *interpellation* or hailing, and which can be imagined along the lines of the most commonplace everyday police (or other) hailing: 'Hey, you there!'.

The significance of this is that the individual becomes the subject in the moment of interpellation, through the process of recognition and interaction. Therefore, interpellation represents a 'double constitutive' moment. The first moment is the construction of a subject position that creates the possibility of identity. The second is the moment in which the concrete individual is interpellated or 'hailed' into the constructed subject position and takes on that identity (Althusser 1971: 160). This second moment is insertive, as an individual's intentionality is projected into a position and takes on the 'role' that a particular identity provides. In this moment it is possible to take on a social identity under the subject positions of 'we', 'us', 'America', 'the West' and so on, which provide the basis of social action through collective intentionality. These actions therefore provide the possibility of discourses having communicative and coordinative functions that culminate in ideological effects.

Interpellation is a particularly useful concept within a game-play metaphor. Constructed subject positions provide 'gateways' from which to 'enter the game', whilst additionally inscribing a set of social rules and expectations that can be followed by the strategic actor in the strategically selective context. This is significant because it draws attention to representations of identity and the adoption of subject positions, but also demonstrates that 'identity is an inescapable dimension of Being, rather than an epiphenomenal property, for both individual and collective subjects' (Campbell 1998: 226). This is all the more important because this inescapable property of Being means that all strategic actors adopt a subject position or identity, which carries with it 'particular ways of functioning in the world' (Weldes 1999a: 104), but is simultaneously embedded in rule(s) and power relations.

The power of narratives greatly relies on the process of interpellation. Through emplotment, subject positions are asserted and members of the audience are being asked to insert themselves into the horizon being articulated. This is crucial because the power of the articulator lies not in direct indoctrination but in the seduction of the audience. The power of a strategic political agent's articulations lies in the agent's ability to *encode* and 'frame the discursive context within which political subjectivities are constituted, reinforced and re-constituted' (Hay 1996b: 261). However, 'the basis of interpellation lies in the inherently imaginative process of *decoding* through which we, the readers, inject ourselves into the narrative structure' (ibid.: 262). The moment of dialogue is therefore a political moment of negotiation in which the articulator and audience fuse in a process that culminates in degrees of recruitment or rejection, which is anything but passive or static. The concept of interpellation therefore helps highlight both the conflictual and the cooperative side of politics, which is an integral part of any society.

By introducing the concept of interpellation it is possible to stress the importance of the '9/11' crisis narrative in constructing consent for the war on terrorism. The power of a narrative 'stems from its complexity' (Polletta 2006: vii), in its ability to fill a storyboard by articulating multiple aspects of social reality. Indeed, 'even the most "simple" of stories is embedded in a network of relations that are sometimes astounding in their complexity' (Cobley 2001: 2). Yet, despite the complexity of its construction, to be successfully interpellated the narrative needs to resonate with a broad audience (see Weldes 1999a: 104). This generates a milieu in which identities are concurrently both a product of and the justification for foreign policy. Given this, the manner in which identities are articulated in the crisis narrative is of crucial importance, not least as a starting point for any systematic textual analysis.

The process of interpellation is inherently linked to narratives and identity through the process of subjectification and identification. To stipulate a decoder is to raise questions concerning the politics of location, in which the subject is 'dislocated' but interpellated into subject positions made possible within discourses.[32] When identity is defined in this way, it is possible to see how 'identity is the understanding of oneself in relation to others' (Barnett 1999: 9; see also Huntington 2005: 21–33), something that both individuals and groups can take possession of rather than something intrinsic or essential. Identity, as an expression of socially recognised differences, is, *ipso facto*, overwhelmingly constructed. Under such circumstances identities are never unified, but 'fragmented and fractured'; the interactive process itself helps produce multiple constructions, which can be antagonistic as they intersect (Hall 2000: 17). 'National identity', which underlies the very concept of the *national* interest, is one such construction (see Anderson 1983). Moreover, by virtue of being relational, identities depend on the construction of an 'inside' and 'outside' status and collectively an 'us' and a 'them' that exist in the socially negotiated imagination of the identity holder. This contingency highlights not only the historical nature of 'the nation', but also the manner in which identities are in constant motion as the process of interaction and negotiation unfolds. National identities must themselves be narrated and (re)presented in a collectively understood 'geo-biography'. This relies on strategic agents articulating the constitutive inside and outside, which relies on logics of equivalence and difference to open and close the boundaries of the nation. The notions of articulation and interpellation therefore highlight the communicative, coordinative, cognitive and normative functions of IDFs in (re)constructing the 'United States' as much as the 'foreign Others'; nation-building is therefore a constant two-way process 'internally' and 'externally'. Thus it is possible to agree with Richard Jackson's assertion that

> the language of the 'war on terrorism' is not simply an objective or neutral reflection of reality; nor is it merely accidental or incidental . . . Rather, it is a deliberately and meticulously composed set of words, assumptions, metaphors, grammatical forms, myths and forms of knowledge – it is a carefully constructed discourse – that is designed to achieve a number of key political

goals: to normalise and legitimise the current counter-terrorist approach; to empower the authorities and shield them from criticism; to discipline domestic society by marginalising dissent or protest; and to enforce national unity by reifying a narrow conception of national identity. The discourse of the 'war on terrorism' has a clear political purpose; it works for someone and for something; it is an exercise of power.

(Jackson 2005: 2)

Once conceived in this manner the Freedom Agenda should be understood not simply as a policy of promoting democracy in the MENA, but rather as an exercise of power in US–MENA relations. Therefore answering how and why the policy was constructed, and why it developed and evolved in a particular way, informs us of something much greater than a simple analysis of the policy itself; it reveals how 'democracy promotion' is inherently bound with conceptions and projections of American power over the region and its peoples.

Methods: computer-assisted narrative discourse analysis and ethnography

The research methods adopted in this volume are a logical corollary of the constructivist institutionalist methodology. By positing the importance of narratives in the construction of crises, and the role of articulation and interpellation in underpinning IDFs, a set of methods necessarily followed on that provided a dual function. The first was to conduct a theoretically informed *process-tracing* of the emergence of the Freedom Agenda. This allowed the evolutionary logics of the Freedom Agenda to be rendered apparent; it was therefore explicitly concerned with how the policy was formed and evolved over time. The second function of the methods adopted was to allow a *textually oriented discourse analysis* to be conducted. This allowed the hermeneutic dimension to be rendered apparent, and was therefore concerned with the IDFs that underpin the Freedom Agenda.

The adoption of this dual function takes a wide interdisciplinary perspective that combines social and textual analysis (see Fairclough 2003: 2–3; Fairclough 1992, 1995). This perspective recognised that textual analysis was insufficient in edifying the relationship between discourse and social practice, and therefore reinforced it by combining a textually oriented discourse analysis with a social approach to the study of foreign policy. Such a method maintained the premises that:

- Language is an irreducible part of social life, and therefore of foreign policy.
- One way of doing foreign policy research is through a focus on language, and therefore the deployment of discourse analysis.
- This deployment can be reinforced by other analytical strategies, and in this research this is done with a social and institutional analysis to foreign policy, as set out by the constructivist institutionalist methodology.

52 A constructivist institutionalist methodology

Accordingly, this research adds value to other approaches used to analyse American foreign policy through its emphasis on a detailed diachronic analysis of post-crisis transformation in US foreign policy discourse. Discourse is therefore seen as dynamic and transforming, which recognises that a distinctive quality of 'discourse' is in fact embedded in the etymology of the term. Discourse, which has its roots in the Latin *discursus*, literally means to 'run about' or to 'run here and there', which captures a sense of movement, interaction, haste and disturbance (see Virilio 1991: 113–14). A diachronic analysis allowed this sense of movement to be captured, and highlighted how the Freedom Agenda is the result of political processes; it is a social response to a crisis and, consequently, the focus of this study is to foreground the lexicon of definitions, rules and discourses that construct the Freedom Agenda as a policy paradigm, and elucidate the ideological effects of constructing a policy in this way at the level of policy implementation.

Significantly, positing a constructivist institutionalist methodology raised a series of research questions that could not be easily dismissed. Such questions concern authority, such as 'whose articulations are important in the construction of crisis narratives?' and 'whose articulations are important in the (re)construction of the Freedom Agenda?' This volume is based on the analytical decision to regard foreign policy production as an elite project. This accepts the premises of securitisation theory more broadly, but in particular Richard Jackson's theoretically based but empirically informed premise that 'the war on terrorism is an elite-led project and these elites have provided the primary justifications and overall vision. It thus seems logical to focus primarily on their words' (Jackson 2005: 26). Thus, it is with caution that it is noted that US foreign policy is run by contingently bound elites; this expression refers to the limited number of strategic agents located in specific parts of the state system: custodians of the machinery of the state. Consequently, this research fits within broader literature employing discursive methods in Foreign Policy studies that focuses on the discursive productivity of elites (see Milliken 1999: 236). It therefore adopted a qualitative approach, focusing on interpreting the Bush administration's discourses as they pertain to the Freedom Agenda and its evolutionary logic. However, this was widened to include other 'political elites'. Thus, although this research focused on President Bush and senior members of his administration, it moved vertically down through the executive branch, but also horizontally across the legislature and judiciary, and across borders to policy practitioners and aid recipients in the MENA region itself.

Once this analytical decision was made, 'texts' were selected and generated. A text was considered to be an act of spoken or written language. It is therefore an umbrella term for speeches, interviews, hearings, legislation, web postings, government documents, internal government reports and documents, press releases, letters, emails and written articles by leading figures within the administration in Washington, DC, and its embassies throughout the MENA region. Thus, as Richard Jackson (2005: 17) argues:

> Text . . . sets out the parameters of official thinking and forms the basis of policy and action; it establishes the core principles, assumptions and

knowledge ... implies the kind of actions that will be undertaken and provides the overall story or narrative for public understanding of the issue.

On the premise that foreign policy is an elite project, a logical consequence was to gather texts that pertained to the Freedom Agenda but were produced by elite actors within the state system. Text selection was based on the two key criteria. First was the importance of the source, which was determined by either a high level of public attention or symbolic importance. The second was relevance to the Freedom Agenda policy. This produced around 2,500 texts ranging from the time when G. W. Bush was running for presidential office to subsequent efforts by the former administration at legacy construction. This database also included texts produced by the Barack Obama campaign, and the Obama administration until December 2011. The database therefore covered a more than 12-year period from September 23, 1999, to December 31, 2011. Undoubtedly, this favoured analysing texts produced/delivered by President Bush and President Obama, because of their central role in communicating the Freedom Agenda to the public. Moreover, the role of President allowed them to be privileged storytellers, with the authority to utilise the power of the state to garner media attention. However, text selection was not isolated to presidential speeches and public addresses; it included remarks and speeches made by senior officials within the administration, congressional hearings, legislation and official documents produced by the administration and the collective bureaucratic organisations in the US government that promote democracy. There was a high level of access to such sources in the forms of speeches, interviews, press briefings, press releases, policy documents, fact-sheets, reports to Congress, legislation and congressional debates. Notably, in many cases, these sources intentionally target a public audience and were transcribed into public records and official department websites.

By selecting sources based on their association with the foreign policy elite, text selection was highly specific. However this was supplemented with semi-structured interviews carried out at multiple points throughout 2008 to 2011 in Washington, DC, and various countries in the MENA region. In Washington, this focused on elites who either were within or had been within the White House, the Department of State and the Department of Defense throughout the Bush and/or Obama administrations. Semi-structured interviews were conducted with policy experts outside government, at institutions such as the *Carnegie Endowment*, the *Brookings Institute*, the *Council on Foreign Relations, the American Enterprise Institute* and the *National Endowment for Democracy* (NED). The interview length varied from 20 minutes to two hours, and proved fruitful because of targeting individuals that had worked on issues regarding the Freedom Agenda. Within the MENA, interviews were also carried out with multiple recipients of Freedom Agenda funding and research was conducted in Tahrir Square from July to October 2011 with social movements and protestors involved in the removal of the Mubarak regime.

Once texts were selected, and interviews transcribed, they were placed into a QSR NVivo 8 database. This helped with the analysis of just under 2,500 documents within an NVivo project. This allowed a computer-assisted qualitative data

54 A constructivist institutionalist methodology

analysis (CAQDAS) to be conducted. This method was specifically chosen to allow a large volume of texts to be made more physically manageable. Thus, the software does not, and cannot, carry out analysis. Rather it is a tool that allows manual labour to be cut, so that more time can be spent focusing on the analysis of texts in a fluid, consistent and dynamic manner.

When each text was entered into the NVivo project, it was given a title. The title started with the year, month and day in which the text was produced. This allowed the texts to be ordered temporally, and chronologically analysed within the software. Accordingly, a theoretically informed process-tracing of the Freedom Agenda was conducted, which allowed significant periods of policy formation and alteration to be identified. Examples of the title format include:

- 1999_09_23 Citadel Period of Consequences (G. W. Bush);
- 2000_10_05 Vice Presidential Candidate Debate (R. Cheney & J. Liberman);
- 2006_08_07 ME Crisis between Lebanon and Israel (G. W. Bush & C. Rice).[33]

Step one of the data analysis process was to conduct a detailed review of the texts, to maintain consistency of format throughout the database. *Step two* required subjecting the text to analysis, in which sections of the text were manually coded. This was done by making extensive notes using the DataBit function and coding the data at each source. Thus, a 'Code whilst Browsing' method was adopted that created a series of 'free nodes'. Once this had been completed, *step three* was undertaken, which reviewed the complete series of free nodes for overlaps and inconsistencies. Consequently, the coding process was an active research process culminating in iterative yet cumulative manoeuvres. *Step four* consisted of a series of computer-assisted searches, notably focusing on word frequency and co-occurrence between nodes, and to ensure completeness. *Step five* consisted of converting free nodes into 'tree nodes', which created clusters of nodes around hierarchical concepts. For example, nodes pertaining to the construction of American identity were brought together under tree node title 'Representations of American Identity'. Once this had been completed, *step five* was to review the project to ensure accuracy, detail and consistency. Adopting these steps allowed greater familiarity with the texts and a rigorous analysis to take place.

This analysis focused on *process-tracing* whilst conducting a *textually oriented narrative discourse analysis*. Ultimately, this allowed the IDF that underpins the Freedom Agenda to be identified. To conduct a narrative discourse analysis and code each individual text within the NVivo project, each text was subjected to a series of questions:

- How are actors in the text represented and how are identities constructed?
- What forms of argument structures are used?
- How are events sequenced within the text, and how are the past, present and future represented?
- Is there a plot running through the text and cases of emplotment?
- How are causal relationships explicitly, or implicitly, represented in the text?

- What ontological and epistemological claims are being made within the text?
- What assumptions, beliefs and values underlie the language of the text?
- What articulations are being made within the text?
- What meanings are implied by the context of the text, and how does this context alter the meaning of the words?
- What patterns can be observed in the language, and how do different parts of the text relate to each other?
- How consistent are the discursive constructions within the text?
- What regulative and constitutive 'rules' are (re-)constructed within the text?
- What are the power functions of the discursive constructions?
- What knowledge or practices are normalised and legitimised by the language of the text?
- How does the current text relate to the previous texts?

As a direct result of these questions individual free nodes were created, which were then organised into hierarchical tree nodes. Specific attention was paid to recurring themes and the manner in which a narrative was constructed and framed. This latter stage was completed by analysing small parts of texts, whole texts and across texts. The purpose of which was be to rigorously reconstruct the dominant logics, representations and intentions that were put forward in relation to the Freedom Agenda. The fruits of this labour produced the empirical analysis that follows.

3 From candidate to crisis
Laying the discursive tracks of the Freedom Agenda

The constructivist institutionalist methodology, set out in the previous chapter, is particularly fruitful in setting out a starting point for the analysis that follows. If it is the construction of September 11, 2001, that ultimately culminated in the construction of the Freedom Agenda, then it is analysing the post-Cold War context within which the George W. Bush administration was strategising that should instigate this analytical account. This allows for a more systematic analysis of continuity and change, whilst permitting this chapter to highlight how the initial phase of the 'war on terror' was constructed, and contributed to the eventual institutionalisation of the Freedom Agenda. Moreover, from the process-tracing narrative analysis conducted to generate this empirical account, it was evident that as a presidential candidate, Bush publicly set out an IDF that would in many ways characterise his administration's tenure in office. It was this IDF that was in place before September 11, 2001, and would evolve after the moment of punctuation and the construction of the crisis, albeit within the context of a new policy paradigm. Consequently understanding the shape of its various definitions and articulations is an important way of helping to contextualise the Bush administration's response to the crisis and the subsequent construction of the Freedom Agenda. This point is particularly pertinent to the construction of the Freedom Agenda, as it was between late 1999 and early 2001 that Bush began to articulate and define concepts such as 'freedom', 'power', 'peace' and the 'national interest'.

Candidate G. W. Bush and the post-Cold War era

That the collapse of the Soviet Union had a profound impact on American foreign policy throughout the 1990s has become something akin to received wisdom. Gone was the overarching rationale of containment, and in swept a period of uncertainty about how to use American global supremacy. In effect, the fall of the Soviet Union led to a collapse of an ideational orthodoxy used to guide US foreign policy, leaving policy-makers deprived of consensus and an overarching policy paradigm for routine puzzle-solving. This was reflected in American's wider political discourse, as the desire for a 'peace dividend' fractured both the Democratic and Republican parties on Capitol Hill. Whilst the Democrats were struggling to compose a method of marrying progressive policies with American power, the Republican Party fractured into isolationists, contract Republicans, realist pragmatists and neoconservative idealists (Chollet and Goldgeier 2008: 318–26; Bowen and Dunn 1996: 1–29). This made achieving a foreign policy consensus on most issues highly problematic, as this period became defined by the mêlée being waged in Washington and the nation more generally.

This is to argue not that a radical reform had taken place, but rather that the 'marketplace of ideas' was filled with policy prescriptions that would have been contentious in the Cold War period. Accordingly, exactly where on the political agenda foreign policy should feature was being re-examined and redefined. Yet, given the profound nature of the change within the international system, numerous critics have argued that many of the broader objectives in the post-Cold War era resembled those in place before the collapse of the Soviet Union, which included a rejection of isolationism, support for democracy, and a tendency to see the new order as conterminous with American national interests (Cox 1995: 5).

However, without an overarching policy paradigm or strategic narrative underpinning US policy, the USA appeared to have lost its sense of purpose, which was captured by the very term 'post' Cold War; people knew where they had been, but not where they were, much less where they were heading (Haass 1997: 21). This allowed two predominant temperaments to prevail in this period of uncertainty: *pessimistic declinism* and *triumphant exhilaration*. The first of these temperaments was captured in Paul Kennedy's (1987) bestseller, *The Rise and Fall of the Great Powers*. Spanning from 1500 to 1980 Kennedy laid out a pattern of rise and decline that Great Powers have undergone. Yet he extended his analysis through to the end of the twentieth century, predicting the rise of powers such as China, Japan and the European Economic Community, and the decline of the Soviet Union and the United States. This decline was regarded as an 'enduring fact' given US 'imperial overstretch' and the notion that the 'United States' global interests and obligations [were] far larger than the country's power to defend them all simultaneously' (see Kennedy 1987: 565–698).

Conversely, it was Francis Fukuyama's (1989) article 'The End of History?' that came to represent triumphant exhilaration. In an attempt to understand the importance of the end of the Cold War, Fukuyama sought to place the events into a 'larger conceptual framework'. Consequently, drawing on Hegel and Kojève, he set out an argument that described a new stage of history characterised by the 'triumph of the West, of the Western *idea*'. For Fukuyama this represented an 'unabashed victory of economic and political liberalism' evident in the 'total exhaustion of viable systematic alternatives to Western liberalism'. This constituted the 'end of history', defined as the 'the end point of mankind's [sic] ideological evolution and the universalisation of Western liberal democracy as the final form of human government'. This was a bold and encouraging argument, which placed the 'West' into the category of 'post-historical' whilst the 'Rest' was classified in the 'historical' phase of this teleological progression (see Chollet and Goldgeier 2008: 21–3; Callinicos 1995: 15–43). Philosophical problems aside, this was a deeply influential article that permeated post-Cold War America.

These two temperaments offered contrasting views of the politically feasible, practical and desirable, for America's foreign policy. On the one hand, pessimistic declinism suggested a cautious more prudent foreign policy, and if taken to the logical extreme it could even be used to advocate neo-isolationism. Yet, on the other hand, triumphant exhilaration suggested a bold inevitability of Western superiority; cautious or not, the 'historical' bloc would inevitably arrive at the 'post-historical' phase of human existence. In essence, triumphant exhilaration seemed to provide a purpose: to ensure that other countries arrive at, and accept, the dominance of economic and political liberalism. However parsimonious this dichotomy may appear, it does provide a heuristic device for understanding the prevailing circumstances in which the 2000 presidential campaign was fought, and in helping explain George W. Bush's campaign platform.

That G. W. Bush ran for presidential office claiming that he would re-invent a national purpose was not unusual. All American presidencies aspire to provide symbolic leadership and a re-invention of national purpose, whether it is in the form of a New Deal, New Frontiers, New Foundations, New World Order, New Covenant or Democratic Enlargement (Dumbrell 1997: 54–6; Chollet and Goldgeier 2008: 315). Bush declared his early offering at the Ronald Reagan Presidential Library, proposing a 'Distinctly American Internationalism' (Bush 1999, November 19). This stagecraft was intended to stake Bush's claim to be the heir of the Republican darling Ronald Reagan, as the candidate set out a philosophy of limited government, tax cuts and 'peace through strength'.[1] Given such circumstances, it is perhaps somewhat inaccurate to label 'pre-9/11' Bush as a 'realist', as many commentators have sought to do. Indeed, Thomas Carothers has argued:

> [D]uring the 2000 presidential campaign Bush and his advisers had made it very clear that they favoured great-power realism over idealistic notions such as nation-building or democracy promotion.
>
> (Carothers 2004: 63)

That Bush and his team were seen as realists was certainly helped by Bush claiming, in his 'Distinctly American Internationalism' speech, that 'a president must be a clear-eyed realist' whilst asserting that enemies are put in 'check by strength and purpose and the promise of swift punishment' (Bush 1999, November 19). Yet a closer analysis of that speech reveals a series of caveats:

> Some have tried to pose a choice between American ideals and American interests – between who we are and how we act. But the choice is false. America, by decision and destiny, promotes political freedom – and gains the most when democracy advances . . . I will address these responsibilities . . . To each, I bring the same approach: A distinctly American internationalism. Idealism, without illusions. Confidence, without conceit. Realism, in the service of American ideals.
>
> (Bush 1999, November 19)

Such a statement gives pause for thought, not least because it seems to suggest a much more complex vignette than the label 'realist' captures. Bush's 'Distinctly American Internationalism' openly inscribed a tension between realism and idealism. This dialectic is unsurprising given the extent to which the battle between idealism and realism has shaped the history of American foreign policy. However, upon closer analysis of the Bush campaign it is clear that these two larger philosophical bodies of thought were playing out through the temperament of pessimistic declinism and triumphant exhilaration embedded in a very distinct IDF.

The prevalence of pessimistic declinism was certainly evident in the Bush campaign's critique of President Clinton. During the 2000 presidential campaign, Bush ran on a foreign policy platform that sought to discredit the Clinton administration, and therefore undermine the appeal of his political opponent Al Gore. At the 2000 Republican National Convention, he asserted that:

> Our current president embodied the potential of a generation . . . to what end? . . . no great purpose . . . Little more than a decade ago, the Cold War thawed . . . But instead of seizing this moment, the Clinton/Gore administration has squandered it. We have seen a steady erosion of American power and an unsteady exercise of American influence.
> (Bush 2000, August 15)

In juxtaposition to Al Gore's Clintonesque platform, the Bush campaign began to frame a narrower definition of what constituted the nation's interests, emphasising American power and primacy as the lone superpower (see Krauthammer 2001). Evidently, Carothers was correct in asserting that the Bush campaign derided nation-building. In the first presidential candidate debate, when questioned directly about when it would be appropriate to use force, Bush replied:

> Well, if it's in our vital national interest, and that means whether our territory is threatened or people could be harmed, whether or not . . . our defense alliances are threatened, whether or not our friends in the Middle East are threatened . . . I don't think we can be all things to all people in the world. He [Al Gore] believes in nation-building. I would be very careful about using our troops as nation builders . . . I believe we're overextended in too many places. And therefore I want to rebuild the military power.
> (Bush 2000, October 3)

By making reference to an overextended and declining military Bush certainly appealed to pessimistic declinism. Bush sought to construct an image of himself as a more prudent candidate, willing to use force, but if and only if more traditional security threats presented themselves. Yet embedded in the candidate's response was something of a paradox. Why was it necessary to rebuild military power, if the number of military missions was to be lower as a result of abandoning smaller nation-building exercises?

In part, the Bush campaign's answer to this came in the form of a stark description of deep military decline:

> Not since the years before Pearl Harbor has our investment in national defense been so low as a percentage of GNP. Yet, rarely has our military been so freely used – an average of one deployment every nine weeks in the last few years. Since the end of the Cold War, our ground forces have been deployed more frequently, while our defense budget has fallen by nearly 40 percent.
> (Bush 1999, September 23)

Invoking Pearl Harbor is a powerful discursive tool. In this context, Bush was clearly trying to invoke a sense of danger and the potential results such military weakness could invite. Conspicuously, this depiction of military decline was silent on the fact that the USA had the world's largest defence expenditure and between 1999 to 2000 outspent the next six nations combined (Chamberlin 2004: 5).[2] Nor was it mentioned that defence cuts began under President Bush Snr, or that 1999 saw the Pentagon receive the biggest financial boost since the end of the Cold War (Chollet and Goldgeier 2008: 297). The prevailing narrative was simply that:

> Eight years ago, the Clinton–Gore administration inherited a military ready for dangers and challenges facing our nation. The next president will inherit a military in decline. But, if the next president is George W. Bush, the days of decline will be over.
> (Bush 2000, November 3)

What is perhaps more interesting about the narrative presented by the Bush campaign, however, is that it embedded a deeper, more ideological answer to why the USA should rebuild military power. In particular, Bush's 'Distinctly American Internationalism' articulated the need for American primacy inspired by the ideals of hegemonic stability theory. It was throughout the late 1980s and early 1990s that advocates of a primacy strategy had drawn on hegemonic stability theory to begin advancing an alterative policy to containment. Their interpretation had led to the conclusion that peace is a collective good which is best secured by the unqualified and unchallenged preponderance of US power. The logic being espoused was that peace and stability could be secured by having such overwhelming preponderance that others would not dare attack (see Nye 2007: 64–5). This was the view put forward in President Bush's inaugural address in January 2001:

> *we will build our defenses beyond challenge, lest weakness invite challenge* ... The enemies of liberty and our country should make no mistake: America remains engaged in the world by history and by choice, *shaping a balance of power that favors freedom.*
> (Bush 2001, January 20)[3]

Much has been made about the last part of this quote, notably because the phrase 'a balance of power that favors freedom' was later used by the Bush administration in its 2002 *National Security Strategy of the United States*, which attempted to legitimise the 2003 Iraq war. That this phrase was used in President Bush's inaugural address has been widely overlooked. Yet what is important about the notion of a 'balance of power' in the context used by President Bush is that it was not referring to an equilibrium. The superficial articulation of the two terms 'balance of power' and 'favors freedom' creates an oxymoron. That this balance favours freedom would suggest imbalance and a forward-leaning approach to foreign policy; not equilibrium. This rules out the most typical manner in which a 'balance of power' is traditionally used by Realists in International Relations theory. That is to say that it is not being used in a classical realist sense, whereby states consciously adjust their alliances to ensure that no single state dominates the international system. Rather, as Christian Reus-Smit points out, the phrasing suggests primacy because 'it is sustained American ascendancy that will favour human freedom' (Reus-Smit 2004: 35).

Once understood in this context, it is clear that from the moment it took office the Bush administration sought to maintain US supremacy in what Charles Krauthammer termed the 'unipolar moment'. This was deemed to be in both the American national interest and the interest of the world; or, more boldly expressed, what was good for America was good for the world. This US-centric approach was advocated by Bush, who argued that when in power he would be led by 'what's in the best interests of the United States' (Bush 2000, October 11).

In part this US-centric position reflected the Bush campaign's perceived need to reassert American interests and 'renew America's purpose' (Bush 1999, September 23, 2000, August 15). As Bush narrated the past he described the USA's post-Cold War foreign policy as drifting, and failing to develop an overarching rationale to utilise American supremacy. This position also reflected appeals to the Reaganesque premise of 'peace through strength'. Such sentiments were expressed in claims that the US military should be used to 'fight and win war and therefore prevent war from happening in the first place' (Bush 1999, September 23) and 'I know that the best defense can be a strong and swift offense' (Bush 2000, October 3). Yet instructively, because such statements were being articulated through the prism of primacy inspired by hegemonic stability theory, it is possible to conclude that throughout the 2000 campaign, and taken into office, was a desire to ensure that America would maintain freedom of action and preserve its position of preponderance (see Rice 2000).

Such a position infers a noteworthy definition of 'power'. In particular, 'power' was described as something quantifiable and derived from the possession of military and economic superiority. This wrote out conceptions of 'social power', or rather deontic powers, such as rights, duties, obligations, commitments, authorisations, requirements, permissions and privileges (see Searle 2007: 93; Reus-Smit 2004: 45–50). Such factors were dismissed as a product of 'discomfort' and 'reflexive appeals' or as being of 'second-order' importance, rather than seen as possessing intrinsic value for the pursuit of foreign policy goals. This position underpinned the unilateral emphasis that would accompany the Bush administration into office, manifesting itself in policies towards the Anti-Ballistic Missile (ABM) Treaty, the International Criminal Court, global climate change, and distrust of the United Nations, North Korea and Iran (see Buzan 2004: 166–70). This was, in a term coined by Richard N. Haass, 'à la carte multilateralism'. The term reflects the 'unilateral bias' and 'ideological leanings' of the Bush administration, which was 'too quick to dismiss the benefits of multilateralism and legal frameworks and too quick to go it alone' (Haass 2009: 182–3). In essence, the Bush administration put forward a narrow definition of power, which made military and economic factors its main preoccupation. This was done in the expectation that this form of power would maintain US preponderance, because '*America's* pursuit of the national interest' was expected to deliver global conditions for 'freedom, markets and peace' (Hassan 2008: 271).

Notably, this narrow quantifiable theory of power was not the only conception of power put forward throughout the Bush campaign. Many accounts of this campaign have written out the extent to which the Bush team put forward a conception of power that was directly related to the triumphant exhilaration of the post-Cold War era. In particular the Bush campaign articulated a conception of 'freedom' with 'power':

> Now, *we trust freedom. We know freedom is a powerful, powerful, powerful force*, much bigger than the United States of America.
>
> (Bush 2000, October 11)

This conception of 'power' is clearly not the same as that of military or economic power. Rather, power here is seen to be a property of 'freedom', which was described as having an ontological status in the 'human spirit':

> Military power is not the final measure of might. Our realism must make a place for the *human spirit*. This spirit, in our time, has caused dictators to fear and empires to fall ... *The most powerful force in the world is not a weapon or a nation but a truth: that we are spiritual beings, and that freedom is 'the soul's right to breathe'*.
>
> (Bush 1999, November 19)

In part, the Bush campaign represented its ontology of Being through allusions to Fukuyama's teleological argument. This was done by claiming that the USA was on the 'right side of history' (Bush 1999, November 19; Rice 2000). This was buttressed with claims that history has a 'direction' and 'current', and invoking an intertextuality with George Washington's claim that 'Liberty, when it begins to take root, is a plant of rapid growth' (Bush 1999, November 19). Such claims would also be invoked after September 11, when the President argued 'there is a *current in history* and it *runs toward freedom*' (Bush 2001, November 10). In addition to this teleological argument, the 'power of freedom' in the 'human *spirit*' was also given a theological tone; freedom was the '*soul's* right to breathe', and American was on 'the right side of history – the side of man's dignity and *God's justice*' (Bush 1999, November 19). As this shows, 'freedom's power' was an articulation of both the teleological and the transcendental.

Unsurprisingly, Bush and his team were vague when it came to explaining exactly what was meant by the term 'freedom'. It was simply asserted that 'the basic principles of human freedom and dignity are universal' (Bush 1999, November 19). To the extent that these 'universal' values were elucidated, it was simply asserted that:

> People should be able to *say what they think. Worship as they wish. Elect those who govern them.* These ideals have proven their power on every continent . . . We value the elegant structures of our own democracy – but realise that, in other societies, the *architecture will vary*. We *propose our principles, we must not impose our culture*.
>
> (Bush 1999, November 19)

The tone of this statement is certainly modest, and appears to be respectful of cultural plurality albeit bound by some form of democratic legitimacy. Yet, further to this, the Bush campaign did make some remarkably telling statements concerning its guiding definition of 'freedom' and how it would be promoted. Once again Bush appealed to the legacy of Ronald Reagan, and in particular the notion that the free market was a necessary foundation for individual freedom:

> America believes in *free markets and free trade* – and benefits most when markets are opened . . . We believe, with Alexander Hamilton, that the 'spirit of commerce' has a tendency to '*soften the manners of men.*' . . . I view free trade as an important ally in what Ronald Reagan called '*a forward strategy for freedom.*' The case for trade is *not just monetary, but moral. Economic freedom creates habits of liberty. And habits of liberty create expectations of democracy.* There are no guarantees, but there are good examples, from Chile to Taiwan. *Trade freely with China, and time is on our side.*
>
> (Bush 1999, November 19)

What is particularly striking about this passage, and many other statements made throughout the campaign, is that Bush was espousing a dedication to the modernisation thesis and articulating this with 'a forward strategy of freedom'. This strategy has a direct intertextuality with the policy Bush would declare as the precursor to the Freedom Agenda after September 11, when the Bush administration announced a 'forward strategy of freedom'. Notably, the articulation of this strategy with the modernisation thesis put forward a particular understanding of how liberalisation and democratisation are linked to political economy. The benefits of free trade and free markets were portrayed as a method of reducing poverty and unemployment, and fundamentally as a method of linking economic and political liberalisation. This is a theory of political change, which posits modernisation as a functionalist and economistic outcome of capitalism. Moreover, modernity is seen as a single universal model in which democratisation is achieved through pursuing economic growth that results from integration into the global market (Grugel 2002: 47–8; Lockman 2004: 133–40).

The rationale behind the modernisation thesis is that free-market reforms act as a tool for democratisation. By supposedly generating economic growth, economic liberalisation is seen as a method of creating a strong middle class that will sequentially demand liberal rights from its government. This is certainly what Bush meant by the phrase '*soften the manners of men*' and the assertion that '*habits of liberty create expectations of democracy*'. Within this schema economic freedom is paramount, and capitalism is seen as the heart of democracy because it produces wealth that is assumed will 'trickle down' and lead to a higher level of mass consumption, economic growth and a well-educated middle class that will demand cultural changes favourable to democracy. This was Bush's '*vision of freedom . . . nurtured by free markets*' (Bush 1999, September 23).

That Bush was espousing the modernisation thesis as a premise for his future administration's foreign policy should come as no surprise. US foreign policy has long drawn on this 'old thinking in academia' (Goldgeier 2008). It was institutionalised into the US foreign policy bureaucracy when the U.S. Agency for International Development (USAID) was established. USAID drew on the ideas of Walt Whitman Rostow, who served as deputy national security assistant and national security adviser under the Kennedy and Johnson administrations respectively (Wiarda 1997: 16). Rostow's work as an economist had set out a teleological argument in *The Stages of Economic Growth: A Non-communist Manifesto* (Rostow 1960), in which he asserted that societies go through five distinctive stages of economic growth and social change. Most notably he posited a 'takeoff into growth' stage that provided the link to turn traditional societies into high mass consumption societies characteristic of the West. When USAID was established it premised much of its development planning on Rostow's argument and focused on the 'takeoff into growth' stage (USAID 2005). By institutionalising the ideas of Rostow in USAID, US foreign and security policy has since embodied an explicit teleological link between economic growth and democratisation. Furthermore, the modernisation thesis is now institutionalised in the growing democracy bureaucracy in the United States. As James Goldgeier explained:

> [I]n Washington, the extent to which people think about it [democracy promotion], it is modernisation theory. The economic development comes first, and then you can have democracy. And the fact that that is hugely debated now within academia, I don't think it has penetrated . . . I mean there is a lot of work in academia now that challenges that, but that debate isn't known in Washington. There is not a lot of thinking about that. And I think that if you compare the economists to the other, to the people doing democracy stuff, you know people serving at the Treasury and working at the IMF, their economists, they know economic theory. They know what they think is necessary to build markets and they follow from that. People doing democracy promotion, they are not political scientists, and they don't know the political science literature.
>
> (Goldgeier 2008)

Strikingly, the difference between Bush's espoused modernisation thesis and its Cold War anti-communist archetype is that the Bush campaign had fused it with a staunch neoliberal philosophy (see Antonio and Bonannolt 2006). This is unsurprising given that Bush wanted to emulate and expand the 'Reagan revolution'. The term 'neoliberalism' clearly requires explaining, as it is an allusive term, which is often conflated with globalisation. Although related, the two terms are not equivalent. Notably, neoliberalism is a theory of political economic practices that places a heavy emphasis on an institutional framework characterised by strong private property rights, free markets and free trade. For neoliberals, such an institutional framework is seen as the best method of securing human well-being as it liberates individual entrepreneurial freedoms and skills. Within such a schema, the role of the state is to create and preserve an institutional framework appropriate for strong private property rights, free markets and free trade. As a result, the state has the duty of securing the quality and integrity of money and setting up military, defence, police and legal structures required to secure private property rights. The ultimate purpose of the state is therefore to secure the proper functioning of markets; by force if necessary. As David Harvey explains:

> [I]f markets do not exist (in areas such as land, water, education, healthcare, social security or environmental pollution) then they must be created, by state action if necessary. Beyond these tasks the state should not venture. State interventions in markets (once created) must be kept to a bare minimum because, according to the theory [neoliberalism], the state cannot possibly possess enough information to second-guess market signals (prices) and because powerful interest groups will inevitably distort and bias state interventions (particularly in democracies) for their own benefit . . . It holds that social good will be maximised by maximising the reach and frequency of market transactions, and it seeks to bring all human action into the domain of the market.
>
> (Harvey 2005: 2–3)

The importance of neoliberalism is that the philosophy is accompanied by a particular understanding of freedom. This philosophy is inspired by Friedrich A. Hayek and Milton Friedman's 'Chicago Boys' and their notion that all forms of state intervention undermine individual freedom by removing an individual's right to choose. This is not just in monarchies, dictatorships and oligarchies, but also in 'momentary majorities' (Friedman 1962 [2002]: 15). Consequently the philosophy embodies antistatism as an approach to political and economic affairs, in favour of allowing markets to rule. As Friedman argued, 'the private sector is a check on the powers of the governmental sector and an effective protection of freedom of speech, of religion, and of thought' (Friedman 1962 [2002]: 3). Freedom is understood as decentralised political power, limited government and a free market economy because:

> [C]ompetitive capitalism . . . [is] a system of economic freedom and a necessary condition for political freedom . . . economic freedom, in and of itself,

is an extremely important part of total freedom . . . the kind of economic organisation that provides economic freedom directly, namely competitive capitalism, also promotes political freedom because it separates economic power from political power and in this way enables the one to offset the other.
(Friedman 1962 [2002]: 3, 8, 9)

As Eric Foner points out, 'what set these "libertarian" conservatives apart from other social critics . . . was their equation of individual freedom with unregulated capitalism' (Foner 1998: 309). More fundamentally they turned the philosophy of nineteenth century 'radicals' such as Jeremy Bentham on its head; no longer was it political freedom that delivered economic freedom, but 'economic freedom as a means to political freedom' (Friedman 1962 [2002]: 10–12). In this attempt to capture what Hayek (1944) called 'the almost indispensable term' from 'the left', freedom was now defined in individualistic and economic terms, with political freedom being described as 'the absence of coercion of a man by his fellow men [sic]' (Friedman 1962 [2002]: 15). When Ronald Reagan brought this definition of freedom into the presidential office, succeeding where Barry Goldwater failed in the 1964 campaign, he shifted the 'official' discourse of freedom. Freedom was articulated no longer through the vernacular of civil rights, free expression and equal opportunity but rather through tax cuts, deregulation and military superiority. Special interests were not the economic elites of big business corporations and finance, but those in favour of state-run social welfare programmes, unions and environmental groups. Democracy was no longer the realm of public goods and citizens, but the domain of entrepreneurial market consumers and a dedication to private property (Antonio and Bonannolt 2006: 11; Foner 1998: 307–32). This was a radical shift in the manner in which freedom had been conceived though various stages of US history, but it was a definition that G. W. Bush keenly articulated into his IDF, and a definition that would prove key to constructing the Freedom Agenda.

This definition of freedom was embedded in Bush's appeals to 'compassionate conservatism' and proclamations that 'big government is not the answer'. The solution proposed to social problems was 'helping the helper' because 'Government cannot do this work' (Bush 2000, August 15). That Bush had a dedication to a neoliberal conception of freedom is unquestionable. Bush himself attributes it to a trip to China he undertook in 1975:

> I'll never forget the contrast between what I learned about the free market at Harvard and what I saw in the isolation of China. Every bicycle looked the same. People's clothes were all the same – drab and indistinguishable. Central planners restricted choices; a free market frees individuals to make distinct choices and independent decisions. The market gives individuals the opportunity to demand and decide, and entrepreneurs the opportunity to provide. It was clear that China's restrictions of markets limited individuality and competition . . . My visit underscored my belief in the power and promise of the marketplace, and deepened my belief that by introducing capitalism and the market place, China will free her people to dream and risk.
> (Bush 2001: 61)

The lessons Bush learnt at Harvard Business School, or what he termed 'the West Point of capitalism', were not just limited to the benefits that capitalism could bestow to others. Free markets, he alleged, would also benefit the United States:

> I believe the best way to help American oilmen and farmers and producers and entrepreneurs is to open new markets by tearing down barriers, everywhere, so the whole world *trades in freedom*.
> (Bush 2001: 66)

The phrase 'trades in freedom' is a particularly suggestive *double entendre*. One interpretation suggests that the world trades without restraint, yet, a second meaning is clearly neoliberal in its suggestion that freedom is being exchanged like a currency through trading. Bush deployed this double meaning consistently, arguing that it was in fact a president's duty to 'promote a fully democratic Western Hemisphere, bound together by free trade . . . [and] lead toward a world that *trades in freedom*' (Bush 1999, November 19), and that

> The cause of freedom rests on more than our ability to defend ourselves and our allies. *Freedom is exported* every day, as we ship goods and products that improve the lives of millions of people. *Free trade brings greater political and personal freedom*.
> (Bush 2001, February 27).

By articulating 'freedom' as both a transcendental value and an ontological property of Being, the Bush campaign constructed an object that could be transplanted through free trade mechanisms. This often led to freedom being equated with free trade. In essence, this led to the essentially contested concept becoming a nominalisation, which undermined the adjectival quality of 'freedom'. In turn, this marginalised social and agential qualities. Freedom was simply a set of 'universal values', predominantly defined and delivered by free trade, the adoption of which, it was argued, would not only produce global prosperity but also 'extend peace' and security:

> Our world, shaped by American courage, power and wisdom, now echoes with American ideals. We won a victory, not just for a nation, but for a vision. A *vision of freedom* and individual dignity – defended by democracy, *nurtured by free markets, spread by information technology, carried to the world by free trade. The advance of freedom . . . is creating the conditions for peace* . . . Building a *durable peace* will require strong alliances, *expanding trade* and confident diplomacy.
> (Bush 1999, September 23)

By understanding free trade as the engine of modernisation, the Bush campaign put forward a utopian vision of an interdependent, prosperous, secure and peacefully organised world, which it would encourage from a 'position of strength' (Bush 1999, November 19). This vision also propagated a mode of democracy promotion, albeit understood as the product of free trade. This challenges the notion that the Bush administration came into office without a 'democracy promotion agenda' per se. Rather, a closer inspection of the espoused IDF, underpinning the campaign's narrative, reveals a desire to promote democracy vis-à-vis modernisation through free trade and free markets.

President Bush in the post-Cold War era

With his accession to the Presidency, it became highly apparent that G. W. Bush's initial approach to foreign policy lacked any grand vision. Although the shift in Washington's elites in early 2001 had the impact of modifying the operational definition of the national interest, the new administration did not view the strategically selective context radically differently from the Clinton administration. Throughout the campaign it had put forward a distinguishable IDF, but within the first months the Bush foreign policy was discernible only by a modification of settings and instruments. There was no large paradigm shift, and it became increasingly evident that the new President found himself charting a course without the advantage of an overarching foreign policy rationale. Instead, domestic policy took precedence, with tax cuts at home being the mantra of the new administration. Even areas that Bush had promised to place more emphasis on were not stressed. Particularly noticeable was the fact that the Clinton administration had been derided for its supposed chronic underfunding of the military, yet when it came to defence spending the new President informed Congress that 'there will be no new money for defense this year' (Krugman 2001). In turn many in the military noted that 'it sounds like campaign promise No. 1 being broken' (Krugman 2001; see also Daalder and Lindsay 2003: 63).

The lack of an overarching rationale manifested itself in US–MENA relations. This is unsurprising given that, although deemed strategically important, US–MENA relations were not a key issue in the 2000 campaign. Moreover, it is not unusual for an incoming administration to take a few months to formulate its Middle East policy through the NSC process. Thus, despite criticism of the Clinton administration, the Bush administration was largely abiding by long-established policies towards the region. This lack of focus on the region was symbolised by the administration taking three months to appoint a senior director for Middle Eastern affairs to the NSC staff (Daalder and Lindsay 2003: 66). To the extent that there was an alteration in US–MENA policy within the first eight months, it came in the form of disengaging from the Palestinian–Israeli conflict and asserting the need to focus on Saddam Hussein's regime in Iraq.

On January 30, 2001, 10 days after being inaugurated, President Bush called his first meeting of the NSC. The overriding focus of the meeting was on Middle East policy. It was at this meeting that the President declared to all the principals of his NSC staff that his administration was going to abandon Clinton's efforts at peace talks in the region, and 'tilt back towards Israel' (Suskind 2004: 71–2). Effectively, this meant disengaging from the peace process, whilst the second Intifada, which had begun on September 28, 2000, continued. Violence had not just broken out between Israeli soldiers and stone-throwing Palestinian youths, but also involved Fatah's paramilitary Tanzim fighters and sections of the Palestinian Authority police force. The violence was later exacerbated by Ariel Sharon being elected Israeli Prime Minister in February 2001. Yet, far from an even-handed disengagement, it was clear that the Bush administration was adopting a hard-line stance against the Palestinian leader Yasser Arafat (Reporters Sans Frontières 2003: 7–8).[4] Whilst the new National Security Adviser, Condoleezza Rice, was arguing that 'we shouldn't think of American involvement for the sake of American involvement' (in Usborne 2001), President Bush was asserting that

> [Israel is] a small country that has lived under the threat throughout its existence. At my first meeting of my National Security Council, I told them that a top foreign policy priority of my administration is the safety and security of Israel. My administration will be steadfast in supporting Israel against terrorism and violence, and in seeking the peace for which all Israelis pray.
> (Bush 2001, May 3)

The Bush strategy towards the conflict clearly placed Israeli security concerns first, with an emphasis on containing the conflict rather than urging both parties towards a resolution.[5] This was certainly evident at the United Nations Security Council, where the Bush administration continued the historical trend of stymieing any attempts at condemning Israeli policy (Zunes 2003: 116).

Yet, whilst the Bush administration was making the case for lowering the priority of resolving the Palestinian–Israeli conflict, it was prioritising a harder approach on Iraq. As Scott McClellan, the former White House Press Secretary, has argued:

> [E]ven at the outset, Iraq was looming in the background. The very first Monday [January 22, 2001], the *New York Times* . . . ran a front-page story about Iraq rebuilding factories 'that the United States has long suspected of producing chemical and biological weapons' . . . The *Times* called it an early test of Bush's pledge to 'take a tougher stance against' Saddam Hussein than his immediate predecessor had . . . Iraq would continue to be a top issue of the administration's focus and media interest in months to come. The National Security Council made Iraq an early priority of the policy formulation process. As for that first day, with no new policy yet firmly in place, we simply told the press that the president expected Saddam Hussein to live up to his agreement with the United Nations that his regime not produce weapons of mass destruction.
> (McClellan 2008: 89)

From Paul O'Neil's account of the January 30, 2001, NSC meeting, it is clear that the President, and key advisers such as Rice, Tenet and Cheney, viewed Iraq as a destabilising force in the region, and that 'ten days in . . . it was about Iraq . . . Getting Hussein was now the administration's focus' (Suskind 2004: 70–6).

70 *From candidate to crisis*

This is not to suggest that a plan to attack Iraq was established. Despite Donald Rumsfeld, Paul Wolfowitz and Dick Cheney advocating regime change before coming into office, once in office these calls were muted as no consensus emerged concerning an overthrow strategy. This was reflected in Paul Wolfowitz's confirmation hearing when he argued that overthrowing Saddam Hussein 'I think would be worthwhile', but conditioned this with the claim that he had not seen a 'plausible plan' for changing the regime (in Katzman 2003: 7). Instead, Iraq policy was largely run by Colin Powell's State Department, and the 'new purpose' promised throughout the 2000 campaign manifested itself in a commitment to 'smart sanctions', which attempted to alter the conditions of the UN-led oil-for-food programme. Clinton's Iraq policy was seen as a failure and Saddam Hussein as 'a danger', but Bush argued that it was necessary to rebuild the 'coalition to keep the pressure on him [Saddam Hussein]', and 'absolutely not' abandon sanctions, but make them 'tougher' (Bush 2000, October 11).

This was not an administration determined on military-induced regime change, but rather an administration that had no overarching rationale and no plan in place to deal with Iraq. There were certainly a few senior individuals who wanted to overthrow Saddam Hussein, in particular Paul Wolfowitz. However, they had no plan and these individuals were marginalised by Colin Powell's State Department, which was arguing that the UN and USA had contained Saddam Hussein and 'kept him in his box', and therefore the policy ought to be declared a success (Powell 2001, February 23). Without a consensus on US Iraqi policy in place, ultimately the Bush administration was drifting whilst trying to appear 'tougher' on Iraq. The prevailing narrative put forward by Bush as a candidate was that 'our coalition against Saddam is unravelling. Sanctions are loosened. The man . . . may be developing weapons of mass destruction, we don't know because inspectors aren't in' (Bush 2000, October 17). The 'smart sanctions' policy was an 'amend it, don't end it' policy, which focused on military goods, but was relaxed on trade more generally. However, once in office, the Bush administration pursued many elements of the Clinton administration's policy, favouring sanctions in conjunction with the 1998 Iraq Liberation Act, which had the stated goal of removing the Saddam regime by funding Iraqi exile groups. However, even this was not taken to the extreme, as evident in the Treasury Department's Office of Foreign Assets Control granting Ahmed Chalabi's Iraqi National Congress (INC) a licence for information gathering but withholding backing for the group's plan to rebuild its presence in Iraq (Katzman 2003: 8).

The most significant attempt to look more decisive against Iraq occurred on February 16, 2001, when, without the usual build-up and brinkmanship, the USA bombed close to the Iraqi capital, sending Saddam 'a clear message' of the new administration's willingness to use force (Asser 2001; Teimourian 2001). However, rather than the bombings themselves being seen as a deviation from US policy, the prevailing message put forward by the Bush administration was concern over Chinese workers helping the Iraqi military install a fibre optic communication network in the Iraqi air defence system (Ricks 2006: 26–7). The attacks were as significant a message to China about its encroachment into the

Middle East as they were towards the Iraqi regime. Moreover, the attacks marked an escalation in the willingness to use military power more readily as a method of deterrence, but ultimately the instruments and indeed the broad goals of US Iraqi policy remained unaltered. Evidently, the Bush administration had a grand strategy neither for Iraq in particular nor for the MENA more broadly. Maintaining regional stability remained the overarching rationale, and there was a conspicuous silence concerning both freedom and democracy in the region.

To the extent that there was a noteworthy shift from past policy it was not immediately obvious. The new administration's policies towards Israel and Iraq were not substantive in and of themselves, if taken in isolation. Rather, what the first NSC meeting demonstrated was an effort to pursue a 'de-coupling' strategy. Throughout the 1990s, the Clinton administration held the view that events in the eastern Mediterranean impacted on the Gulf. Consequently, securing Israeli security and the flow of oil from the region was seen to require active engagement in the peace process. However, the Bush administration reprioritised its Middle East focus, seeing peace as desirable but not vital to securing long-term security interests. That is to say that the Palestinian–Israeli conflict was perceived as less destabilising to the region than it had been considered by American administrations over the previous three decades. Iraq, however, was seen as the greatest threat to US national interests because of its 'destabilising' effect throughout the region. As a logical corollary, the two issues were de-coupled as one was seen as important and the other not (Mohamedi and Sadowski 2001: 14). The importance of the new administration's stance towards Israel and Iraq is that it isolated them from each other, which set the backdrop of the Bush administration's policy towards the Middle East before September 11, 2001. Although this was a significant modification in how previous administrations had viewed regional politics and configured US strategy, it was certainly not a paradigm shift in US–MENA relations; continuity was largely the watchword of this pre-September 11, 2001, period. Yet this radically changed on September 11, 2001. The day's events provided a moment of punctuation in political time leading to the strategic construction of a war on terror, which cumulatively evolved into the Freedom Agenda as a transformative liberal grand strategy for the MENA. It is to explicating the first stage of this evolution that this diachronic research must now turn, and, as the constructivist institutionalist methodology elucidated, there is no better place to start than what President Bush has termed 'a moment of crisis' (Bush 2010: 128).

The moment of punctuation: stabilising uncertainty and securing authority

The brute facts of September 11, 2001, are widely known and well documented, starting at 8:46 a.m. Eastern Standard Time (EST), when American Airlines Flight 11 crashed into the North Tower of the World Trade Center in New York City. At 9:03 EST United Airlines Flight 175 struck the South Tower of the World Trade Center. At 9:37 EST, American Airlines Flight 77 crashed into the Pentagon building, and at 10:02 EST United Airlines Flight 93 crashed into an empty field

72 *From candidate to crisis*

in Shanksville, Pennsylvania (NCTAUS 2004: 1–14). It is tempting to think of these events as merely 'reflecting' reality; to argue that the events 'speak for themselves'. Indeed this is a temperament aided by the ubiquitous representations of the events. At the ontologically objective level, the 'facts' are not contentious; aircraft had been used as kinetic weapons, which crashed into prominent buildings, which were either totally or partially destroyed. Yet the *meaning* of these events is not easy to determine. Rather *meaning*, and therefore the *interpretation* of the events, exists at an ontologically subjective level; they are human constructions. What the events signified is a hermeneutic question, which once answered exists at an observer-dependent level. This is a level that exists in and through language; a result of establishing post hoc 'readings' of the events through the deployment of discourses. Once understood in this manner, the ontologically objective events can be considered as constituting part of the *fabula* of any narrative, as the 'material or content' that is worked into a narrative (see Bal 1997; Fairclough 2003: 83–6). In the case of historical narratives, this represents 'referential intention' (Fairclough 2003: 85).

Yet to appropriate this fabula into a narrative requires what Paul Ricoeur has termed an act of 'productive invention'. These events must be ordered by and within the human imagination. Within a narrative, *plot* serves this function, as it is the plot that

> 'grasps together' and integrates into one whole and complete story multiple and scattered events, thereby schematising the intelligible signification attached to the narrative as a whole.
>
> (Ricoeur 1984: x)

Indeed, the initial plot put forward by the Bush administration in the immediate aftermath of September 11, 2001, was one of 'tragedy'. Within hours of the attacks occurring, President Bush and members of his administration began framing the events in this way:

> Today we've had a national *tragedy*.
>
> (Bush 2001, September 11a)

> Today America has experienced one of the greatest *tragedies* ever witnessed on our soil.
>
> (Ashcroft 2001, September 11)

> The President's focus right now is on helping those who have lost their – the families of those who have lost their lives and those who are suffering in this *tragedy*; and then on taking whatever the appropriate next steps should be.
>
> (Fleischer 2001, September 12)

> We are gathered here because of what happened here on September 11th. Events that bring to mind *tragedy*.
>
> (Rumsfeld 2001, October 11)

To construct the plot as a tragedy is significant, notably because it provided the first steps in filling what some analysts have termed a 'void of meaning' (see Jackson 2005: 29; Der Derian 2002: 107). The sheer visceral horror of the events created an *aporia*; the events marked a breach in the expected state of things, generating uncertainty as the *peripeteia* awoke the audience. Thus, it was out of this chaos, a sense of order under attack, vulnerability and surprise that the events were constructed as a tragedy, which transformed the 'inexpressible' into the 'expressible' in an attempt to stabilise the uncertainty created. As Pierre Macherey points out, the function of the tragic is to reduce elusive silence into regulated knowledge; it is the 'art of overcoming unmeaning' (Macherey 1978: 6).

To refer to the events as a 'tragedy', however, has larger implications related to further stabilising the uncertainty condition that emerged out of this moment of punctuation. It provided the initial understanding of the events, whilst inviting a set of instructional rules. At a basic level, it could be argued that the events were to be understood as tragic at the level of human emotions: as 'distressing', or a signification of 'suffering'. As Terry Eagleton points out, 'in everyday language, the word "tragedy" means something like "very sad"' (Eagleton 2003: 1). This, as President Bush made clear, was certainly articulated as part of its meaning:

> The pictures of airplanes flying into buildings, fires burning, huge structures collapsing, have filled us with *disbelief, terrible sadness, and a quiet, unyielding anger.*
>
> (Bush 2001, September 11b)

> We are here in the middle hour of our *grief*. So many have *suffered* so great a *loss*, and today we express our nation's *sorrow*.
>
> (Bush 2001, September 14)

In addition to this, the Bush administration made it very clear who was supposed to feel these emotions. This was a 'national tragedy' in which 'we', meaning Americans, were to undergo these emotions and be interpellated into the emerging crisis narrative.[6] This is a significant discursive move as it constructed a focalisation from the local to national, and provided an instructional rule on what should be felt and how to behave. This act of interpellation was directly intended to allow the audience to identify with the events, thereby urging participation within the tragedy itself. Members of the audience were not merely spectators, but rather directly invited to be involved within the tragedy. This represented what Friedrich Nietzsche referred to as the Dionysian aspect of a tragedy, in which interaction helps 'forget the self' and experience a more mystical communal union. This unifying experience is thus intended to provide an intoxicating and therapeutic outlet through the response (Nietzsche 2008 [1886]: 119–38).

This emotional aspect of the tragedy plot, once framed as a *national tragedy*, allowed a more political dimension to be secured (see Falk 2002: 130). National unity and patriotism[7] had become the order of the day, with members of the Bush administration arguing that

> now is the time for us to *come together as a nation* ... for *every one of us* that has been changed forever by this horrible *tragedy*.
>
> (Ashcroft 2001, September 11)

> *Americans* showed a deep commitment to one another, and an *abiding love for our country* ... we feel what Franklin Roosevelt called the warm courage of *national unity* ... It has *joined together* political parties in both houses of Congress ... *Our unity is a kinship of grief.*
>
> (Bush 2001, September 14)

This mix of emotion, uncertainty, tragedy, unity, and patriotism allowed the Bush administration to establish a series of regulative rules. This began with the President asserting that

> Americans are asking: What is expected of us? *I ask you to live your lives and hug your children* ... I ask you to *be calm and resolute* ... *I ask you to uphold the values of America* ...We are in a fight for our principles, and our *first responsibility is to live by them.* .. The thousands of *FBI agents who are now at work in this investigation may need your cooperation, and I ask you to give it* ... I ask your *continued participation and confidence in the American economy.*
>
> (Bush 2001, September 20)

Of particular interest about these instructional rules is the manner in which, in the name of patriotism, they encourage submission to the state at this tragic time. By October 2001, the Bush administration had been able to pass a sweeping piece of legislation called the *USA PATRIOT Act*. This acronym reveals the temperament of the time. Public Law Pub. L. 107-56 articulated the desire of *Uniting and Strengthening America*, under the banner of *patriotism*. This established a direct challenge to civil liberties under the banner of *unity* and *patriotism*, whilst allowing the demarcation of binaries such as patriot/unpatriotic, American/un-American and 'with us or against us' (see Andrews 2007: 99–107).

Moreover, the rules put forward by the Bush administration were not controversial in and of themselves, but when articulated through the prism of patriotism worked to 'depoliticise' the events and establish non-critical practices. For example, the first instructional rule 'live your lives and hug your children' appears to be benign. Yet, as Maja Zehfuss argues:

> What might at first have appeared to be an alternative approach to dealing with the experience of an inevitable insecurity, turned out in fact to be a deeply patronising comment, the ultimate closure of debate. Concentrate on your families. Do not concern yourselves with the difficult business of politics. The state will provide security.
>
> (Zehfuss 2003: 525)

The second set of instructional rules, 'uphold the values' and 'live by them', are, upon reflection, equally strategic. Such rules encouraged the unconditional celebration of American life, values and institutions in a benignant manner; rather than encouraging inquiry into the anti-American grievances so prevalent in the Arab world (Falk 2003: 131). Furthermore, the third notion of what Americans should do is troubling, as it was suggested that American's patriotic duty was now to spend and invest (see Lowenstein 2001: 20). This notion was anathema to the temperament of the time as 'the events of September 11 had renewed nonmaterial values' (Silberstein 2002: 124). Yet this conflation of consumerism and patriotism sent a simple message: focus your attention on spending, not politics, as the latter will be handled by the state.

What was evident from these instructional rules was that they were not coupled with notions of inquiry, critique and introspection. There was no attempt made by the Bush administration to compel the American public to evaluate for themselves why the events had happened. Indeed, if as Nicolas Onuf argues 'rules yield rule' (Onuf 1998: 74), a tangible reason for not compelling inquiry and critique was that this would threaten the interpellative effect of the narrative presented by the Bush administration. In turn, this would challenge the legitimacy of the narrative being presented and the political hierarchy it sought to maintain; the President and his administration therefore sought to stabilise their authority and remain the main storytellers. In effect, the events of September 11, 2001, had created a moment of punctuation in political time, which not only mobilised 'America' as an imagined community, through the process of interpellation, but also provided the Bush administration with manoeuvrable space to redirect policy by constructing and developing a strategic narrative that would underpin the construction of a new policy paradigm.

From tragedy to morality play: articulating God, freedom and an exceptional nation

Once the events of September 11, 2001, were constructed as a 'national tragedy', the Bush administration was able to build upon this plot and seamlessly construct a morality play. This is a significant dynamic that had far-reaching consequences throughout the Bush administration's political tenure. In the immediate aftermath of September 11, 2001, the Bush administration bestowed the events with metaphysical meaning:

> Tonight, I ask for your *prayers* for all those who grieve, for the children whose worlds have been shattered, for all whose sense of safety and security has been threatened. And *I pray they will be comforted by a power greater than any of us, spoken through the ages in Psalm 23: 'Even though I walk through the valley of the shadow of death, I fear no evil, for You are with me.'*
>
> (Bush 2001, September 11b)

This discursive manoeuvre is significant because its intended purpose was to provide comfort in a time of grief. Once again the Dionysian aspect of a tragedy was evident: the implication was to forget the self and experience a more mystical communal union; albeit now the intoxicating and therapeutic outlet was endowed with religious meaning. Comfort was now to be found by the nation embracing God in a time of suffering:

> *Scripture* says: '*Blessed are those who mourn for they shall be comforted.*' ... We will persevere through this *national tragedy* and personal loss. In time, we will find healing and recovery; and, in the face of all this evil, we remain strong and united, '*one Nation under God.*'
>
> (Bush 2001, September 13)

> *[T]he prayers of private suffering*, whether in our homes or in this *great cathedral, are known and heard, and understood* ... *This world He created is of moral design. Grief and tragedy and hatred are only for a time.* Goodness, remembrance, and love have no end. And *the Lord of life holds all who die, and all who mourn.* It is said that *adversity introduces us to ourselves. This is true of a nation as well.*
>
> (Bush 2001, September 14)

> A Marine chaplain, in trying to explain why there could be *no human explanation* for *a tragedy such as this*, said once: 'You would think it would *break the heart of God.*' We stand today in the *midst of tragedy* – the *mystery of tragedy*. Yet a mystery that is part of that *larger awe and wonder that causes us to bow our heads in faith* and say of those we mourn, those we have lost, the words of scripture: '*Lord now let Thy servants go in peace, Thy word has been fulfilled*'.
>
> (Rumsfeld 2001, October 11)

This was clearly an act of *deus ex machina*, as God was lowered into the narrative to provide meaning to the events. The catastrophe was presented as a 'reversal of fortune', and, once tragedy was articulated with a theological discourse, meaning was conferred upon the dead and their 'eloquent acts of *sacrifice*' (Bush 2001, September 14).[8] With speeches being delivered in symbolic terrain, such as the National Cathedral, the loss of life was given meaning through a Christian theological discourse. The loss of life was not constructed as part of the 'absurdity', 'inexplicability' or 'unpredictability' of Being, which would clearly have provided the basis of an alternative narrative. Morality and divine purpose were not portrayed as part of the human imagination, which is a readily available discourse from the works of Nietzsche, Kierkegaard, Sartre or Camus.[9] The Bush administration had made a metaphysical move, appealing to theological ideas.

This theological move could be seen as following 'American tradition'. It is possible to argue that, given the circumstances presented by September 11, 2001, this theological appeal was the result of a 'logic of appropriateness'. This is not meant as a culturally deterministic or structuralist argument. Given the relationship between Dasein and temporality, what one inherits from one's forefathers one must win again anew. However, the prominence of religiosity in the USA makes a Christian theological discourse present itself as an attractive option for strategic agents working in a strategically selective context. Yet what is significant about framing the tragedy in theological terms is the manner in which it seamlessly allowed acts of 'emplotment' to become transcendental. 'God' was cast as an actor in what was transformed into a morality play:

> God's signs are not always the ones we look for. We learn in tragedy that his purposes are not always our own.
> (Bush 2001, September 14)

> Many have discovered again that *even in tragedy – especially in tragedy – God is near*.
> (Bush 2002, January 29)

This act of emplotment is crucial to understanding the manner in which characters were constructed within the narrative. Indeed, theological ideas are politically illuminating, and, when articulated with identity politics, have dramatic consequences. Once the premise is accepted that God is an ontological reality, then as a logical corollary it is possible to posit a world of *moral realism*. This is a world where there is a moral reality independent of moral beliefs; morality has an ontologically objective status independent of Being. Through this prism, actions have moral properties, which are genuine properties that are simply part of the furniture of the world (see McNaughton 1988: 3–65; McDowell 1978; Mackie 1977). This premise is part of the IDF that President Bush brought with him into office. In reference to what as Governor he termed the 'American story', he argued that this was a

> story in which *evil is real*, but courage and decency triumph . . . America has determined enemies, who hate our values and resent our success – terrorists and crime syndicates and drug cartels and unbalanced dictators. The Empire has passed, but *evil remains*.
> (Bush 1999, November 19)

Similarly, in President Bush's November 2001 speech to the United Nations General Assembly, he argued that 'we know that *evil is real*, but *good will prevail against it*. This is the teaching of many *faiths*, and in that assurance we gain strength for a long journey' (Bush 2001, November 10).

This is a powerful and far-reaching meta-ethical claim that has political consequences. By casting God as an actor within the tragedy plot, it was possible to foreground normative characterisations and make them appear organic. Consequently, the Bush administration began constructing the events of September 11, 2001, and its perpetrators as a product of 'evil':

> Thousands of lives were suddenly ended by *evil*, despicable acts of terror ... Today, our nation saw *evil*, the very worst of human nature ... The search is underway for those who are behind these *evil acts* ... 'Even though I walk through the valley of the shadow of death, I fear no *evil*, for You are with me.'
> (Bush 2001, September 11b)

Instructively, by understanding that the Bush administration was using the term 'evil' as part of a moral realist claim, it is possible to infer that the term is not merely being used to denote strong disapproval. Rather, an ontological claim was being made that depoliticised the acts. As Richard Jackson argues, the reason for the attacks was being 'firmly rooted in the identity and nature of the attackers' (Jackson 2005: 54). The source of the attacks, and the uncertainty they produced, was diagnosed and constructed as being intrinsic to the identity of the enemy. Accordingly, the events of September 11, 2001, were portrayed not as a product of political grievances, but as part of an ongoing moral battle:

> This will be a monumental struggle of *good versus evil*. But *good* will prevail.
> (Bush 2001, September 12)

This binary is instructive as it established the demarcation of identities that would dominate the Bush administration's political tenure. Moreover, this was accompanied by a series of binary identity constructions that essentialised the identity of the 'terrorists' and 'Americans' (Table 3.1).

This constructed vernacular was extended to other strategic actors. In President Bush's address to the nation on September 11, the President personally included the statement, in consultation with Condoleezza Rice:

> We will make no distinction between *the terrorists* who committed these acts and *those who harbor them*.
> (Bush 2001, September 11b)[10]

This logic of equivalence is significant because it disregarded conceptions of national sovereignty with regards to terrorism. In what some have termed the 'first Bush doctrine' the 'evil' enemy was not just 'terrorists' but also states that collaborated or permitted terrorist training on their soil (see Singer 2004: 144–53). This was a significant articulation, in which the Bush administration began characterising the enemy as 'terrorists and states'. Moreover, it established a new set of rules concerning how other states should behave, as Ari Fleisher declared when asked 'when Mr. Wolfowitz talked about putting an end to states that harbor terrorists, did he mean to say that U.S. policy is to wipe out governments that sponsor terrorists?' His response was:

> Well, I can only say, in the President's words and as the President said, the U.S. will use all our resources to conquer the enemy. *And anybody who chooses to be America's enemy will have to think about what that means.*
> (Fleischer 2001, September 13)

Table 3.1 Sample of binary identity constructions deployed by the Bush administration between September 11, 2001, and January 20, 2009

Description of 'terrorists'	Description of 'America'
Terrorists	Liberators
Evil	Good
Tyrannical	Free
Unjust	Just
Barbaric/uncivilised	Progressive/civilised
Violent	Peaceful
Cowardly	Daring/brave/heroic/courageous
Weak	Strong
Intolerant	Tolerant
Cruel	Kind
Brutal	Loving
Indifferent	Caring
Mad	Reasonable

Note: This list of adjectives is by no means exhaustive, but rather provides an attributive vernacular that essentialised the identities of the 'terrorists' and 'America', taken from multiple texts within the NVivo 8 database that underpins this research.

Evident in the construction of an American 'we' and the terrorist 'Other', in a binary formation, was the extent to which the Bush administration attempted to attribute depoliticised motivations for the attacks. The terrorist's actions were portrayed as deriving from this binary identity structure: 'they' acted because 'they' are 'evil' and 'we' were targeted because 'we' are 'good'. As Donald Rumsfeld argued:

> [I]n targeting this place [the Pentagon] . . . and those who worked here, the attackers, *the evildoers* correctly sensed that *the opposite of all they were*, and *stood for, resided here.*
>
> (Rumsfeld 2001, October 11)

Indeed, 'good', as the Bush administration deployed the term, was inextricably articulated with the concept of 'freedom'. Consequently, notions of 'good' were conflated with 'freedom', whilst notions of 'evil' were conflated with 'tyranny':

> In every generation, the world has produced enemies of human freedom. They have attacked America, because we are freedom's home and defender.
>
> (Bush 2001, September 14)

> Americans are asking: Why do they hate us? *They hate* what we see right here in this chamber [the US Capitol Building] – *a democratically elected government. Their leaders are self-appointed. They hate our freedoms* – our

freedom of religion, our freedom of speech, our freedom to vote and assemble and disagree with each other ... These terrorists kill not merely to end lives, but to disrupt and *end a way of life.*

(Bush 2001, September 20)

This is a long-standing discourse that the Bush administration appropriated and deployed. As Eric Foner expounds:

[N]o idea is more fundamental to Americans' sense of themselves as individuals and as a nation than freedom. The central term in our political vocabulary, 'freedom' – or 'liberty' ... is deeply embedded in the documentary record of our history and the language of everyday life.

(Foner 1998: xiii)

This point is instructive because it demonstrates how the Bush administration re-appropriated the *American exceptionalist* myth, and through semantic innovation interwove it within the tragedy plot. Thus, lying behind the deployment of a 'language of evil' there are political functions, made possible by its ability to encode 'a reservoir of cultural forms and meanings' (Hariman 2003: 513). The Bush administration was invoking the myth that Americans were God's chosen people and that America represented a beacon of light in the world: a city upon a hill. Such sentiments were echoed in a prayer given by Donald Rumsfeld in the aftermath of 9/11:

Ever-faithful God, in death we are reminded of the precious *birthrights of life and liberty You endowed in Your American people* ... We seek Your special blessing today for those who stand as sword and shield, *protecting the many from the tyranny of the few* ...We pray this day, Heavenly Father, the prayer our nation learned at another time of righteous struggle and noble cause – *America's enduring prayer: Not that God will be on our side, but always, O Lord, that America will be on Your side.* Amen.

(Rumsfeld 2001, September 14)

Of particular interest in this passage is the manner in which there is an articulation between being God's chosen people and the concept of liberty. It reflects an insight made by Alexis de Tocqueville, who asserted that,

I have already said enough to put the character of Anglo-American civilisation in its true light. It is the product ... of two perfectly distinct elements that elsewhere have often made war with each other, but which, in America, they have succeeded in incorporating somehow into one another and combining marvellously. I mean to speak of the *spirit of religion* and the *spirit of freedom*.

(Tocqueville 2002 [1835]: 43, emphasis in original)

This articulation of religious doctrine and political theory is insightful, because it captures what is meant by the myth of American exceptionalism. At a simplistic level, it could be construed as a comparative label of difference; however, the term is far more than this. It captures the profoundly religious origins of the 'chosenness vision' and an ideological vision of a way of life centred upon 'freedom' (see Hughes 2004: 19; Deudney and Meiser 2008). Further still, it captures the manner in which many Americans believe that the United States is a force for 'good' in the world because its political system represents the acme of political progress at the centre of the international order. Consequently, when members of the Bush administration began to construct a morality play between good/evil and freedom/tyranny they were not merely making normative judgements. Rather, these strategic actors were re-articulating and assimilating the events of September 11, 2001, into a well-established narrative constructed at the birth of the American nation. The importance of this to the eventual formation of the Freedom Agenda cannot be overestimated. Once the tragedy plot was articulated with an American exceptionalist discourse, the narrative presented by the Bush administration was able to provide meaning to the events in the image of a morality play whilst also providing characterisations of both 'America' and the 'terrorists'. This helped construct a set of foreign policy goals that were 'far broader and more ambitious than a simple response to the immediate attacks would have suggested' (McCartney 2004: 400). Moreover, by invoking American exceptionalism the concept of 'freedom' was foregrounded, which provided a significant stepping-stone on the road to the eventual formation of the Freedom Agenda. The narrative presented was simplistic and obscured any political motivations for the attack, but it provided a sufficient description of the situation and endowed the events with meaning. It therefore laid the foundations for how the Bush administration was to market its response to the attacks; that is to say, the decisive intervention that would follow.

4 September to December 2001
The decisive intervention

The Bush administration's representation of September 11, 2001, within a religious, tragic and moral narrative provided meaning to the events, and constructed characterisations of the actors involved. The significance of such factors is that they laid the groundwork for the Bush administration's decisive intervention to be readily accepted. Not only do they reveal the perceptions that helped constitute the ontologically subjective observer-dependent dimensions of the 'crisis' in the first instance, but they also defined the boundaries of what was politically feasible and what would be considered to be in the national interest. This articulated framing laid the foundations for the Bush administration's decisive intervention that followed. As President Bush would later state, he had three objectives at this stage of the crisis: 'mourn the loss of life, remind people there was a loving God, and make clear that those who attacked our nation would face justice' (Bush 2010: 146).

The nature of that decisive intervention, or how 'justice' would be sought, was through the construction of the crisis as a declaration of war. Indeed, President Bush's personal account of the events of that day are that 'instinct kicked in', and that as his 'thoughts clarified', within an hour of the events taking place, his interpretation of events was that this crisis constituted an act of war: 'The first plane could have been an accident. The second was definitely an attack. The third was a declaration of war' (Bush 2010: 128).[1] Evidently, the decision to cast the events as a declaration of war was not a well-considered analytical decision based on a well thought-out plan. It was a construction made without the full knowledge of the situation, in what Bush would term 'the fog of war'.[2] As President Bush would later argue in his autobiography:

> The first step of any successful crisis response is to project calm . . . over time, we had to devise a strategy to bring the terrorists to justice so they would not strike again . . . our first priority was to make it through the crisis.
> (Bush 2010: 129, 133)

The President never considered plausible alternative readings of the events, such as constructing them as 'criminal exploits' or 'crimes against humanity', which could have placed the response into the international litigious realm (see Lawler

2002: 171; Jackson 2005). Nor, at the point of deciding this was a 'war', was the President aware who had perpetrated the attacks. Rather, the state of 'America' was instantly deemed the victim and, consequently, 'America' would respond with a state-based military response. Thus, at 9:45 a.m. EST, September 11, 2001, the President told Vice-President Cheney, 'Sounds like we have a minor war going on here, I heard about the Pentagon. We're at war . . . somebody's going to pay' (NCTAUS 2004: 39; see also Woodward 2002: 17–18).

With the discursive deployment of 'war' as a response, the events were unsurprisingly constructed as a 'crisis' for the state. President Bush became the key strategic interpreter in this decision, essentially making a judgement that set a new trajectory for US foreign and security policy. Accordingly, this marked an abrupt systemic transformation, caused by the perceived failure of past policy to provide security on American soil and protect the state apparatus. From destruction came the need for construction, as 'war' became the perceived method of dealing with the uncertainty and complexity that September 11, 2001, presented. Immediately following the terrorist attacks, President Bush laid discursive tracks that would help move towards constructing a 'war plot'. This was done firstly at the Booker Elementary School, where the phrase 'Terrorism against our nation will not stand' was declared (Bush 2001, September 11a). The importance of this phrase is its clear intertextuality with President G. H. W. Bush's declaration that 'This will not stand. This will not stand, this aggression against Kuwait', made before the first Gulf War (Bush 1990, August 5). Moreover, in the President's address to the nation on September 11 he asserted that:

> Immediately following the first attack, I implemented our government's emergency response plans. *Our military is powerful, and it's prepared.* America and our friends and allies join with all those who want peace and security in the world, and we stand together to win the *war against terrorism.*
> (Bush 2001, September 11b)

This certainly demonstrates that the Bush administration was preparing to construct a 'war' plot. However, what is apparent from multiple accounts is that the wider implications of a 'war' plot were withheld from public disclosure. In the evening address, the line 'This is not just an act of terrorism. This is an act of war', which reflected the President's discussions with his NSC staff, was cut from the public address. The reason for this was that the President saw his administration's mission as one of 'reassurance' (see Woodward 2002: 30–1; Frum 2003: 124–33). Thus, the President saw his role as allowing the Dionysian aspect of a tragedy to unfold, and therefore not to make apparent the nature of his conceived decisive intervention in the immediate aftermath of the events. The exclusion and inclusion of text within the speech is therefore highly significant. It demonstrates strategic thinking on behalf of the President and members of his administration, and a deliberate attempt to shape a message. Constructing the national tragedy plot and morality play was to take precedence over an abrupt assertion of how to directly respond. The administration was describing the paradise lost through tragedy, before asserting how it would be regained. To the extent that this was done by the administration, it reveals a deliberate attempt to frame the events in a manner that resonated with the American public and allowed for the interpellation of the narrative, and therefore provide the foundations for its eventual decisive intervention to be widely accepted.

This factor was not lost upon members of the Bush administration. Before September 11, 2001, Karl Rove, as head of the Office of Strategic Initiatives, saw his job as one of ensuring that broad support was used effectively, and his objective was to 'shape and manipulate sources of public opinion, much as in a political campaign, to help advance the Bush agenda and policies' (McClellan 2008: 77). The events of September 11 provided the perfect milieu for this, because Rove calculated that, 'in the past, when the public rallied around the president in times of crisis, the boost in popularity lasted seven to ten months' (in Woodward 2006: 81; see also Woodward 2002: 206).[3] Similarly, Donald Rumsfeld was all too aware of the lessons of the Second World War, and the institutions created out of that crisis, and readily drew comparisons with September 11, 2001:

> there was a war [the Second World War] that shifted relationships between nations dramatically. That created new institutions that grew out of that conflict. It is easier to do it if there's an event . . . is it possible that what took place on September 11th . . . that maybe out of this tragedy comes opportunity. Maybe, just maybe, the world will sufficiently register the danger that exists on the globe and have this event cause the kind of sense of urgency and offer the kind of opportunities that World War II offered, to refashion much of the world.
>
> (Rumsfeld 2001, October 12)

This notion of 'opportunity' was echoed by President Bush himself on September 11, 2001, when he remarked that 'This is an opportunity . . . we have to think of this as an opportunity' (in Woodward 2002: 32; see also NCTAUS 2004: 330).

Evidently, within hours of the September 11, 2001, attacks an internal administration discourse was developing, as the key strategically selective actors began to diagnose, proselytise and impose on themselves a notion of what this crisis was, before they could recommend what collective state-based action to take. To the extent that the President did begin scripting a direct response more publicly, it initially muted reference to war. The President asserted that:

> The search is underway for those who are behind these evil acts. *I've directed the full resources of our intelligence and law enforcement communities to find those responsible and to bring them to justice.*
>
> (Bush 2001, September 11b)

Such a response clearly left policies alternative to 'war' as possible options. This point was not lost on certain members of the Bush administration that wanted to forge ahead and make the decision to go to war immediately public. For David Frum 'the speech Bush had delivered was not a war speech. It was a hastily revised compassionate conservatism speech' (Frum 2003: 128). Relatedly, the decision to construct the acts as a 'declaration of war' was initially an area of political contestation. Rather than a 'war construction' being inevitable, it is important to note that early objections to it were voiced. On September 12, 2001, Senate Majority Leader Tom Daschle cautioned the President to take care with his rhetoric, noting that the word 'war' had powerful implications (Bush 2010: 142; Woodward 2002: 45).

Despite such objections, on September 12, 2001, President Bush deployed the line he had formerly suppressed:

> The deliberate and deadly attacks which were carried out yesterday against our country were *more than acts of terror. They were acts of war.* This will require our country to unite in steadfast determination and resolve. Freedom and democracy are under attack.
>
> (Bush 2001, September 12)

This marked the first public construction of a war plot, and signified the nature of the Bush administration's decisive intervention. This intervention would be consistently reinforced by articulating it with historical analogy, and in particular the bombing of Pearl Harbor in 1941. The President's diary entry made on September 11 stated: 'The Pearl Harbor of the 21st century took place today' (in Woodward 2002: 37). This became a commonly deployed strategic analogy throughout the Bush administration's tenure, with assertions such as:

> We've had oceans which have protected us over our history. *Except for Pearl Harbor, we've never really been hit before. And yet, on September 11th, this great land came under attack.*
>
> (Bush 2001, October 24)

The use of this historical analogy is important. It rendered the attacks comprehensible by not allowing the meaning of the events to remain in flux, and it framed the events within a particular interpretation. This was an undeserved attack on an innocent nation, which necessitated that the USA fight a 'just' war. Such a comparison allowed a seamless elicitation of the USA's collective understanding of the Second World War. Such a construction established a very specific rule structure within the narrative presented by the administration: America should not appease the perpetrators and America must confront them through violent means if necessary. This rule structure was heavily reinforced in and through assertions such as:

> *[W]e have seen their kind before. They are the heirs of all the murderous ideologies of the twentieth century.* By sacrificing human life to serve their *radical visions* – by abandoning every value except the will to power – *they*

follow in the path of fascism, and Nazism, and totalitarianism. And they will follow that path all the way, to where it ends: in history's unmarked grave of discarded lies.

(Bush 2001, September 20)

In a second world war, we learned there is no isolation from evil. We affirmed that some crimes are so terrible they offend humanity, itself. And we resolved that the aggressions and ambitions of the wicked *must be opposed early, decisively, and collectively, before they threaten us all. That evil has returned, and that cause is renewed.*

(Bush 2001, November 10)

The rule structure, derived from these historical analogies, remade and reinforced the notion that the events of September 11, 2001, were an 'act of war', and provided guidance on how the USA should proceed. The Bush administration, through the figurative use of the Second World War, was assimilating the events into a wider historical narrative. The discursive link to the Second World War tied the framing of September 11, 2001, to the same plot, and popularly held beliefs over why the USA went to war in 1941. It created a sense of American innocence as a peaceful nation reluctant to engage in international affairs, but that when attacked had no choice but to respond against this evil enemy. Just as the Nazis embodied 'evil' and could not be appeased, the same must be true of these new 'enemies of liberty'. The parallels with Hitler's Germany were encoded in the '9/11 crisis' narrative, and once decoded through interpellation suggested the need for a war-based decisive intervention to stop the enemy at all costs. This framing rendered negotiation an illegitimate action; 'appeasement' was not a solution to this threat derived from 'evil' just as it was not a solution to dealing with Nazi Germany.

Simultaneously, the figurative use of the Second World War informed the audience about what action must be taken in the future. Just as the former 'evil' regimes with totalitarian ideologies were strategically engaged and defeated in the past, the same must be done to defeat terrorism and its state sponsors. This opened the door for terrorists to be assimilated into contemporary understandings of the Nazis, with expansionist intentions driven by an evil ideology, therefore constituting a global threat to liberty and freedom:

I believe *this war is more akin to World War II . . . This is a war in which we fight for the liberties and freedom of our country.*

(Bush 2002, March 13)

Intertextual appeals to the Second World War further supported the notion that the attackers carried out their attack because they were 'evil'. Thus, it was through an interpretation of the past, once applied to the events of September 11, that 'going to war' was cast as a legitimate and rational response. Simply put, the construction of a war plot, articulated with a commonly understood narrative of the Second World War, turned a tragedy and morality play into a moralistic crusade.

To use the term 'moralistic crusade' is provocative, as it conjures historical images of a religiously driven military campaign particularly targeted against Muslims.[4] However, using this term is appropriate given the President's assertions that

> We need to be alert to the fact that these evil-doers still exist. We haven't seen this kind of barbarism in a long period of time ... *This crusade, this war on terrorism* is going to take a while.
> (Bush 2001, September 16)

Moreover, the term 'moralistic crusade' captures a specific dimension of American exceptionalism and its relationship with eschatological philosophies of war. This has been best elucidated by Seymour Martin Lipset, who argued that

> Americans are utopian moralists who press hard to institutionalise virtue, to destroy evil people, and eliminate wicked institutions and practices. A majority even tell pollsters that God is the moral guiding force of American democracy. They tend to view social and political dramas as morality plays, as a battle between God and the Devil, so that compromise is virtually unthinkable ... A sense of moral absolutism is, of course, part of what some people see as problematic about American foreign policy.
> (Lipset 1996: 63)

A significant aspect of the moral absolutist discourse, is that, whilst national identity constructs an 'us' and 'them', moral absolutism inscribes characterisations to this dyad. It posits the 'insider status' of the imagined community as morally 'good', and reinforces the notion that God is on America's side, whereas the binary opposite 'outsider status', as a logical corollary, is evil and demonic. Once an expression of difference has been turned into 'Otherness', bifurcated along religious conceptions of good and evil, it becomes coherently possible for Americans to define wars as moralistic crusades.[5] The result of such moralistic crusades is to insist on 'unconditional surrender' of the enemy in war, the reason for which is the ascribed relationship between going to war and the moral righteousness that motivates it. Thus, as Lipset argues:

> we [Americans] set moral goals, such as 'to make the world safe for democracy', as reasons to go to war. We have always fought the 'Evil Empire'. Ronald Reagan was as American as apple pie when he spoke of the evil empire as the enemy. But if we fight the evil empire, if we fight Satan, then he must not be allowed to survive.
> (Lipset 1996: 65)

Once again, the Bush administration appropriated and reconstructed this tradition. It presented a moralistic crusade as the solution to the perceived crisis. Consequently, arguing that the nature of its decisive intervention was clear:

Our responsibility to history is already clear: to answer these attacks and rid the world of evil.

(Bush 2001, September 14)

In every generation, the world has produced enemies of human freedom. They have attacked America, because we are freedom's home and defender. *And the commitment of our fathers is now the calling of our time.*

(Bush 2001, September 14)

This will not be an age of terror; this will be *an age of liberty, here and across the world* . . . In our grief and anger we have found *our mission* and our moment. *Freedom and fear are at war. The advance of human freedom* – the great achievement of our time, and the great hope of every time – now depends on us.

(Bush 2001, September 20)

Several elements require elucidation to generate a greater understanding of this discursive framing. First, what is strikingly clear about this formulation of the initial policy response is that the accompanying narrative was 'utopian, transformative, [and] derived from a perspective that sees history as a contest of ideas and minds more than of battalions and budgets' (Mazarr 2003: 513). Out of the crisis brought on by the September 11, 2001, attacks emerged a dogmatic liberal idealism embodied in the IDF deployed by the Bush administration. In effect, the IDF set out in the 2000 presidential campaign became reinvigorated, and the 'war on terror' was now seen as the overarching rationale in US foreign policy. In this context, the phrase 'the commitment of our fathers is now the calling of our time' is important because it has two interrelated purposes: the first is the manner in which it establishes a sense of America's liberal tradition, and the second is a direct appeal to America's foundational myth. Thus, as Hughes argues, 'Every schoolchild learns that the Puritans settled America for the sake of freedom' (Hughes 2004: 28). It therefore has impact by appealing to the American cultural terrain and creating a discursive relationship between the USA's mission and liberal beliefs (see Hughes 2004: 2). It resonates with, and reconstructs, US identity, consequently rendering US exceptionalism as inextricably linked to how Americans identify themselves in liberal terms (Wittkopf *et al*. 2002: 246).

The second element that requires elucidation is the manner in which the discursive framing allowed a policy response to emerge that was remarkably simplistic in its prescription. To construct a policy based around 'ridding the world of evil' appears absurd at first glance, not least because of the statement's metaphysical nature and sheer scale. This is especially true as the President would later assert that *'anybody* who tries to affect the lives of our *good* citizens *is evil'* (Bush 2001, October 24). However, upon closer analysis it is clear that the Bush administration was constructing the national interest focused upon a broad counter-terrorism strategy that targeted a 'tactic' rather than a specific enemy; a verb, not a noun.

Nations all across the globe have bound with the United States to send a clear message that *we'll fight terrorism* wherever it may exist.

(Bush 2001, October 24)

The men and women aboard Flight 93 . . . if they could see how our country is united to preserve freedom from terror, they'd be proud. Proud of our unity, proud of our strength, and *proud of the determination to find, root out and deal with the evil of terrorism and those who seek to terrorize.*

(Rumsfeld 2001, December 11)

The strategy that the Bush administration was adopting was embedded in the very title 'war against terrorism' (Bush 2001, September 11b). Evidently, this approach was not attempting to address the underlying causes of terrorism, but rather proceeded on the basis that a finite number of 'evil' terrorists existed and could be found and eradicated. Indeed, throughout President Bush's tenure he would constantly require statistical figures, asking 'how many did we kill?' and 'they killed three of ours. How many did we kill of them?' as a sign of 'progress' (see Woodward 2006: 319–20, 482–3). This 'scorecard' approach was a direct consequence of moral realism being embedded within the Bush administration's IDF. Indeed, to 'rid the world of evil' implies an ontologically objective status in the world, and was a rationale that underpinned the initial strategy adopted in Afghanistan.

Justice and the moralistic crusade in Afghanistan

The full implications of the Bush administration narrating the events of September 11, 2001, as a 'declaration of war' became highly evident on October 7, 2001, when the United States launched Operation Enduring Freedom (OEF) in Afghanistan. By asserting that the USA would 'make no distinction between the terrorists who committed these acts and those who harbor them', the Bush administration was able to proceed as if this were a 'traditional war' between sovereign states (Bush 2001, September 11b). In essence, the discursive move allowed geographical boundaries to reify an amorphous transnational terrorist network, and provided the initial target for a moralistic crusade. Yet, before and during the first major combat initiative of the 'war on terror', the Bush administration went to great lengths to construct this as a 'just war', which foregrounded notions of justice within the crisis narrative:

This is a day when all Americans from every walk of life unite in our resolve for *justice* and peace . . . we go forward to defend freedom and all that is good and *just* in our world.

(Bush 2001, September 11b)

Whether we bring our *enemies to justice*, or *bring justice to our enemies, justice will be done* . . . Freedom and fear, *justice and cruelty*, have always been at war, and we know that God is not neutral between them . . . Fellow citizens, we will meet violence with *patient justice* – assured of the rightness of our cause.

(Bush 2001, September 20)

[W]e're making good progress in *a just cause* . . . It may take a long time, but no matter how long it takes, those who killed thousands of Americans and citizens from over 80 other nations will be *brought to justice*, and the misuse of Afghanistan as a training ground for terror will end.

(Bush 2001, November 6)

We are deliberately and systematically hunting down these murderers, and we will bring them to *justice*.

(Bush 2001, November 8)

What is particularly fecund about this range of quotes is the manner in which there are different definitions of justice being appealed to. First, retributive justice in which members of the Bush administration invoked the need to hold individuals accountable and punish the perpetrators of the attacks and the Taliban regime:

All I can tell you is that *Osama bin Laden is a prime suspect, and the people who house him, encourage him, provide food, comfort or money are on notice* . . . we're going to find those who – those evil-doers, those barbaric people who attacked our country and we're going to *hold them accountable*, and we're going to *hold the people who house them accountable*; the *people who think they can provide them safe havens will be held accountable*; the *people who feed them will be held accountable*.

(Bush 2001, September 17)

The Bush administration's espoused narrative asserted that an injustice had been done, and that there was therefore a need to exact a just punishment. Yet, because the concept of justice was embedded within the plot of a moralistic crusade, it is evident that this retributive dimension was not litigious.[6] The terrorists had not committed a 'crime', but rather 'declared war'. Within the narrative presented by the Bush administration the notion of a criminal trial was deliberately written out as a likely or desirable option.[7] There was not to be any cross-examination or study of forensic evidence in a courtroom prior to punishment, as the US military in Afghanistan would be used for counter-terrorism operations.

In place of any litigious dimension being applied to the concept of justice, the Bush administration articulated retributive justice with 'frontier justice' (McCarthy 2002: 128–9). This is justice taken into an individual or group's own hands irrespective of the legal ramifications. It represents a lawless state of nature, and conjured romantic notions of the Wild West, which were often invoked by the administration:

I want justice. There's an old poster out west, as I recall, that said, 'Wanted: Dead or Alive'. . . . All I want and America wants him brought to justice.
(Bush 2001, September 17)

Well, the president's policy is *dead or alive*. And, you know, I have my preference but that's not a government position . . . We'll have to keep, as the president said, *closing the noose*.
(Rumsfeld 2001, November 21)

In this context the Bush administration had deemed itself the judge and jury that would 'bring our enemies to justice, or bring justice to our enemies' (Bush 2001, September 20). This image was reinforced by the President's repeated assertions that the US would 'hunt' those responsible:

The United States will *hunt down and punish those responsible* for these cowardly acts.
(Bush 2001, September 11c)

We hunt an enemy that hides in shadows and caves.
(Bush 2001, November 6)

Our military is pursuing its mission . . . We are *deliberately and systematically hunting down these murderers, and we will bring them to justice* . . . Our government has a responsibility to *hunt down our enemies* – and we will.
(Bush 2001, November 8)

The manner in which the term 'hunting' was used was deeply provocative as it helped reinforce the characterisation of the enemy as sub-human. As Erin McCarthy argues, 'the repeated use of the word "hunting" cannot be meant but to evoke images of hunting animals and shooting to kill' (McCarthy 2002: 131). When the terms 'justice' and 'hunting' are articulated together, the two terms seek to legitimise coercion; it is acceptable to kill because it is just, and justice is deliverable through killing.

This is significant because the Bush administration posited moral realism as a philosophical tenet, suggesting that moral values have an ontologically objective status. Yet, at the same time, the administration sought to legitimise the use of violence as a means of bringing about justice. Given this, there is a tension in the narrative presented by the administration between the subscribed philosophical tenets and the recommended practice. To square this circle, the Bush administration utilised a third conception of justice to legitimise the war, by construing it as a 'just war'. This was certainly the implication intended when the Department of Defense originally titled the Afghanistan campaign *Operation Infinite Justice*,[8] and by the repeated affirmations by the Bush administration that the war was just:

> Our military action is also designed to . . . drive them out and bring them to *justice* . . . To all the men and women in our military . . . I say this: Your mission is defined; your objectives are clear; *your goal is just*.
>
> (Bush 2001, October 7)

> Our cause is necessary. *Our cause is just*.
>
> (Bush 2001, December 11)

> I assure you and all who have lost a loved one that our *cause is just* . . . *Our cause is just*, and it continues . . . We seek a *just* and peaceful world beyond the war on terror.
>
> (Bush 2002, January 29)

The implication of invoking Just War theory clearly added to the moralistic crusade plot constructed by the Bush administration, and reinforced the characterisation of the USA as a moral actor. Indeed, the Bush administration was keen to recognise the long-standing distinction in Just War theory between *jus as bellum* and *jus in bello*; the justice *of* war and justice *in* war (Walzer 2006: 21–2). This was done though assertions such as:

> The United States respects the people of Afghanistan – after all, we are currently its largest source of humanitarian aid – but we condemn the Taliban regime.
>
> (Bush 2001, September 20)

> The oppressed people of Afghanistan will know the generosity of America and our allies. As we strike military targets, we'll also drop food, medicine and supplies to the starving and suffering men and women and children of Afghanistan.
>
> (Bush 2001, October 7)

> Our efforts are directed at terrorist and military targets because – unlike our enemies – we value human life. We do not target innocent people, and we grieve for the difficult times the Taliban have brought to the people of their own country.
>
> (Bush 2001, November 6)

The notion that Operation Enduring Freedom (OEF) constituted a Just War has been all too readily accepted. Yet serious questions remain about the applicability of Just War theory to OEF, when the Bush administration's first response to the attacks was to cast them as an act of war; this was therefore the first recourse and not the last resort. This point is particularly pertinent because one of the key tenets of Just War theory is that all non-violent alternatives should be exhausted before initiating the war. Nevertheless, whether one agrees with the applicability of Just War theory to Afghanistan or not, it is clear that through the lexicon of 'justice' the

Bush administration was utilising American power and setting out a rule structure for the international system. This initially came in the form of 'demands' and ultimatums to the Taliban:

> The United States of America makes the following *demands* on the Taliban: Deliver to United States authorities all the leaders of al-Qaida who hide in your land. Release all foreign nationals – including American citizens – you have unjustly imprisoned, and protect foreign journalists, diplomats, and aid workers in your country. Close immediately and permanently every terrorist training camp in Afghanistan and hand over every terrorist, and every person in their support structure, to appropriate authorities. Give the United States full access to terrorist training camps, so we can make sure they are no longer operating. *These demands are not open to negotiation or discussion.* The Taliban must act and act immediately. *They will hand over the terrorists, or they will share in their fate.*
> (Bush 2001, September 20)

> *There is no need to negotiate. There's no discussions. I've told them exactly what they need to do. And there is no need to discuss innocence or guilt. We know he's guilty* . . . I said *no negotiations* . . . *There's nothing to negotiate about.* They're harboring a terrorist. And they need to turn him over, and not only turn him over, turn the Al Qaeda organisation over, destroy all of the terrorist camps – actually, we're doing a pretty good job of that right now.
> (Bush 2001, October 14)

The rule structure presented by the Bush administration was therefore essentially one of compulsion, whereby the Taliban either complied or faced America's military power. As Peter Singer has argued:

> The intention behind the ultimatum was not to find a satisfactory solution to the problem, but to provide an excuse for going to war. War was not the last resort . . . It was the most aggressive choice amongst a range of options that had never been adequately explored.
> (Singer 2004: 151–2)

The articulation of retributive justice, frontier justice and Just War theory embedded in the Bush administration's official narrative reduced the concept of justice to the raw exercise of coercive power. It mirrored the definition of justice presented by Thrasymachus in Plato's *Republic*: 'Justice is nothing other than the advantage of the stronger' (Plato 1997: 338c). Despite the moralistic crusade plot and grandiose use of moral terms, ultimately justice became a legitimising concept for the projection of US power in an attempt to establish a system of rule that reflected the Bush administration's pre-September 11, 2001, preference for unilateralism. This was certainly echoed in the manner in which the USA responded to the attacks unilaterally, turning down the proposal by the UN Secretary-General,

Kofi Annan, for Security Council authorisation, and bringing NATO forces into the conflict only after the campaign had ended and peacekeeping was necessary (Gurtov 2006: 59). Moreover, the Bush administration was strategically aware that the war in Afghanistan could be used as an example to other regimes opposing US primacy. The notion that a war with Afghanistan could send a message and act as a deterrent to other regimes opposing US power was at the forefront of the strategically selective intervention:

> Let's hit them hard. *We want to signal this is a change from the past. We want to cause other countries like Syria and Iran to change their views.* We want to hit as soon as possible.
> (G. W. Bush in Woodward 2002: 98)

At the start of the campaign, President George W. Bush said, 'We are at the beginning of our efforts in Afghanistan, but Afghanistan is only the beginning of our efforts in the world. This war will not end until terrorists with global reach have been found and stopped and defeated.' You are the men and women who will *hand-carry that message to America's enemies, sealed with the muscle and might of the greatest warrior force on Earth.*
(Rumsfeld 2001, November 21)

> Our military has a new and essential mission. For states that support terror, it's not enough that the consequences be costly – *they must be devastating. The more credible this reality, the more likely that regimes will change their behavior* – making it less likely that America and our friends will need to use overwhelming force against them.
> (Bush 2001, December 11)

This echoed Bush's notion, when a candidate, of 'peace through strength', and Afghanistan presented an opportunity to enforce, and reinforce, a rule structure Bush established in the run-up to the 2000 presidential election:

> My second goal is to build America's defenses on the troubled frontiers of technology and terror . . . *Let me be clear. Our first line of defence is a simple message: Every group or nation must know, if they sponsor such [terrorist] attacks, our response will be devastating.*
> (Bush 1999, September 23)

The events of September 11, 2001, provided a situation in which Afghanistan and its Taliban regime were to be made an example of, and OEF was to demonstrate to the world the consequences of challenging US power and failing to follow instructions given from Washington. It was in essence Bush's 'Distinctly American Internationalism' put into practice. An attack on the USA had been carried out, and it was now time to demonstrate the consequences of invoking US preponderance so that others would not dare to attack or challenge US power.

That this mission was carried out under the banners of 'justice' and 'freedom' clearly demonstrates the extent to which US preponderance became intertwined with these concepts.

The conduct of the Bush administration reflected a new rule structure that members of the administration sought to put in place. Similar to the sentiments of Eliot A. Cohen's '9/11 rules', the Bush administration's declaration that you are either 'with us or against us' created a dichotomy in which the USA promised to 'help our friends, punish those who impede us, and annihilate those who attack us' (Cohen 2001: 16). Once again this resembles Plato's *Republic*, but this time reflecting Polemarchus' notion that justice is 'to treat friends well and enemies badly' (Plato 1997: 332d). This language was not just for public consumption; it was used at the highest diplomatic levels. In General Pervez Musharraf's account, the President of Pakistan brought to power by a coup d'état in 1999 recalls Colin Powell telling him that 'you are either with us or against us'. The nature of this threat became all the more evident when Richard Armitage added that, if Pakistan chose to be on the side of terrorists, then they should be 'prepared to be bombed back to the Stone Age' (Musharraf 2006: 201).

In addition to dividing the world into a simplistic dichotomy and therefore establishing a rather simplistic rule structure for the other states to follow, the Bush administration sought to disembed itself from long-established legal norms as part of its counter-terrorism strategy. This created a situation in which the USA was creating a rule structure that it alone was permitted to follow: a do as we say, not a do as we do, rule structure. This was certainly the logic presented by the Bush administration as it began to bypass laws and principles of legality. In the months after September 11, 2001, the USA increasingly began to appeal to friendly regimes in the Middle East to cooperate with the CIA, in particular Egypt, Morocco, Syria and Jordan (Williams 2006: 124). The result of this was an expansion of America's willingness to pursue a policy of 'extraordinary rendition'. This extrajudicial practice, which started under President Clinton,[9] was intensified as a result of the war on terror, and, as J. Cofer Black, the former head of the CIA's counter-terrorism centre, testified, by late 2002 'there were at least 3,000 terrorist prisoners being held worldwide' (see Grey 2004). The procedure of 'rendering' terrorist suspects to third countries allowed US officials to bypass American laws prohibiting torture and the right of habeas corpus (see Mani 2003: 101). This established a policy of 'torture-by-proxy'.[10] The practical logic of this policy was clearly set out by a former CIA agent, Bob Baer:

> If you want a serious interrogation, you send a prisoner to Jordan. If you want them to be tortured, you send them to Syria. If you want someone to disappear – never to see them again – you send them to Egypt.
>
> (in Grey 2004)

Clearly, within the articulation of justice presented by the Bush administration, and under the lexicon of security, domestic and international laws were seen to work against the sort of justice that the Bush administration wanted to deliver.

Once again this action demonstrates the Bush administration's willingness to send a message to those that oppose American power:

> the White House and the Department of Defense had adopted a policy of fighting terror with terror . . . More so than other modes of torture, this type of contract crime may be ordered mainly for reasons of deterrence – i.e., to teach an object lesson to all people who fall afoul of the U.S., regardless of their national origin.
>
> (Bix 2005)

The war in Afghanistan, in combination with the greatly expanded use of 'extraordinary rendition', therefore marked a point of acceleration in the Bush administration's desire to disembed itself from international institutions and international law. This created a situation in which 'the strong do what they have the power to do and the weak accept what they have to accept' (Thucydides 1972: 401–2). This manifested itself with the Bush administration introducing new characters into the narrative, labelled 'unlawful enemy combatants' and 'battlefield detainees'. The introduction of these characterisations caused a deep public split within the administration, between the State Department on one side and the Defense Department and Vice President's office on the other. Notably this divide concerned whether the Geneva Conventions applied to these characters or not. Despite this divide in the administration, it became clear that official policy favoured the Vice President's view that 'They don't meet the requirement of the laws of war' (Cheney 2002, January 27). The Vice President summed up the situation concisely when he argued that:

> the legal question is, is there a category under the Geneva Convention for unlawful combatants, and one argument, the State Department argument, is, they ought to be treated within the Geneva Convention . . . The other argument is, the Geneva Convention doesn't apply in the case of terrorism, and that leads you down a different track from a legal standpoint . . . The ultimate result is, they will be treated humanely, but they are not going to be accorded the treatment you would accord, for example, the Iraqis that we captured in the Gulf War . . . These are bad people. I mean, they've already been screened before they get to Guantanamo. They may well have information about future terrorist attacks against the United States. We need that information, we need to be able to interrogate them and extract from them whatever information they have.
>
> (Cheney 2002, January 27)

What is interesting about the Vice President's statement is that it sought to construct the USA as a moral actor, by claiming that detainees will 'be treated humanely', and cast the USA as working within legal boundaries, albeit 'down a different track from a legal standpoint'. Evidently, habeas corpus had been suspended under the administration's retributive definition of justice. In place of legal norms, the Bush administration was simply able to declare that those rendered were 'bad people'. In effect, the crisis narrative constructed a state of exception, which allowed the USA to *rule by law* 'constructed by Bush lawyers' and not under the *rule of law* (see Robertson 2006: 537). The Bush administration had created a 'legal limbo' that it sought to legitimise around a specific characterisation of the enemy and a specific definition of justice articulated within its narrative.

Tensions in the moralistic crusade: freedom versus justice

The period between September 11, 2001, and December 2001 demonstrated serious tensions within the Bush administration's IDF. At the level of grand strategic narrative the concept of freedom was foregrounded. This was very much in keeping with liberal notions of post-Cold War triumphant exhilaration, according to which the idea of the West would inevitably triumph over all other global models. Yet, although the concept of freedom was strategically central to the crisis narrative, it was clear that OEF was not launched to nation-build or democratise Afghanistan. That is to say, there was a disjunction between references to freedom and the so-called 'calling of our fathers' and the manner in which the Bush administration engaged in OEF.

Throughout October to November 2001, the upper echelons of the Bush administration were reluctant to construct a post-Taliban political plan. The administration was focused on the objectives of regime change and counterterrorism because, as President Bush argued, OEF was 'designed to disrupt the use of Afghanistan as a terrorist base of operations, and to attack the military capability of the Taliban regime' (Bush 2001, October 7). When asked about any responsibility that a policy of regime change might have on US commitments to Afghanistan, Secretary of Defense Donald Rumsfeld argued at length that:

> The United States of America, and certainly the United States military ... are simply doing exactly what the president indicated, trying to root out terrorists ... because we have that concern and we go in and root out terrorists, I don't think [this] leaves us with a responsibility to try to figure out what kind of government that country ought to have ... I don't know people who are smart enough from other countries to tell other countries the kind of arrangements they ought to have to govern themselves.
>
> (Rumsfeld 2001, October 9)

As a result of the Bush administration's initial approach, when Ambassador James F. Dobbins was announced as the Bush administration's representative to the Afghan opposition, and tasked with putting together and installing a post-Taliban regime, he 'had no particular instructions' regarding how to fill the political vacuum left once the Taliban was removed. Far from a commitment to spreading freedom and democracy, Dobbins argued that the Bush administration would have been 'happy for the King [Mohammed Zahir Shah] to come back and make it a monarchy or whatever' (Dobbins 2008a). It was only once King Zahir

Shah, who was residing in Rome and aged 87, made it clear that he had no desire to seek a formal role in any post-Taliban administration, that the Bush administration's discourse shifted towards embracing a more representative outcome, but remained determined not to become embroiled in a post-conflict nation-building role. Consequently, the Bush administration asserted the aspiration of a 'new Afghan government' that would 'adhere to accepted international principles' and therefore be 'broad-based, represent all Afghans, men and women, and be drawn from all ethnic groups'. Yet this was conditioned with assertions that the USA would not 'create the future government of Afghanistan' because 'it is up to the Afghans themselves to determine their future' (Bush 2001, November 13). The Bush administration made clear that it wanted to maintain a low military presence throughout the country, focusing on counter-terrorism, and leaving the country as soon as its military objectives were achieved (Wolfowitz 2001, December 6). As Ambassador Dobbins explained:

> No one in the Bush administration wished to see an American military occupation of Afghanistan on the model of post-World War II Germany or Japan. Neither did anyone want to see an international administration on the model of Bosnia or Kosovo. Instead, everyone hoped the Taliban could be succeeded by a broadly based, moderate Afghan regime that would unify the country, reassure its neighbours, and cooperate with the United States in stamping out any residual terrorist threat. Determining how to achieve that outcome was the problem.
> (Dobbins 2008b: 19–20)

The US solution was to invite the United Nations (UN) to take the lead in calling for a conference, from which a new Afghan government would be formed, thereby initiating the Bonn Process under the leadership of Lakhdar Brahimi, Special Adviser to the Secretary-General. With UN Security Council Resolution 1378, passed on November 14, 2001, the USA was able to purse its moralistic crusade to hunt down al-Qaeda and the Taliban, whilst UN peacekeepers delivered aid, attempted to maintain stability and began planning a roadmap for Afghanistan's political future. Thus, during the early phase of the war there were two conflicting strategies. The USA pursued its counter-terrorism strategy, which assumed that there were a finite number of terrorists who could be identified and destroyed, whilst the UN began to formulate a democratisation agenda for post-Taliban Afghanistan (Dunn and Hassan 2010; Hassan and Hammond 2011).[11] Of course such a clear distinction is problematic to the extent that the USA is a key strategic actor on the UN Security Council itself, and was heavily involved in the Bonn Process. As such, it was through the UN that the USA demonstrated a formal, albeit tacit, commitment to democratisation that permitted the UN to pursue a transformative agenda for Afghanistan. However, in areas where the objectives of democratisation and counter-terrorism collided, the USA privileged and pursued the latter. The US position was one in which it would tacitly support nation-building and democratisation, through the UN, if and only if this did not collide with the immediate interests of the war on terror. This was certainly evident in the initial months of the war, revealing not only how the US and UN strategies were in tension, but also how the concepts of freedom and justice defined within the administration's own IDF conflicted rather than complemented one another.

The US counter-terrorism strategy in Afghanistan was predicated on retributive frontier justice. This definition of justice, combined with the Bush administration's earlier pessimistic declinism, circumscribed any notion that the Bush administration itself should commit to nation-building and democratisation. Thus, the administration's very conception of justice was in tension with other elements of its post-crisis narration, as freedom simply came to mean the removal of al-Qaeda and of oppression by the Taliban regime. That is to say, it was not merely perceptions of short-term national interests that were trumping long-term interests, but the primary definitions of freedom and justice deployed by the Bush administration were in fact, despite being articulated together, in an often conflictual relationship within the overarching crisis narrative. American identity was constructed around the USA as a moral agent spreading 'freedom' to defeat 'evil', but seeking 'justice' was tied to eradication; where they overlapped was around the manner in which both were tied to the concept of US primacy.

This tension was clearly evident on a range of issues surrounding the Bonn Agreement. For example, it was Javad Zarif, the Iranian representative at Bonn, who insisted that the term 'democracy' be included in the agreement, whilst the Bush administration's core concern was ensuring that the emergent Interim Authority was chaired by Hamid Karzai, whom the USA had lobbied vigorously to secure (Dobbins 2008b: 83).[12] Moreover, with the Bonn Agreement being heavily influenced by the USA, the Bush administration was able to remove reference to the originally drafted 'International Security Force' and have it renamed the 'International Security Assistance Force' (ISAF), which would only 'assist in the maintenance of security for Kabul and its surrounding areas'. This discursive transformation clearly demonstrated the Bush administration's emphasis on Afghans providing their own security and was designed to 'eliminate any suggestion that international soldiers might themselves provide security for the Afghan population' (Dobbins 2008b: 102).

Notably, with the Bush administration's moralistic crusade swiftly removing the Taliban from power, by December 20, 2001, ISAF was mandated by UNSCR 1386, and proved to be relatively successful in providing security in and around Kabul (see McNerney 2005). This led to interim Prime Minister Hamid Karzai personally appealing to both the UN and President Bush for a greater number of peacekeepers beyond Kabul, which was a clear acknowledgement of an emergent 'security gap' beyond the nation's capital (Hassan and Hammond 2011). Brahimi, the chief UN envoy, acknowledged that far from ISAF being seen as illegitimate, as some commentators had feared, he had heard demands for the expansion of ISAF 'even from the warlords', and Kofi Annan, UN Secretary-General, declared that 'security was the number one preoccupation of everyone we met in Afghanistan' (in Orme 2002). In spite of this, the Bush administration remained firmly committed to placing counter-terrorism at the core of US objectives and argued that with respect to ISAF 'such a force must do nothing that would in any way inhibit the coalition from carrying out the primary objectives of ridding

Afghanistan of terror' (Haass 2001, December 6). Such a position ultimately led to the Bush administration failing to answer pleas for help from Karzai's Interim Authority, and demonstrated the tensions between the UN objectives of nation-building and democracy and the US objectives of seeking justice and security through counter-terrorism. The impact this had on UN democratisation objectives is that it further undermined what was already an extremely difficult, if not highly unlikely, democratisation exercise. Moreover, as the Bush administration gradually came to see the promotion of democracy as a fundamental American national interest, throughout 2002 and 2003, these initial decisions began to raise issues that contended with the Freedom Agenda (Hassan and Hammond 2011).

Laying discursive tracks for the Freedom Agenda to evolve

The first three months after September 11, 2001, proved remarkably fluid as the Bush administration responded to the terrorist attacks. From the construction of the events as a tragedy, to casting God as an actor in a morality play, through to the construction of war and a moralist crusade, the Bush administration was able to articulate a crisis narrative and formulate its decisive intervention in Afghanistan. Indeed, one of the striking features of this narrative was how seamlessly it was able to iteratively and cumulatively construct the 'war on terror' through articulating multiple concepts, identities, temporalities and plot structures to reconstruct the past, present and future. Thus, September 11, 2001, certainly provided a moment of punctuation in political time, and the Bush administration was able to construct a narrative that shaped the nature of political change to come.

Accordingly, as explained by the constructivist institutionalist methodology, this tells us something about September 11, 2001, in particular, but also something more broadly about the nature of political crises. Simply put, the construction of crises represents an opportunity for foreign policy transformations, because such moments of abrupt systemic punctuation require strategically selective actors to come together and act within a strategically selective context. The narrative that emerges from such action is crucial because, as demonstrated above, the narrative provides both policy makers and the wider audience with answers to questions such as 'what has gone wrong?' and 'what is to be done?' Consequently, the context of post-crisis action cannot be divorced from an understanding of the crisis. In defining the events as an 'act of war', the Bush administration was reacting to the events, but also prescribing the form of political change that was to follow. Crucially, as Richard Jackson has argued:

> [T]he important point is that this construction of the attacks as 'war' . . . was probably the most significant and far reaching aspect of the entire official discourse. It set the foundations for almost everything that followed . . . it was in no sense inevitable and the use of different words would have given an entirely different understanding to September 11, 2001 – which in turn would have altered the entire response to the attacks.
>
> (Jackson 2005: 40)

This is certainly the case with the emergence of the Freedom Agenda. The declaration that the USA was attacked because of its status as a 'beacon for freedom and opportunity' is not a neutral discursive act. It is a (re)construction of US identity emplotted within a strategic narrative. Yet, by declaring this, discursive tracks were laid that gave rise to the notion that the USA must defeat 'evil' and 'advance freedom'. This was an idealist vision of history and of the USA's role in the world, which was increasingly giving rise to a utopian orientation and moralistic crusade. Accordingly, whilst it was highly evident that US foreign policy radically changed following the terrorist attacks on September 11, 2001, the idealist narrative that emerged as part of the '9/11 crisis' narrative assimilated the events into a longer historical understanding of US foreign policy. This was done by directly appealing to the international idealism of the Wilsonian legacy, and its transformational vision, which became popular in the USA after the Second World War (see Nye 2007). Moreover, in a world of triumphant exhilaration and Fukuyama's 'end of history', the Bush administration presented the need to bring others into the so-called post-historical phase. In effect, the Bush administration's narrative had articulated the concepts of freedom and security together through an American exceptionalist discourse. The implications of this would not be seen in the initial months of the war in Afghanistan, as the articulation of security and justice led to the initial counter-terrorism strategy, but slowly over time the importance of this initial construction was to become all the more pressing as the Freedom Agenda would slowly emerge.

This slow construction of the Freedom Agenda was certainly evident within the first months after the attacks. By deploying the concept of freedom as the utopian goal of the war on terrorism, the President had invited contestation within the administration itself. Thus, before the Freedom Agenda was officially sanctioned, individuals within the Bush administration, such as Paula J. Dobriansky, the Under Secretary of State for Global Affairs, declared that:

> [O]ur overall goal is not just fighting against terrorism; it is fighting for civilization and democracy ... the advancement of human rights and democracy is important in its own right. At the same time, these efforts are the bedrock of our war on terrorism. The violation of human rights by repressive regimes provides fertile ground for popular discontent. In turn, this discontent is cynically exploited by terrorist organisations and their supporters. By contrast, a stable government that responds to the legitimate desires of its people and respects their rights, shares power, respects diversity, and seeks to unleash the creative potential of all elements of society is a powerful antidote to extremism.
>
> (Dobriansky 2001, December 21)

The ideas expressed by Secretary Dobriansky were not widely espoused within the administration, but would soon gather momentum and become institutionalised as the rationale for the Freedom Agenda. Equally, a competing view of how to combat terrorism and promote freedom began to emerge from the Office of the United States Trade Representative. Just nine days after the terrorist attacks, Robert B. Zoellick wrote an op-ed in the *Washington Post* arguing that:

> Our enemy's selection of targets – the White House, the Pentagon and the World Trade Towers – recognises that America's might and light emanate from our political, military and economic vitality. Our counteroffensive must advance U.S. leadership across all these fronts . . . America is the economic engine for freedom, opportunity and development . . . Trade is about more than economic efficiency. It promotes the values at the heart of this protracted struggle . . . Congress needs to complete action on the U.S. free trade agreement with Jordan, our first such commitment in the Arab world . . . The terrorists deliberately chose the World Trade towers as their target. While their blow toppled the towers, it cannot and will not shake the foundation of world trade and freedom.
>
> (Zoellick 2001, September 20)

In effect, Zoellick was espousing the neoliberal definition of freedom set out during the 2000 presidential campaign, in which freedom and free trade were indivisible. Yet, under the banner of 'raising the flag of economic leadership', Zoellick was asking Congress to pass 'Fast Track' legislation that would allow the administration to bypass committee deliberations and full congressional debate. Articulating the need for 'free trade' under the proviso of combating terrorism and spreading freedom was largely derided by Congress. Consequently, Charlie Rangel, the Democratic Congressman form New York, asserted that:

> to appeal to patriotism in an effort to force Congress to move on Fast Track by claiming it is needed to fight terrorism would be laughable if it weren't so serious.
>
> (in Juhasz 2006: 18)

Yet this was the first articulation by a prominent member of the Bush administration that free trade was needed to fight terror and spread 'freedom'. This is an idea that would lead the Bush administration to declare the *Middle East Free Trade Area* initiative on May 9, 2003. Thus, the construction of crisis resulting from September 11, 2001, clearly has implications on the construction of the Freedom Agenda. It opened up a political space for contestation within the administration over what exactly 'the calling of our fathers' entails, albeit with the prevailing narrative inscribing the need for a 'war on terrorism' to achieve it. What is notable about this political space is that it was bound by a binary between those who believed the response should be to focus on the 'eradication' of terrorism and those, such as Zoellick and Dobriansky, who saw the need for a wider response that addressed the 'causes' of terrorism. This tension was at the heart of the war on terror as a US foreign policy paradigm, but it was clear that although at the level of grand narrative the concepts of freedom and security were providing a cognitive function, which helped the decisive intervention seem conceptually sound whilst resonating with national values, the concepts of justice and security were providing a coordinative policy function with regards to policy in Afghanistan. Given this situation, the apparently swift success in Afghanistan and then the formulation of the war in Iraq would play a crucial role in tipping the balance in favour of freedom and security as the '9/11 crisis' narrative evolved into the Freedom Agenda and a new policy paradigm for the MENA emerged.

5 Constructing the Freedom Agenda for the Middle East

With the Bush administration having laid discursive tracks in response to the crisis constructed out of September 11, 2001, the perceived early successes in Afghanistan only helped the administration move closer to constructing the Freedom Agenda as a policy paradigm towards the MENA. With the Taliban removed from power and al-Qaeda being 'hunted down', some of the immediate elevated tensions between the administration's definitions of freedom and justice were resolved in favour of the former. Yet, just as significantly, important lessons were learnt in the first few months of the war in Afghanistan that both the administration and the US military would seize upon and appropriate into the war on terror narrative. As President Bush argued:

> These past two months have shown that an innovative doctrine and high-tech weaponry can shape then dominate an unconventional conflict . . . *our military are rewriting the rules of war* . . . The conflict in Afghanistan has *taught us* more about the future of our military than a decade of blue ribbon panels and think-tank symposiums.
>
> (Bush 2001, December 11)

In essence the President was arguing that the USA had developed military supremacy through technological innovation, which was powerful, swift and effective enough to be projected across the world and achieve a desirable outcome. This certainly appeared to be the case as the Northern Alliance, with US support, was able to take the city of Mazar-e-Sharif by November 9, 2001, and then capture Kabul by November 12, 2001 (Katzman 2005: 9; Struck 2001). The rapid collapse of the Taliban regime appeared to vindicate the Rumsfeld–Franks strategy of combining the indigenous Northern Alliance with US Special Forces and airpower (Call 2007: 25–41). This not only silenced critics, but fundamentally altered how the Bush administration viewed the strategically selective context; it altered what was seen as politically feasible, practical and desirable. No longer was the military seen as 'declining', which had been the position put forward in the 2000 presidential campaign (see also Rumsfeld 2011: 331–3). Rather, a military strategy had supposedly been constructed by the Pentagon and the CIA, which made fears of military overstretch appear redundant.

Constructing the Freedom Agenda for the Middle East 105

The pessimistic declinism embedded in the administration's espoused IDF had been vanquished by swift military success. As a consequence, the triumphant exhilaration born out of the end of the Cold War became dominant. Afghanistan facilitated this roll, because the rapid success of the operation offered a low-cost option of regime change, and provided a model for future military action (Woodward 2004: 5, 30; Dunn 2005: 18). In effect, the Afghanistan campaign, and subsequent rapid regime change, facilitated the conditions for the USA to foster and narrate a new hubris, which helped dispel the myth of US weakness, which had been a lasting legacy of the Vietnam War. The war in Afghanistan represented an *anagnorisis* moment in the narrative presented by the Bush administration:

> When I committed U.S. forces to this battle, I had every confidence that they would be up to the task. And they have proven me right. The Taliban and the terrorists set out to dominate a country and intimidate the world. Today, from their caves, it's all looking a little different. And no cave is deep enough to escape the patient justice of the United States of America. We are also beginning to see the possibilities of a world beyond the war on terror. We have a chance, if we take it, to write a hopeful chapter in human history.
> (Bush 2001, December 11)

Furthermore, this turning point was assimilated into the American exceptionalist narrative. Having removed the Taliban regime, the Bush administration by the spring of 2002 narrated the reasons for removing them as 'liberation', and increasingly began to align its stated mission objectives with those of the UN nation-building efforts. It thus began to alter its narrative, assimilating the events into a privileged genealogical past; for the Bush administration the war represented a continuation of America's democracy promotion tradition:

> None of us would ever wish the evil that has been done to our country, yet we have learned that *out of evil can come great good.*
> (Bush 2001, November 8)

> *There's jubilation in the cities that we have liberated.* And the sooner al Qaeda is brought to justice, the sooner Afghanistan will return to normal.
> (Bush 2001, November 19)[1]

> Part of that cause was to *liberate the Afghan people from terrorist occupation, and we did so . . . In Kabul, a friendly government is now an essential member of the coalition against terror.*
> (Bush 2002, March 11)

> The first phase of our military operation was in Afghanistan . . . *You've got to understand that as we routed out the Taliban, they weren't sent in to conquer; they were sent in to liberate . . .* America seeks hope and opportunity for all people in all cultures. And *that is why we're helping to rebuild Afghanistan*

> ... The Marshall Plan, rebuilding Europe and lifting up former enemies, showed that America is not content with military victory alone. Americans always see a greater hope and a better day. And America sees a just and hopeful world beyond the war on terror ... by your effort and example, *you will advance the cause of freedom around the world.*
>
> (Bush 2002, April 17)

The importance of this transformation should not be understated. Whereas the Bush administration had originally rejected the need for nation-building, its objectives in Afghanistan had incrementally transformed to the point at which the Bush administration would repeatedly declare that the success of a free Afghanistan was a large rationale behind the reasons for war. Such is the prominence of these assertions that in President Bush's memoir *Decision Points* he argues that he changed his mind about nation-building after September 11, 2001, and that 'Afghanistan was the ultimate nation-building mission' (Bush 2010: 205) – although, rather disingenuously, the former President also edits out the length of time it took to arrive at this decision, arguing that 'helping a democratic government emerge' was a *cause célèbre* of the original 'comprehensive' strategic vision for OEF (Bush 2010: 205).

Nonetheless, that as early as 2002 the war in Afghanistan was being constructed as a 'war of liberation' is instructive. It demonstrates how the projection of US power, and the US construction of a crisis, could be assimilated into the rubric of democracy promotion and liberation. That is to say, the two discourses, and objectives, could coexist within an IDF. The meaning and usage of the concept of justice was consequently subtly changed, and came to legitimise a nation-building project under the banner of 'freedom', whilst also continuing to be a central discursive structure underpinning anti-democratic practices, such as indefinite detention, torture and targeted assassinations. This proved to be a critical dynamic in the evolution of the Freedom Agenda, which posited both the need for US primacy over, and the democratisation of, the Middle East.

Moreover, with the removal of the Taliban regime, under the banner of justice and peace, the Bush administration was now characterising US military intervention as strong, resolute, credible, anti-imperialistic and able to deliver a nation, to freedom. However, with the dispelling of the myth of American weakness, a fundamental shift in the power structure of the US corporate bureaucracy occurred. No longer was Colin Powell's State Department seen as the key institution with regard to foreign policy in the MENA region; the door had been opened for other strategically selective actors in the state system to reassert themselves. The military success created a shift in power from the State Department, which was increasingly being accrued by Pentagon officials and the Vice President's office; this laid the foundations for 'phase two' of the administration's moralistic crusade in Iraq and the institutionalisation of the Freedom Agenda. That is to say, there was a shift in the perceived deontic power of the players statuses within these institutional settings, which had began as a result of the crisis narrative but was reified in light of the perceived success in Afghanistan. Moreover, this shift in institutional statuses empowered officials inclined to use military power to reshape the Middle East in its image, and set the scene for the Bush administration to make its most controversial foreign policy decision.

The decision to launch Operation Iraqi Freedom in March 2003 generated a considerable level of debate and confusion around the world, and events in Iraq did little to relieve the original sense of puzzlement. This was most instructively demonstrated when Richard N. Haass, the former director of the Policy Planning Staff at the State Department and President of the Council on Foreign Relations, was asked why President Bush had decided to go to war. He replied:

> I will go to my grave not knowing that . . . I can't answer it. I can't explain the strategic obsession with Iraq – why it rose to the top of people's priority list. I just can't explain why so many people thought this was so important to do.
> (in Lemann 2004: 157)

This is a sentiment Haass would repeat in his memoir *War of Necessity; War of Choice*. Haass points out that the decision to invade Iraq in 2003 was not the product of a definitive moment in which principles met to discuss the pros and cons of the invasion before a final decision was made. Rather, the decision was the product of a cumulative process (Haass 2009: 234). To the extent that Haass does offer a modicum of an explanation, he argues that

> after 9/11, the President and those closest to him wanted to send a message to the world that the United States was willing and able to act decisively. Liberating Afghanistan was a start, but in the end it didn't scratch the itch. Americans had no long standing history of feud with Afghanistan . . . Iraq was fundamentally different. The President wanted to destroy an established nemesis of the United States. And he wanted to change the course of history, transforming not just a country but the region of the world that had produced the lion's share of the world's terrorists and had resisted much of modernity.
> (Haass 2009: 234–5)

This explanation is one that resonates with many academics' and political commentators' accounts (Bacevich 2008: 59–60; Lieven and Hulsman 2006; Traub 2008: 118–19; Monten 2005; Jervis 2003). Embedded in this explanation is an answer to why the Freedom Agenda emerged: it was, in conjunction with the Iraq war, an attempt to transform the Middle East with the aim of countering terrorism and delivering 'modernity'. However, such a position is not without its critics. Tamara Cofman Wittes, in her sustained and highly detailed account of the Freedom Agenda, *Freedom's Unsteady March: America's Role in Building Arab Democracy,* excludes any analysis of Iraq, arguing that:

> [I]n the public discourse both in the United States and abroad, the Bush administration's policy of advancing Middle Eastern democracy is inextricably linked to the war in Iraq. Yet this conflation misunderstands both the

Iraq war and Bush's policy of democracy promotion. Humanitarian intervention to topple a brutal dictatorship was a distant third among rationales put forward by the Bush administration and its allies for the invasion; the primary arguments had to do with Iraq's weapons of mass destruction, both past and presumed, and its alleged links to terrorist groups. Hope that Saddam's fall would produce a democratic 'domino effect' in the region was expressed by the president and other senior officials as a hope, and not as a war aim. The United States would not have gone to war simply to create a democracy in Iraq, absent what was then viewed as a compelling security rationale.

(Wittes 2008a: 8–9)[2]

In an interview at the Brookings Institute, she expanded this argument by asserting that:

the marketing of the war was number one WMD, number two links to terrorism, number three humanitarian intervention . . . If the core motivation of Iraq was to set up a democracy and create this domino effect then the military implementation would have looked very different, because, you do not create a democracy with that kind of post-invasion force structure . . . if the President were whole-heartedly committed to setting up a democracy in Iraq that would create this domino impact throughout the region, he would have . . . at some point during the process when he and his advisers were being briefed on the military planning for the war, [President Bush] would have said how are we going to create a democracy afterwards? There is no evidence in anything that has been written so far about the planning for the war that that question was ever asked.

(Wittes 2008b)

Evidently, there is a clear divergence of opinion between proponents who articulate a close relationship between the Iraq war and the Freedom Agenda and those who view them as separate policies. Moreover, it is clear from the two positions that the relationship between the Iraq war and the Freedom Agenda requires an analysis of the period leading up to the Iraq war. Instructively, the constructivist institutionalist methodology sheds light on this issue through its commitment to process-tracing narrative analysis.

Diagnose, proselytise and impose: Iraq and the Freedom Agenda

The shift in bureaucratic influence within the Bush administration away from the State Department's policy of smart sanctions, and towards the Defense Department's regime change policy in Iraq, came shortly after the Northern Alliance had captured Kabul. According to President Bush, he asked Donald Rumsfeld to turn his attention to Iraq for an assessment of possible military options on November 21, 2001 (in Woodward 2004: 30). Thus, before the Bonn

Agreement was signed the Bush administration was already turning its attention away from Afghanistan towards the build-up to war with Iraq. Symptomatic of this was the manner in which Tommy Franks was told to conduct war-planning against Iraq, whilst he was in Kabul, and briefed the President on December 28 2001, just days after the Interim Authority had come to power in Afghanistan.

For many commentators the shift from focusing on Afghanistan to Iraq has been seen as a product of the Vice President's office, where Dick Cheney adopted the role of 'examiner of worst case scenarios' in which he had to 'think about the unthinkable' (Woodward 2004: 29). In this role, Vice President Cheney began to focus on weapons of mass destruction (WMD) being used by terrorists against the US. The fear of such an occurrence was compounded by intelligence gathered before September 11, 2001, which appeared to show Osama bin Laden meeting with Sultan Bashiruddin Mahmood in Kandahar. This meeting was of great significance, as Mahmood was the former chairman of Pakistan's Atomic Energy Commission and an expert on uranium enrichment (Suskind 2006: 27; Overbye and Glanz 2001). In light of the events of September 11, 2001, this meeting was interpreted as a 'nightmare' by George Tenet and consequently presented to Dick Cheney and other principals of the US intelligence community. The result of this meeting was dramatic, as it provided the first articulation of what the Pulitzer Prize winner Ron Suskind termed *The One Percent Doctrine.* Suskind quotes the Vice President's assertion that

> If there's a one percent chance that Pakistani scientists are helping al Qaeda build or develop a nuclear weapon, we have to treat it as a certainty in terms of our response . . . It's not about analysis, or finding a preponderance of evidence . . . It's about our response.
>
> (Suskind 2006: 62)

This was an extraordinary assertion, which fundamentally altered the rules of the game. No longer was policy to be led by evidence, but rather a dichotomy had been constructed between analysis and action. This disarticulation created a scenario in which the possible was to be deemed more important to strategic policy action than the probable. Within such a context the causes for action fundamentally changed, as the strategically selective actors viewed the strategically selective context differently. Ultimately, policy became heavily reliant on the productive imagination, which in turn became embedded in the Bush administration's narrative through semantic innovation. The consequences of this were highly apparent to Sir Richard Dearlove, head of the UK intelligence agency MI6, who briefed Prime Minister Blair nine months before the invasion commenced in Iraq. In his assessment he argued that war was 'inevitable' and that 'the facts and intelligence' were being 'fixed round the policy' by the Bush administration (Rycroft 2005; Fielding 2005).

Instructively, the Bush administration was concerned about possible links between WMD and 'terrorism' before September 11, 2001. The administration framed its argument for withdrawing from the 1972 Anti-Ballistic Missile

(ABM) Treaty by arguing that it was concerned about the link between 'missiles and terror' and the possibility of 'attack and blackmail' (Bush 1999, September 23). The need for a Ballistic Missile Defense (BMD) shield was marketed as necessary for maintaining US primacy and preventing the perceived threat from 'rogue nations' willing to 'blackmail', 'threaten' or 'attack'. The importance of this discursive structure is that it was a readily available discourse, which was expanded after the September 11, 2001, attacks. In particular this discourse was assimilated into the Bush administration's moralistic crusade plot in light of the anthrax attacks that followed September 11:

> *We have faced unprecedented bioterrorist attacks delivered in our mail . . .* And tonight, *we join in thanking a whole new group of public servants who never enlisted to fight a war, but find themselves on the front lines of a battle nonetheless: Those who deliver the mail – America's postal workers. We also thank those whose quick response provided preventive treatment that has no doubt saved thousands of lives* – our health care workers . . . *The first attack against America came by plane . . . The second attack against America came in the mail.*
>
> (Bush 2001, November 8)

> *America's next priority to prevent mass terror is to protect against the proliferation of weapons of mass destruction and the means to deliver them . . .* One former al Qaida member has testified in court that he was involved in an effort 10 years ago to obtain nuclear materials. And the leader of al Qaida calls that effort 'a religious duty.' Abandoned al Qaida houses in Kabul contained diagrams for crude weapons of mass destruction. *And as we all know, terrorists have put anthrax into the U.S. mail . . . And almost every state that actively sponsors terror is known to be seeking weapons of mass destruction and the missiles to deliver them at longer and longer ranges.* Their hope is to blackmail the United States into abandoning our war on terror.
>
> (Bush 2001, December 11)

The anthrax attacks provided a physical incarnation of 'terrorists' using WMD on American soil. Thus, although the origin of the attacks was unknown, they were articulated as a 'second wave', a phrase which alludes to causality on the basis of succession in time.[3] This created a *post hoc, ergo propter hoc* fallacy rooted in a conflation between the 'terrorists' who carried out the September 11, 2001, attacks and the 'terrorists' who sent anthrax in the postal system (see Egan 2002; Vulliamy 2002). Through doing this, the Bush administration was able to reify an association of ideas between WMD and terrorism, and sell this as an immediate threat to the US populace. This was an audience that no longer thought in the abstract of such attacks, but rather through collective fear had 'experienced' the attacks and was readily interpellated. As a direct consequence, US counter-terrorism and counter-proliferation policies were increasingly portrayed in synergy as the Bush administration's narrative amalgamated them together.

The linguistic embodiment of such an articulation was delivered through phrases such as 'mass terror', 'catastrophic harm', 'catastrophic terrorist violence', 'turn their hatred into holocaust', 'technologies to kill on a massive scale', 'massive and sudden horror', 'maximum death and destruction', and 'unprecedented dangers'. This list is by no means complete, but rather provides a sample of the language used to represent the alleged danger facing the USA. This tendency to inflate danger was evident during the anthrax attacks, when the Bush administration portrayed them as threatening 'thousands of lives', rather than the five deaths and 15 sicknesses that actually resulted from the attacks (Bohn *et al.* 2008). The propensity to inflate threat was increasingly utilised and assimilated within the Bush administration's 'war on terror' narrative. As a consequence the characterisation of the 'enemy' began to undergo a process of metamorphosis. Claims were increasingly made concerning terrorism and the use of WMD:

> These same terrorists are searching for weapons of mass destruction, the tools to turn their hatred into holocaust. They can be expected to use chemical, biological and nuclear weapons the moment they are capable of doing so ... We face enemies that hate not our policies, but our existence.
>
> (Bush 2001, November 10)

> [S]ome states that sponsor terror are seeking or already possess weapons of mass destruction; terrorist groups are hungry for these weapons, and would use them without a hint of conscience. And we know that these weapons, in the hands of terrorists, would unleash blackmail and genocide and chaos. These facts cannot be denied, and must be confronted.
>
> (Bush 2002, March 11)

> Our adversaries have now shown their willingness to slaughter thousands of innocent civilians in a devastating strike. If they had the capacity to kill millions of innocent civilians, do any of us believe they would hesitate to do so?
>
> (Wolfowitz 2002, October 4)

> We don't want the smoking gun to be a mushroom cloud ... that would make September 11 look small in comparison ... We're in a new world. We're in a world in which the possibility of terrorism, married up with technology, could make us very, very sorry that we didn't act.
>
> (Rice 2002, September 8)

Highly observable in these quotes is the manner in which the characterisation of the enemy changed from merely 'evil terrorists' to a triad of 'evil terrorists, WMD and rogue states'. This was accompanied by a narration of a possible future that was not only apocalyptic, but a dystopia in which the 'American way of life', 'civilization' and 'freedom' were destroyed and 'fear', 'evil' and 'tyranny' replaced them. This imagined future was seen as a possibility because, as the Bush administration argued, there were 'evil states' and 'evil terrorists' working together to challenge and destroy the USA with WMD. This conflated an essentialised identity of 'terrorists' and 'rouge states':

> Our second goal is to prevent regimes that sponsor terror from threatening America or our friends and allies with weapons of mass destruction . . . *we know their true nature . . . Iraq continues to flaunt its hostility toward America and to support terror.* The Iraqi regime has plotted to develop anthrax, and nerve gas, and nuclear weapons for over a decade . . . *States like these, and their terrorist allies, constitute an axis of evil.*
> (Bush 2002, January 29)

> *Terror cells and outlaw regimes building weapons of mass destruction are different faces of the same evil.* Our security requires that we confront both.
> (Bush 2002, October 7)

Evidently, the Bush administration's narrative continued along the plot of a moralistic crusade. However, by expanding the characterisation of the enemy to an essentialised 'evil' triad, the Bush administration began reforming the boundaries of what constituted the national interest and how to pursue it. The original response to the war on terror was abstractly defined as 'ridding the world of evil' and defeating 'every terrorist group of global reach' (Bush 2001, September 20). However, by late 2001 this had changed, and now the national interest was expanded to dealing with terrorism and proliferation, through 'pre-emptive' force, to 'prevent mass terror' and the 'proliferation of weapons of mass destruction and the means to deliver them' (Bush 2001, December 11). Problematically, this distinction would be written out of the official narrative as the President began claiming that the objective was 'always the same' (Bush 2002, April 17). This shift in the construction of the national interest is fundamentally important to understanding the evolution of the Freedom Agenda. Whereas the moralistic crusade in Afghanistan was conducted under the banner of Just War theory, the build-up to the Iraq war was constructed as a prudent measure, given the possibility of 'mass terror'. However, whilst the administration was focusing on 'mass terror', it also began to focus on the MENA region more broadly.

On November 29, 2001, the issue of Iraq and the idea of democratising the Middle East began to be developed as two distinct, but conjoined, ideas. In another demonstration of the influence the Department of Defense had gained through the President's decision to construct a decisive intervention as a war, Donald Rumsfeld asked Paul Wolfowitz to bring together scholars from the American Enterprise Institute (AEI) and John Hopkins School of Advanced International Studies (SAIS) (Rumsfeld 2006, July 6). This meeting, which Wolfowitz and Rumsfeld's consultant Steve Herbits termed 'Bletchley II', was called together to answer broader questions that the Pentagon was unable to answer, such as 'Who are the terrorists? Where did this come from? How does it relate to Islamic history, the history of the Middle East, and contemporary Middle East tensions? What are we up against here?' (Woodward 2006: 83).[4]

Constructing the Freedom Agenda for the Middle East 113

The goal of this meeting was to construct post-9/11 policy towards the Middle East,[5] which would be drawn up as a memo and circulated around the Bush administration (see Bosman 2006). Although this memo remains classified, what little information is available is highly revealing. The title of the memo was *Delta of Terrorism*. Significantly, the metaphor of a *delta* was chosen to conjure images of the mouth of a river from which terrorism flows from the entire MENA region. According to Christopher DeMuth, an instrumental actor in the meeting:

> the general analysis was that Egypt and Saudi Arabia, where most of the hijackers came from, were the key, but the problems there are intractable. Iran is more important, where they were confident and successful in setting up a radical government . . . We concluded that a confrontation with Saddam was inevitable. He was a gathering threat – the most menacing, active and unavoidable threat. We agreed that Saddam would have to leave the scene before the problem would be addressed.
>
> (in Woodward 2006: 84–5)

DeMuth's description of the meeting's conclusion is instructive as it put forward a wide-ranging plan for US–MENA relations. Countries that were deemed important to long-term national interests, such as Saudi Arabia and Egypt, were highlighted as important to transforming the region, but as part of a gradual process resulting from the removal of Saddam Hussein. Iran was believed to be a threat, but too difficult to deal with. Consequently, Saddam Hussein was seen as an easier, more vulnerable target that could be removed. At the meeting Baathism was seen as 'an Arab form of fascism transplanted to Iraq' and that the Bush administration should consider itself 'facing a two-generation war' starting 'with Iraq'. This, it was believed, would be 'the only way to transform the region' (Woodward 2006: 83–5).

This memo certainly proved to be a tipping point for many in the administration, as it provided a broad vision, strategy and alternative policy paradigm for dealing with the MENA region. When the memo was hand-delivered to members of Bush's war cabinet, Rice said that the memo was 'very, very persuasive', Cheney was 'pleased with the memo' and the President was now focused on the 'malignancy' of the Middle East (Woodward 2006: 85). Moreover, the memo reveals an important chain of events. First, the notion of invading Iraq was set in motion before any conception of its wider impact on transforming the region. However, within less than a fortnight after the President asked Donald Rumsfeld to look into invading Iraq, a much wider policy paradigm was being established that would transform the MENA, starting with an invasion of Iraq. This was the ideational birth of a liberal grand strategy for democratising the MENA region. Consequently, it is possible to concur with Andrew Bacevich's assessment of the situation:

> [T]hrough a war of liberation, the United States intended to convert Iraq into what Deputy Secretary of Defense Paul Wolfowitz termed 'the first

Arab democracy'. Yet, as they prepared for a final showdown with Saddam, Wolfowitz and others in the administration were already looking beyond Baghdad . . . The ultimate aim of the strategy was nothing less than 'to remake the world' or at least what the administration referred to as the Greater Middle East. Here was an imperial vision on a truly colossal scale, a worthy successor to older claims of 'manifest destiny' . . . President Bush's 'freedom agenda' updated and expanded upon this tradition.

(Bacevich 2008: 59–60; see also Lieven and Hulsman 2006; Traub 2008: 118–19; Monten 2005; Jervis 2003)

Indeed, by the autumn of 2002 it was clear that the Bush administration was increasingly associating regime change in Iraq with a much larger and more far-reaching transformation of the entire region (see Ottaway 2005: 178). In an interview with the *Financial Times* on September 23, 2002, Rice explicitly claimed that the USA would be 'completely devoted' to democratising Iraq in the event of an invasion and that democratisation would not 'stop at the edge of Islam'. Further still, Rice asserted that the USA had a commitment to the 'democratisation or the march of freedom in the Muslim world' (Harding *et al.* 2002). Rice's assertion was echoed by the President, when he asserted that:

If we meet our responsibilities, if we overcome this danger, *we can arrive at a very different future.* The people of Iraq can shake off their captivity . . . *inspiring reforms throughout the Muslim world.* These nations can *show by their example that honest government, and respect for women, and the great Islamic tradition of learning can triumph in the Middle East and beyond.*

(Bush 2002, September 12)

The current Iraqi regime has shown the power of tyranny to spread discord and violence in the Middle East. *A liberated Iraq can show the power of freedom to transform that vital region,* by bringing hope and progress into the lives of millions. *America's interests in security, and America's belief in liberty, both lead in the same direction: to a free and peaceful Iraq* . . . *A new regime in Iraq would serve as a dramatic and inspiring example of freedom for other nations in the region.*

(Bush 2003, February 26)

This demonstrates that within the narrative presented by the Bush administration there was a vision of the future that made a commitment to democracy in Iraq, and that this would act as an exemplar for the rest of the region. The Iraq war was increasingly being narrated as the method of creating a 'very different future' for the region: the utopian ending of the moral crusade plot that was juxtaposed with a possible dystopia resulting from terrorists possessing WMD. It was with this utopian ending of the moral crusade in mind that the President met with Iraqi exiles to discuss post-invasion democratisation on January 10, 2003. Similarly, in an NSC meeting on February 14, 2003, when considering what would happen if a coup to replace Saddam with another dictatorship occurred, the President made it clear that he would insist on authority being turned over to a publicly supported Iraqi authority to ensure some movement towards democracy (in Woodward 2004: 258, 315; see also Bush 2003, February 26). As Dick Cheney said of the President at the time, 'Democracy in the Middle East is just a big deal for him. It's what's driving him' (in Woodward 2004: 412).

Consequently, far from viewing the Freedom Agenda and the Iraq war as distinct entities, the Bush administration itself portrayed these two policies as part of the same larger policy paradigm, which had been formulated over time as a result of September 11, 2001, but constructed as a strategy for delivering 'freedom' throughout the entire MENA region. This makes it evident that the centrepiece of the Bush administration's ideological vision of the Middle East began with attacking Iraq. In the belief that the USA had unprecedented power to wield, Iraq was seen as the route through which to transform the entire region. Unlike the Clinton administration, which believed peace was achievable through solving the Palestinian–Israeli conflict, the Bush administration viewed regional transformation as achievable through the removal of Saddam Hussein (see Indyk 2002). This was evident in the decoupling strategy outlined in the first NSC meeting in February 2001, and became all the more prominent after the September 11, 2001, terrorist attacks.

Understanding the relationship between the Freedom Agenda and the Iraq war as two reinforcing policies, embedded within the same policy paradigm, allows a more cogent appreciation of why the President's narrative asserted the importance of Iraq for transforming the region. Evident in the Bush administration's appeals that Iraq would become an exemplar for the region was an appeal to 'domino theory'. As a dominant metaphor throughout the Cold War, the theory resonates with the US public and is widely understood: the fall of one country to an ideology would stimulate the fall of those adjacent to it. However, in the post-Cold War era when the exhilaration of victory led to claims of the 'end of history' in which the USA stood vindicated as the sole remaining superpower, the Bush administration sought to deploy the metaphor for inspirational purposes: push Baghdad, and 'unfriendly tyrannies' in the MENA will fall with it.

From the view of those within the higher echelons of the Bush administration there appeared only one direction in which the dominos would fall. As Paul Wolfowitz explained, ' "Export of democracy" isn't really a good phrase . . . we're trying to remove the shackles on democracy' (in Smith 2007). This was coupled with Dick Cheney's claims that 'after liberation, the streets in Basra and Baghdad are sure to erupt in joy in the same way throngs in Kabul greeted the Americans' (in Lockman 2004: 251). In the Bush administration's espoused narrative, it was highly evident that democracy was seen as the 'natural' order a society would adopt; if tyranny was removed democracy would surely follow. At the 'end of history', when liberal democracy is the 'final form of human government' and the teleological 'end point of mankind's [sic] ideological evolution' (Hassan 2008: 272–3) what other way could Iraq and the rest of the MENA region fall? This established one of the most ideological premises of the Bush administration's vision for the future of the Middle East. If Iraq could be emancipated from Saddam Hussein it would become a pro-American bastion of freedom in the region. It was believed that it would provide a 'model' for pro-American forces in the region to rise up and demand similar levels of democracy and freedom. This was, as John Lewis Gaddis declared, a formula of 'Fukuyama plus force' (Gaddis 2004: 90). However, as events in Iraq began to challenge the Bush administration's teleological understanding of history, demonstrating problems within the administration's IDF, the Freedom Agenda would come to evolve distinctively and become the defining feature of the new policy paradigm.

The incremental evolution of a new policy paradigm for the Middle East

By understanding the Iraq war and the Freedom Agenda as part of a grand vision for the MENA region, articulated together by the vision set out at 'Bletchley II', it is possible to trace the gradual evolution of the Freedom Agenda back to within months of the September 11, 2001, crisis. Indeed, by early 2002, policy practice began to catch up with the initial transformative discourse the administration set out in its initial crisis narrative. Yet the evolution of the policy itself was not a smooth process, as the Bush administration needed to adapt its crisis narrative to events, setbacks and challenges to the policy's institutionalisation. This became all the more apparent throughout the end of 2002 when long-term MENA allies, such as Egypt, began facing increasing pressure from the administration to reform. Equally, as the build-up to the war in Iraq was unfolding, the administration's thinking about the Freedom Agenda was evolving to provide a more distinctive policy coupled with a distinctive set of institutions. Thus, although the Iraq war was intended to create a domino effect, the Freedom Agenda was departing from relying on the fall of 'dominos' alone.

Long before the Freedom Agenda was declared the leitmotif of Bush's second term in office, the policy came into fruition through a slow gestation of ideas. What distinguishes the period between early 2002 and the launch of Operation Iraqi Freedom in March 2003, and why it is important to the evolution of the Freedom Agenda, is that the Bush administration began to shift the definition of the national interest. No longer was simply 'eradicating terrorism' at the core of the definition, but at the same time as the administration began to include the use of 'pre-emptive' force to 'prevent mass terror' it also slowly began to see a national interest in addressing wider social conditions in the MENA. What emerged was a definition of the national interest that sought to deal with what the administration saw to be the causes of terrorism. As strategically selective actors within the state bureaucracy began to interpret the strategically selective context differently, as a result of a crisis, the construction of the national interest shifted to solve the puzzle the crisis appeared to present. The Freedom Agenda in its final evolutionary form is the product of this shift.

That the Bush administration's post-crisis narrative was evolving to include a more prescriptive approach to dealing with the causes of terrorism before the Iraq war was launched became highly evident in the President's West Point speech. As early as June 2002, the President declared to West Point candidates that

> the 20th century ended with a single surviving model of human progress, based on non-negotiable demands of human dignity, the rule of law, limits on the power of the state, respect for women and private property and free speech and equal justice and religious tolerance. America cannot impose this vision – yet we can support and reward governments that make the right choices for their own people ... A truly strong nation will permit legal avenues of dissent for all groups that pursue their aspirations without violence. An advancing nation will pursue economic reform, to unleash the great entrepreneurial energy of its people. A thriving nation will respect the rights of women, because no society can prosper while denying opportunity to half its citizens. Mothers and fathers and children across the Islamic world, and all the world, share the same fears and aspirations. In poverty, they struggle. In tyranny, they suffer. And as we saw in Afghanistan, in liberation they celebrate.
> (Bush 2002, June 1)

These sentiments were repeated in the *National Security Strategy* published in September 2002. Such assertions represented an evolutionary step in the moral crusade plot presented by the administration. In narrating a future utopian vision 'beyond the war on terror', the President asserted the need to confront 'poverty' and 'tyranny' by supporting and rewarding 'governments that make the right choices for their own people'. This was to be done by countries adopting the 'single surviving model of human progress'. Such a statement is notable for its teleological understanding of 'progress' towards a single vision, and the prescription of democratisation as a solution to terrorism. This added a much more complex understanding of how to 'fight' the 'war on terror' than had been initially constructed.

The implications of this statement became all the more evident in US–MENA relations. Chiefly, US–Egyptian relations were symptomatic of the coming problems that would prove highly troublesome for the Freedom Agenda when it was formally institutionalised. On June 8, 2002, President Bush held a joint press conference with President Mubarak in which he thanked Egypt for its 'strong support in our war against terror', claiming that 'we've got a good friend, Americans have a good friend, when it comes to this war on terror, in Egypt' (Bush 2002, June 8). However, by August 2002 the White House refused to honour an Egyptian request for $130 million in supplementary aid. This was a direct protest against the July sentencing of the prominent Egyptian-American democracy activist Saad Eddin Ibrahim and his colleagues for apparent fraud and defamation. This was the first time the USA had linked the provision of aid to a human rights case in the Arab world (Hawthorne 2003a: 23). As the Bush administration became increasingly concerned by the internal politics of regimes it regarded as allies, tensions began to surface. This saw the creeping insurrection of the 'conflict of interests' problem, which slowly began to ferment in US–MENA relations.

Within the early evolutionary phase of the Freedom Agenda, it became abundantly clear that the Bush administration was asserting the need to promote 'freedom' in the region, but that the narrative failed to provide a robust and consistent understanding of why this applied to the entire region. Consequently, it failed to set out a strategy other than deploying the 'domino' metaphor. This became all the more evident when the Bush administration began re-engaging in the Palestinian–Israeli conflict, seeking an end to the second Intifada. Indeed, President Bush argued that,

> if liberty can blossom in the rocky soil of the West Bank and Gaza, it will inspire millions of men and women around the globe who are equally weary of poverty and oppression, equally entitled to the benefits of democratic government.
> (Bush 2002, June 24)

This vision was narrated as the end point of the President's proposed two-state solution, which would be supported if 'a new and different Palestinian leadership' was elected. Evidently, Washington wanted 'regime change' in the Palestinian Authority, and argued that this would allow 'democratic reforms' to move forward (Bush 2002, June 24). Removing Arafat had now become US policy in an effort to restart negotiations between the Palestinians and Israelis; this later culminated in the 'Road Map' (see Mearsheimer and Walt 2007: 199–228; Hudson 2005).

Without a coherent narrative of why the USA needed to promote 'freedom' in the region, the Bush administration once again narrated the 'universal value' of freedom within an exceptionalist discourse:

> Prosperity and freedom and dignity are not just American hopes, or Western hopes. *They are universal, human hopes.* And even in the violence and turmoil of the Middle East, America believes *those hopes have the power to transform lives and nations.*
> (Bush 2002, June 24)

> Americans are a free people, who know that *freedom is the right of every person and the future of every nation. The liberty we prize is not America's gift to the world, it is God's gift to humanity.*
> (Bush 2003, January 28)

That 'freedom' was 'God's gift to humanity' was an articulation that was often deployed to legitimise the Freedom Agenda. Without a coherent rationale or strategy in place, the phrasing legitimises the Freedom Agenda by implying that God demands such a policy. Not only does it provide a sense of moral mission, but it places God on the USA's side in that mission. To promote freedom is to do God's altruistic work, and, consequently, human actions imitate God's will whilst building a utopia on Earth. Evidently, through rationalising the policy in these transcendental terms the Bush administration was attempting to maintain the interpellative resonance of the war on terror as a moral crusade, whilst silencing critics.[6]

This transcendental argument, derived from a US exceptionalist discourse, underpinned the Freedom Agenda's social engineering project. This was social utopianism par excellence. As Donald Rumsfeld had explained:

> we have a choice, either to change the way we live, which is unacceptable, or to change the way that they live . . . we chose the latter.
> (Rumsfeld 2001, September 18)

Yet failure to assert a coherent rationale proved highly problematic for the Freedom Agenda throughout the early phase of its institutionalisation. At the launch of MEPI in December 2002, the flagship programme underpinning the Freedom Agenda, Colin Powell argued that focusing on development would fill the 'hope gap' in the region and that:

> [U]ntil the countries of the Middle East unleash the abilities and potential of their women, they will not build a future of hope. Any approach to the Middle East that ignores its political, economic, and educational underdevelopment will be built on sand.
> (Powell 2002, December 12)

However, with an initial budget of only $29 million, this was derided in the region as tokenism (Sharp 2005a: 3). This fact was not lost on US officials, who increasingly argued that MEPI represented a 'philosophical commitment' towards reforming the region (Sharp 2005a: 3). Accordingly, as the administration tried to justify its position, claiming that this was a strategy of 'partnerships' and 'principle' (Powell 2004), it became all the more evident that the Freedom Agenda was not a direct challenge to MENA allies. Rather, the Freedom Agenda's intended purpose was to work with regional allies, in 'partnerships', to try and alleviate the social conditions that were undermining their legitimacy.

The rise of the Freedom Agenda: consolidating the paradigm

Whilst the Iraq war was being fought, the Bush administration toned down the prominence of the Freedom Agenda in its espoused narrative. Instead, the Bush administration concentrated on explaining its operational doctrine and focused on the particulars of the conflict rather than the wider regional strategy. However, after the swift collapse of the Iraqi regime, the Freedom Agenda began to be increasingly seen as the overarching rationale for US policy. Thus, although the Iraq war was a point of origin for the Freedom Agenda, it also served as a point of departure that ultimately led to the Freedom Agenda becoming deemed the central policy paradigm of the Bush administration's tenure in office.

The rise in the Freedom Agenda's prominence was directly linked to failures in Iraq. The celebration of the liberated masses, which the administration had promised prior to the invasion, failed to materialise. In its place came a growing insurgency and increasing instability in the country. This fundamentally challenged the simplicity of the 'war on terror' narrative; far from removing the 'shackles on democracy', the removal of Saddam Hussein brought with it sectarian violence and the possibility of the territorial integrity of the country being split along Shia, Sunni and Kurdish lines. As a result, the Bush administration faced increasing problems in securing its war on terror narrative. The facts on the ground directly contradicted its parsimonious assertions that an invasion of Iraq would increase the security of the USA. On the contrary, reports from the country were showing that supporters of al-Qaeda were increasingly infiltrating the country and seeking to set up a 'kind of safe haven for jihad against the West that Afghanistan was before September 11' (Diamond 2005: 320).

This represented a crisis of its own in the post-crisis narrative, which opened up space to criticise the Bush administration's foreign policy, and the narrative it espoused. It is important to recognise that, as Stuart Croft argues:

> Any new policy programme prescribed in and through this new discourse [the war on terror] would inevitably be challenged over time. Policy programmes decay in the normal course of debate as issues and attitudes change over time; and new crises are constructed, ones that produce different discourses that take different directions.
>
> (Croft 2006: 2)

The growing unease about the moral crusade plot the Bush administration had put forward was evident in speeches the President began to make. In an attempt to defend the war on terror as an overarching rationale he began arguing that:

> [A]s democracy takes hold in Iraq, the enemies of freedom will do all in their power to spread violence and fear. They are trying to shake the will of our country and our friends, but the United States of America will never be intimidated by thugs and assassins. The killers will fail, and the Iraqi people will live in freedom.
>
> (Bush 2004, January 20)

This, and many other statements to the same effect, attempted to assimilate the growing insurgency into the original narrative in an attempt to salvage the original construction of the war on terror. Those who opposed the US occupation were deemed the 'enemies of freedom', masking a divergent set of political objectives. Similarly, the original decision to cast the terrorist attacks as an 'act of war' began to be challenged in a manner that had not been done in 2001, leading the President to assert in his 2004 State of the Union address:

> I know that some people question if America is really in a war at all. They view terrorism more as a crime, a problem to be solved mainly with law enforcement and indictments. After the World Trade Center was first attacked in 1993, some of the guilty were indicted and tried and convicted, and sent to prison. But the matter was not settled. The terrorists were still training and plotting in other nations, and drawing up more ambitious plans. After

Constructing the Freedom Agenda for the Middle East 121

the chaos and carnage of September the 11th, it is not enough to serve our enemies with legal papers. The terrorists and their supporters declared war on the United States, and war is what they got.

(Bush 2004, January 20)

The strength of the counter-narrative, however, was too persuasive in the face of evidence throughout 2004. This led to active and retired military leaders charging that the war on terror was too simplistic in its prescriptions, and that the term conveyed the impression that military power alone could address the threat (see Chollet and Goldgeier 2008: 314). The result of this pressure gave the President cause to assert that:

We actually misnamed the war on terror. It ought to be the struggle against ideological extremists who do not believe in free societies who happen to use terror as a weapon to try to shake the conscience of the free world. And, you know, that's what they do. They use terror, and they use it effectively.

(Bush 2004, August 6)

Similarly, as Donald Rumsfeld was leaving office he argued that:

I don't think I would have called it the war on terror . . . I don't mean to be critical of those who have or did or – and certainly I've used the phrase frequently . . . it's not a war on terror. Terror is a weapon of choice for extremists who are trying to destabilise regimes and impose their . . . dark vision on all the people that they can control. So 'war on terror' has a problem for me.

(Rumsfeld 2006, December 7)

Such statements marked a significant alteration in the Bush administration's espoused narrative. When faced with increasing challenges to the simplicity of the narrative, the Bush administration chose not to abandon it, but rather to modify it to become more accommodating to the challenges. The enemy was no longer defined by its 'evil' nature alone, but rather by an 'ideology'. The logical conclusion of this alteration was delivered by President Bush when he asserted that:

While the killers choose their victims indiscriminately, their attacks serve a clear and *focused ideology, a set of beliefs and goals that are evil, but not insane. Some call this evil Islamic radicalism; others, militant Jihadism; still others, Islamo-fascism.* Whatever it's called, this *ideology* is very different from the religion of Islam. *This form of radicalism exploits Islam to serve a violent, political vision: the establishment, by terrorism and subversion and insurgency, of a totalitarian empire that denies all political and religious freedom . . . Islamic radicalism* is more like a loose network with many branches than an army under a single command.

(Bush 2006, October 6)[7]

The change in the characterisation of the enemy had a profound impact on the manner in which the Freedom Agenda evolved. It was no longer portrayed as a policy to prevent terrorists being recruited, but rather as a 'foreign policy based on liberty' motivated by 'hopeful ideology called freedom'. It was no longer just a strategy to transform the Middle East, but rather a challenge to a 'hateful ideology' (Bush 2006, July 28). The shift in focus to an ideological struggle re-invented the importance of the Freedom Agenda. It built on the original narrative, presented after September 11, 2001, to include more than just military means, therefore answering critics of the war on terror. Yet, in doing so, the Freedom Agenda was presented as the overarching rationale for US foreign policy. Accordingly, the President argued that:

> *The war we fight today is more than a military conflict; it is the decisive ideological struggle of the 21st century.* On one side are those who believe in the values of freedom and moderation... And on the other side are those driven by the values of tyranny and extremism.
>
> (Bush 2006, August 31)

> *We are engaged in the defining ideological struggle of the 21st century.* The terrorists oppose every principle of humanity and decency that we hold dear. Yet in this war on terror, there is one thing we and our enemies agree on: *In the long run, men and women who are free to determine their own destinies will reject terror and refuse to live in tyranny. And that is why the terrorists are fighting to deny this choice to the people in Lebanon, Iraq, Afghanistan, Pakistan, and the Palestinian Territories. And that is why, for the security of America and the peace of the world, we are spreading the hope of freedom.*
>
> (Bush 2008, January 28)

Within this iteration of the war on terror narrative, ideological struggle was seen to be the central plot and the Freedom Agenda as America's method of victory. This was an implicit recognition of the limitations of the previous narrative; the narrative was cumulatively yet iteratively adapted so that the Freedom Agenda transformed into the central paradigm in what remain a moral crusade.

Making the spread of liberty central to US foreign policy was explicitly the goal of President Bush's second term in office. When informing Michael Gerson, the President's chief speech writer, of what he wanted to be included in his upcoming second inaugural address, President Bush explicitly told him that he needed to get across a single idea: 'The future of America and the security of America depends on the spread of liberty' (see Woodward 2006: 371). This was to be as central to the war on terror as containment had been in the Cold War. The President was explicitly trying to modify the war on terror narrative so that the Freedom Agenda would become the single overarching policy paradigm for US foreign policy. Through claims that the regional status quo had not provided security, the President increasingly asserted that:

As long as the Middle East remains a place of tyranny and despair and anger, it will continue to produce men and movements that threaten the safety of America and our friends. So America is pursuing a forward strategy of freedom in the greater Middle East. We will challenge the enemies of reform, confront the allies of terror, and expect a higher standard from our friends.
(Bush 2004, January 20)[8]

Given the centrality of the Freedom Agenda, it was no longer sufficient to argue that it was a product of transcendental values or based on principle alone. Rather, the policy was endowed with a more complex security rationale. Throughout 2004 until the end of Bush's tenure in office, the Bush administration increasingly began to narrate the Freedom Agenda as a method of securing a global democratic peace. To substantiate these claims the Bush administration increasingly justified the pursuit of the Freedom Agenda by appropriating the logic of democratic peace theory. In the President's own words:

The freedom agenda is based upon our deepest ideals and our vital interests . . . We [Americans] *believe that freedom is a gift from an almighty God . . . And we also know, by history and by logic, that promoting democracy is the surest way to build security. Democracies don't attack each other or threaten the peace. Governments accountable to the voters focus on building roads and schools – not weapons of mass destruction. Young people who have a say in their future are less likely to search for meaning in extremism. Citizens who can join a peaceful political party are less likely to join a terrorist organisation. Dissidents with the freedom to protest around the clock are less likely to blow themselves up during rush hour. And nations that commit to freedom for their people will not support terrorists – they will join us in defeating them.*
(Bush 2006, July 28)

This was coupled with continuous assertions such as 'in Europe, as in Asia, as in every region of the world, the advance of freedom leads to peace' (Bush 2003, November 6) and 'we believe democracy yields peace' (Bush 2006, August 7). Such calls appeared to give Washington's national security liberalism the guise of a scientific imperative, because of the empirical strength of the thesis. Indeed, many academic studies have demonstrated that the number of wars between democracies during the past two centuries has been low, ranging from 'zero to less than a handful depending on precisely how democracy is defined' (Levy 1988: 661). Consequently, as Jack Levy argues, the 'absence of war between democracies comes as close as anything we have to an empirical law in international relations' (Levy 1988: 662).

Significantly, the appeal to democratic peace theory is not new to American foreign policy, as similar sentiments have been expressed by successive administrations since the end the Cold War.[9] However, the G. W. Bush administration was the first to suggest that this could be implemented in the Middle East and create institutions in the foreign policy bureaucracy to pursue this end. The vision that the Bush administration increasingly espoused was one in which the national interest is satisfied by creating a 'zone of peace' in the Middle East, in which the nature of democracy creates a reluctance to go to war with other states in the region, whilst also undermining the appeal of terrorism. This created a cocktail in which democratic peace theory not only was the route to peace but had universal applicability, and democracy promotion was seen as the silver bullet to problems ranging from terrorism to proliferation. Democratic peace theory therefore played a significant role in justifying the direction of US strategy. It provided part of the administration's IDF that motivated and legitimised a liberal grand strategy for the MENA region.

The shape and content of post-crisis continuity and change

By attempting to answer how and why the Freedom Agenda was constructed, using a constructivist institutionalist approach, the empirical chapters thus far have set out the results of a textually orientated process tracing discourse analysis. They have presented a narrative of the Bush administration's strategic narrative, which traced the institutional and discursive processes of the Freedom Agenda's construction and highlighted the key events that helped the Freedom Agenda develop as a policy paradigm. What they reveal is that the shape of political time can best be described as punctuated evolution, in which an existing policy paradigm (status quo) was interrupted by a moment of crisis (September 11, 2001), and a new policy paradigm ultimately emerged (the Freedom Agenda) (see Figure 5.1).

However, although this characterises the shape of political time, and clearly demonstrates the importance of crises in policy more generally, it says nothing about the content of political continuity and change. For this, it was necessary to focus on how strategically selective actors, situated within the institutional bureaucracies of the state, first narrated the crisis (tragedy, morality play, moralistic crusade), second engaged in puzzle-solving (post-crisis meetings, Afghanistan, Bletchley II, Iraq) and third articulated elements of their IDF together (such as primacy, hegemonic stability theory, unilateralism, neoliberalism, modernisation thesis, teleological understanding of history, American exceptionalist identity, moral realism, transcendentalism, domino theory and democratic peace theory). All of this contributed to the construction of the Freedom Agenda as central to US national interests. Moreover, although these categories are analytically distinct,

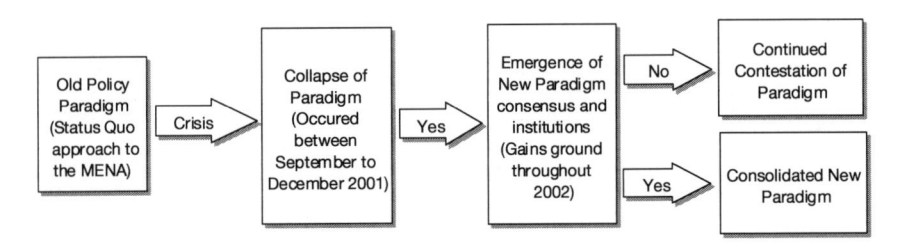

Figure 5.1 The shape of post-crisis political change: old paradigm, crisis, new paradigm.

the nature of narratives is that those espousing them combine elements with ease, masking the enormous complexity of what is being presented. However, by asking questions about the Freedom Agenda's construction, it has become possible to demonstrate some of this complexity and reveal how the narration of the war on terror was particularly dynamic, and ultimately gave birth to the Freedom Agenda as a policy paradigm.

Rather than the Freedom Agenda lacking a coherent rationale, which was a consistent critique of the Freedom Agenda when the administration was in office, these chapters have shown how the Bush administration increasingly articulated various discourses together to justify and construct its policy (see Hawthorne 2003a: 22). Indeed, this was a distinguishable feature of the crisis narrative presented, which was clearly a product of the administration laying discursive tracks as it expanded, enhanced, refined and even contradicted its initial construction of its war on terror. This fact is unsurprising given that, in the immediate years following September 11, 2001, the USA undertook two foreign wars, re-engaged in the Palestinian–Israeli conflict and constructed a strategy that would 'democratise' the Middle East. The birth of the Freedom Agenda is not separate from these developments; it is a direct product of them. It is the result of strategically selective agents arguing, diagnosing, proselytising and imposing various notions of what caused the crisis in the first place, and how to deal with such a threat to provide 'security'. The Freedom Agenda was the institutionalisation of such processes, which although somewhat obvious has been missed within a considerable amount of literature. Indeed, as David H. Dunn argued:

> while it is widely recognised that American foreign policy changed quite radically following the terrorist attacks of 9/11, what is less obvious in the commentaries of these events is how much the foreign policy strategies adopted by the United States have continued to evolve and change since that time. This is the case in part because America's responses are often presented, especially by the Bush administration, as part of one relatively continuous or seamless approach.
>
> (Dunn 2005: 1)

All too often the decision to 'democratise' the MENA has been described as a direct result of September 11, 2001, but the nature of its development as the war on terror unfolded has been ignored. This gap in the literature has been problematic because it is only by analysing the creeping insurrection of the policy, and the ideas and narratives that underpinned it, that it is possible to understand *how* it was constituted and *why* it was done in this way. This pre-formative analysis of the Freedom Agenda's institutional development is instructive because it provides a more holistic understanding of the policy, and establishes a basis from which to explore the policy paradigm's institutionalisation, consolidation and evolution. It is to elucidating the nature and effectiveness of these institutions that the next chapter turns, but it is clear from the analysis that follows that the Bush administration's IDF and crisis narration of the war on terror had a dramatic impact on the shape and nature of the Freedom Agenda's institutions.

6 Institutionalising the Freedom Agenda
A policy of conservative radicalism

The institutionalisation of the Freedom Agenda had a considerable number of milestones throughout the Bush administration's time in office. Starting with the creation of the MEPI in December 2002, the administration would go on to construct and institutionalise the Middle East Free Trade Area (MEFTA) and the Broader Middle East and North Africa initiative (BMENA), as well as passing the ADVANCE Democracy Act and National Security Presidential Directive 58, entitled *Institutionalising the Freedom Agenda*. It was through these institutions that the Bush administration attempted to divert and utilise American resources, capabilities and foreign and security policy instruments towards promoting democracy and reforming the MENA, in addition to the nation-building exercises in Afghanistan and Iraq.

The institutionalisation of the Freedom Agenda significantly affected the Department of State and USAID in particular, but had an important effect on the US foreign policy bureaucracy as its institutionalisation evolved and expanded. The impact of this was to divide parts of the foreign policy bureaucracy, between and within departments, as the policy paradigm faced an initial period of contestation. Indeed, the notion of the 'Freedom Agenda' implies more unity than there initially was. There was in fact considerable divergence within the Bush administration about why democracy should be promoted and if it should be promoted at all. The official narrative asserted that it was out of 'principle' and in the 'national interest' and would create a 'democratic peace' between the MENA region and the West. However, three distinct democracy promotion groups existed within the administration. First, there were those who believed that September 11, 2001, demonstrated the need to transform the MENA into a zone of pro-American democracies, and were willing to use force if necessary. Second, there was a group that believed democracy promotion could be used as a method of winning 'hearts and minds' in the region, and therefore called for public diplomacy programmes and democracy assistance funding. Third, there was a group that believed undemocratic governance was the cause of terrorism, but recommended engaging existing governments to promote reform (Hawthorne 2003a: 22). Accordingly, the Freedom Agenda was not held together by a coherent rationale, but rather was an agreement between various strategic actors within the state bureaucracy. These strategic actors saw the strategically selective context differently, but largely subscribed to the Freedom Agenda because it satisfied notions of what they believed was in the national interest. This masked not only the considerable disagreement within the administration about the nature of the policy, but also the extent to which the Bush administration found itself lacking the ability to promote democracy in the region. As a direct consequence of both of these factors, the Bush administration found itself adopting a policy of *conservative radicalism*.

As the Freedom Agenda's institutions evolved, the policy became *radical* to the extent that it insisted on political democracy, drawing on a combination of foreign policy tools ranging from financial backing to diplomatic pressure and the presidential pulpit. Yet the policy was also extremely *conservative* in its desire to safeguard the socio-economic privileges and power of the established order to secure regional stability. What emerged was a policy caught between free trade liberalisation, as the positive route to eventual democratisation, and domination, to the extent that it increasingly favoured regional stability, the continuation of long-term security interests and the undermining of regimes that challenged its hegemony over the region. As the Bush administration oscillated between emphasising both of these elements it enabled a double standard in the Freedom Agenda to emerge. For MENA allies, the Bush administration relied on the definition of freedom it set out on the 2000 campaign trail and proposing a gradualist sequential policy with the neoliberal modernisation thesis at its core. However, for regimes that opposed US power in the region a more hostile approach was taken that led to some of the MEPI's funding being diverted to support regime change by internal dissidents and exiled groups. Ultimately, this led to the Freedom Agenda lacking coherence and ultimately failing. As the policy paradigm evolved, it proved to be too ad hoc and unable to sufficiently navigate the strategically selective context set out by the conflict of interests problem.

Challenging MEPI from within: the bureaucratic resistance to the Freedom Agenda

The Bush administration's flagship programme for promoting democracy in the Middle East and North Africa was MEPI, based within the US Department of State's Bureau of Near East Affairs (NEA). MEPI was originally conceived of by Elizabeth (Liz) Cheney, and was officially launched on December 12, 2002, by Secretary of State Colin Powell.[1] The intention behind MEPI was stated at its official launch, when Colin Powell declared that:

> It is time to lay a firm foundation of hope. I am announcing today an initiative that places the United States firmly on the side of change, of reform, and of a modern future for the Middle East . . . Through the *U.S.–Middle East Partnership Initiative*, we are adding hope to the U.S.–Middle East agenda. We are pledging our energy, our abilities, and our idealism to bring hope to all of God's children who call the Middle East home.
>
> (Powell 2002, December 12)

Liz Cheney saw MEPI as a method of pushing for institutional reform in the region, and it was argued that this programme would 'broaden' the US approach to Middle East reform by focusing on factors highlighted in the *2002 UN Arab Human Development Report*. This report outlined a 'freedom deficit' in the MENA, and argued that a new strategy to deliver 'freedom from fear' and 'freedom from want' was needed, in conjunction with educational improvements and women's empowerment to the people in the region (AHDR 2002). Significantly, this report was constructed by Arab scholars from the region, and MEPI was portrayed as building on regional desires (see Bush 2003, May 9; Powell 2002, December 12). Indeed, the impact of the 2002 report cannot be underestimated, because as Condoleezza Rice argues:

> The intellectual origins of the link between the freedom gap and terrorism are complex. The works of Bernard Lewis and Fouad Ajami were influential with all of us, but the single most impactful document for the President, and certainly for me, was the 2002 Arab Human Development Report ... By identifying the primary sources of the problem, the report helped clarify the way forward.
>
> (Rice 2011: 327)

Accordingly, the report resonated with the administration's narrative about freedom and the war on terror, and was consequently appropriated by the Bush administration. Therein, MEPI identified four pillars into which it divided its programme funds: Political, Economic, Education and Women's issues.

These four pillars were specifically designed to generate short-term grants, lasting for two years or less, which focused on addressing specific challenges to democratisation in the region. Accordingly, they sought to overcome problems that stymied longer-term development projects run by the United States Agency for International Development (USAID) (see McInerney 2008: 11; Wittes 2008b: 89). To meet this goal, MEPI officials often worked with Arab governments, especially in the first two years, to invest funds in programmes geared towards 'strengthening Arab civil society, encouraging micro-enterprise, expanding political participation, and promoting women's rights' (Sharp 2005a: 2). In practice, this translated into a plethora of programmes in each pillar, which were undertaken simultaneously and justified by their ability to complement and facilitate progress between each other.[2]

To fund these programmes in fiscal year (FY) 2002 and FY2003, MEPI originally relied on emergency supplemental appropriations from Congress, which combined into a total of $119 million (see Sharp 2005a: 4). However, from FY2004 to FY2008 MEPI received funding from Economic Support Funds (ESF) in the annual rounds of Congressional Foreign Operations Appropriations legislation. This peaked at a single-year high of $114.2 million in FY2006, but from FY2002 to FY2008 cumulatively totalled $497.7 million (see Table 6.1).

Evidently, these were meagre sums of money for the task at hand, and demonstrate that the monumental goal of transforming the conditions in the region

Table 6.1 Requested and actual MEPI funding FY2002–FY2009 (US$ millions)

Financial year	Requested	Actual	Cumulative Actual Total
FY2002	n/a	29	n/a
FY2003	n/a	90	119
FY2004	145	89.5	208.5
FY2005	150	74.4	282.9
FY2006	120	114.4	397.3
FY2007	120	50.8	448.1
FY2008	75	49.6	497.7

Source: McInerney (2008).

were never met with a sufficient proportion of means (see Hawthorne 2003b).[3] Of course some activities that MEPI was running were cheaper than others, such as supporting political party organisation or skills training for women candidates in Regional Campaign Schools across the MENA. However, the disjuncture between the overall rationale of MEPI and the sums allocated was reflected by the manner in which some members of the State Department and the wider Bush administration referred to the programme as 'reinforcing trends' and 'working alongside' democratic movements whilst not alienating friends and allies in the region (Senior State Department Official A 2011).

That MEPI received such meagre sums did not, however, save the institution from controversy within the Bush administration. Between the groups that believed democracy promotion was the right course of action there was serious bureaucratic infighting. Those that were calling for public diplomacy programmes were 'incredibly angry' as the creation of MEPI, which many of them saw take funds away from already existing programmes and reallocate them to Liz Cheney's 'incredibly ideological project' (Senior State Department Official B 2011). Thus, there was a clear tension between approaches within the Bush administration itself. However, with the institutionalisation of MEPI it became clear that, under Liz Cheney, those who favoured a new approach of working with existing MENA governments in 'partnerships' had won the bureaucratic battle.

Further institutional battles occurred once MEPI was established, but this time between those who worked in MEPI and those who saw the Freedom Agenda as damaging to long-term national interests. This set the stage for a significant power struggle among MEPI, the State Department and the Defense Department, as clearly not all strategically selective actors within the state bureaucracy agreed that the Freedom Agenda would satisfy perceived national interests. Accordingly, when MEPI was establishing its office in late 2002 and early 2003, it was placed in the State Department's Bureau of Near East Affairs (NEA). However, a defining feature of the new MEPI staff was that they were drawn from the National Endowment for Democracy and its 'children', the National Democratic Institute (NDI) and the International Republican Institute (IRI). They had developed their expertise in democracy assistance from their experiences in Eastern Europe after the fall of the Soviet Union. Herein, upon coming into the MEPI offices, their main understanding of democracy promotion was through the Freedom Support Act that had been applied to former Soviet satellite states. Consequently, they had expertise in the form of a template of programmes, such as improving the rule of law, strengthening parliaments and political parties, and training political candidates. This was strongly reflected in the MEPI programmes. However, this group lacked expertise in the Middle East, and sought to acquire this with the aid of other members of NEA. This proved highly problematic, as many members of the NEA resisted the implementation of the Freedom Agenda. Rather than providing help to MEPI, many long-term officials in the NEA sought to undermine it. Indeed, Tamara Coffman Wittes described them as 'pushing back really hard against this policy', and portrayed the situation as one in which

> they [NEA Staff] didn't like it and so you have a bunch of people going in who need regional information and expertise, and the people who are giving it to them are trying to undermine them at the same time . . . [Also] you had a bunch of ambassadors who when MEPI was first announced, saying 'well what the heck is this and why am I now responsible for doing this. This is going to mess up my relations with the host government, why am I being forced to create tension in this relationship. That's not my job'. And we're just trying to ignore it or do the minimum.
>
> (Wittes 2008b)

Moreover, resistance to the Freedom Agenda was not only the preserve of various factions within the State Department. Similar opposition came from the Department of Defense, as the Freedom Agenda began to conflict with other long-term regional interests. This was especially the case with Egypt and Morocco, but applied to other regional allies with significant military relationships with the USA. Thus, although at the higher levels of the Department of Defense individuals such as Paul Wolfowitz clearly wanted to promote democracy throughout the region, and were willing to use force where necessary, mid-level officials were above all important in pushing back against the Freedom Agenda (Senior State Department Official B 2011). Indeed, often these mid-level officials were not given talking points and notes on how to engage regimes on the issues of human rights and democracy. Similarly, the interagency process acted as a locale for the conflict of interests problem to surface. On issues such as US aid to authoritarian regimes, the interagency process brought together multiple parts of the foreign policy bureaucracy, and it was the Department of Defense that would often argue for the status quo over democracy promotion. For example, over aid to Egypt, it was the Department of Defense that was arguing that aid should not be altered, because it was too important to the Mubarak regime, which was 'providing logistical support to our operations in Afghanistan . . . and . . . giving the spare material to the Lebanese army to fight Fatah al-Islam'. As Wittes points out, this was an important 'source of push back against the policy, and an important one because it gets to the substantive policy conflicts in democracy promotion' (Wittes 2008b). Moreover, in spite of this internal resistance to MEPI, since its institutionalisation in 2002 it has been able to become the 'central hub' for interagency discussions under the Freedom Agenda and significantly impacted the US 'democracy bureaucracy'.

Reinforcing MEPI: US–Middle East Free Trade Area

Once MEPI had become the central institutional hub of the Freedom Agenda, the Bush administration sought to buttress this institution by proposing a US–Middle East Free Trade Area (MEFTA) and launching the Broader Middle East and North Africa initiative. Thus, on May 9, 2003, President Bush proposed that MEFTA be established by 2013, arguing that:

> The combined GDP [gross domestic product] of all Arab countries is smaller than that of Spain. Their peoples have less access to the Internet than the people of Sub-Sahara Africa. The Arab world has a great cultural tradition, but is largely missing out on the economic progress of our time. Across the globe, free markets and trade have helped defeat poverty, and taught men and women the habits of liberty. So, I propose the establishment of a U.S.–Middle East free trade area within a decade, to bring the Middle East into an expanding circle of opportunity, to provide hope for the people who live in that region . . . By replacing corruption and self-dealing, with free markets and fair laws, the people of the Middle East will grow in prosperity and freedom.
>
> (Bush 2003, May 9)

MEFTA was perceived as an end goal of a series of cumulative measures targeted at 20 countries in the MENA.[4] On June 23, 2003, at the World Economic Forum held in Jordan, the US Trade Representative (USTR), Robert B. Zoellick, outlined a six-step process for MENA countries to create MEFTA:

1 joining the World Trade Organization (WTO);
2 participating in the Generalised System of Preferences (GSP) programme to increase US trade linkages with the MENA;
3 negotiating and entering into new trade and investment framework agreements (TIFAs);
4 negotiating formal bilateral investment treaties (BITs) with interested countries;
5 negotiating comprehensive free trade agreements (FTAs) with the USA, which would be combined into a sub-regional FTA and ultimately a single MEFTA;
6 participating in trade capacity building, by allowing the USA to provide financial and technical assistance to realise the creation of open markets (see Zoellick 2003, June 23; Bolle 2006: 7–9; Lawrence 2006a: 1–2).

132 *Institutionalising the Freedom Agenda*

Eligibility for entering into this six-step process required minimal concessions from MENA countries. The opportunity of joining MEFTA was left open to countries that met the following criteria:

- 'peaceful' and seeking to increase trade relations with the USA;
- prepared to participate in economic reform and liberalisation;
- not participating in primary, secondary or tertiary boycotts of Israel (Bolle 2006: 9).

The USA already had FTAs established with Israel and Jordan before September 11, 2001, and it subsequently concluded FTA agreements with Morocco, Bahrain, the West Bank and Gaza, and Oman. Moreover by the end of President Bush's tenure in office the USA had 15 TIFAs and six BITs in place with MEFTA eligible countries, and was assisting Arab governments that had not joined the WTO to reach this goal.

The motivation behind MEFTA was not primarily economic. Evidently, this institution drew on the IDF set out by Bush before he came to office in 2001, but it also united the multiple democracy promotion factions within the administration. Some perceived MEFTA as a method of dealing with 'freedom from want' in the region. Others saw it as a method of winning 'hearts and minds' by creating greater prosperity and peace through trade. Some saw it as a method of laying foundations for liberal reform in the region, whereas others perceived it as a counter-terrorism strategy. Further still, some within the administration perceived MEFTA as a method of cementing influence in region. Thanks to these last, MEFTA was able to avoid being attacked by those within the administration who opposed the democratisation of the region. Thus, in addition to envisaged economic benefits, MEFTA sought to work with MEPI to use FTAs as a democratising tool, by promoting structural, economic and governance reforms. Accordingly, trade promotion and trade-related technical assistance programmes were established, focusing on teaching better methods of making government regulation transparent, promoting the rule of contract law and protecting intellectual property (see Wittes 2008b: 85–92).

Reinforcing MEPI: the BMENA initiative's multilateral dimension

Along with MEPI and MEFTA, the USA also launched the *Broader Middle East and North Africa* initiative during its 2004 G8 presidency, intending to add a multilateral dimension to the Freedom Agenda's 'forward strategy'. The initiative was the product of a working paper which suggested that the G8 create a *Greater Middle East Initiative* (GMEI), which agreed upon a set of common reform priorities towards the MENA.[5] As such, BMENA attempted to replicate many of MEPI's ambitions at a multilateral level, including the objectives of 'promoting democracy and good governance, building a knowledge society, and expanding economic opportunities' (G8–BMENA 2006) for the MENA. As a result, the BMENA initiative was marketed as a 'partnership' between the G8, the USA and

Institutionalising the Freedom Agenda 133

European nations, on the one hand, and the governments, business and civil society of the MENA region, on the other. Through what was described as 'genuine co-operation', BMENA officials asserted that the initiative would 'strengthen freedom, democracy and prosperity for all' in the region (see G8–BMENA 2006; DOS 2004).

The central initiative that emerged from the Sea Island summit of June 8–10, 2004, was the *Forum for the Future*. This was intended to be an annual meeting in which governments, business and civil society groups from the G8 and MENA would meet and discuss reform measures. The first of these meetings took place in December 2004 in Morocco, the second in November 2005 in Bahrain, the third in December 2006 in Jordan and the fourth in 2008 in the United Arab Emirates. Although there was intended to be a forum in Yemen in 2007 this was not held because of US efforts to rejuvenate Israeli–Palestinian peace talks at the Annapolis Conference in Maryland (Wittes 2008a: 96).

In addition to the Forum for the Future, the BMENA initiative was composed of several small multinational and national projects. Out of the subsequent Forums for the Future four main 'working groups' were established:

- 'Tax Administration and Policy', led by Egypt;
- 'Financial Systems', combining Banking System, Financial Sector Reform and Regulation, Financial Services and Capital Market Development, led by Bahrain;
- 'Microfinance', led by Jordan;
- 'Financing Poverty Alleviation', led by Yemen (see G8–BMENA 2006).

In addition to these developments and private enterprise endeavours, the BMENA initiative attempted to promote literacy by creating 'The Literacy Hub'. This was designed to provide policy-makers and programme developers in the BMENA region with an extensive database of exemplary practices and programmes in literacy (see LiteracyHub 2008).

A further multilateral dynamic that the BMENA initiative launched was the *Foundation for the Future*. The Foundation was created as an autonomous institution, which is supported by the Forum for the Future but autonomous from the Forum's processes. Announced in November 2005, the Foundation was intended to pool and distribute international funds to non-governmental organisations (NGOs) in the region, with the specific goal of creating a MENA-based mechanism for channelling technical and financial assistance. As Condoleezza Rice announced:

> The Foundation will provide grants to help civil society strengthen the rule of law, to protect basic civil liberties, and ensure greater opportunity for health and education. But most importantly, the Foundation is a sign that citizens have to be trusted who are working for democratic reform in particular countries, and cities, and villages to use their grant money for the greatest good that they see fit.
>
> (Rice 2005, December 12)

134 *Institutionalising the Freedom Agenda*

The largest donations to this fund came from the USA, which in FY2006 dedicated $35 million of MEPI's funding to the foundation, but other donors included Denmark, the European Commission, Germany, Greece, Hungary, Jordan, Spain, Switzerland, Turkey and the United Kingdom (FFF 2008; Wittes 2008b: 97). In total the fund raised approximately $60 million, and by the end of 2008 the foundation had a net total of $26 million in assets available for future projects (FFF 2009: 43–54; DOS 2009; Sharp 2005b).

Strategic actors in the strategically selective context: push for elections and retreat

With the creation of MEPI, MEFTA and the BMENA between 2002 and 2004, the Bush administration had effectively institutionalised the Freedom Agenda. Moreover, with these institutions in place, in addition to efforts being pursued in Afghanistan and Iraq, the President would personally place the Freedom Agenda centre stage of his second term in office, announcing at his inaugural address:

> America's vital interests and our deepest beliefs are now one . . . Across the generations we have proclaimed the imperative of self-government . . . Advancing these ideals is the mission that created our Nation. It is the honourable achievement of our fathers. Now it is the urgent requirement of our nation's security, and the calling of our time. *So it is the policy of the United States to seek and support the growth of democratic movements and institutions in every nation and culture, with the ultimate goal of ending tyranny in our world.*
>
> (Bush 2005, January 20)

This declaration formalised the Freedom Agenda, whilst clearly elevating it to the central policy paradigm of President Bush's foreign policy agenda. Unlike its institutionalisation in 2002–4, which focused on the MENA, the Freedom Agenda was now claimed to be the overarching rationale for policy towards all parts of the globe. Moreover, what is distinguishable about this address was that it repeated many of the sentiments of the original crisis narrative put forward immediately after September 11, 2001, and seamlessly narrated the Freedom Agenda as the logical conclusion of that original response. This was certainly the position of Condoleezza Rice, who has subsequently argued that:

> The second inaugural address made the choice of promoting freedom in the Middle East and elsewhere explicit . . . Realists ran to the barricades to sound the alarm that 'interests,' not 'idealism,' should guide the United States' interactions with the world. What they failed to see was the Freedom Agenda was not just a moral or idealistic cause; it was a redefinition of what constituted realism, a change in the way we viewed U.S. interests in the new circumstances forced upon us by the attacks of that horrible day. We rather quickly arrived at the conclusion that US interests and values could be

linked together in a coherent way, forming what I came to call a distinctly American realism.

(Rice 2011: 325)[6]

With the formal announcement of the Freedom Agenda in early 2005, the administration was particularly keen on demonstrating the effectiveness of its new institutions and obtaining concrete results. Given this, many in the upper echelons of the administration were particularly vocal about pushing for elections in the region. Secretary of State Condoleezza Rice publicly confronted close allies Egypt and Saudi Arabia to hold fair elections, release political prisoners, and allow free expression and rights for women (see Weisman 2005). Moreover, with the death of Yasser Arafat in late 2004, the Bush administration supported swift elections for a new President of the Palestinian Authority and urged new parliamentary elections in the West Bank and Gaza. Within the Freedom Agenda narrative, the Bush administration had put forward a vision of the future in which democracy would be the cure to the Palestinian plight, and that open and free elections would give cause for the USA to support a viable Palestinian state. With the electoral victory in January 2005 of Mahmoud Abbas, Washington's preferred candidate, it appeared that the Bush administration had a new more 'moderate' President of the Palestinian Authority to work with in the peace process.

The period between 2004 and 2006 looked promising for regional reform; indeed the Bush administration was keen to point out that an 'Arab Spring' was taking place in which there were broad-based elections in Afghanistan and Iraq, limited elections in Egypt and Saudi Arabia, the 'Cedar' revolution in Lebanon, which removed Syrian occupational forces, political reforms in Morocco and Jordan, and women's suffrage introduced in Kuwait. For the Bush administration such acts constituted 'extraordinary progress in the expansion of freedom' (NSC 2006: 2). This was supported in 2005 by Freedom House, which measured 'modest positive trends' taking place throughout the region (see Abrams 2005). What were by any measure moderate successes were being trumpeted by the Bush administration and some members of the political commentariat as vindication for the Iraq war and the Freedom Agenda more generally. The *New York Times* had articles expounding 'Unexpected whiff of freedom proves bracing for the Mideast' and 'For Bush, a taste of vindication in Mideast' (MacFarquhar 2005; Purdum 2005), whilst Charles Krauthammer boldly asserted that:

[H]istory has begun to speak, and it says that America made the right decision to invade Iraq . . . Right on what? That America, using power harnessed to democratic ideals, could begin to transform the Arab world from endless tyranny and intolerance to decent governance and democratisation.

(Krauthammer 2005)

Such emboldening statements were particularly short-lived as the warnings of the Islamist dilemma became all the more apparent in early 2006. By emphasising open elections in order to demonstrate 'progress' visibly, the Bush administration proved to have considerable blind-spots in its IDF. Imbibing the belief that democracy and freedom were the natural state of human affairs, and that the universal appeal of 'God's gift to humanity' would trump all, senior members of the administration did not consider the possibility of the 'Islamist dilemma'. That is to say, they fundamentally misunderstood the strategically selective context in which they were operating. Thus, when Hamas won the parliamentary elections on January 25, 2006, with a 'landslide' the result was one of shock within the administration. Indeed, when Condoleezza Rice heard that Hamas had won, her initial response was 'well, that's not right', followed by 'oh my goodness, Hamas won?' (in Bumiller 2007). That the Secretary of State could be caught off guard compounds the fact that the administration had a poor understanding of the challenges faced in democratising the region, and interpreted the strategically selective terrain incorrectly.

Pushing for elections was not just limited to the Palestinian territories. With the assassination of the former Lebanese Prime Minister Rafik Hariri in February 2005, there appeared to be a 'Beirut Spring', with large crowds marching in the streets and sympathetic police aiding them in avoiding police blockades. The response from Washington was that this marked a milestone in the Freedom Agenda, as the President argued that

> anyone who doubts the appeal of freedom in the Middle East can look to Lebanon, where the Lebanese people are demanding a free and independent nation. In the words of one Lebanese observer, 'Democracy is knocking at the door of this country and, if it's successful in Lebanon, it is going to ring the doors of every Arab regime.'
>
> (Bush 2005, March 8)

This was accompanied by pressure on Syria to withdraw its military occupation, as the Bush administration imposed an array of sanctions on Syria's government and banks, and froze the assets of Syrian officials implicated in Mr Hariri's killing (Cooper and Sanger 2006). Moreover, in this milieu, the Bush administration also pushed for swift parliamentary elections, in the hope of securing the apparent national consensus. The result of these elections, however, gave Hezbollah increased political power, in the form of cabinet slots in a new coalition government (see Pressman 2009: 161). Once again the Islamist dilemma, ignored by the Bush administration, proved to be problematic for the aspiration of creating a democratic peace with the West, and once again the Bush administration demonstrated the extent to which it was struggling to navigate the conflict of interests problem.

The pattern of elections won by Islamic groups hostile to Washington was repeated throughout the first so-called 'Arab Spring'; these included the Muslim Brotherhood in Egypt and Shiites backed by militias in Iraq (Weisman 2006a). This was coupled with the 2006 Israel–Hezbollah war in Lebanon and increasing civil violence in Iraq despite hopes that the elections would calm the insurgency

(Kurth 2006). Thus, in 2006, Freedom House measured a fall in the previous year's gains as many autocrats in the region began to withdraw what little political and civil openings they had made available, with Egypt delaying municipal elections by two years, Yemen cracking down on the news media and Jordan abandoning many reform plans (Noland and Pack 2007: 273; Fattah 2006). By placing a procedural understanding of democracy at the forefront of the Freedom Agenda the Bush administration proved that its IDF was woefully inadequate at understanding the strategically selective context. Although the administration had established an ideological justification for why reforming the Middle East was in the national interest, it had failed to appreciate how the original strategically selective context that led to previous administrations supporting friendly regimes remained in place and needed to be more thoughtfully navigated.

These setbacks led to growing dissent in the Republican Party, with Representative Henry Hyde, the Chairman of the International Relations Committee, condemning the Bush strategy because of its emphasis on democracy as a 'magic bullet'. Moreover, the electoral success of Islamists gave 'realists' in the Republican Party cause to challenge the Bush administration's approach and condemn the emphasis on democracy promotion at the expense of other American interests (Weisman 2006b). The results of this challenge were stark. Whereas Condoleezza Rice had once pronounced the need to move towards democracy, by 2007 there was near silence on pressuring for domestic reform; the void was filled with appreciative comments about Egypt's support in the region and Saudi Arabia was now referred to as 'moderate' (Diehl 2007: 15; Slackman 2007). Indeed, embassies were told by senior officials in the administration not to mention the Freedom Agenda in their diplomatic engagements with important allies (State Department Official A 2011; Ottaway 2011).

The impact of this conflict of interests was dramatic. It created a series of contradictions within the Freedom Agenda. At the same time as the Department of State and USAID were conducting a joint review, to ensure that all USAID programmes in the MENA region complied with MEPI's goals and objectives, the administration was de-emphasising the Freedom Agenda (see Epstein *et al.* 2007: 1–3; Sharp 2005a: 3; Wittes 2008b: 89). Given this, no sooner had the results of this review been published in the *Joint Strategic Plan* (JSP) *for Fiscal Years 2007–2012*, and a policy of 'Transformation Diplomacy' been proposed, than the administration fell conspicuously silent on the issue of political reform in the region. As a result, throughout 2007, many members of the Freedom Agenda institutions were increasingly sidelined by mid-level State Department officials who had not wanted to pursue democracy promotion and now appeared to have their hostility to the Freedom Agenda vindicated. As the Bush administration lowered the level of pressure it applied to MENA regimes, it became evident that members of the Freedom Agenda institutions were not getting the support from the higher echelons of the administration, resulting in some high-profile advocates leaving their posts (see Rozen 2008).

This of course is not to suggest that 2007 was not in and of itself an important year for the Freedom Agenda. Whilst the Bush administration was re-evaluating the Freedom Agenda, Congress added an additional legislative layer to the policy's institutionalisation through the ADVANCE Democracy Act of 2007 (ADA). On August 3, 2007, as part of H.R.1. *Implementing Recommendations of the 9/11 Commission Act of 2007*, ADA was ratified, and asserted that:

> It is the policy of the United States to promote freedom and democracy in foreign countries as a fundamental component of United States foreign policy, along with other key foreign policy goals.
>
> (*ADA* 2007: 22 USC 8202)[7]

The significance of ADA is multifaceted. The bill was originally proposed in 2005, and attributed to Mark Palmer, who had attended 'Bletchley II', and his book *Breaking the Real Axis of Evil: How to Oust the World's Last Dictators by 2025* (see Lantos 2005; Palmer 2003).[8] The importance of the legislation is that, for the first time in US history, supporting democracy abroad has the force of law as a fundamental component of US foreign policy (Mann 2007). Moreover, far beyond simply being a rhetorical commitment to democracy promotion, the ADA legislated institutional changes, such as the creation of a *Democracy Liaison Office* (DLO), with new officers to serve under the supervision of the Assistant Secretary of State (*ADA* 2007: 22 USC 8211). Additionally, the ADA formally instructed Chiefs of Mission in non-democratic and democratic transition countries to:

> Develop, as part of annual program planning, a strategy to promote democratic principles, practices, and values in each such foreign country and to provide support, as appropriate, to nongovernmental organizations, individuals, and movements in each such country that are committed to democratic principles, practices, and values.
>
> (*ADA* 2007: 22 USC 8211)[9]

These instructions were accompanied by orders to publicly condemn violations of internationally recognised human rights, to visit local landmarks associated with non-violent protest, and to meet with government leaders to discuss human rights and democratisation. Thus, part of the central importance of the ADA is that it has created a lasting legacy of bureaucratic changes that emphasise democracy promotion in US foreign policy, requiring:

- the creation of a *Democracy Fellowship Program* to allow Department of State (DOS) officers to work with relevant congressional committees, NGOs and multilateral organisations;
- enhanced training for Foreign Service Officers on protecting human rights and supporting democratisation;
- making support for democracy and human rights a criterion for awards, performance pay and promotions within the DOS;
- establishing an Office for Multilateral Democracy Promotion;

- the change of title for the annual report on *Supporting Human Rights and Democracy: The U.S. Record*, to the *Annual Report on Advancing Freedom and Democracy*.

In addition to these official requirements, the ADA also presented a 'sense of Congress':

- urging the Community of Democracies to establish a headquarters and formalise its organisation;
- urging USAID and the Secretary of State to develop guidelines to direct and coordinate U.S. democracy promotion efforts;
- commending the Secretary of State for creating an *Advisory Committee on Democracy Promotion*[10] (ACDP), and asserting that this committee 'should play a significant role in the Department's [DOS] transformational diplomacy' (*ADA* 2007: 22 USC 8231).

In spite of the importance of the ADA, however, 2007 clearly marked a period of withdrawal from the Freedom Agenda, signified by the failure to hold the intended Forum for the Future meeting in Yemen, and the increased silence from the administration in its bilateral engagements with autocrats in the MENA. Given such insights it is difficult to agree with both critics and proponents of the Freedom Agenda who allege that the Bush administration put democracy promotion at the forefront of its policy. Indeed, as the Freedom Agenda insider J. Scott Carpenter has argued, the Freedom Agenda was a 'tertiary concern' for the Bush administration;[11] it came behind regional security and, by 2007, a renewed interest in the Palestinian–Israeli conflict (Carpenter 2008). A more accurate analysis of the situation is that America's core objective in the Middle East remained regional stability to secure its long-term interests, because the Bush administration

> was never able to delineate how it would handle perceived trade-offs between the long-term project of democracy promotion and the shorter term imperatives such as counter-terrorism, assistance in stabilising Iraq, and support for the Middle East peace process.
>
> (Wittes 2008a: 79)

As the conflict of interests problem began to challenge the Freedom Agenda, the Bush administration began to increasingly reshape its policy in a manner that sought to maintain stability and secure the more immediate goals of the war on terror. This point was reinforced by the policy of extraordinary rendition. The Bush administration was willing to send contradictory messages to MENA regimes, and, under the rubric of security demands, the Bush administration sought to utilise for its own purposes the very conditions it claimed were the cause of terrorism. The starkness of this contradiction was evident as members of the CIA such as Michael F. Scheuer, the former Chief of the CIA's Bin Laden Unit, were asserting that there were no qualms at all about sending people to Cairo and kind of joking up our [the CIA] sleeves about what would happen to those people in Cairo in Egyptian prisons ... I don't care what happens to the people who are targeted and rendered ... Mistakes are made ... They are not Americans. I really don't care ... I never got paid, sir, to be a citizen of the world.

(see HCFA 2007)

The contradiction between claims of promoting freedom in the Middle East and using Middle Eastern prisons for 'torture, indefinite detentions, and disappearances' did not go unnoticed. As Representative Bill Delahunt, Chairman of the Subcommittee on International Organizations, Human Rights and Oversight, pointed out:

These extraordinary renditions are utterly inconsistent with our broader foreign policy goals of promoting democracy and the rule of law, the very foundations of civil society. These practices have brought us universal condemnation and have frustrated our efforts to work in a concerted way with our allies in fighting terrorism.

(HCFA 2007)

Moreover, the policy of extraordinary rendition demonstrated a dependency on the very regimes the Bush administration claimed to want to reform by offering an 'ideology of freedom'. This raised serious credibility issues regarding the sincerity of its Freedom Agenda to observers in the Middle East and beyond. The Freedom Agenda was far from the overarching rationale the Bush administration narrated it to be. This demonstrated not only that the prominence of the Freedom Agenda was being considerably overstated by the administration, but that the Bush administration failed to pursue the policy with a modicum of coherence. Placing a sign on the entrance gate of Guantánamo Bay detention facility, which read 'Honour bound to defend freedom', strongly illustrates this point – if not an acute sense of irony.

The Freedom Agenda: a policy of conservative radicalism

Although the Bush administration increasingly outlined a more complex understanding of why pursuing the Freedom Agenda was in the national interest, and claimed to be making democracy promotion a central part of the Bush doctrine, this was clearly re-evaluated in light of the 'Islamist dilemma'. That is to say, throughout 2002–6, the Bush administration had managed to secure the Freedom Agenda as the dominant paradigm in US–MENA relations, and promoting reform and elections was considered to be in the national interest. However, predominantly as a result of Hamas being successful in elections, contestation over the paradigm was reopened. The administration's response was to increasingly fund 'softer' projects that would not be opposed by authoritarian governments in the region. Pushing for more open political systems, radically supporting opposition parties or providing robust election observation rapidly fell from the foreign policy agenda along with the Bush administration's willingness to challenge friendly MENA regimes (Ibrahim 2006: 15). This became highly evident in US–Egyptian relations, in which the USA certainly sent mixed messages between 2005 and 2007. For example, Congress specified in the *FY2005 Consolidated Appropriations Act* [P. L. 108–447] that:

> [D]emocracy and governance activities shall not be subject to the prior approval of the GoE [government of Egypt]. The managers intend this language to include NGOs and other segments of civil society that may not be registered with, or officially recognized by, the GoE. However, the managers understand that the GoE should be kept informed of funding provided pursuant to these activities.

This was the first time that the US had decided to give independent funding to NGOs in Egypt, therefore bypassing the Egyptian government's highly restrictive legislation on funding civil society groups (Sharp 2007: 13; see Elbayar 2005). This was a direct challenge to the Mubarak regime. However, by June 2006, the Egyptian government responded by ordering the International Republican Institute (IRI) and the National Democratic Institute (NDI) to cease all activities in Egypt until they formally registered with the government and obtained a licence. Under the rubric of 'national security' concerns the Egyptian government forced all programmatic activity to a halt. As Bahieddin Hassan, director of the Cairo Institute for Human Rights Studies, noted at the time:

> the decision to halt the activities of the two institutes has to do with the regime's new agenda to curb public dissent and is not in any way linked to press claims that they are threatening national security.
>
> (in Shahine 2006)

This crackdown was part of a larger approach adopted by the Mubarak regime, in which judges were intimidated, bloggers arrested, local elections were postponed and emergency laws were renewed (see Wittes 2008b: 78). The response from the White House was muted at best, with the President and Vice President meeting with Mubarak's son, Gamal Mubarak, but refusing to comment on what was said (NYT 2006). By July 2006 events in the region began to require Egyptian help in trying to diffuse a war between Israel in Lebanon. As a result Condoleezza Rice poured praise on the Egyptian regime for its 'very positive role ... in trying to diffuse the crisis' (Rice 2006, July 13). Ultimately it appeared that the Freedom Agenda's credibility was being challenged, and the Bush administration had retreated.

The Egyptian example is informative of a much wider quality possessed by the Freedom Agenda. Notably, with a lack of strategic guidance, the Freedom Agenda institutions funded democratisation projects in a 'hodgepodge' manner (Hawthorne 2005). As J. Scott Carpenter confessed in his role of overseeing MEPI:

We don't know yet how best to promote democracy in the Arab Middle East. I mean we just don't know. It's the early days ... I think there are times when you throw spaghetti against the wall and see if it sticks.

(in Finkel 2005)

By 2006, through to the end of the Bush administration's tenure in office, it became highly evident what exactly had 'stuck' as an approach to US–MENA relations; namely, the Bush administration had adopted a policy of conservative radicalism as the central dynamic in its post-crisis policy paradigm. The approach was *radical* to the extent that it insisted on political democracy, yet *conservative* in its desire to safeguard the socio-economic privileges and power of the established order to secure regional stability. However, what was noticeable about such a strategy was that the radical side was being targeted at regimes that opposed US influence in the region, whereas the conservative side was the approach adopted for friendly allies in the MENA. As the Bush administration oscillated between emphasising each of these elements, it enabled a double standard in the Freedom Agenda to emerge.

Regimes that challenged *pax Americana* in the region, such as Iran and Saddam Hussein's Iraq, had become labelled 'Axis of Evil' states. The price of such opposition was the Freedom Agenda's radical side, which insisted on regime change and political democracy. In Iraq this had been forcibly brought about by military coercion, followed by the idea of J. Scott Carpenter, at the time working in the America's Coalition Provisional Authority in Iraq, that sovereignty should be transferred quickly and unexpectedly to the Iraqi people to catch insurgents off guard. Subsequently, the Bush administration would try to 'shape' the outcome of elections, rather than 'dictate' them (Woodward 2006: 313–4, 436). However, in Iran and Syria, strong diplomatic pressure was coupled with the *Iran Democracy Program* and the *Syria Democracy Program*, which sought to utilise MEPI funds and personnel to bolster internal dissidents and exile groups wanting US-supported regime change (see DOS 2006b; Ganji 2006; Sharp 2009). Accordingly, without a credible military solution for preventing Iran developing its nuclear weapons capability, the State Department in conjunction with the Defense Department set up a new *Iran–Syria Operations Group* that reported to Elizabeth Cheney (Dinmore 2006; Baxter 2006). From early 2006, the Freedom Agenda institutions were not simply 'supporting democratic trends' in the region, but were additionally backing covert action and opposition movements attempting to instigate regime change (see Weisman 2006c).

The radical side of the Freedom Agenda demonstrated the prominence of primacy as a node in the Bush administration's IDF. Challenging US power in the region was met with attempts at regime change. No clearer example of this can be demonstrated than in the Palestinian territories. Having been surprised by the electoral success of Hamas in 2006, the Bush administration speedily overturned its dedication to democracy promotion and set about its archetypal response to the rise of such a regime. Despite the Palestinian Authority's being democratically elected, the US along with the EU responded swiftly by cutting off aid and refused

Institutionalising the Freedom Agenda 143

to work with the Hamas-led government (see Turner 2006). More troublesome, however, was the covert initiative from within the Bush administration to supply new weapons and training to Fatah, designed to remove the democratically elected Hamas-led government from power, building on the Bush administration's 'counter-insurgency surge' strategy (see Rose 2008; Greenway 2007; Murphy 2007; IISS 2007; Black and Milne 2011). Although this attempt failed, it demonstrated a guiding rule underpinning the Freedom Agenda. The United States would aspire to promote democracy in the Middle East if and only if the results of this did not challenge its influence and other interests in the region. Thus demonstrating how 'making other people free is said to be the goal of US foreign policy; but the natives are expected not only to accept the offer of freedom but also to show their gratitude' (Ingram 2007: 3).

For regimes that helped maintain *pax Americana* and secure America's historical interests, the *conservative* approach was put forward and the Freedom Agenda was designed to generate stability through liberalisation, with democratisation being a secondary long-term goal. This distinction is crucial because, whereas 'democratisation' signifies a move towards greater degrees of political participation in existing governmental systems, 'liberalisation' can mean any reform that enhances the individual freedom enjoyed by a citizen. Thus, unlike Iraq, Iran and Syria, when it came to regimes such as Saudi Arabia, Egypt, Jordan, Kuwait, Morocco and Yemen, the Bush administration never advocated regime change through military action, democratic populism or civil disobedience. That is to say, under no circumstances did the Freedom Agenda seek to deliver the sorts of scenes that have accompanied the 2011 revolutions. This was reflected in the Freedom Agenda programmes, which showed an overwhelming emphasis on low-risk gradualist policies that emphasised promoting evolutionary reform of existing status quo regimes; not mass uprisings opposing allies in the region. This was not democratic reform as much as it was the *promotion of the conditions for eventual democratic reform*, highlighting that the Freedom Agenda was a policy that construed democracy as a long-term project emerging out of a 'social and economic context that should be prepared' (Wittes and Yerkes 2006: 17).

The grand liberal strategy that the Bush administration espoused, rejecting the status quo in favour of freedom, came with some strong caveats. President Bush consistently made clear that the war on terror and the Freedom Agenda were a 'generational commitment', and that the promotion of 'working democracies always need time to develop . . . and this makes us patient and understanding as other nations are at different stages of this journey' (Bush 2003, November 6). Moreover, as a senior Bush administration official hastened to add after the launch of the MEPI, the USA was not planning 'to abandon long-term allies such as Saudi Arabia and Egypt because of their lack of democracy' but would offer 'positive reinforcement for emerging reform trends' (in Ottaway 2005: 182). This factor was consistently reinforced by the use of the term 'partnerships'. This was not only explicitly asserted in the very naming of the Middle East *Partnership* Initiative, but unambiguously set out by Condoleezza Rice in the *Joint Strategic Plan*:

The joint mission of the Department of State and USAID is to '*Advance freedom for the benefit of the American people and the international community by helping to build and sustain a more democratic, secure, and prosperous world composed of well-governed states that respond to the needs of their people, reduce widespread poverty, and act responsibly within the international system.*' It is a vision rooted in partnership, not paternalism – in doing things with other people, not for them.

(JSP 2006: 4, italics in original)

These partnerships effectively blunted the Freedom Agenda's edge and led to its various programmes conforming with the very regimes the policy claimed to be attempting to democratise. The most high-profile example of this was MEPI's project in Saudi Arabia, where money was given to a breast cancer awareness campaign endorsed by the Saudi government and figureheaded by the First Lady, Laura Bush; a clear instance of public diplomacy efforts, in coordination with autocratic regimes, 'hijacking' and blunting the aims of MEPI (Wittes 2008a: 93–4). Indeed, when this author interviewed recipients of MEPI funding about their relationship with democratisation efforts, a shockingly large number responded with a variation of 'Democracy? We don't really do that', often followed by a list of activities that would be considered extremely tangential to any models of democratisation.[12] Such findings resonate with observations Thomas Carothers and Marina Ottaway made in the early period of the Freedom Agenda:

> the softer, long-term side of the US push for democracy in the Middle East is, at best, a work in progress. Its slow advance is in part due to the unfamiliar territory to be traversed and uncertainty about how to proceed. But it is also due to the fact that, as urgent and serious as the pro-democracy imperative appears to many in the US policy community, the stubborn reality remains that the United States has other important security related and economic interests, such as cooperation on antiterrorism enforcement actions and ensuring secure access to oil. Such interests impel it to maintain close ties with many of the authoritarian regimes in the Middle East and be wary of the possibility of rapid or unpredictable political change.

(Carothers and Ottaway 2005: 5)

In juxtaposition to the gradualist conservative side of the policy, when the radical side of the agenda was emphasised, the Bush administration was portraying 'freedom' as something that could be engineered from the outside, and in the case of Iraq brought to the country by coercion. Emphasis was placed on the universality of freedom, which merely required tyrannical regimes to be removed and the natural aspirations of the 'human spirit' to come forth. Yet with the conservative side of the approach it was argued that the inherent nature of democracy meant that it could not be imposed from the outside and that America simply did not have the power to decree that MENA regimes obey its demands to reform. As Richard Haass argued before the launch of the MEPI, 'while it can be encouraged from outside, democracy is best built from within' (in Ottaway 2005: 182). Given this juxtaposition, it became highly evident that the Bush administration was legitimising its gradualist approach through appealing to the neoliberal conception of freedom, and the modernisation process it would inspire. This remained a defining feature of the Bush administration's approach to global affairs from the IDF set out in the 2000 presidential campaign, through to Robert B. Zoellick's proposal that democracy could be brought about by free trade just days after September 11, 2001, and the eventual institutionalisation of MEFTA.

The 'neoliberal' Freedom Agenda: freedom as markets and modernisation

Although the conservative radicalism approach to the MENA demonstrated two divergent approaches to dealing with the region, as the Freedom Agenda progressed it became highly evident that they had a common core. Notably both approaches utilised the same neoliberal conception of 'freedom' embedded within the Bush administration's IDF. The first signs of the practical application of neoliberalism in the Freedom Agenda manifested themselves in Iraq. Whilst insurgency was rife and personal security was largely absent throughout most of the cities in Iraq, Paul Bremer, the head of the Coalition Provisional Authority, decided that it was time to 'teach influential Iraqis the basics of a free-market economy' (Bremer and McConnell 2006: 63). On September 19, 2003, Bremer ordered:

> The full privatisation of public enterprises, full ownership rights by foreign firms of Iraqi businesses, full repatriation of foreign profits ... the opening of Iraq's banks to foreign control, national treatment for foreign companies, and the elimination of nearly all trade barriers.
>
> (in Harvey 2005: 6)

These orders were to apply to all areas of the economy, including public services, the media, manufacturing, transportation, finance and construction. Whereas the labour market was to be strictly regulated, strikes were effectively outlawed in key sectors and the right to unionise restricted (see Juhasz 2006). Notably, this neoliberal agenda ignored the advice of Milton Friedman, who in 2001 admitted that a decade earlier he would have advised that any economy moving from a socialist economy, much like Iraq's, should follow three words: 'privatise, privatise, privatise'. However, he then conceded that 'I was wrong ... It turns out that the rule of law is probably more basic than privatisation' (in Fukuyama 2004: 25). This advice had not reached the higher echelons of the Bush administration and the Coalition Provisional Authority, which placed marketisation before securing the cities in Iraq. As Donald Rumsfeld declared at a tribute to Friedman, 'Milton is the embodiment of the truth that "ideas have consequences." ... So, yes, he has changed the course of history' (Rumsfeld 2002, May 9). Iraq had become a test case for American-style free-market capitalism in the Middle East (see Looney 2003). Whereas Thomas Friedman (2005) of the *New York Times* was keen to point out that 'we are not doing nation-building in Iraq. We are doing nation-creating', Naomi Klein asserted that:

> Overnight, Iraq went from being one of the most isolated countries in the world, sealed off from the most basic trade by strict UN sanctions, to becoming the widest-open market anywhere.
>
> (Klein 2007: 339)

With the Bush administration espousing domino theory it became clear exactly what type of exemplar 'model' Iraq was supposed to set for the rest of the region. This was a far cry from President Bush's assertion that:

> as we watch and encourage reforms in the region, we are mindful that modernisation is not the same as Westernisation. Representative governments in the Middle East will reflect their own cultures. They will not, and should not, look like us.
>
> (Bush 2003, November 6)

With full scale neoliberalisation taking place in Iraq, it was evident that the Iraqi people had not decided to take their economy down this path. Consequently, Iraq's interim trade minister, Ali Abdul-Amir Allawi, argued that:

> We suffered through the economic theories of socialism, Marxism and then cronyism . . . Now we face the prospect of free-market fundamentalism . . . This push to sell everything is the political stance of economic fundamentalism . . . A plan based on ideology, not economics is, of course, naturally wrong . . . By no means should we preserve all state-owned enterprises . . . But there are some sectors that are more natural for government involvement or rehabilitation . . . We understand the need for foreign investment . . . But we worry that, too, many people will be driven out of business before they have a chance to organise . . . [The Iraqi people are] sick and tired of being the subjects of experiments. There have been enough shocks to the system, so we don't need this shock therapy in the economy.
>
> (in Crampton 2003)

Condemnation of adopting this neoliberal strategy in Iraq came from diverse corners. Paul Krugman, of the *New York Times* and winner of the Nobel Prize for economics, argued that by introducing free-trade, supply-side tax policy and privatisation into Iraq, the Coalition Provisional Authority 'undermined the chances for a successful transition to democracy' and reinforced 'the sense of many Iraqis that we [America] came as occupiers, not liberators' (Krugman 2004a). Krugman later added that by turning Iraq into 'a playground for right-wing economic theorists . . . the administration did terrorist recruiters a very big favor' (Krugman 2004b). Similar discord was echoed by Newt Gingrich, the former speaker of the House of Representatives, who told Vice President Cheney that 'Bremer's [economic] model was totally wrong. Totally' and added that 'Bremer is the largest single disaster in American foreign policy in modern times' (in Woodward 2006: 252).

What the Iraq experiment showed, however, was that the Bush administration was trying to establish its 'single sustainable model' in Iraq. Such sentiments had been codified in the 2002 National Security Strategy (NSS), which argued that:

> [T]he great struggles of the twentieth century between liberty and totalitarianism ended with a decisive victory for the forces of freedom – and a single sustainable model for national success: freedom, democracy, and free enterprise.
>
> (NSC 2002)

Consequently, it was through the appropriation of academic theories, articulated with the constant repetition of the word 'freedom', that the administration legitimised both its intervention and its strategy in the region. Importantly, this essentially contested concept was rarely utilised alone. It was part of a collocation that became defined by the 'company' that it kept, and habitually and predictably being articulated with terms such as 'peace', 'democracy', 'free trade' and 'free markets'. Thus, as the NSS 2002 set out:

> [T]he U.S. will use this moment of opportunity to extend the benefits of *freedom* across the globe . . . We will actively work to bring the hope of *democracy, development, free markets, and free trade* to every corner of the world.
>
> (NSC 2002, emphasis added)

As a result the abstract boundaries of the term 'freedom' were reified and conditioned by ideologically framing the debate around a triumvirate of widely understood American values: 'freedom, democracy and free enterprise' (see Reus-Smit 2004: 34–8; Steger 2005). By articulating the triumvirate together, what appear to be pluralistic concepts were sutured together in an attempt to close their political contestability. Such an act legitimised the notion that they combine into 'a single sustainable model for national success' (NSC 2002: 1). This created a paradox in which 'freedom' became the choice of a single ethnocentric pre-configuration of both the political and economic realms, and not the desire on the part of individuals and groups for autonomy. As Eric Foner points out, 'There is no sense that other people may have given thought to the question of freedom and arrived at their own conclusions' (Foner 2003: 21). The utopianism inscribed in the Bush administration's post-crisis narrative embedded a teleological vision of the world, resulting in a 'single model'. This was a 'hard' form of Hegelianism, rather than a 'softer' form, which would have promoted a move away from tyranny to a destination established by the strategically selective agents within the political process being transformed; a move *towards* a utopian vision and not *away from* tyranny.

Within this scenario, 'freedom' implied the existence of intervention from the United States to help Middle Eastern regimes achieve the 'single sustainable model'. This was a defining feature of the post-crisis narrative presented by the

Bush administration, and applied as much to the conservative strategy it adopted as it did to the radical strategy it had pursued in Iraq. Despite the diverse nature of programmes initiated by MEPI and the BMENA it was economic reform, exemplified in MEFTA, that came to provide the Freedom Agenda's nucleus (see Table 6.2).

The emphasis on economic reform running throughout all the Freedom Agenda programmes, was that this was seen as a method of reforming the region and delivering 'good governance', whilst ultimately providing a means to combat terrorism. Thus, as President Bush declared:

> *Across the globe, free markets and trade have helped defeat poverty, and taught men and women the habits of liberty.* So I propose the establishment of a U.S.–Middle East Free Trade Area within a decade, *to bring the Middle East into an expanding circle of opportunity, to provide hope for the people who live in that region.*
>
> (Bush 2003, May 9)

The argument put forward by the Bush administration was that a lack of economic opportunities in the Middle East helped foster resentment towards Western affluence and generated conditions that favoured Islamist extremism. As a logical corollary, it was argued that:

> The advance of freedom and peace in the Middle East would drain this bitterness and increase our own security ... The Arab world has a great cultural tradition, but is largely missing out on the economic progress of our time. *Across the globe, free markets and trade have helped defeat poverty, and taught men and women the habits of liberty.*
>
> (Bush 2003, May 9)

Table 6.2 Areas addressed by the Freedom Agenda

Programme	Political reform	Economic reform	Educational reform	Women's empowerment
Middle East Free Trade Area	Conceptual commitment no-programming	Core programme focus		
Broader Middle East and North Africa Initiative	Conceptual commitment no-programming	Core programme focus	Conceptual commitment no-programming	
Democracy Assistance Programmes (MEPI, DRL, USAID)	Core programme focus	Core programme focus	Core programme focus	Core programme focus

Source: Adapted from Wittes and Yerkes (2006: 6).

Instructively, embedded within this vision was a notion that free trade and free markets would provide a mechanism for modernisation and ultimately the democratisation of the MENA.[13] The President was setting out the lessons he had learned at the 'West Point of capitalism', but articulating them through the prism of counter-terrorism: 'We fight against poverty because hope is an answer to terror' (Bush 2002, March 22). Moreover, as Colin Powell would declare when launching MEPI, 'Hope begins with a paycheck' (Powell 2002, December 12). Thus, the Freedom Agenda was proposing the model of the 'Asian Tigers' to be implemented in the Middle East (see Wittes and Yerkes 2006). The proposed economic strategy at the heart of the Bush administration's conservative approach to the MENA consequently embodied a gradualist and sequential understanding of how political economy relates to democratisation in the region. This was the same theory of political change that was posited by Bush in the 2000 presidential campaign, but as a result of September 11, 2001, had been applied to US–MENA relations. Modernity was seen as a single universal model in which democratisation was reachable through pursuing economic growth, and integrating the MENA into global markets (Lockman 2004: 133–40). Within this schema, economic freedom was being promoted because it was seen as a method of slowly loosening the statist grip that many authoritarian regimes have over their economies.

The promise of such a strategy was that it would create wealth that it was assumed would 'trickle down' and produce a well-educated middle class that would demand cultural changes favourable to democracy, such as increased secularism, and therefore weaken the role of Islamic identities (see Grugel 2002: 47). This was the quintessential expression of the modernisation thesis that lay at the heart of the Bush administration's IDF. As a result, the 'ideology of freedom' that the Bush administration presented drew an explicit connection between the MENA's economic stagnation, its failure to democratise and terrorism. Consequently, recognition was given to the 'demographic time bomb' MENA regimes face. For a typical regime in the region the unemployment rate is often in double digits and may rise to above 20 per cent. This is coupled with a growing number of young and fairly well-educated workers finding themselves without jobs (Lawrence 2006a: 13; Wittes 2008a: 30–55).

From such a diagnosis it became apparent that, within the conservative side of Bush's Freedom Agenda, it too would adopt a neoliberal prognosis. MEPI reinforced this process by promoting economic reform and private sector development, with the aim of enhancing the region's competitiveness, encouraging investment, and facilitating the growth of private enterprise by creating a market-driven framework and private sector-led economy (USDS–BNEA 2003).[14] Similarly, the BMENA initiative sought to support such activities through several small multilateral projects designed to assist the development of private enterprise and promote job training and literacy in the Middle East (Wittes and Yerkes 2006: 8). Yet ultimately it was MEFTA that personified the neoliberal agenda.

With other areas of the Freedom Agenda being rejected by MENA regimes, it became highly evident that by the time the Bush administration left office it was in effect pursuing an 'economics-first' strategy. This prescribed standard market-orientated measures, which the USA and international financial institutions have advocated around the world, such as increased privatisation, fiscal reform, banking reform, tax reform and investment liberalisation (Carothers 2005: 198–200). Rather than challenging the political power of friendly regimes, the Bush administration was working with them to carefully and slowly create the conditions for reforming their autocracies. This was hardly the radical policy that the Bush administration described it to be, as in many ways it simply built on similar policies undertaken by the Clinton administration throughout the 1990s, such as the 1994 Gore–Mubarak Commission, the 1998 US–North Africa Economic Partnership (USNAEP) and the 1985 US–Israel Free Trade Agreement amended in 1996 to include the West Bank, Gaza and Qualified Industrial Zones in Jordan (Dunne 2005: 210). The distinction was, however, that these were now elevated to become the basis of the administration's policy paradigm central to US–MENA relations. The focus of these previous talks was very similar in emphasis to those being discussed under the MEFTA talks, with a focus on 'dismantling and privatising statist economic structures, facilitating trade and foreign investment (including through accession to the WTO), and generating employment' (Dunne 2005: 210; see also Lawrence 2006a). Such efforts demonstrate a notable continuity between the Clinton administration and G. W. Bush's MEFTA initiative. To this extent, it is evident that the Bush administration's democracy promotion rationale, which apparently broke with the past, drew significantly on the 'one size fits all' logic of the 'Washington Consensus' in which *democracy* (mainly meaning elections), *open markets* (which follow the prescriptions of neoliberal economics) and *free trade* (within larger interdependent markets) all fit together and reinforce one another (Wiarda 1997: 16; Thomas 2005: 328–34; Williamson 2004; Goldgeier 2008).

Moreover, as the Freedom Agenda became 'watered down' and the Bush administration retreated, it became evident that what remained was an ad hoc set of policies held together by a neoliberal core; economic reform was the order of the day and it did not directly challenge, or necessitate serious political reform from, friendly allies in the MENA. This was in effect a set of policies that friendly regimes in the MENA desired. As Robert Z. Lawrence argued:

> [T]he US interest in MEFTA is not primarily economic. Rather it reflects geopolitical and security considerations. The MEFTA initiative reflects the judgement that US interests cannot be best advanced through purely military or political initiatives. To be effective in the battle for hearts and minds in the region the policy needs an economic component. By contrast, for Arab countries the interest in MEFTA is primarily economic.
>
> (Lawrence 2006b: 2)

The appeal of this approach was located in the manner in which it created the illusion of favouring both parties. Middle Eastern regimes were able to accept such an agreement in the belief that economic reforms would allow them to alleviate the poor social conditions that threaten their power, whereas the USA was able to pursue a strategy that many believed would dilute the appeal of Islamist groups and move the region slowly to stable, liberalised democracies. This apparently symbiotic relationship was appealing because of its gradualist emphasis, in which the USA need not directly challenge friendly regimes, consequently allowing cooperation to ensue on security and other economic concerns. In effect, it provided the default foundations upon which the Freedom Agenda's final iteration was constructed, by offering an illusionary 'silver bullet' to Middle East reform. Accordingly, it mirrors Edward Ingram's insight about *pax Americana*, which favours 'trade and investment without rule whenever possible, but with rule when unavoidable' (Ingram 2007: 7).

This mixed relationship between domination and democracy promotion, which attempted to secure American primacy through neoliberal democracy promotion, ultimately resembles what James Tully has referred to as the 'imperial right'. As Tully describes it:

> This is the right of [Western] states and their companies to trade freely in non-European societies and the duty to civilise non-European peoples, together with the duty of hospitality of non-European peoples to open themselves to trade and civilisation. If indigenous peoples resist and defend their own constitutional forms and constituent powers and civilisations, and thus violate the international duty of hospitality, the imperial powers have the right and duty to impose coercively the conditions of trade, hospitality and civilisation: namely, the appropriate features of modern constitutional forms and constituent powers. The right and two duties – in their many formulations from Francisco de Vitoria through Locke and Kant to the GATT/WTO and the restructuring policies of the World Bank, and the norm of democratisation under international law – serve to legitimate the coercive imposition and protection of the legal and political conditions of western imperialisation on the non-west. I will call the right and two duties the 'imperial right'.
>
> (Tully 2008: 210)

For Tully this imperial right has evolved through three historical stages: colonisation, indirect rule and informal rule. First, colonisation required the implantation of European settler colonies, which imposed 'legal and political systems' on indigenous populations and 'dispossessed them of their territories' (Tully 2008: 211). Second, indirect rule is based on 'imperial powers establishing a small colonial administration or trading company to rule over a much larger indigenous population indirectly, by establishing a formal infrastructure of imperial law' (Tully 2008: 211). Indirect rule also allowed for the preservation and modification of existing indigenous customary constitutions but notably ensures that 'resources and labour are privatised and opened to trade, labour discipline, and investments and contract law dominated by the [imperial] trading companies'. Under such a legal system resistance is deemed illegal. The means of ensuring that this situation arises include:

recognising local rulers as quasi-sovereigns and making unequal treaties with them, civilising or westernising local elites and making them dependent on imperial economic and military power and bribes, dividing and conquering opposition, training indigenous armies to protect the imperial system of property and trade law to fight proxy wars for them, inciting resistance so the trading companies can claim compensation for damages and lost profits (as in Iraq after 2003), and so on. This is the major way the imperial right was exercised in India, Ceylon, and Africa prior to its violent recolonisation after 1885, and in the Middle East in the twentieth century.

(Tully 2008: 211–12)

The third form of imperialism, that of 'informal or free trade imperialism' however is 'one step beyond indirect rule', as:

The imperial power permits the self-rule and eventual self-determination of indigenous peoples within a protectorate or sphere of influence while exercising informal paramountcy (hegemony) to induce them to open their resources, labour and markets to free trade by establishing the appropriate legal and political forms, thereby combining 'empire and liberty', the oldest rallying cry of British and US imperialism. The informal ways and means include the recognition of quasi-sovereignty and unequal treaties, economic and aid dependency, bribes, sanctions, the 'civilisation of natives' by voluntary and religious organisations and by Western legal, political economic and military experts, and threats of military intervention and actual military intervention if all else fails.

(Tully 2008: 212)

Given such a framing, Tully's conception of the imperial right is particularly adept at capturing the dynamics underlying the construction and institutionalisation of the Freedom Agenda. The status quo policy of the twentieth century was a form of direct rule, but, as a result of September 11, 2001, the Freedom Agenda was constructed as a policy paradigm to move US–MENA relations into a period of informal rule. Thus, the conservative and radical dimensions of the Freedom Agenda were part of the same IDF that was attempting to transform the nature of American hegemony over the region: from indirect rule to informal rule. This form of imperialism was typified by Robert B Zoellick's calls for a 'competitive liberalisation strategy' to be at the heart of US–MENA relations. For Zoellick, under the guise of fighting terrorism and democratically transforming the region, this strategy would be used to make an assault on protectionism, whilst countries eager for greater access to US markets would vie for Washington's attention and approval (Magnusson 2003: 94; Lawrence 2006a: 4–12). This form of economic statecraft was highly significant for pursuing primacy in the Middle East because it sought to increase American influence in the region by creating interdependence between the US and Middle Eastern economies, therefore strengthening US hegemony. However, for the MENA's autocratic regimes this form of liberalisation has typically been part of a regime-driven survival strategy, which in the past allowed governments to avoid legitimisation crises by defusing popular dissatisfaction. This apparently symbiotic relationship provided the default foundations upon which the Freedom Agenda was constructed, demonstrating that, whereas 'democratisation' was portrayed as being in the national interest, economic liberalisation inspired by the modernisation thesis was seen by the Bush administration as the best way to achieve it. The importance of this cannot be overstated, as the Freedom Agenda, although sounding emancipatory, was in fact being used as a technology to secure a new form of imperial security governance over the region.

Once the Freedom Agenda is in fact understood as a modality of control, it is possible to observe one of its defining features, and the implications of its neoliberal definition of 'freedom'. Discernibly, such a definition falls into what Isaiah Berlin defined as a 'positive' conception of freedom. Indeed, using Berlin's conceptions of negative and positive liberty as a heuristic tool is illustrative:

> I am normally said to be free to the degree to which no man or body of men interferes with my activity . . . If I am prevented by others from doing what I could otherwise do, I am to that degree unfree; and if this area is contracted by other men beyond a certain minimum, I can be described as being coerced, or, it may be, enslaved . . . Coercion implies the deliberate interference of other human beings within the area in which I could otherwise act.
> (Berlin 2006: 34)

The implications of this are important as it can be argued that to the extent that the USA pursued its strategies of both indirect and informal rule throughout the twentieth and twenty-first centuries, and through doing so supported autocratic regimes with military and economic aid packages over popular opposition, the USA was complicit in removing that population's negative liberty under the rubric of US national interests. Consequently, the inhabitants of the MENA cannot be said to have negative liberty to the extent that US imperialism has implications for, and structures, areas of their everyday lives. Notably, this is the form of freedom that is undermined by the US desire for primacy over the region to secure its long-term interests.

Yet the USA, through the Freedom Agenda, was offering the MENA a positive conception of liberty. Embedded in the Freedom Agenda's teleological vision was a rule structure that bestows a pattern of action.[15] Freedom was the name of an end state: the 'single sustainable model' of democracy, development, free enterprise and free trade. The dangers of offering such a positive conception of liberty were strongly pronounced by Berlin, and are worth quoting at length:

> The 'positive' and 'negative' notions of freedom historically developed in divergent directions . . . until, in the end, they came into direct conflict with each other . . . The perils of using organic metaphors to justify the coercion of some men by others in order to raise them to a 'higher' level of freedom have been pointed out . . . we recognise that it is possible, and at times justifiable,

to coerce men in the name of some goal . . . which they would, if they were more enlightened, themselves pursue, but do not because they are blind or ignorant or corrupt. This renders it easy for me to conceive of myself as coercing others for their own sake, in their, not my, interest. I am then claiming that I know what they truly need better than they know it themselves . . . Once I take this view, I am in a position to ignore the actual wishes of men or societies, to bully, oppress, torture them in the name, and on behalf of their 'real' selves.

(Berlin 2006: 44–5)

This is a prophetic vision of what happened in Iraq, not only through the adoption of neoliberal policy, but more profoundly in events in Abu Ghraib prison and beyond. More widely, what Berlin's distinction provides is a method of understanding how the Freedom Agenda became stuck between a policy of domination and democracy. To accept that the USA has a legitimate right to intervene in the region, especially to secure its own primacy, is to accept domination. Indeed, if one consults the etymological roots of the term, *dominus* and *dominari*, 'a lord' and 'to be lord over', such control can legitimately be termed domination. However, such a position is not strictly contradictory if it is understood that the Freedom Agenda is based on a positive conception of liberty, in which freedom is not based on autonomy, but rather a pattern of action and an end state that is seen to be conducive to *pax Americana*. The grand liberal strategy the Bush administration put forward can therefore be seen as a policy of ensuring primacy but also as propagating a positive conception of liberty. The strategy was caught between free trade, as the positive route to liberty, and domination, to the extent that negative liberty is undermined in favour of stability.

The contradiction between democracy and domination is not a new phenomenon in US foreign policy. It is as old as the USA's first democratisation project, carried out in the Philippines in 1892, when a policy of democratisation emerged as part of a compromise between proponents of a US empire and anti-imperialists (LaFeber 1994: 212–7; Schmidt 2005: 38–42). As Tony Smith maintains about the first democratisation project:

> Imperialists could . . . tout the superiority of the Anglo-Saxon race, while anti-imperialists could reassure themselves that the ideals of self-government would not be endangered . . . the democratisation of the Philippines came to be the principal reason the Americans were there; now the United States had a moral purpose to its imperialism and could rest more easily . . . democracy would become the moving faith of the forty-eight years of American control.
> (Smith 1994: 43)

These genealogical origins are revealing. They highlight not only the less than benign way in which American foreign policy originally adopted democracy promotion as a strategy, but additionally the manner in which 'democratisation' can be utilised as a discourse to justify a policy of subjugation, authority and rule.

Indeed, it is worth reflecting on Abraham Lincoln's assertions in Baltimore in April 1864:

> The world has never had a good definition of the word liberty, and the American people, just now, are much in want of one. We all declare for liberty; but in using the same word we do not all mean the same thing. With some the word liberty may mean for each man to do as he pleases with himself, and the product of his labor; while with others the same word may mean for some men to do as they please with other men, and the product of other men's labor. Here are two, not only different, but incompatible things, called by the same name – liberty. And it follows that each of the things is, by the respective parties, called by two different and incompatible names – liberty and tyranny.
>
> (Lincoln 2003: 17)

These are pertinent words given that in effect the Freedom Agenda came to offer a form of 'low-intensity democracy' (see Gills *et al*. 1993). Thus, as Barry Gills points out:

> there may be a deep seated antagonism between the extension of American power through accelerated and intensified neoliberal economic globalisation and the realization of social progress through meaningful democratization. The economic policies pursued by the US tend to pre-configure the political, narrowing the range of regime type to a form called 'low-intensity democracy', which itself is a political form not necessarily conductive to real economic progress for the majority. Low-intensity democracy has, however, emerged as a characteristic political form of the post-cold war era, in which formal electoral democracy is promoted, but the transformatory capacity of democracy is limited in order to facilitate neoliberal economic policies.
>
> (Gills 2000: 326)

Many authors have illustrated that low-intensity democracy has been a model adopted by many parts of the developing world (see Gills *et al*. 1993: 127–257). With it, neoliberal policy has brought increased inequality, social polarisation and the predominant sum of the world's wealth being held by the few. Consequently economic power is concentrated, whilst labour is increasingly exploited, leading to alienation and various attempts at resistance. It is therefore no coincidence that, in multiple interviews with young people of varied social and political movements in Tahrir Square throughout 2011, these same complaints arose about Egyptian society following the Mubarak regime's accelerated economic neoliberalisation from 2006 onwards. Thus, whilst individuals such as Thomas Friedman of the *New York Times* have argued that President Bush's 'aggressive engagement' should be backed as the best strategy for 'leading the Arab world into globalisation' (Friedman 2003: 314–15), it is well worth ruminating on the implications of this. The Freedom Agenda was narrated as the method of providing a utopian peace, delivering greater prosperity and security to the region and the world; yet it may well have laid the foundations for something radically different. If Gills is correct, and the 'simultaneity of economic liberalisation and democratisation creates particular problems of transition for all these societies and generally exacerbates the problems of maintaining social and political stability' (Gills 2000: 331), then it would appear that the final iteration of Bush's Freedom Agenda may well achieve neither democratisation nor domination. A strategy of economic reform first was perceived by the Bush administration as a method of slowly transforming the region, securing US primacy and maintaining regional stability in 'partnership' with its allies. This strategy was specifically designed to avoid the unpredictability, uncertainty and instability of the 2011 revolutions. Far from Bush's Freedom Agenda inspiring such events, as some revisionist accounts have argued, the 2011 revolutions represent the ultimate failure of this economics-first strategy and the Freedom Agenda's attempts to maintain stability. Yet it was a lack of stability that the Obama administration inherited along with the institutional legacy of the war on terror and the Freedom Agenda it gave birth to.

7 Obama's Freedom Agenda

Conservative pragmatism and the 2011 revolutions

On January 15, 2009, a ceremony to commemorate the foreign policy achievements of the G. W. Bush administration was held in the Department of State. With President Bush sitting centre stage, Secretary of State Condoleezza Rice declared that 'today is a very special day. We are going to commemorate many of the achievements of our nation over the last eight years in furthering the Freedom Agenda' (Rice 2009, January 15). The Secretary of State also added that there were now 'democratically elected leaders in Kosovo, Lebanon, Liberia, Afghanistan, and Iraq', and that these countries 'have experienced a new birth of freedom . . . Because when impatient patriots looked for support in their struggle for liberation, America and you, Mr. President, stood with them' (Rice 2009, January 15). This was just one event that followed a flurry of activity in mid to late 2008, where the Bush administration sought to narrate the Freedom Agenda as the central platform of his foreign policy legacy. Indeed, on October 9, 2008, the Bush administration elected to partially declassify *National Security Presidential Directive* (NSPD) *58*: *Institutionalising the Freedom Agenda*, which stated that:

> It is the policy of the United States to seek and support the growth of democratic movements and institutions in every nation and culture, with the ultimate goal of ending tyranny in the world. This policy goal was established and elaborated in the 2006 National Security Strategy of the United States of America, which declares the promotion of freedom, justice, human dignity, and effective democratic institutions to be central goals of our national security.
>
> (DOS 2008)[1]

However, the Bush administration's legacy, and its relationship with democracy promotion, was represented by the newly elected President Obama somewhat more pejoratively. Keenly aware that for many observers the Freedom Agenda had been exclusively conflated with the war in Iraq, albeit incorrectly, President Obama asserted the need for a 'new beginning' in a speech made at Cairo University, arguing that:

> I know there has been controversy about the promotion of democracy in recent years, and much of this controversy is connected to the war in Iraq. So let me be clear: No system of government can or should be imposed by one nation on any other.
>
> (Obama 2009, June 4)

Such a statement was indicative of the Obama administration's attempts to both publicly distance itself from the Iraq war and downplay the Freedom Agenda as a central platform of US–Middle East relations. This was the position taken throughout the 2008 campaign and in the initial months of coming into office, when the Obama administration publicly narrated the Iraq war as a 'war of choice' (Obama 2009, June 4). Indeed, there was a conspicuous silence on the issue of democracy promotion from the Obama campaign. However, when the *Washington Post* directly asked 'should democracy promotion be a primary US goal?' a much more nuanced narrative emerged. Candidate Obama replied:

> We benefit from the expansion of democracy . . . Our greatest tool in advancing democracy is our own example. That's why I will end torture, end extraordinary rendition and indefinite detentions; restore habeas corpus; and close the detention facility at Guantanamo Bay . . . I will significantly increase funding for the National Endowment for Democracy (NED) and other nongovernmental organizations to support civic activists in repressive societies . . . I recognize that our security interests will sometimes necessitate that we work with regimes with which we have fundamental disagreements; yet, those interests need not and must not prevent us from lending our consistent support to those who are committed to democracy and respect for human rights.
>
> (Obama 2008, March 2)

This narrative suggested that, once successful, Obama's approach would be to downplay the vindicationalist policies of the Bush administration in favour of a more stealthy and modest exemplarist strategy, whereby the administration would attempt to restore the USA as an example to the rest of the world on democracy and human rights. In effect the Obama administration had recognised that the deontic power of the USA had been damaged by the Bush administration's record in office, and sought to restore its credibility as a symbol of democracy. This was not an abandonment of the Freedom Agenda per se, as the institutions of the Freedom Agenda remained actively in place, but rather recognition that the radical dimension of the Freedom Agenda had delegitimised and damaged America's reputation. The Obama administration's approach was to be more pragmatic and downplay the radical dimension, whilst steadily allowing the conservative side of the agenda to evolve and expand as it was articulated within the new administration's IDF. This approach was unsurprising given that as early as 2005 Senator Obama signalled a clear dedication to the Freedom Agenda. The Senator had co-sponsored an early version of the ADA introduced by Senator John McCain, which went further than that eventually adopted as part of the *Implementing Recommendations of the 9/11 Commission Act of 2007*.[2] Whereas the ratified 2007 version qualified democracy promotion, by asserting that democracy would be promoted 'along with other key foreign policy goals', the 2005 version had contended more assertively that 'It shall be the policy of the United States to promote freedom and democracy in foreign countries as a fundamental component of United States foreign policy' (*ADA* 2005: Sec. 3).

Once elected to office, it was clear that the new administration was remaining conspicuously silent on the issue of democracy promotion, whilst attempting to start Obama's exemplarist strategy. The limited references to 'democracy' and 'freedom' in President Obama's inaugural address were widely commented upon (Carothers 2012: 9). This silence was also noticeable across much of the administration, as democracy promotion was disarticulated from public announcements of American foreign policy and policy makers' everyday lexicon more generally. This impression was compounded when Hillary Clinton was willing to assert the need for a 'comprehensive plan' for 'diplomacy, development and defense', in her Senate confirmation hearing, but reduced 'advancing democracy' to a mere background 'hope' (Clinton 2009, January 13). This had left some analysts wondering if the 'fourth "D" of democracy promotion was being abandoned' (Bouchet 2010: 572). Further still it became clear that, whereas President Bush had underpinned the plot of the war on terror with a temperament of triumphant exhilaration, the Obama administration was altering the narrative and beginning to pragmatically deal with an increasing sense of US decline: an increased sense that the USA was being challenged by rising powers in a multipolar world, combined with the shock of the global economic crisis, a recession in the US economy, fears about global climate change, the threat of nuclear proliferation, the continued wars in Iraq and Afghanistan and a new front in Pakistan. Within this context the Freedom Agenda was removed from the overarching narrative of US foreign policy, until the Obama administration began rethinking its approach in light of an unsuccessful policy in Iran and the events of 2011. The Obama administration removed notions that the USA was on a moralistic crusade, and replaced Bush's policy of conservative radicalism with a policy of conservative pragmatism.

Obama's Freedom Agenda: a conservative pragmatist approach

The pragmatic approach adopted by the Obama administration certainly sent mixed messages, which gave the impression that US foreign policy had jettisoned the Freedom Agenda. Accordingly, many analysts argued that Obama had returned to a status quo policy that existed before the September 11, 2001, crisis. Some simply asserted that 'Obama is a realist, by temperament, learning, and instinct' (Zakaria 2009) and that before the 2011 revolutions he had said 'almost nothing about broader goals like spreading democracy, protecting human rights, or assisting in women's education' (Kagan 2009). Further still, other analysts simply dismissed what the administration had said on these issues as 'lip service', arguing that President Obama simply returned to a traditional policy of 'reliance on Arab strongmen' (Fukuyama 2010). Yet a deeper analysis of Obama's foreign policy reveals a much more nuanced relationship with democracy promotion. Although initially silent on the issue the administration secured increased Congressional support, which manifested itself with improved funding for Freedom Agenda institutions at a time of serious financial and budgetary constraint for the US government over all. In FY2009, MEPI was granted $50 million, which rose significantly in FY2010 to $65 million and $80 million in FY2011 (McInerney 2011: 7). Moreover, President Obama also made some high-level appointments that clearly indicated that democracy promotion was not being jettisoned from the political agenda. Within the State Department Anne-Marie Slaughter, the Princeton University professor who had been on Condoleezza Rice's Advisory Committee on Democracy, was appointed Director of Policy Planning. Similarly, Tamara Coffman Wittes, who had long argued that democracy promotion needed to be a fundamental component of US foreign policy in the MENA and predicted the increasing instability in the region, was appointed Deputy Assistant Secretary for Near Eastern Affairs. This was complemented by appointing Samantha Power, author of *A Problem from Hell: America and the Age of Genocide*, and Michael McFaul, author of *Advancing Democracy Abroad: Why We Should and How We Can*, to the National Security Council. With these appointments it was highly unlikely that democracy promotion was going to be removed from the Obama administration's agenda, even if these individuals had to fight bureaucratic battles with more realist appointments within the administration. Rather, as McFaul explained, in the early days of the administration, given how contaminated the term 'democracy promotion' had become, the aim was to 'talk less and do more' (Cooper 2009).

Obama's reforms of the Freedom Agenda, from Bush's conservative radicalism to a policy of conservative pragmatism, began immediately upon his coming into office. The radical side was downplayed as the administration signalled a desire to pragmatically engage with the regimes in Syria and Iran. At the President's inauguration he asserted that:

> To the Muslim world, we seek a new way forward, based on mutual interest and mutual respect. To those leaders around the globe who seek to sow conflict, or blame their society's ills on the West – know that your people will judge you on what you can build, not what you destroy. To those who cling to power through corruption and deceit and the silencing of dissent, know that you are on the wrong side of history; but that we will extend a hand if you are willing to unclench your fist.
>
> (Obama 2009, January 20)

Just two days later, the President appointed George Mitchell as Special Envoy for Middle East Peace, and, by January 26, Mitchell was sent to the region for a 'listening tour' (Lander 2009). Moreover, signalling the importance of engaging with the Middle East and changing the tone of US–MENA relations, President

Obama elected to give his first televised interview at the White House to the news channel Al-Arabiya. He announced that Mitchell's tour would launch the administration's 'holistic' approach to the region, arguing that:

> I do think that it is impossible for us to think only in terms of the Palestinian–Israeli conflict and not think in terms of what's happening with Syria or Iran or Lebanon or Afghanistan and Pakistan . . . These things are interrelated . . . if we are looking at the region as a whole and communicating a message to the Arab world and the Muslim world, that we are ready to initiate a new partnership based on mutual respect and mutual interest, then I think that we can make significant progress.
>
> (Obama 2009, January 26)

The pragmatic nature in which the Obama administration began engaging with the MENA demonstrated an acute sensitivity to perceptions of the USA in the region and a desire to 'restore' good relations that 'America had with the Muslim world as recently as 20 or 30 years ago' (Obama 2009, January 26). This mix of an exemplarist strategy and acknowledgement of the USA's damaged reputation was a trope of the Obama campaign, and once in office Obama was able to issue three executive orders which called for the closure of Guantanamo Bay within one year, a ban on the CIA's controversial interrogation techniques and a review of detention policy options. Thus, within just a week of taking office, the administration had set itself upon what it believed to be a more pragmatic path to engaging with the MENA and restoring America's reputation in the world; albeit these policies proved to be more difficult to enact than originally perceived.

Whereas the shift towards engagement itself represented a break with the Bush administration, it was the manner in which the Obama administration asserted that there would be no 'preconditions' for such talks that made the policy distinctive. The Bush administration had long held that engaging with Iran was possible if and only if Iran suspended its uranium enrichment programme. However, in a pragmatic move President Obama, having sent two personal letters to Iran's supreme leader, Ayatollah Ali Khamenei, asserted that it would 'talk to our foes and friends', breaking the convention of setting conditionality for open talks (see Borger 2009). By April, however, Hillary Clinton was threatening tougher sanctions against the regime in Tehran, if the Iranian regime failed to acknowledge the offer to engage in 'constructive dialogue' (Clinton 2009, April 22).

The pattern of offering talks, but threatening sanctions, was combined with reassurances that the USA was not attempting to push for regime change in Iran; it was simply attempting to 'engage and change the behaviour of advisories' (Clinton 2009, July 10). However, by June the Obama administration faced its first serious challenge to this policy, as the Iranian regime began to blame the USA and UK for protests breaking out in major cities across Iran against the re-election of President Mahmoud Ahmadinejad. The 'Green Revolution', or as some have called it the 'Twitter Revolution', marked a significant moment for the administration as it presented a tension between engaging the Iranian regime, in the hope of halting uranium enrichment, and openly supporting the protesters and questioning the legitimacy of the election. Much to the chagrin of many members of congress and political commentators, the White House selected the former, opting for a policy of non-interference (MacAskill 2009). In part the construction of this strategically selective strategy reflected a cornerstone of the Obama administration's preference not to align with protesters, for fear that this would damage the legitimacy and domestic image of protesters. Indeed, openly supporting protesters does risk playing directly into the hands of regimes that have typically appealed to the colonial policies of the West in their narratives.

With increasingly violent images being seen around the world, the President's response was to condemn the violence and call for it to stop, deny Iranian claims that the revolution was inspired by the West, and assert recognition of Iranian sovereignty. It was not until Obama's engagement strategy was seen as problematic, and other Western powers led with strong criticism of the Iranian regime, that the USA toughened its discursive posture towards the regime. Thus, in what would be a precursor to the 2011 revolutions, the Obama administration made it clear that, where engagement and supporting democratic struggles conflicted, on Iran his pragmatic position favoured the former. This was made all the more evident when the White House discovered that Jared Cohen, a member of the Policy Planning Staff in the State Department, had 'interfered' in the revolution by contacting Twitter's chairman, Jack Dorsey. Cohen urged Dorsey to reschedule planned maintenance, so Iranians could continue tweeting, and 'he almost lost his job over it' (Lizza 2011: 9). Cohen was, however, protected by a State Department that was increasingly concerned with democracy promotion and experimenting with new strategies to reform and reinvigorate the conservative side of the Freedom Agenda. Indeed, one of the characteristics of the Obama administration's inherited Freedom Agenda was a tension between the White House and the Department of State over if, how and why democracy should be promoted in the Middle East.

Many elements of the conservative side of Bush's Freedom Agenda remained under the Obama administration before the 2011 revolutions, in part because of institutional inertia, but also because the Freedom Agenda, as inherited from Bush, did not conflict with the desire to listen and engage with the region. The neoliberal backbone of the Freedom Agenda made it amenable to the MENA regimes that Obama was now 'listening' to. These relationships were made easier by virtue of the Obama administration's continued downgrading of elections as an important indicator for democratic progress, which was a continuation of Bush's policy following the electoral success of Hamas. Indeed, although Obama was touting the need for engagement and 'talking to foes', it was clear that this was not to apply to Hamas despite its elected status. For the Obama administration, winning an election did not confer democratic legitimacy and an automatic right to engagement, as the administration increasingly articulated democracy promotion with the concepts of justice, dignity, human rights and the rule of law. There were limitations to Obama's pragmatism.

Where the Obama administration did, however, begin to reform the conservative side of the Freedom Agenda was by increasingly articulating democracy promotion with development. What the Obama administration was proposing before the 2011 revolutions was a more complex strategy, whereby a modernisation process for the region would be spurred on not simply by free trade, but also through a gradual process of development. Thus, as Obama had argued when a candidate:

> In the 21st century, progress must mean more than a vote at the ballot box – it must mean freedom from fear and freedom from want. We cannot stand for the freedom of anarchy. Nor can we support the globalization of the empty stomach. We need new approaches to help people to help themselves.
> (Obama 2007: 2)

The Obama administration was proposing to shift from 'democracy promotion' signified by elections but spurred on by free trade modernisation, to what has been termed 'dignity promotion' that would seek to 'fix the conditions of misery that breeds anti-Americanism and prevent liberty, justice, and prosperity from taking root' (Ackerman 2008). Whereas G. W. Bush saw the Freedom Agenda as eradicating terrorism through the promotion of the free market, the Obama administration increasingly saw the same role for development. This position was widely held within the Obama administration. As Susan Rice, the US Permanent Representative to the United Nations, wrote critiquing the Freedom Agenda:

> Promoting both development and democracy in far away countries is a 21st century security imperative. We need a dual strategy. We must combine effective formulas for fostering freedom though building civil society and transparent democratic institutions with a determination to 'make poverty history'. If we fail to do so, we will have squandered a crucial chance to accomplish what President Bush boldly staked out as his ambitious legacy: 'to advance the cause of liberty and build a safer world'.
> (Rice and Graff 2009: 51)

Just as in the Cold War development had been narrated as a method of containing communism, the Obama administration now articulated development as a method of engaging with the MENA and eradicating terrorism. This rationale was also partly behind the launch of the first Quadrennial Diplomacy and Development Review (QDDR) to look at how development and diplomacy could be coordinated, integrated and complemented by each other, and make use of what Hillary Clinton termed 'smart power' (Clinton 2009, July 10). Indeed, when the QDDR process was announced, it was clear that evaluating US development policy's relationship with democracy promotion was in the administration's sights. The Secretary of State declared that:

> we are working for a world in which more people in more places can live in freedom, can enjoy the fruits of democracy and economic opportunity and have a chance to live up to their own God-given potential . . . instead of

simply trying to adjust to the way things are, we need to get in the habit of looking to the horizon and planning for how we want things to be ... We will be doing this quadrennial review, which will be, we hope, a tool to provide us with both short-term and long-term blueprints for how to advance our foreign policy objectives and our values and interests.

(Clinton 2009, July 10)

The release of the QDDR in late 2010 simply reaffirmed the administration's previous assertions that a more sustainable form of democracy support was needed, and set out the rationale for articulating democracy support and development policy:

Through an aggressive and affirmative development agenda and commensurate resources, we can strengthen the regional partners we need to help us stop conflict and counter global criminal networks; build a stable, inclusive global economy with new sources of prosperity; advance democracy and human rights; and ultimately position ourselves to better address key global challenges by growing the ranks of prosperous, capable and democratic states that can be our partners in the decades ahead.

(QDDR 2010: ix)

The importance of what some have termed Obama's 'sustainable democracy promotion' approach is multifaceted (see Patterson 2012). It represents a partial shift away from neoliberal modernisation thesis, as development was seen as an approach to democratisation. This, however, does not necessarily deal with issues of informal rule that were part of the Bush administration's institutionalised imperial right. The approach remained conservative and shared a similar goal of ensuring gradual transformation in the region that was compatible with US interests. Whilst the USA was pursuing its neoliberal approach in partnerships with governments top-down, it was also now conceptualising a modernisation approach that was bottom-up. This demonstrated a shift in the proposed *means* of informal rule, rather than representing any paradigm shift. It was an adjustment of the of settings and instruments within the Freedom Agenda paradigm. The objective of such a strategy was to replace the technology of 'free-market democratisation' with the technology of foreign assistance and development to achieve continued domination of the region and the continued pursuit of American interests. This is an adjustment of means to meet the same ends as the Freedom Agenda constructed by the Bush administration. The USA, whether through a strategy of promoting free trade or development, was still not going to abandon long-term partners in the region, but rather would continue to work with them in 'partnerships'. The development strategy did not challenge the power of MENA regimes, and was still reliant on a gradualist strategy. Its focus, in the MENA context, was on undermining extremist Islamist groups by using development as a tool for socially engineering the region. Thus, as Samantha Power had argued:

Look at why these baddies win these elections ... it's because [populations are] living in climates of fear ... Their fears of going hungry, or of the thug on the street. That's the swamp that needs draining. If were to compete with extremism, we have to be able to provide these things that we're not.

(in Ackerman 2008)

Although the Obama administration was attempting to change the modality of the Freedom Agenda, the narrative they constructed still articulated democracy promotion as a method of eradicating extremism and fighting terrorism (see Al-Anani and Patkin 2008). The Obama administration had not entirely jettisoned the narrative that underpinned the Freedom Agenda, and the President regularly made appeals to the universality of democracy, and to teleological notions of progress and being on 'the right side of history'. As the President explained in his Cairo speech:

I do have an unyielding belief that all people yearn for certain things: the ability to speak your mind and have a say in how you are governed; the confidence in the rule of law and equal administration of justice; government that is transparent and doesn't steal from the people; the freedom to live as you choose. These are not just American ideas; they are human rights. And that is why we will support them everywhere.

(Obama 2009, June 4)

In this respect there was a considerable amount of continuity between Bush's Freedom Agenda and the overarching approach adopted by the Obama administration. They both predominantly adopted conservative strategies when approaching allies and friendly regimes in the MENA. Of course the Obama administration's conservative strategy is somewhat complicated by the timing of the 2011 revolutions. It was just as the administration's thinking on this issue was maturing and the State Department began developing a more novel and dynamic approach to democracy support, through digitising the Freedom Agenda and engaging beyond the state, that the 2011 revolutions began.

Engaging beyond the state: civil society partnerships and the digitisation of the Freedom Agenda

The first steps towards the digitisation of the Freedom Agenda started in 2008, as the Bush administration began to transfer power to President-elect Obama and his new administration. It began with the Obama campaign team's cooperation and participation in the December 3–5, 2008, *Alliance for Youth Movements* (AYM) Summit held at Columbia University Law School. The AYM Summit was the brainchild of Jared Cohen in Condoleezza Rice's Policy Planning Staff. In October 2008, just weeks before Barack Obama was elected President, Cohen persuaded the Under Secretary of State for Public Diplomacy and Public Affairs, James K. Glassman, to take a trip to the Republic of Colombia. The purpose of the trip was to meet with the founder of a Facebook group called *No More FARC Movement* and observe how social media could be used as a tool for combating extremism. Subsequently, Glassman instructed Cohen to run with his idea of

> Put[ting] people together, shar[ing] best practices, produc[ing] a manual that will be accessible online and in print to any group that wants to build a youth empowerment organisation to push back against violence and oppression around the world.
> (Cohen 2008, November 24)

The result was the AYM Summit, which partnered the Department of State with the private sector companies Howcast, Google, Facebook, YouTube and MTV, and brought civil society activists from all over the world together in New York City. This included representatives of Egypt's April 6th Movement and others from around the MENA (Glassman 2008, November 24). Notably, this summit, in light of the 2011 revolutions, should not be overemphasised in terms of its importance to inducing the revolutions themselves, as has been attempted by individuals such as Paul Wolfowitz (2011, February 11). The April 6th movement launched its Facebook page on March 23, 2008, to support a textile workers' strike planned on April 6 in Mahalla al-Kobra, to protest against low wages and high food prices. The group had formed and then studied 'the American civil rights movement' and in particular 'Martin Luther King, Rosa Park and Malcolm X', along with the struggles in 'Poland, Georgia, Ukraine and Serbia', which led them to develop relations with Otpor! in Belgrade (Rashed 2011). From its founding, the group was particularly savvy at using Facebook as a tool for communication and organising protest (see Wolman 2008). Indeed, it is clear from Wikileaks papers that April 6th regarded the AYM Summit as 'interesting', but plans to remove Mubarak from power were already under way. Thus, as Cohen argued, regarding the AYM Summit 'we wanted to partner with as many people as possible to help *what was already happening* on a larger scale' (Cohen 2008, November 24).

The importance of the AYM Summit, however, was threefold. First, Joe Rospars, Obama's New Media Director, and other members of Obama's campaign team participated, demonstrating that on the issue of democracy promotion and counter-extremist measures there was a willingness to cooperate with the departing administration. Second, Jared Cohen's role proved pivotal to the AYM summit, and it was therefore important that Hillary Clinton retained Cohen on her Policy Planning Staff before he became director of Google Ideas in 2010. Finally, and most importantly, this marked the intellectual beginning of the Obama administration's *Internet Freedom Agenda*, which would be formally announced by Hillary Clinton in January 2010; in it the Web 2.0 techniques that helped President Obama get elected were articulated with international relations and civil struggles around the globe.

From the AYM Summit, a website called *movements.org* was constructed, which seeks to 'identify', 'connect' and 'support' '21st century activism' and provide a 'new model of peer to peer training' (www.movements.org/pages/

about/). Indeed, it is highly evident that this site has connections with multiple civil society organisations within the MENA, and helps put groups in contact with one another within countries, across regions and globally. Amongst other things, the site also acts as a hub for information in publication form such as *Creating Grassroots Movements for Change: A Field Manual* and *How to Bypass Internet Censorship*, and the site was touted as particularly useful during the 2011 revolutions for providing information that helped circumvent the Mubarak and Gaddafi regimes' internet closures. The particular importance of this site is that it appears to be an effective tool for putting groups in contact with one another, whilst facilitating discussions of best practice. In effect it allows groups to learn from one another, from across the globe, and then use these lessons to aid with their own indigenous forms of resistance.

Shortly after the AYM Summit in April 2009, having remained at the State Department, Cohen began heading up routine 'technology delegations', in which he would assemble delegations of US technology company chief and senior executives and go to Iraq and Syria, amongst other countries, in an effort to develop technology-based solutions with local stakeholders in these countries. In essence such practices amounted to what Hillary Clinton and Jared Cohen termed '21st Century Statecraft', which entailed 'building connections' to 'empower citizens, promote greater accountability and transparency, and capacity build' (Cohen 2010, September 7).

The next iteration of the Obama administration's digitisation of the Freedom Agenda came in November 2009, when in a speech at the Forum for the Future, in Morocco, Hillary Clinton launched the *Civil Society 2.0* initiative. The Secretary of State announced that:

> We seek to support civil society efforts worldwide because we believe that civil society helps to make communities more prosperous and stable. It helps to drive economic growth that benefits the greatest number of people. And it pushes political institutions to be agile and responsive to the people they serve. So the United States is launching an initiative called Civil Society 2.0. This organized effort will provide new technologies to civil society organizations. We will send experts in digital technology and communications to help build capacity . . . Now, these are some of the ways that the United States is pursuing President Obama's vision for a new relationship. Our work is based on empowering individuals rather than promoting ideologies; listening and embracing other ideas rather than simply imposing our own; and pursuing partnerships that are sustainable and broad-based.
>
> (Clinton 2009, November 3)

Conspicuously, the Obama administration became at ease with using the term 'partnership', which carries intertextuality with the Bush administration's discourse. Discernibly, however, the Obama administration began broadening the concept. No longer were 'partnerships' simply between the US and MENA governments, as had been the usage under Bush's conservative dimension of the

Freedom Agenda, but rather partnerships under Obama were increasingly understood as a triangular relationship between the US government, MENA regimes and civil society organisations. Along with an emphasis on 'engagement' announced in Cairo, 'engaging in partnerships' with civil society groups provided the intellectual basis of Obama's digitised Freedom Agenda and the reforms made to existing Freedom Agenda institutions. Thus, whereas in 2009 the Obama administration made the decision to provide bilateral funding to only those Egyptian NGOs that were registered with the government, by 2010 there were increased calls by the administration for 'civil society dialogues' and need to 'engage beyond the state' (QDDR 2010: vii; McInerney 2010: 24). Such an approach increasingly built on some of the activities conducted in the Forum for the Future, where in 2009, for example, government ministers from the region were placed on the same platform as civil society leaders, to talk about common issues.

The emphasis on civil society partnership was also consolidated as a commitment within MEPI. Since 2004 MEPI had developed a local grant programme, which would provide funds to indigenous NGOs in the region through US embassies averaging around $50,000 per NGO. However, this remained a limited proportion of MEPI's overall programme portfolio. The Obama administration significantly increased both the average total amount given under the local grant programme and its proportion of MEPI's total portfolio. This led to 'a lot more funding of indigenous NGOs close to the ground in the region . . . backed up by branch management staff in regional offices in Tunis and Abu Dhabi' (Wittes 2011). Yet the most dramatic alteration in this programme is the extent to which funding began shifting from being allocated through a 'call driven' process to being 'demand driven'. When this author interviewed MEPI grant recipients, the most dramatic shift many of them highlighted was that increasingly, as MEPI has reformed and evolved, potential recipients have been able to design projects and directly appeal to US embassies for funding consideration. Moreover, many recipients commented on their ability to change budgets and project design once grants have been approved, which MEPI often allows within their two-year projects as long as there is a justifiable rationale. Given this, many recipients described MEPI as 'flexible', whilst also commending the institution for 'risk taking', and being a core funding source for new and innovative NGOs.

This of course is not to suggest that there are no problems in MEPI's shift to focusing more on civil society. At a practical level, there continue to be problems with MEPI funding only short-term projects. Many grant recipients aired their frustration with a lack of 'continuation' funds, even in projects that by the standards initially agreed with MEPI would be considered highly successful. Indeed, the rationale for MEPI's local grant programme was that it did not overlap with USAID, but all too often once grants had expired it was evident that 'USAID won't step in' and was not 'interested'. MEPI does of course make the terms of its grant clear, but the local grants programme creates only limited 'start up' partnerships with civil society organisations that can seriously struggle to find funds once MEPI funding runs out. This raises a range of sustainability and budgeting issues, and has led many organisations to seek greater funding from the private sector, which all too often ends up being large multinational companies, and in particular corporate sector companies. However, some grant recipients noted that their golden standard was to receive funds from local indigenous business, with one in Egypt commenting that 'getting local money is very powerful ... [it shows] Egyptians are working on their own development' (Hassan 2011b). This has been particularly important since the 2011 revolutions, as some international donors have withdrawn from funding projects in the region.

Beyond the practical short-term issues, however, more theoretical concerns were raised by grant recipients, not least the problem that, although prospective grant recipients could design projects and take them to MEPI, there is a tendency for MEPI to fund things 'specific to their view of development'. As one grant recipient noted, 'this isn't helping, it's meddling' (ibid.). This was followed by complaints that MEPI was not 'doing evaluations of their own performances because they are the ones with the money'(ibid.). There were further complaints that grants were being made from embassies based on existing personal relationships and networks, and that it was difficult for small NGOs to 'break into this' and cultivate the same sorts of relationships required in the donor–recipient nexus. Evidently, although MEPI is increasingly funding civil society organisations, there are still issues regarding the power relationship this represents in a region with strong colonial awareness and sensitivity. Grant recipients were clearly aware of these issues as they often provided a frame of reference during discussions, but, as one grant recipient argued, 'I don't care about the source [of funding], it is [about the] purpose ... you have to ask yourself, what [is] my project [about], what is my strategy for helping the human right situation here; that need[s] money'(ibid.).

The shift towards further engaging with civil society in a more sustained and frequent basis, through the Forum for the Future, the Internet Freedom Agenda and MEPI's local grants programme, was making the Obama administration's Freedom Agenda more distinctive and marked a partial evolution of the Freedom Agenda's institutionalisation. There has, of course, always been a focus on reform-orientated programming, but under the Bush administration this was often limited and conservative and was clearly not digital given that sites such as Facebook and Twitter had little momentum until the last years of the Bush administration.[3] Thus, the Obama administration's policy was more salient and distinctive in the manner in which it quantitatively and qualitatively engaged with civil society. This shift has been noted by grant recipients, with one commenting that under Obama there was a less 'imperialist and colonial way of thinking of things'. These perceptions appear to reflect the Obama administration's more amenable and consultative approach, and demonstrate certain benefits gained from the administration's insight that 'fundamentally change comes from within. If you believe that, then that is where you have to invest' (Wittes 2011). The Obama administration's strategy represents the beginning of a partial shift from a Freedom Agenda focusing on 'democracy promotion', to a policy of 'democracy support'. This has powerful implications because as this strategy is further developed it may well offer an innovative route for US policy to take in the region. Such a strategy offers the possibility of potentially removing the imperialist modalities of informal rule and seeking to genuinely empower the peoples of the region to take charge of their own politics and economics. The possibilities of the 2011 revolutions would therefore offer the chance not only for the region to transition to democracy, but also for the USA to transition from a policy of informal rule to genuine dialogue, engagement and empowerment.

With the Freedom Agenda beginning to demonstrate a more pragmatic approach, less driven by utopian visions of remaking the region to fit neoliberal principles, it may well be able to escape the serious issues the Bush administration's imperial strategy brought with it. Indeed, supporting the people of the region to reach their goals and achieve their aspirations is dramatically different to socially engineering the societies of that region to fit US interests. Providing access to information and tools to empower and mobilise people against oppressive regimes, through open access on the internet, does not carry the same problems as seeking to impose an imperial right on the region. Indeed, the importance of the tactics and guidance provided on movements.org, for example, is that it does not discriminate between groups. Provided they have access to the internet the information about best practice is free and openly available to liberal civil society movements and Islamist movements. The site does not limit access to information based on ideology or geography in the same way that direct civil society work with the US government does. This creates an important distinction in what promises to be an expanding area of democracy support in the digitised twenty-first century. There is a difference between supporting people to be free through their own labours to achieve the type of society they demand and want to construct and a society that is subjugated to the social experiments and rules of another. It is the difference between supporting the rights of a people to have their own negative liberty and move *away from tyranny*, rather than the USA attempting to impose its own positive conception of liberty upon the region and attempting to steer it towards a US-inspired free market utopia. Given this, it is unfortunate that the Obama administration was late in developing this approach and that it was such a limited part of the Obama administration's Freedom Agenda.

The Obama administration's incremental emphasis on 'engaging beyond the state', 'civil society partnerships' and partial digitisation of the Freedom Agenda is indicative of the way the Obama administration was attempting to develop new strategic thinking before the 2011 revolutions. Thus, as President Obama declared to the UN General Assembly:

> Civil society is the conscience of our communities and America will always extend our engagement abroad with citizens beyond the halls of government. And we will call out those who suppress ideas and serve as a voice for those who are voiceless. We will promote new tools of communication so people are empowered to connect with one another and, in repressive societies, to do so with security.
>
> (Obama 2010, September 23)

This was part of what some within the administration referred to as developing the 'long-term plan' for democracy promotion in the MENA (State Department Official B 2011). As these developments began to lay discursive tracks, the

President increasingly began to concern himself with what this would mean for the MENA, issuing a five-page memorandum called *Political Reform in the Middle East and North Africa* to senior members of his foreign policy team on August 12, 2010. Accounts of the memo assert that it began by arguing that 'progress toward political reform and openness in the Middle East and North Africa lags behind other regions and has, in some cases, stalled' (in Lizza 2011). The President continued by arguing that there was, however, 'evidence of growing citizen discontent with the region's regimes . . . [and] if present trends continue . . . [MENA allies would] opt for repression rather than reform to manage domestic dissent' (in Lizza 2011). This marked the beginnings of the President seriously attempting to strategise how to deal with the conflict of interests problem and move the Freedom Agenda forward. He argued that:

> Increased repression could threaten the political and economic stability of some of our allies, leave us with fewer capable, credible partners who can support our regional priorities, and further alienate citizens in the region . . . our regional and international credibility will be undermined if we are seen or perceived to be backing repressive regimes and ignoring the rights and aspirations of citizens.
>
> (in Lizza 2011)

Obama's solution was to instruct Samantha Power, Gayle Smith, the Special Assistant to the President and Senior Director at the NSC, and Dennis Ross, the Special Assistant to the President and Senior Director for Central Region at the NSC, to develop a 'tailored' approach to the region looking at 'country by country' strategies for political reform. In essence the President had asked them to evaluate the costs and benefits of undertaking a conservative approach to the region. The results of this review challenged the assumption that modernisation or sequencing, through the free market or development, was a prerequisite for democratisation. Rather 'all roads led to political reform'. Moreover, it began challenging the 'conflict of interests' problem itself, asserting for example that Egyptian cooperation on counter-terrorism and relations with Israel were in fact in the regime's interest too, which would provide more room for the Obama administration to challenge the regime without greatly jeopardising these other interests (Lizza 2011). However, just as this review was being finished in mid-December 2010, events triggering the removal of Ben Ali were being set in motion that would culminate in the precise form of instability the conservative side of the Freedom Agenda was designed to avoid.

The 2011 revolutions: a pragmatic approach to regional instability

The sudden collapse of Ben Ali's regime in Tunisia, followed by the fall of Mubarak in Egypt, the removal of Colonel Gaddafi in Libya and the multiple resistance struggles sparked throughout 2011, marked a period of crisis in the MENA. Protracted problems with changing demographics, economic stagnation, alienation and human rights abuses generated enough anger within these countries to challenge long-standing autocratic regimes and ferment instability. Notably, these were the conditions that the Bush administration had highlighted as problematic when constructing the Freedom Agenda, and they were the problems that the Obama administration was increasingly recognising as troublesome throughout 2009 and 2010. They were the problems that the conservative side of the Freedom Agenda, within both administrations, intended to militate against, and therefore prevent the instability of 2011 taking shape. That is to say, the long-term gradual reform of these regimes was intended to ensure that the events of 2011 did not unfold, and that the region remained stable, with 'partnerships' amenable to US interests. The revolutions started in 2011 may well represent a serious step forward for the MENA eventually becoming more democratic, although this remains to be seen, but equally they represent the ultimate failure of the Freedom Agenda and the gradualism that underpinned its strategic thinking. Simply put, the Freedom Agenda was attempting to control the uncontrollable, and the USA failed to recognise the speed at which these transformations would take shape; as is often the case, events outpaced policy.

Both the surprise and the strategic challenges presented by the 2011 revolutions were evident in the Obama administration's reactions. Although Mohammed Bouazizi's self-immolation had occurred on December 17, 2010, and there were growing protests throughout Tunisia by early January, it was clear that the holiday season in Washington, DC, left the administration ill prepared to keep pace with events (Ghattas 2011). Moreover, there was a low US diplomatic profile in the country, in spite of MEPI having a regional office in Tunis, which reflected the low priority the US government afforded the Ben Ali regime (State Department Official C 2011). Before the revolution, the basis of this relationship was largely around counter-terrorism and Ben Ali's attempts to eradicate the main political opposition party in the country, the Islamic Tendency Movement (*Mouvement da la Tendance Islamique*, MTI), also known as En-Nahda (Renaissance). As Yahia H. Zoubir argues:

> Ben Ali, a resolute enemy of political Islam, sought to counter En-Nahda through an economic modernisation program and the mobilisation of the middle class . . . The regime imprisoned and tortured thousands of En-Nahda sympathisers . . . the Tunisian government obtained support from the US and France for its policy of eradicating Islamists.
>
> (Zoubir 2009: 254)

Once the protests were under way, the Obama administration resorted to its default approach of not taking sides, but urged the Ben Ali regime to demonstrate restraint and respect the right of protesters to assembly. With the removal of Ben Ali on January 14, the Obama administration moved forward by voicing its wish for free and fair elections in Tunisia. Just 11 days later, however, the onset of a much larger policy issue for the USA began to take hold, as hundreds of thousands of Egyptians took to the streets on the January 25 'Day of Revolt'.

Once again, the Obama administration appeared surprised and thoroughly underprepared as events began to unfold. Hillary Clinton's initial reaction was to assert that:

> We support the fundamental right of expression and assembly for all people, and we urge that all parties exercise restraint and refrain from violence. But our assessment is that the Egyptian Government is stable and is looking for ways to respond to the legitimate needs and interests of the Egyptian people.
> (Clinton 2011, January 25)

As one senior state department official told this author, 'we were expecting something to happen eventually, as there was a problem with the model in region, but we didn't expect it in 2011; to happen so soon' (Senior State Department Official B 2011). Nevertheless, as violence in and around Tahrir Square increased, and the protests began to swell around the country, the administration broke with its non-interference strategy and, on February 1, Obama spoke with Mubarak and made a public statement on the situation. He asserted that:

> Throughout this period, we've stood for a set of core principles. First, we oppose violence . . . Second, we stand for universal values, including the rights of the Egyptian people to freedom of assembly, freedom of speech, and the freedom to access information . . . Third, we have spoken out on behalf of the need for change . . . the status quo is not sustainable and . . . change must take place . . . what I indicated tonight to President Mubarak – is my belief that an orderly transition must be meaningful, it must be peaceful, and it must begin now.
> (Obama 2011, February 1)

The following day, pro-Mubarak demonstrators rode into Tahrir Square on camels and horses to beat protesters, in what was the start of a protracted battle, lasting until the military stepped in to restore relative calm. This merely added to Washington's sense of frustration with the Mubarak regime and on February 10, after Mubarak made a speech but failed to announce his departure, President Obama unequivocally declared that:

> The Egyptian people have been told that there was a transition of authority, but it is not yet clear that this transition is immediate, meaningful or sufficient . . . The Egyptian government must put forward a credible, concrete and unequivocal path toward genuine democracy, and they have not yet seized that opportunity . . . We therefore urge the Egyptian government to move swiftly to explain the changes that have been made, and to spell out in clear and unambiguous language the step by step process that will lead to democracy and the representative government that the Egyptian people seek.
> (Obama 2011, February 10)

The next day Mubarak finally stepped down, leaving the Supreme Council of the Armed Forces (SCAF), headed by Field Marshall Mohamed Hussein Tantawi, to oversee Egypt's future. Within less than three week the USA was forced to abandon an autocrat it had supported for 30 years. Serious uncertainty had been introduced into US–Egyptian relations and questions were being raised about how the USA was going to navigate the 'conflict of interests' problem in this moment of transformation.

The situations in Tunisia and Egypt were, however, only compounded by the outbreak of protests in Libya and the sudden deterioration into civil war. As an armed opposition group emerged to challenge Colonel Gaddafi's regime, it became increasingly clear that this was not going to be the start of a peaceful transition process. The Interim Transitional National Council was able to establish its authority over the cities of Benghazi and Tobruk, whilst claiming to have taken control of many other major cities throughout the country, only to be met by Colonel Gaddafi's forces. By late February and early March, Gaddafi's forces had driven the rebels back to Benghazi in a counter-offensive, and by the middle of March were threatening to take Benghazi. With European governments, the Arab League and the Gulf Cooperation Council all calling for the establishment of a no-fly zone, in response to Gaddafi's threats to crush the rebellion, the Obama administration finally decided to intervene to prevent a humanitarian disaster. Crucial to this decision were the cases made by Samantha Power and Hillary Clinton, who were able to persuade the President, over more sceptical colleagues, that intervention was the best course of action (Stolberg 2011). Consequently, the administration supported UN Security Council Resolution 1973, which authorised NATO intervention to protect civilians (see Bellamy and Williams 2011). By March 19, the Obama administration was 'leading from behind' in a NATO intervention that would last seven months and decisively contribute to the rebel victory (Lizza 2011).

The importance of the initial months of 2011 with regards to US–MENA relations was that, for the first time, the USA was faced with the practical implications of supporting democracy and breaking partnerships. No longer was this a choice concerning how best to reform the status quo and navigate the 'conflict of interests' problem. The 2011 revolutions mark a serious shift in the strategically selective context, in which strategically selective actors were operating. Events in Iran during June 2009 certainly acted as a precursor, but unlike the revolutions in 2011 there was no partnership to break. Throughout 2011 the Obama administration was forced to intervene in the unfolding crises, and, as Thomas Carothers notes, 'the administration faced a defining question of democracy support: Should it now shift gears and put democracy at the core of its policy in the Middle East?' (Carothers 2012: 29). As the conservative side of the Freedom Agenda was increasingly challenged the Obama administration once again demonstrated its preference for pragmatism. The administration sought to maintain the conservative side of the Freedom Agenda where possible, but jettisoned it in favour of pushing for democratic openings where either the USA had an interest in the transformation removing a hostile regime, or transition looked highly probable and would restore some semblance of stability. The Obama administration therefore supported democratic transitions, but tried to remain a background character in the unfolding narrative; it did not attempt to get in front of events. What the Obama administration has demonstrated is cautious, restrained and careful strategising. For example, in Morocco the USA has remained a supportive partner, largely because of intensely close security cooperation, having conferred major non-NATO ally status on the country, and King Mohamed VI's monarchy's constitutional referendum and reforms. Further still, with Saudi Arabia responding to the 2011 revolutions with financial distribution and mobilisation of security forces in the Kingdom and Bahrain, the USA has remained largely silent on human rights abuses and sought to reassure the regime that it was not going to abandon it as it had Mubarak. Yet, with Syria and Yemen, the Obama administration increasingly moved towards pushing for change as human rights abuses mounted and it was clear that Bashar al-Assad and the USA's long-time ally President Ali Abdullah Saleh were facing protracted problems with protests.

Nonetheless, once the USA had embraced the transitions in Tunisia, Egypt and Libya, the Obama administration moved swiftly to buttress democratic trends. In Tunisia and Egypt, for example, the administration spoke out in favour of democratic transitions and provided multiple sources of funding to support a new range of programmes from 'elections administration, civic education and, and political party development' (Carothers 2012: 31). As a senior state department official explained:

> the decision was made to do a lot more work with local civil society as soon as we could. . . . In Tunisia and Egypt we have done a lot of work this year . . . there has been a lot of focus on those two countries.
> (Senior State Department Official B 2011)

Before the revolution in Tunisia, for example, MEPI was dealing with around five NGOs, but afterwards demand 'skyrocketed' from both local and international NGOs. As a result MEPI began pushing out grants, and replicated this process in Egypt. The flexibility of MEPI allowed it to respond to the crises relatively swiftly, but as some admitted the fear was that in the rest of the region, 'where demand has skyrocketed, we haven't been able to respond quickly' (Senior State Department Official A 2011). The response from MEPI was first to 'throw money at Egypt and Tunisia', followed by 'coalition building amongst NGOs' and 'establish regional networks' (Senior State Department Official B 2011). Indeed, with MEPI having 10 years of institutional experience to draw from, it mobilised the MEPI alumni network, rolled out seminars on using social media as a tool for advocacy, ensured that activists met at conferences and ultimately attempted to ensure that learning was occurring throughout the ongoing revolutionary transition processes. Indeed, MEPI's response has been to consider a lot more regional programming, and establish more detailed sector-by-sector analyses of where it can strengthen networks to help continue the sharing of information that drives change. The aim is to 'grow and sustain the demand for change' (Wittes 2011).

These initial steps were intended to contribute to what the President would announce, on May 19, 2011, as a 'bold new approach to foreign policy' and US relations with the MENA. Taking centre stage in the Department of State's Benjamin Franklin room, the President argued that the 2011 revolutions were caused by a denial of dignity, a lack of political and economic self-determination throughout the region, the role of new media and the region's young demographic. He argued that Tunisia and Egypt were entering years of transition and that this process of transition would have ups and downs potentially challenging America's core interests, but that the administration would continue to 'keep our commitments to friends and partners'. However, he clearly signalled that such partnerships were problematic in the long term if autocratic regimes did not embrace reform:

> The status quo is not sustainable. Societies held together by fear and repression may offer the illusion of stability for a time, but they are built upon fault lines that will eventually tear asunder. So we face a historic opportunity ... There must be no doubt that the United States of America welcomes change that advances self-determination and opportunity.
> (Obama 2011, May 19)

What was highly evident about this apparently 'new approach to foreign policy', however, was that it was remarkably similar to Bush's Freedom Agenda and downplayed many of the incremental innovations the Obama administration had made throughout its time in office. It appealed to similar premises to those of Bush's liberal grand strategy, arguing that, 'after decades of accepting the world as it is in the region, we have a chance to pursue the world as it should be'. Within such a context, the President began to construct more of an overarching narrative for its approach to the region, setting out a liberal, albeit pragmatic, grand strategy under the headings of political reform, human rights and economic reform. The supposed new strategy would be to help support reform across the region starting with the Tunisian and Egyptian transitions to democracy, and noted the serious problems in Libya, Syria and Iran, whilst also condemning partners such as Yemen and Bahrain for their use of force; and by implication Saudi Arabia.

The President, at considerable length, detailed how the USA would support change in the region through economic reforms for nations that are transitioning to democracy, asserting that:

> America's support for democracy will therefore be built on financial stability, promoting reform, and integrating competitive markets each other and the global economy ... starting with Tunisia and Egypt.
> (Obama 2011, May 19)

He continued to argue that the problem with the region was its 'closed economies' and that the region needed 'trade' and 'not just aid'; 'investment' and 'not just assistance'; and that 'protectionism must give way to openness'. President

Obama's strategic narrative had all the hallmarks of proposed informal rule and the expectations of the imperial right, as it was announced that:

- The World Bank and IMF were to construct a plan to present to the G8 Summit about what would be needed to stabilise and modernise the economies of Tunisia and Egypt.
- Egypt would be relieved of $1 billion in debt and allocated $1 billion in loans for infrastructure.
- The USA would help to recover assets that had been stolen by members of the former regimes in Tunisia and Egypt.
- Enterprise Funds would be set up to invest in Tunisia and Egypt, modelled on the funds that helped transitions in Eastern Europe.
- OPEC would create a $2 billion facility to help support private investment.
- The USA would work with allies to refocus the European Bank for reconstruction and development so it provides the same support for democratic transitions and economic modernisation in the MENA as it has in Europe.
- It would establish a comprehensive trade and investment initiative with the MENA, working with the EU to facilitate more trade from within the region, and build on existing agreements to provide integration with the US and EU markets.
- It would help these transition countries 'tear down the walls' that stand in the way of progress and help them fulfil their 'international obligations' (see Obama 2011, May 19).

Conspicuously, shortly after this speech Egypt rejected the IMF offer of a $3.2 billion loan, arguing that it would be an infringement of Egyptian sovereignty to accept a loan requiring 'mandatory reforms and austerity measures, like cutting food and fuel subsides' (NYT 2012). Although Egypt wanted the money, it did not want to accept the neoliberal logic that underpinned the loan. It had rejected the offer of informal rule. However, by early 2012, with falling foreign currency reserves, Egypt was succumbing to reopening the loan request with an IMF delegation (Kirkpatrick 2012). This was indicative of the Obama administration's emphasis on the same rationale that underpinned MEFTA and much of the Bush administration's Freedom Agenda. In spite of all the grand assertions of a 'new approach' the administration had returned to the logic of the imperial right that underpinned the Bush administration's IDF. The overarching narrative presented by Obama foregrounded the typical aspects of a neoliberal approach, at a time when neoliberalism was facing a serious crisis as an approach to political economy in the USA and Europe. In effect the Obama administration's new approach was remarkably similar to that institutionalised by the Bush administration throughout the post-crisis period of September 11, 2001, demonstrating how entrenched the logic of the Freedom Agenda had become as a policy paradigm.

This demonstrated that, in spite of the evolutionary steps the new administration had made to make its own agenda distinctive, ultimately these were largely peripheral to the default appeal of neoliberalism, and the definition of freedom that had underpinned the conservative dimension of the Freedom Agenda. Such a definition was at odds with the problems and the solutions being presented by protesters in Tahrir Square. It was not a definition of freedom underpinned by economic liberalisation that they were willing to die for, but rather a plethora of messages surrounding issues of human rights, social justice, adherence to the Islamic faith in one form or another and equality (Hassan 2011a). Economic issues were of course a large part of why these protests took place; Mohammed Bouazizi's self-immolation was after all in part a protest against economic helplessness which resonated beyond Sidi Bouzid. However, it was the former Egyptian regime that had embraced the neoliberal logic of Bush's Freedom Agenda most swiftly, and, as protesters in Tahrir Square complained, all it brought was inequality whereby the Egyptian Army and members of the Mubarak regime profited, creating greater inequality throughout the country (Hassan 2011a).

Given the profound nature of the 2011 revolutions, it was therefore a major problem that the Obama administration was unable to construct a new paradigm for the region and the US approach to democracy promotion. This was not because the USA was pursuing a sound policy programme, but rather that there was a serious lack of grand policy innovation within the administration, and the Obama administration has been unable to develop a strategy for dealing with the landscape presented by the conflict of interests problem. With the USA constructing its interests around conceptions of global military reach, its security relationship with Israel and access to the region's resource in the carbon economy, the strategically selective context in which the Obama administration could strategise remained limited. Ultimately, US policy choices remain shaped by the landscape set out by the conflict of interests, and, in spite of multiple efforts to reform the status quo, the Freedom Agenda failed. The USA has lost the grand strategy 'gradualism' provided, and has little by way of an alternative strategy in response. To substitute this, the Obama administration was pragmatic in its response, but has ultimately failed in constructing a policy that allows it to delineate when to push regimes towards democratisation, and when to ensure continued cooperation on economic and security issues. This of course is not to say that the administration did not attempt to adjust, but rather that the administration was slow to do so.

Attempting to adjust to the new strategically selective context, wherein Islamist parties have proved to be successful in elections, Israeli security is less guaranteed by allies and Iran has increasingly behaved provocatively, did, however, rise up the administration's agenda by late 2011. Having appointed William B. Taylor as Special Coordinator for Transitions in September 2011, the Obama administration sought to move beyond the traditional approach to the region and help support transitions across the region. As Ambassador Taylor argued, 'it is important to us that the transitions succeed' (Taylor 2011), and consequently the administration has constructed a position from which to coordinate policy between the US government and other global and regional actors. Taylor has also been placed in charge of efforts to coordinate the efforts of America's democracy bureaucracy, spread out across the Department of State, USAID, the DRL and MEPI, to ensure a greater level of coherence. Thus the Obama administration's approach increasingly attempted to coordinate the Freedom Agenda institutions in combination with other parts of government, and therefore ensure that the response is done in what has been considered a 'whole government way'. This brings 'the assistance side' together with 'trade policy, whilst [also] seeing what the private sector can do, what we can do with our diaspora communities here in the US . . . and bring a lot of different pieces together' (Senior State Department Official B 2011). The newly established coordination office does not implement programmes, but rather strives to better synchronize and harmonise programme implementers, to make the democracy bureaucracy more efficient. Taylor acknowledges, however, that the US government does not have the same resources it had during previous attempts to support transitions 'in Central Europe and the former Soviet Union for example', and that the USA must therefore support transitions 'more efficiently and more creatively' (Taylor 2011). Moreover, when asked about the conflicts of interests problem and how the Obama administration was attempting to overcome it, Taylor argued at length that:

> This is a big issue that is very important. We are looking at it very carefully and giving it a lot of attention, to deciding how can we do both our principles, the principles of democratic transitions and democratic governance and minority rights, women's rights, assembly, expression; those principles that are important to us. Reconciling those with our interests, in the Egypt–Israel peace treaty, transit rights, over flight rights etc. . . . in particular with Egypt. Finding the right balance, in each individual country is going to be important, but I think that this administration has been very clear that it puts a very high importance on the principles side, and democratic government, and democratic ideals. In the past we let interest dominate, but this administration has been clear that principles will guide us. We have problems all the time and we will have compromises in the short term, but in the medium to long term the focus is on democratic governance in this part of the world, like other parts of the world, will be in our interest.
>
> (Taylor 2011)

Nonetheless, when pressed about whether this will be done on an ad hoc basis or through an institutional mechanism, it was clear that the National Security Council and the interagency process would continue to govern such decisions on an ad hoc basis. Moreover, as a senior State Department official added:

> All of those other interests we pursued over the decades are still our interests. They haven't changed, but the environment in which we pursue them has changed fundamentally, therefore our foreign policy has to change in response. That's the way the President articulated it in May [2011], that's the new policy. We are working on the premise that these things will come into alignment, and we will work to bring them into alignment by helping to cultivate the changes that are needed which will bring them into alignment.
>
> (Senior State Department Official A 2011)

This echoed the message presented by Hillary Clinton in her keynote address to the National Democratic Institute on November 7, 2011, in which the Secretary of State argued that:

> transitions are filled with uncertainty . . . We believe that real democratic change in the Middle East and North Africa is in the national interest of the United States . . . Why does America promote democracy one way in some countries and another way in others? Well, the answer starts with a very practical point: situations vary dramatically from country to country. It would be foolish to take a one-size-fits-all approach and barrel forward regardless of circumstances on the ground . . . Our choices also reflect other interests in the region with a real impact on Americans' lives – including our fight against al-Qaida, defense of our allies, and a secure supply of energy. Over time, a more democratic Middle East and North Africa can provide a more sustainable basis for addressing all three of those challenges. But there will be times when not all of our interests align. We work to align them, but that is just reality . . . As a country with many complex interests, we'll always have to walk and chew gum at the same time.
>
> (Clinton 2011, November 7)

In essence, the Secretary of State's address asserted many of the ideas that had underpinned the construction of the Freedom Agenda back in 2002. This demonstrated how the Bush administration had laid the discursive tracks leading to the institutionalisation of the Freedom Agenda in the crisis narrative set out after September 11, 2001, but over a decade later the USA was struggling with the same 'conflict of interests' problem. Only now, with the conservative side of the Freedom Agenda having demonstrably failed, the USA was faced with the Islamist dilemma it had been reluctant to embrace, and the increased level of instability that it sought to avoid. Ultimately the Freedom Agenda, born out of crisis, had failed as a policy paradigm and the Obama administration was pragmatically attempting to navigate the contours of yet another crisis in a period of the USA's declining influence in the region.

Conclusion

In the immediate aftermath of the 2011 revolutions there was considerable debate concerning the role the USA had played in bringing about these events. Multiple media outlets and commentators were asking whether the Bush administration's Freedom Agenda contributed directly or indirectly to the uprisings. Whereas the Bush administration was keen to suggest that this may well be the case, and that events had vindicated their strategy, a closer analysis of the Freedom Agenda reveals a far more problematic picture than the one they have chosen to narrate. Having traced the construction and institutionalisation of this policy by the Bush administration, it is clear that the policy recognised the symptoms, but ultimately failed to prescribe the right policy. Thus, although former members of the Bush administration may well be attempting to construct a legacy underpinned by a simplistic mythology of the Freedom Agenda, it is clear that, just as Reagan did not bring down the Berlin Wall, G. W. Bush did not lead the protests in Tahrir Square. Moreover, it should be stated that the removal of heads of state in Tunisia, Egypt, Libya and Yemen is not equivalent to predestined democratic transition. It may well be a useful start to such a process, but there is no guarantee that these states will inevitably transition to democracy. Within this context, the 2011 revolutions may have done more for international democracy support than international democracy support ever did for the 2011 revolutions.[1]

By challenging the official representation of the Freedom Agenda, the research presented here reveals the imperial pitfalls of the approach the Bush administration constructed, the limitations of the approaches to institutionalisation and ultimately the conservative manner in which the policy was pursued. The importance of this cannot be overstated given that the Obama administration not only inherited these problems, but has largely embraced them in its response to regional unrest. Yet, beyond these empirical issues, what this research has shown, through the development of the constructivist institutionalist approach, is that there is a benefit in theorising and analysing post-crisis policy making. By tracing the IDF that underpins policy construction, it was possible to generate a highly detailed and rigorous understanding of how and why the Freedom Agenda was developed, and what cumulative and evolutionary steps and obstacles led to its institutionalisation. It simultaneously allowed a return to first-order questions, to address what the Bush administration meant by the terms 'freedom' and 'democracy', and how these definitions translated into a policy of conservative radicalism.

Conclusion

By setting out an approach that was explicit in detailing its ontological and epistemological foundations, the manner in which it conceptualised the role of structure and agency, ideas and material, and continuity and change, an ordering framework was established that drove this empirically rich research. Its strength lies in the fact that it is philosophically rigorous, has an interdisciplinary focus and is capable of theorising the complex processes of continuity and change. By combining critical and historical analysis, the strengths of this methodology have come to fruition in this research, and have proved intrinsic to guiding its empirical focus and findings. Notably, the constructivist institutionalist methodology was able to theorise the relationship between the events of September 11, 2001, and the development of the Freedom Agenda, rather than simply asserting a relationship based on their succession in time. This is a meaningful contribution, as it highlights the central role of September 11, 2001, and the manner in which it marked a moment of punctuation in US–MENA relations. The implications of this assertion are evident throughout this research, in which it was shown that the 2000 presidential campaign set the stage for the future Bush administration to outline a distinctive IDF. This appropriated and articulated primacy, hegemonic stability theory, neoliberalism and modernisation thesis into a distinctive formation, which in turn, sedimented particular definitions of concepts such as 'power', 'peace', 'democracy' and 'freedom'. The importance of this cannot be overestimated.

From January to September 2001, President Bush was asserting the need for continuity in US–MENA relations. The most prominent reform in this interregional relationship was Bush's decoupling strategy vis-à-vis the peace process and Iraq. However, this situation changed as a result of the events of September 11, 2001, generating a moment of punctuation in political time. This moment of punctuation created a space for Bush's distinct IDF to be strategically embedded within a post-crisis narrative, which laid discursive tracks for the evolution of the Freedom Agenda. This post-crisis narrative foregrounded the concept of 'freedom' and asserted that America was attacked because it was 'free'. What was remarkable about such a depoliticising conclusion was the absence of detailed expansive studies into the 'causes' of terrorism to justify this assertion. To deal with the uncertainty created as a result of September 11, 2001, the Bush administration primarily utilised logics arising out of the post-Cold War era, the perceived need for an overarching rationale for US foreign policy, and a reconstructed sense of America as 'exceptional'. That is to say, the form of change that followed the moment of punctuation was largely an endogenous product of how strategically selective actors viewed the strategically selective context. Consequently, it is safe to conclude that post-Cold War identity politics proved to be a critical dynamic in shaping the post-crisis narrative, and played a vital role in the eventual evolution of the Freedom Agenda.

Understanding the role of post-Cold War identity politics allows a more generalisable point to be made. September 11, 2001, was not epochal and certainly did not, as the Bush administration argued, 'change everything'. Rather, the nature of political change is more akin to that of a 'kaleidoscope'. Indeed, this is a metaphor deployed by the British Prime Minister Tony Blair in his response to September 11, 2001:

Conclusion   183

This is a moment to seize. The kaleidoscope has been shaken. The pieces are in flux. Soon they will settle again. Before they do, let us reorder this world around us.

(Blair 2001, October 2)

This vignette is instructive because it captures a certain quality about political continuity and change that was evident in the process-tracing narrative discourse analysis carried out through this research: namely, that discourses are important in the conduct of foreign policy, and when moments of punctuation occur they can be reconstructed by articulating them into a different formation. This suggests that there is always a binding with the past, as these discourses have genealogies, but when placed in a different formation they can lead to political change.[2] The Freedom Agenda was a product of exactly this sort of situation, in which a new strategically constituted narrative grasped together multiple factors to construct a plot that guided a new policy paradigm towards the Middle East policy.

Understanding the Freedom Agenda required reconstructing the context from which it arose, and fundamentally analysing the post-crisis narrative that guided its institutionalisation. From doing so, this research has demonstrated that the Freedom Agenda constituted a new policy paradigm in US–MENA relations, which was a product of a cumulative post-crisis policy making process. Thus, events following September 11 were analysed in this research not based on the notion that 'history is just one damn thing after another', but rather, because events, such as the war in Afghanistan, the Bletchley II meeting and the Iraq war, all added to how strategically selective actors viewed the strategically selective context. As a result, what was considered feasible, practical and desirable changed, and out of this reformulation the Freedom Agenda was perceived to be in America's national interest, and institutionalised as a new paradigm. The historical narrative presented in this research, therefore, demonstrates that policy evolves over time as policy-makers try to solve policy puzzles in conditions of uncertainty. Consequently, they develop and deploy specific IDFs (embedded within narratives) to support their strategic actions, and legitimise the policy directions they have constructed within institutional settings.

Policy making is not, however, an exact science. Herein, despite the Bush administration attempting to make democracy promotion *the* central objective of US–MENA relations, both in the form of creating a domino effect after the Iraq war and through the Freedom Agenda institutions, it became clear that the new paradigm was problematic. Whilst the administration gradually recognised that the war on terror could not be fought through military means alone, promoting democracy in the MENA proved to be more difficult than the Bush administration had originally conceived. In the belief that 'freedom' was a universal value, and the natural political arrangement societies would adopt if authoritarian rule was removed, the Bush administration lowered the bar of how difficult promoting democracy in the MENA would be. Indeed, with a growing insurgency in Iraq, and the democratic victory of Hamas in the 2006, it was clear that the Freedom Agenda withdrew to relying on its neoliberal core, and became characterised by both conservative and radical dynamics. As a result, the Freedom Agenda was strongly committed to regional stability and the gradual reform of ally regimes, whilst seeking to challenge regimes hostile to the USA. This realisation adds to the existing debate about the Freedom Agenda, because it generates a more complex understanding of the policy, and consequently moves the debate forward. Indeed, the Bush administration's vision for the Middle East is made considerably clearer once it is acknowledged that the United States sought to promote democracy because it believed that this would tip the global 'balance of power' in the USA's favour and subsequently assure continued US preponderance and ascendancy. It was not democracy in and of itself that was being advocated, but rather democracy that would suit perceived US interests. By highlighting the conservative radicalism dyad, this research illustrates a fundamental tension in US–MENA relations: September 11 may have changed the manner in which the USA viewed the Middle East, but it merely compounded the perceived need for short-term cooperation in the pursuit of other more immediate security goals. Where this occurred, the Bush administration consistently gave priority to the latter, justified with particular definitions of justice and the need for security. Consequently, this research has demonstrated that the Freedom Agenda was contradictory at best, and, at worst, a legitimising concept for the pursuit of US preponderance over the MENA. It was ultimately a policy caught between pursuing democracy and domination. The implications of this clearly demonstrate that, despite the constant repetition of the word 'freedom', which became the trope of the war on terror, elevated to chief purveyor of legitimacy and idol of the tribe, it was necessary to look past this essentially contested term and return to first-order questions about how the Freedom Agenda was constituted.

The narrative presented by the White House obfuscated the degree to which there were tensions in the administration over the institutionalisation of the Freedom Agenda. Indeed, the 'official' narrative wrote out the extent to which members of the Department of Defense and Department of State were hostile to the Freedom Agenda. This was a particularly fecund finding of this research, as it reveals how the 'conflict of interest' problem was difficult for the administration to address throughout its time in office, and in spite of its proclaimed new policy paradigm. Moreover, it demonstrates how a mismatch between regional specialists and the growing democracy bureaucracy proved to be an obstacle in coordinating and entrenching the Freedom Agenda. Herein, it is safe to conclude that, despite President Bush's grand rhetoric, a more complex reality was unfolding within the administration itself. More generally, however, it has been shown that the USA struggles to promote democracy, because it is not clear how best to do so. This accounts for the ad hoc programmes the Freedom Agenda institutions pursued, and was reflected in J. Scott Carpenter's assertion that 'we don't know yet how best to promote democracy . . . there are times when you throw spaghetti against the wall and see if it sticks' (Finkel 2005). Despite this insight, however, it was unambiguously clear that the Bush administration relied on ideological convictions, rather than detailed empirical subscriptions, in its assertions that the democratisation process could be brought about by subscribing to neoliberal reforms and modernisation thesis.

Given such an analysis it is unfortunate that the Obama administration's conservative pragmatist approach has increasingly embraced many of the key notions embedded within the Bush administration's IDF. Many of the universal and exceptionalist notions that underpinned Bush's rhetoric have been evident in Obama administration's thinking, along with a renewed appreciation for the role of neoliberalism, and refreshed appeals to democratic peace theory. This is particularly distressing as the Obama administration had in fact laid the path to a distinctive, less imperial strategy through the digitisation of the Freedom Agenda and the engagement and empowerment of civil society. What is revealed in this analysis is that these strategies may well help move the Freedom Agenda institutions forward in a less imperial fashion, and therefore help provide answers to moral and normative questions about the desire to support democracy in a manner that is respectful of negative liberty and heeds the warnings put forward by Isaiah Berlin about imposing models of positive liberty. In effect they may well lay the foundations for a post-colonial approach to democracy support for the twenty-first century, which embraces dialogue, empowerment and respect. These distinctive approaches seem to lay the foundations for a light footprint approach to democracy support, whereby the focus of the activity is to empower people with tools and networks to move away peacefully from tyranny, rather than seeking to socially engineer peoples towards some outside-inspired utopian end state.

Nonetheless, the prevailing feature of the Obama administrations approach to democracy promotion has been its conterminous nature with that of Bush's Freedom Agenda, and the manner in which the 'conflict of interests' problem dominated the policy before and after the 2011 revolutions. The Obama administration clearly needed to be more innovative than embracing a discredited strategy, and needed to establish a new paradigm for US–MENA relations to deal with the profound nature of change initiated by the 2011 revolutions. The administration was clearly slow in doing this, which was unsurprising given the size of the democracy bureaucracy and the strategically selective context in which US policy operates in the region. However, until the USA creates enough space for policy innovation it will remain stuck with a conservative and reactionary policy; a policy caught between indigenous demands for democracy and the US domination of the region to secure its interests.

Notes

1 American interests and a history of promoting the status quo

1 A term used by William L. Westermann to describe the interwar Middle East (cited in Oren 2007: 380).
2 Of particular importance is Point Twelve of the Fourteen Points Plan presented to Congress in January 1918.
3 For a lineal account of US democracy promotion see Tony Smith (1994).
4 This acronym stands for *Advance Democratic Values, Address Nondemocratic Countries, and Enhance Democracy Act.*
5 Although Britain and France retained influence in the region into the 1960s and the 1970s, their place as the hegemonic external powers was gradually being eroded by the USA (Halliday 2005: 95).
6 This broke an agreement made at the London conference of ministers in September 1945. It had been agreed that Soviet troop withdrawal would be completed no later than March 2, 1946 (Truman 1956: 98).
7 This was originally done in partnership with Britain until the 1950s. Spurred by the failure to establish either the Middle East Command or the Middle East Defence Organisation, US officials increasingly questioned the ability of Britain to protect Western interests in the region (see Hahn 2005: 15). The 1956 Suez Crisis exacerbated this, leading to the USA taking a 'leadership' role and becoming the primary 'Western' power in the region.
8 For a systematic analysis of how economic aid was conceptualised from 1947 through to the 1970s see Packenham (1973).
9 This figure is in constant-dollar data and combines loans and grants given to 'Near East' countries.
10 In 2009, US economic assistance totalled $33946.9 million, and the region received $5439.0 million. In the same year, US military assistance around the globe totalled $13681.3 million, and the region received $6668.9 million (figures available from USAID 2011).
11 In 1955 coal provided 75 per cent of total energy use in Western Europe, and petroleum just 23 per cent. By 1972, coal's share had shrunk to 22 per cent, while oil's had risen to 60 per cent. This was almost a complete reversal (Yergin 1991: 545).
12 Assistance from the USA has consisted of two thirds military assistance to one third economic aid.
13 The Arabic name translates as 'Islamic Resistance Movement'.
14 It should be noted that Mansfield and Snyder (2005: 14, 283) themselves do not oppose democracy promotion, but rather favour a cautious approach.
15 Notably the signatories of this letter included Elliott Abrams, Richard L. Armitage, William J. Bennett, Jeffrey Bergner, John Bolton, Paula Dobriansky, Francis Fukuyama, Robert Kagan, Zalmay Khalilzad, William Kristol, Richard Perle, Peter W. Rodman, Donald Rumsfeld, William Schneider, Jr., Vin Weber, Paul Wolfowitz,

R. James Woolsey and Robert B. Zoellick. Many of theses individuals later became key members of the Bush administration, but not all would be considered neoconservatives.
16 This was evident in the Republican-led House, which voted 296–133, and the Democrat-led Senate, which voted 72–23 (Reid 2002: 20).
17 Here 'sedimentation' refers to the concealment of an original act of institutionalisation, and 'reactivation' is to make such acts visible again (see Laclau and Mouffe 2001: viii).

2 A constructivist institutionalist methodology

1 This has also been termed discursive, ideational, and economic constructivism (see Schmidt 2006: 109; Hay 2006: 56; Campbell and Pedersen 2001: 193–275).
2 This could read as methodological individualism. This is not the intention. To argue that the micro level is ontologically primary is not the same as saying the macro level is ontologically non-existent or constitutive in some way. What is being questioned is the status; actions and conditions must be accounted for. Levels exist in relation to one another through collective intentionality.
3 For an excellent overview of new institutionalist scholarship see Peters (2005), Steinmo, Thelen and Longstreth (1992) and Campbell and Pedersen (2001).
4 Thus, even Kenneth Waltz's neorealist position explicitly asserts that states are not and have never been the only actors, but that they are the *most important actors*. More recently, he has argued that:

> Structures condition behaviours and outcomes, yet explanations of behaviours and outcomes are indeterminate because both unit-level and structural causes are in play... structures shape and shove. They do not determine behaviours... the shaping and shoving of structures may be resisted... with skill and determination structural constraints can sometimes be countered.
> (Waltz 1986: 343)

This is a significant admission highlighting that even the most systemic theories cannot do without both structure and agency if they are to withstand critique (see Hollis and Smith 1991: 92–118). Indeed, as Stanley Rosen (2003: x) points out, the intelligibility of structure requires the 'absence of structure'.

5 This has a striking similarity to Onuf's assertion that:

> When we, as human beings, act as agents, we have goals in mind, even if we are not fully aware of them when we act. If someone asks us to think about the matter, we can usually formulate these goals more or less in the order of their importance to whomever we are acting as agents for, starting with ourselves. Most of the time, agents have limited, inaccurate, or inconsistent information about the material and social conditions that effect the likelihood of reaching given goals. Nevertheless, agents do the best they can to achieve their goals with the means that nature and society (together – always together) make available to them.
> (Onuf 1998: 60)

6 This term is being used because it is an accepted term in philosophy and therefore carries with it a conceptual baggage that I want to introduce. The term literally means 'being-there', referring to an inquiring entity (Heidegger 1967: 28–9):

> The essence of Dasein lies in its existence. Accordingly those characteristics which can be exhibited in this entity are not 'properties' present-at-hand of some entity which looks so and so and is itself more than that... so when we designate this entity with the term 'Dasein', we are expressing not its what (as if it were a table, house or tree) but its being.

7 Relatedly Dasein has free will in the sense of its ability to choose how it will be, and lives through its possibilities. It is always engaged with the world and the entities within it. This conception is fundamental to transcending the Cartesian dualism upon which mind/body and agency/structure are separated.
8 Note that this is intentionality-with-a-t, which is a property of the mind by which it is directed at or about or of objects and states of affairs in the world independent of itself. This should not be confused with intensionality-with-an-s (see Searle 2004: 122–5).
9 Not duality, which implies separation, much like the morphogenetic approach.
10 Weldes notes that the concept of interest is itself a construction. The very notion that interests motivate action and therefore should be referred to in explanations of behaviour and social outcomes is itself a relatively new concept that came with the rise of liberalism and capitalism (Weldes 1996: 306).
11 For alternative constructivist conceptions of the national interest see Wendt (1999), Finnemore (1996b) and Chafetz, Spirtas and Frankel (1999). For an excellent overview of this literature see Burchill (2005).
12 The Weldes version of constructing the national interest places a clear emphasis on agency in constructing the national interest. Finnemore, however, stresses normative structures.
13 The reason I have termed these 'naturalist assumptions' is the manner in which Jepperson, Wendt and Katzenstein (1996: 65) refer to the methodologies espoused throughout the book as explanatory in their engagement with 'normal science', and thus posit 'causal effects either of identities or of the cultural/institutional content of global or domestic environment'. For a more thorough critique see Ruggie (1998b: esp. 38); however, it should be noted that because it is an edited book the extent to which naturalism is subscribed to varies across authors.
14 The emergence of this definition has largely arisen from the observed empirical regularity that 'ideational change invariably precedes institutional change' (Hay 2006: 66).
15 For a detailed account of this and other approaches to social change see Boudon (1986: esp. 16–18).
16 'The crisis which resulted from Khrushchev's decision secretly to install intermediate and medium-range nuclear missiles in Cuba in 1962' (Young and Kent 2004: 236).
17 According to Kennedy's National Security Advisor, McGeorge Bundy, 'most of us agreed with McNamara's summary judgement at the outset, that the Cuban Missiles did not change the strategic balance – not at all' (Weldes 1999a: 95). For an excellent account see Errol Morris's film *The Fog of War*.
18 It involves the encoding and ascription of meaning to events, in order to represent them to the recipient narratees for the process of active interpellative decoding.
19 Since Aristotle's *Poetics*, narrative has been regarded as a temporal sequencing of events into a beginning, middle and end (see Dienstag 1997: 18). The term 'emplotment' refers to the assembly of historical events into a narrative, within a plot.
20 Thus, instead of the Cartesian 'subject–object' divide, this is a distinction between 'organism' and 'environment'.
21 The term 'de-structuring' has been used here as an affinity to Gadamerian method. Notably the term is derived from the Heideggerian method of *Destruktion*. Using this term was a deliberate move by Gadamer to locate a common dimension between his hermeneutical project and the projects of both Heidegger and Derrida (see Michelfelder and Palmer 1989: 6–8).
22 Michael Barnett could be seen as adding to this argument through his assertion that narratives provide a mechanism to 'situate events and to interpret problems, to fashion shared understanding of the world, to galvanize sentiments as a way to mobilize and guide social action, and to suggest possible resolutions to current plights' (Barnett 1999: 15).

23 The impact of adopting this definition may appear to represent a fundamental contradiction to the early appeals to John Searle's work. The key point, however, is to note that with regards to truth claims this research is underpinned by a 'minimal perspectivism' or 'soft philosophical realism' and not relativism (see Prado 2006). This is akin to Richard Bernstein's (1983) *Beyond Objectivism and Relativism*.
24 Within the espoused 'critical' view ideology is not simply reducible to an ideational disposition, but rather is a modality of power (see Fairclough 2003: 9; 1992: 86–96).
25 The ideas that follow from here come from a synthesis of Hall, Weldes, Onuf and Searle. Thus it is crucial to understand that what I have done here is mix vocabularies to construct a worldview, the result of which is that I remain oblivious to the extent to which these authors would individually agree with this synthesis.
26 This research does not reduce all social practices to the discursive, that is to say it does not follow in the footsteps of Laclau and Mouffe's later work in *Hegemony and Socialist Strategy* (Laclau and Mouffe 2001). The 'worldview' stated above is clearly a rejection of anti-foundationalist discursive idealism. Given this, Stuart Hall's definition of the term is particularly instructive as 'he elevates the importance of articulating discourse to other social forces, without going "over the brink" of turning everything into discourse' (Slack 1996: 121).
27 This point reflects Searle's notion of the 'ontologically subjective'. For example we can say that the US Presidency is an observer-relative phenomenon, hence ontologically subjective, but it is an epistemically objective fact that G. W. Bush was the 43rd President (see Searle 2007: 82–4).
28 By extension this should highlight that within FPA this study sits on the hermeneutical side of the divide, and not that of behaviourism (see Hollis and Smith 1991: 68–91).
29 Note that, consistent with the above worldview, such notions are not considered causal factors.
30 To use the language of John R. Searle, the events had an intrinsic quality, but the 'crisis' is an observer-relative phenomena; as such, it is constructed. It is important to note that being a 'construct' does not make it somehow not 'real'; rather it recognises an intrinsic quality of human intentionality to project itself onto the world. Searle's analysis of money provides an excellent analogy.
31 For a more specific use of these categories see Vivien Schmidt (2000).
32 That is, dependent upon an 'outside' that both denies the positions and provides the conditions of their possibility (Du Gay *et al*.2000: 2).
33 Notably, this system was not used for data collected from autobiographies, which are referenced in the standard manner.

3 From candidate to crisis

1 Indeed President Bush later wrote in an autobiographical account of his journey to the White House:

> It was a great honor to meet president-elect Reagan . . . President Reagan was resolute in his goals and confident in his philosophy. He set a clear agenda of limited government, of economic growth through tax cuts, and of peace through strength. His Presidency was a defining one . . . President Reagan realized the greatness of America was found not in government in Washington, but in the hearts and souls of individual Americans.
>
> (Bush 2001: 177)

2 These were mainland China, Japan, France, the United Kingdom, Russia and Germany, which spent a total of approximately US$275,100 million, compared with the US military expenditure of $281,000 million.

3 All italics entered in quotes from this section on have been added by the author for emphasis, unless stated otherwise.
4 This followed advice given by President Clinton, in which he told President-elect Bush not to misjudge Arafat in the same way he had during his own attempts in the Peace Process (Rubin and Rubin 2003: 213).
5 This reflected the Bush campaign's declared approach of being selective over diplomatic engagements. Indeed, in late January 2001, the Bush administration had declined to send an envoy for final attempts at peace talks in Egypt, and later decided to abolish the post of a special envoy to the Middle East. Moreover, when Senator George Mitchell reported back with his report on the causes of the second Intifada in April 2001, his three-step peace plan was endorsed by the administration but given little political support. By June 2001, escalating violence in the region did lead the administration to make a slight reversal on the decision to disengage, leading to the President dispatching the CIA director, George Tenet, to act as a special envoy to negotiate a cease-fire. However, like the Mitchell Plan it was endorsed but given little political support by the higher echelons of the administration (Quandt 2005: 385–96; Daalder and Lindsay 2003: 66).
6 It is particularly worth adding that the Bush administration also consistently made reference to 'civilisation' as under attack, thereby expanding the 'we'. For an excellent analysis of this discourse see Richard Jackson (2005), *Writing the War on Terrorism*.
7 A clear indicator of this level of national unity and patriotism was the extent to which American flag sales increased rapidly: from September 11 to 13, 2001, Wal-Mart alone sold 450,000 and Kmart sold another 200,000 (Andrews 2007: 103).
8 The term 'sacrifice' in modern-day usage often refers to a form of transference: giving one thing for another. Yet the etymological roots of the term are from the Latin *sacrificere*, to perform priestly functions. This is derived from *sacra*, sacred rites, and *facere*, to perform.
9 For a detailed analysis of such authors views of tragedy see Jennifer Wallace's (2007) *Cambridge Introduction to Tragedy*.
10 The word 'harbor' was included after the terms 'tolerated' and 'encouraged' were considered too vague by the President (Woodward 2002: 30). Moreover it is important to note that this passage was not a spontaneous decision. Bush had made a similar claim in the 1999 Republican primaries, and consequently this assertion was drawn from and framed by previously declared policy statements (see Bush 1999, September 23).

4 September to December 2001

1 In Bob Woodward's account of September 11, 2001, he argued that President Bush decided that the day's events constituted an act of war upon being told that 'a second plane hit the second tower'. In an interview with Bob Woodward, President Bush recalled his thoughts at the time; '*They have declared war on us*, and I made up my mind at that moment that *we were going to war*' (see Woodward 2002: 15). This is repeated in G. W. Bush's (2010) autobiography *Decision Points*.
2 Instructively this metaphor is used by many members of the G. W. Bush administration, and is notable in its use because it reinforces the construction of the events of September 11, 2001, as acts of war.
3 Notably, in the immediate aftermath of September 11, 2001, presidential approval ratings soared, going from 51 per cent in a poll conducted from September 7 to 10 to 90 per cent by September 22, 2001 (Gallup 2009).
4 It should be noted that there is an American tradition of using the term 'crusade' in the figurative sense of an aggressive movement or public campaign against some public evil, which was first recorded in Jefferson's 1786 writings.

5 To eliminate monarchical rule (the War of 1812), to defeat the Catholic forces of superstition (the Mexican War), to eliminate slavery (the Civil War), to end colonialism in the Americas (the Spanish–American War), to make the world safe for democracy (the First World War) and to resist totalitarian expansion (the Second World War and Korea) (Lipset 1996: 65).

6 For example, the term 'justice', used by the administration, did not invoke Immanuel Kant's notion of retributive justice as a legal concept, in which punishment is imposed on the guilty party, and not used as a means to promote some other good. Indeed, Kant makes this point rather poignantly when he argues that:

> Judicial punishment can never be used merely as a means to promote some other good for the criminal himself or for civil society, but instead it must in all cases be imposed on him only on the ground that he has committed a crime; for a human being can never be manipulated merely as a means to the purposes of someone else and never be included among objects of the Law of things.
>
> (Kant 1999 [1797]: 331)

The moralistic crusade plot contradicts this, as the war on terror was not just about punishment per se, but described as being motivated for the greater good of 'ridding the world of evil' and 'advancing human freedom'.

7 For a legal argument supporting the case for war see Robertson (2006: 511–21). It is also important to note that the Bush administration was eager to avoid taking this into the litigious realm, which is why, for example, President Bush argued:

> I also had a responsibility to show resolve . . . No yielding. No equivocation. *No, you know, lawyering this thing to death, that we're after 'em.* And that was not only for domestic, for the people at home to see. It was also vitally important for the rest of the world to watch.
>
> (in Woodward 2002: 96)

This is corroborated by Richard A. Clarke's account, in which he asserts that the President declared:

> I want you all to understand that we are at war and we will stay at war until this is done. Nothing else matters. Everything is available for the pursuit of this war. *Any barriers in your way, they're gone.*

Indeed, when Donald Rumsfeld informed the President that international law did not allow retribution, only the prevention of further attacks, he averred that '*I don't care what the international lawyers say, we're going to kick some ass*' (in Clarke 2004: 24). Rumsfeld's specific concern was with General Assembly Resolution 2625 (XXV) (1970) (Declaration on Principles of International Law Concerning Friendly Relations among States).

8 The title Operation Infinite Justice has a clear intertextuality with Operation Infinite Reach, which was President Clinton's response to the US Embassy bombings in Kenya and Tanzania. However, the title was changed because of deeply religious connotations it has in some branches of Islam, in which only Allah can deliver such finality (see BBC 2001).

9 See PDD39, Point Two: Deterring Terrorism (Clinton 1995).

10 This is in spite of US legislation passed in 1998, which codified that:

> The policy of the United States not to expel, extradite, or otherwise effect the involuntary return of any person to a country in which there are substantial grounds for believing the person would be in danger of being subjected to torture, regardless of whether the person is physically present in the United States.
>
> (in Williams 2006: 125)

11 That the UN would favour such an outcome is unsurprising given that it had officially made multiple calls for Afghanistan to move towards democratisation throughout the 1990s, and UN officials saw this as an opportunity to pursue this normative agenda. Moreover, such calls reflect what has become known as 'the New York Consensus' that has flourished since the end of the Cold War. Given this, the UN has increasingly seen the need for a more transformational role in fragile and failed states, and regarded democratisation as the best means of securing so-called international 'goods', such as the creation of liberal democratic polities with vibrant civil societies and market economies.

12 The Bonn Agreement, signed in December 2001, consequently asserted that the Afghan people would 'freely determine their own political future in accordance with the principles of Islam, democracy, pluralism and social justice'.

5 Constructing the Freedom Agenda for the Middle East

1 That the President used the term 'normal' is indicative of his stance that democracy is the natural structure any state would adopt once tyranny was removed. Yet, given Afghanistan's history, 'normal' was certainly not a democratic system.

2 It is interesting to note that Wittes's assertion is contradicted by Strobe Talbott's Foreword in the very same book, in which he argues that:

> Bush's Freedom Agenda faltered in the Arab world because of the instability unleashed by the invasion in Iraq. But the administration also failed to take account of risks to American interests and let itself be lulled into believing that the toppling of a tyrant in Baghdad would vindicate a benign version of the domino theory throughout the region.
>
> (Talbott 2008: x)

3 It was not until August 2008 that these attacks were attributed to the US Army biological researcher Bruce Ivins (Bohn *et al*. 2008).

4 The name 'Bletchley II' was chosen because Wolfowitz wanted to create something akin to Bletchley Park in the Second World War, where a team of mathematicians and cryptologists was set up to try and break German communication codes.

5 Attending on the proviso that the meeting be kept secret, a group of academics assembled in a secured conference centre in Virginia. The attendees included Christopher DeMuth, President of the AEI; Bernard Lewis, a close friend of Dick Cheney and scholar on Islam; Mark Palmer, the former US ambassador to Hungary, who would later be instrumental in authoring the ADVANCE Democracy Act of 2007; Fareed Zakaria, editor of *Newsweek International* and author of *The Future of Freedom*, which sets out the case for the USA to support the democratisation of the Middle East (Zakaria 2004: 150–9); Fouad Ajami, friend of Condoleezza Rice, director of the Middle East Center at SAIS and author of *The Arab Predicament*; James Q. Wilson, former President of the American Political Science Association, specialising in morality and crime; and Reuel Marc Gerecht, senior fellow at the Foundation for the Defense of Democracies, former CIA Middle East expert and former director of the Project for the New American Century's Middle East initiative.

6 Indeed this was certainly the sentiment behind Donald Rumsfeld's quoting the Bible on the front of his briefing papers for the President. Pertinent to this point was quoting the First Epistle of Peter: 'It is God's will that by doing good you should silence the ignorant talk of foolish men' (BBC 2009).

7 What is particularly noteworthy about this passage is that the characterisation of the enemy remains defined as 'evil', yet the concept of evil is articulated with conceptions of rationality and a political vision. That is to say, no longer were the terrorists being defined by their 'apolitical madness' (see Chapter 8), but rather they were being credited with rationality and motivation towards an alternative political vision.

By making this discursive move, the notion that the war on terror was an ideological battle could be put forward, and the official narrative could gain added complexity to maintain its legitimacy in the face of criticism.
8 Note the intertextuality of the 'forward strategy of freedom' with Bush's assertions, when a candidate, about the Reagan presidency (see Bush 1999, November 19).
9 Accordingly, President G. H. W. Bush argued 'In a world where we are the only remaining superpower, it is the role of the United States to marshal its moral and material resources to promote a *democratic peace*. It is our responsibility – it is our opportunity – to lead' (Bush 1993, January 11). Moreover the notion of democratic peace theory was carried through to the Clinton administration and had a significant impact on its foreign policy. Thus, as Michael Cox notes, 'possibly no other academic idea emanating from the academic community exercised as much influence as this one on the White House' (Cox 2000: 326).

6 Institutionalising the Freedom Agenda

1 Elizabeth Cheney is the daughter of former Vice President Richard Cheney and in 2002 was the Deputy Assistant Secretary of State for Near Eastern Affairs.
2 For a more expansive outline of the individual programmes see Hassan (2009).
3 MEPI works in Morocco, Algeria, Tunisia, Libya, Egypt, Jordan, the West Bank and Gaza, Israel, Lebanon, Syria, Saudi Arabia, Kuwait, Bahrain, Qatar, the UAE, Oman and Yemen. After the Bush administration left office Iraq was added as a partner country (see MEPI 2011).
4 These countries were Algeria, Bahrain, Cyprus, Egypt, the Gaza Strip/West Bank, Iran, Iraq, Israel, Jordan, Kuwait, Lebanon, Libya, Morocco, Oman, Qatar, Saudi Arabia, Syria, Tunisia, the United Arab Emirates and Yemen (see Bolle 2006).
5 The GMEI was the original US name given to a more ambitious version of BMENA. The name was changed because MENA governments objected that GMEI was too intrusive in their internal affairs, but also because of objections from the US government that GMEI in its original form replicated European initiatives conducted through the Euro-Mediterranean Partnership.
6 Note the intertextuality with Bush's 'Distinctly American Internationalism'.
7 See H.R.1 Public Law 110-53, 22 USC 8201n; Title XXI, Sections 2101–62, as passed by the 110th Congress.
8 The bill was sponsored by Representative Tom Lantos (D-CA) and Representative Frank Wolf (R-VA) in the House, and Senator John McCain (R-AZ) and Senator Joe Lieberman (D-CT) in the Senate. Moreover, that this author attended the secret Bletchley II meeting that resulted in the Delta of Terrorism paper is in and of itself somewhat suggestive of what this classified document contains.
9 Definitions of non-democratic and democratic transition countries are provided in the legislation.
10 The first meeting of the Advisory Committee on Democracy was held on November 6, 2006. Administration officials that attended were Condoleezza Rice, Randall L. Tobias (USAID), Paula J. Dobriansky (Under Secretary of State for Democracy and Global Affairs), Barry F. Lowenkron (DRL), Stephen Krasner (Director of Policy Planning). The ACDP members include Anne-Marie Slaughter, chair (Princeton University), Lorne Craner (International Republican Institute), Chester Crocker (Georgetown University), Bernard DeLury (formerly of Federal Mediation and Conciliation Service), Aaron Friedberg (Princeton University), Carl Gershman (National Endowment for Democracy), Mary Ann Glendon (Harvard Law School), Donald Horowitz (Duke University), Clifford May (Foundation for the Defense of Democracies), Michael Novak (American Enterprise Institute), Mark Palmer (Council for a Community of Democracies and Freedom House), Richard Soudriette (International Foundation for Election Systems), Vin Weber (National Endowment

Notes

for Democracy), Jennifer Windsor (Freedom House), Richard Williamson (Mayer, Brown, Rowe & Maw) and Kenneth Wollack (National Democratic Institute) (see DOS 2006a; Rice 2006, November 6; Milbank 2007).

11 J. Scott Carpenter served in the Bush administration as assistant secretary of state in the NEA, and oversaw MEPI form 2004 until becoming coordinator of the BMENA in 2006.

12 I have deliberately not listed the activities here because my interviews were conducted on the basis of complete anonymity. Many of the funding recipients I interviewed still use MEPI funding for their programmes, and consequently were reluctant about going on record, but were nonetheless very candid about the benefits and problems surrounding MEPI funding.

13 This argument was not only put forward concerning the MENA, but was also applied to China, in which the President argued that:

> the advance of markets and free enterprise helped to create a middle class that was confident enough to demand their own rights ... Our commitment to democracy is tested in China ... Yet, China's people will eventually want their liberty ... China has discovered that economic freedom leads to national wealth. China's leaders will also discover that freedom is indivisible – that social and religious freedom is also essential to national greatness and national dignity. Eventually, men and women who are allowed to control their own wealth will insist on controlling their own lives and their own country.
>
> (Bush 2003, November 6)

14 This has been implemented on the ground through programmes such as the Partnership for Financial Excellence, Middle East Entrepreneur training, the Commercial Law Initiative and the Middle East Finance Corporation.

15 For an excellent analysis of Berlin's conception of positive liberty see Quentin Skinner's (2006: 243–65) *A Third Concept of Liberty*.

7 Obama's Freedom Agenda

1 NSPD58 codified the policies and practices of the Freedom Agenda on July 17, 2008.

2 This was also co-sponsored by Senators Evan Bayh (IN), Mike DeWine (OH), Joseph I. Lieberman (CT) and Rick Santorum (PA).

3 Facebook and Twitter were launched in 2004 and 2006 respectively. It was not until September 2006, however, that Facebook opened up membership to anyone with a valid email address.

8 Conclusion

1 For this insight I would like to thank my colleague Peter Burnell at the University of Warwick.

2 It is instructive here to recall the concluding words to John Maynard Keynes's *General Theory of Employment, Interest and Money*, in which he asserts that:

> The ideas of economists and political philosophers, both when they are right and when they are wrong, are more powerful than is commonly understood. Indeed the world is ruled by little else. Practical men [sic], who believe themselves to be quite exempt from any intellectual influences, are usually the slaves of some defunct economist. Madmen [sic] in authority, who hear voices in the air, are distilling their frenzy from some academic scribbler of a few years back. I am sure that the power of vested interests is vastly exaggerated compared with the gradual encroachment of ideas.
>
> (Keynes 1936: 383)

Selected bibliography

Abrams, A. (2005) 'Global Survey 2006: Middle East Progress Amid Global Gains in Freedom', Freedom House (Available from: http://www.freedomhouse.org/template.cfm?page=70&release=317).

Abrams, E. (2011) 'In the Streets of Cairo, Proof Bush was Right', *Washington Post*, January 30 (Available from: http://www.washingtonpost.com/wp-dyn/content/article/2011/01/28/AR2011012806833_2.html).

Abrams, E. (2012) 'A Forward Strategy of Freedom', *Foreign Policy*, January 23.

Ackerman, S. (2008) 'The Obama Doctrine', *American Prospect*.

ADA (2005) ADA. – The 109th Congress of the United States; S.516 – IS ADVANCE Democracy Act of 2005 (Introduced in Senate – IS).

ADA (2007) Implementing Recommendations of the 9/11 Commission Act of 2007. – ADVANCE Democracy Act of 2007. The 110th Congress of the United States; H. R.1; PUBLIC LAW 110–53 – AUG. 3, 2007; 6 USC 101 note.

Adler, E. (1997) 'Seizing the Middle Ground: Constructivism in World Politics', *European Journal of International Relations* 3 (3): 319–63.

Adler, E. (2005) 'Constructivism and International Relations'. In Carlsnaes, W., Risse, T. and Simmons, B. A. (eds.), *Handbook of International Relations*. London: Sage, pp. 95–118.

AHDR (2002) *Arab Human Development Report 2002: Creating Opportunities for Future Generations*, United Nations Development Programme: Arab Fund for Economic and Social Development (Available from: http://www.arab-hdr.org/publications/other/ahdr/ahdr2002e.pdf).

Al-Anani, K. and Patkin, T. G. (2008) 'Presidential Candidate Positions Undeclared on Arab Democracy' (Available from: http://www.brookings.edu/research/opinions/2008/07/10-arab-democracy-alanani).

Albright, M. K. (2003) 'Bridges, Bombs, or Bluster?', *Foreign Affairs* 82 (5): 2–19.

Allison, G. T. and Zelikow, P. (1999) *Essence of Decision: Explaining the Cuban Missile Crisis*. 2nd edn. New York: Longman.

Althusser, L. (1971) 'Ideology and Ideological State Apparatuses'. In *Lenin and Philosophy, and Other Essays*. London: New Left Books, pp. 123–73.

Anderson, B. (1983) *Imagined Communities: Reflections on the Origin and Spread of Nationalism*. London: Verso.

Andoni, L. (2010) 'The Rebirth of Arab Activism: How One Young Tunisian Is Emerging as a Symbol of Disenfranchised and Impoverished Arab Youth' (Available from: http://english.aljazeera.net/indepth/opinion/2010/12/20101231161958792947.html).

Andrews, M. (2007) *Shaping History: Narratives of Political Change*. Cambridge: Cambridge University Press.

Selected bibliography

Antonio, R. J. and Bonannolt, A. (2006) 'Periodizing Globalization: From Cold War Modernization to the Bush Doctrine'. In Lehmann, J. M. and Dahms, H. F. (eds.), *Globalization between the Cold War and Neo-imperialism*. Oxford: Emerald Group Publishing, pp. 1–45.

Ashcroft, J. (2001, September 11) 'Press Briefing by Attorney General, Secretary of HHS, Secretary of Transportation, and FEMA Director', The Briefing Room, Washington, DC (Available from: http://georgewbush-whitehouse.archives.gov/news/releases/2001/09/20010911-10.html).

Asmus, R. D. and Pollack, K. M. (2003) 'The Neoliberal Take on the Middle East', *Washington Post*, July 22.

Asser, M. (2001) 'A Tougher Line?', BBC News, February 22 (Available from: http://news.bbc.co.uk/1/hi/world/middle_east/1174771.stm).

Atran, S. (2006) 'The Moral Logic and Growth of Suicide Terrorism', *Washington Quarterly* 29 (2): 127–47.

Bacevich, A. J. (2008) *The Limits of Power: The End of American Exceptionalism*. New York: Metropolitan Books.

Bal, M. (1997) *Narratology: Introduction to the Theory of Narrative*. 2nd edn. Toronto: University of Toronto Press.

Banfield, E. C. (1963) *American Foreign Aid Doctrines*. Washington, DC: American Enterprise Institute for Public Policy Research.

Barnett, M. (1999) 'Culture, Strategy and Foreign Policy Change: Israel's Road to Oslo', *European Journal of International Relations* 5 (1): 5–36.

Baxter, S. (2006) 'Cheney Daughter Leads "Cold War" on Mullahs', *Sunday Times*, March 5 (Available from: http://www.timesonline.co.uk/tol/news/world/article737633.ece).

BBC. (2001) 'Infinite Justice, Out – Enduring Freedom, In', September 25 (Available from: http://news.bbc.co.uk/1/hi/world/americas/1563722.stm).

BBC. (2009) 'Rumsfeld "Bible Texts" Criticised', BBC News Online, May 18 (Available from: http://news.bbc.co.uk/1/hi/world/americas/8056207.stm).

Bell, C. (1971) *The Conventions of Crisis: A Study in Diplomatic Management*. London: Oxford University Press.

Bellamy, A. J. and Williams, P. D. (2011) 'The New Politics of Protection? Côte d'Ivoire, Libya and the Responsibility to Protect', *International Affairs* 87 (4): 845–70.

Benton, T. and Craib, I. (2001) *Philosophy of Social Science: The Philosophical Foundations of Social Thought, Traditions in Social Theory*. Basingstoke, UK: Palgrave.

Berlin, I. (2006) 'Two Concepts of Liberty'. In Miller, D. (ed.), *The Liberty Reader*. Boulder, CO: Paradigm Publishers, pp. 33–57.

Berman, S. (2001) 'Ideas, Norms, and Culture in Political Analysis', *Comparative Politics* 33 (2): 231–50.

Bernstein, R. J. (1983) *Beyond Objectivism and Relativism: Science, Hermeneutics, and Praxis*. Oxford: Basil Blackwell.

Bix, H. (2005) 'Torture, Racism, & the Sovereign President', *Z Magazine*, July 25 (Available from: http://www.zcommunications.org/zmag/viewArticle/13641).

Black, I. and Milne, S. (2011) 'Palestine Papers Reveal MI6 Drew Up Plan for Crackdown on Hamas', *The Guardian*, January 25 (Available from: http://www.guardian.co.uk/world/2011/jan/25/palestine-papers-mi6-hamas-crackdown).

Blair, T. (2001, October 2) 'Blair: In His Own Words' (Available from: http://news.bbc.co.uk/1/hi/uk_politics/3750847.stm).

Blyth, M. (2002) *Great Transformations: Economic Ideas and Institutional Change in the Twentieth Century*. New York: Cambridge University Press.

Blyth, M. (2003) 'Structures Do Not Come with an Instruction Sheet: Interests, Ideas, and Progress in Political Science', *Perspectives on Politics* 1 (4): 695–706.

Bohn, K., Mears, B. and Fiegel, E. (2008) 'U.S. Officials Declare Researcher is Anthrax Killer', CNN International, August 6 (Available from: http://edition.cnn.com/2008/CRIME/08/06/anthrax.case/index.html?eref=rss_topstories).

Bolle, M. J. (2006) *Middle East Free Trade Area: Progress Report.* CRS Report for Congress: Order Code RL32638; Updated July 3.

Boot, M. (2004) *The 'American Empire' in the Middle East.* Berkeley: Berkeley Public Policy Press, University of California.

Borer, D. and Freeman, M. (2007) 'Thinking Strategically: Can Democracy Defeat Terrorism?'. In Forest, J. J. F. (ed.), *Countering Terrorism and Insurgency in the 21st Century: International Perspectives Vol. 1.* Westport, CT: Praeger Security International, pp. 56–79.

Borger, J. (2009) 'Barack Obama: Administration Willing to Talk to Iran "without Preconditions"', *The Guardian*, January 21 (Available from: http://www.guardian.co.uk/world/2009/jan/21/barack-obama-iran-negotiations).

Bosman, J. (2006) 'Secret Iraq Meeting Included Journalists', *New York Times Online*, October 9 (Available from: http://www.nytimes.com/2006/10/09/business/media/09zakaria.html?_r=3&oref=slogin).

Bouchet, N. (2010) 'Barack Obama's Democracy Promotion after One Year', *e-International Relations*, February 25 (Available from: http://www.e-ir.info/?p=3300).

Boudon, R. (1986) *Theories of Social Change: A Critical Appraisal.* Berkeley: University of California Press.

Bowen, J. (2005) *Six Days: How the 1967 War Shaped the Middle East.* London: Simon & Schuster.

Bowen, W. Q. and Dunn, D. H. (1996) *American Security Policy in the 1990s: Beyond Containment.* Aldershot, UK: Dartmouth.

Brecher, M., Wilkenfeld, J. and Moser, S. (1988) *Handbook of International Crises.* 1st edn. Oxford: Pergamon Press.

Bremer, L. P. and McConnell, M. (2006) *My Year in Iraq: The Struggle to Build a Future of Hope.* New York: Simon & Schuster.

Bumiller, E. (2007) 'Rice's Turnabout on Mideast Talks', *New York Times*, November 26 (Available from: http://www.nytimes.com/2007/11/26/washington/26rice.html?pagewanted=1&n=Top/News/World/Countriespercent20andpercent20Territories/Iraq&_r=1).

Burchill, S. (2005) *The National Interest in International Relations Theory.* Basingstoke: Palgrave Macmillan.

Burgat, F. (2003) *Face to Face with Political Islam.* London: I. B. Tauris.

Bush, G. H. W. (1990, August 5) 'Remarks and an Exchange with Reporters on the Iraqi Invasion of Kuwait', South Lawn of the White House (Available from: http://bushlibrary.tamu.edu/research/public_papers.php?id=2138&year=1990&month=8).

Bush, G. H. W. (1993, January 11) 'America's Role in the World', US Department of State Dispatch (Available from: http://findarticles.com/p/articles/mi_m1584/is_n2_v4/ai_13443489).

Bush, G. W. (1999, September 23) 'A Period of Consequences', The Citadel, South Carolina (Available from: http://www.citadel.edu/pao/addresses/pres_bush.html).

Bush, G. W. (1999, November 19) 'A Distinctly American Internationalism', Ronald Reagan Presidential Library, Simi Valley, California (Available from: http://www.globalsecurity.org/wmd/library/news/usa/1999/991119-bush-foreignpolicy.htm).

198   Selected bibliography

Bush, G. W. (2000, August 15) 'Address to The Republican National Convention', *Vital Speeches of the Day* 66 (21): 642–7.

Bush, G. W. (2000, October 3) 'The First Gore–Bush Presidential Debate', Clark Athletic Center, University of Massachusetts, Boston (Available from: http://www.debates.org/pages/trans2000a.html).

Bush, G. W. (2000, October 11) 'The Second Gore–Bush Presidential Debate', Wake Chapel, Wake Forest University, North Carolina (Available from: http://www.debates.org/pages/trans2000b.html).

Bush, G. W. (2000, October 17) 'The Third Gore–Bush Presidential Debate', Field House, Washington University, St. Louis (Available from: http://www.debates.org/pages/trans2000c.html).

Bush, G. W. (2000, November 3) 'George W. Bush Holds Campaign Rally in Grand Rapids, Michigan', Grand Rapids, Michigan (Available from: http://transcripts.cnn.com/TRANSCRIPTS/0011/03/se.04.html).

Bush, G. W. (2001) *A Charge to Keep: My Journey to the White House*. New York: Harper Perennial.

Bush, G. W. (2001, January 20) 'President George W. Bush's Inaugural Address', Steps of the US Capitol Building, Washington, DC (Available from: http://georgewbush-whitehouse.archives.gov/news/inaugural-address.html).

Bush, G. W. (2001, February 27) 'Address of the President to the Joint Session of Congress', The United States Congress, Washington, DC (Available from: http://georgewbush-whitehouse.archives.gov/news/releases/2001/02/20010228.html).

Bush, G. W. (2001, May 3) 'Remarks by the President to the American Jewish Committee', National Building Museum, Washington, DC (Available from: http://georgewbush-whitehouse.archives.gov/news/releases/2001/05/20010504.html).

Bush, G. W. (2001, September 11a) 'Remarks by the President after Two Planes Crash Into World Trade Center', Emma Booker Elementary School, Sarasota, Florida (Available from: http://georgewbush-whitehouse.archives.gov/news/releases/2001/09/20010911.html).

Bush, G. W. (2001, September 11b) 'Statement by the President in His Address to the Nation', The Oval Office, The White House, Washington, DC (Available from: http://georgewbush-whitehouse.archives.gov/news/releases/2001/09/20010911-16.html#).

Bush, G. W. (2001, September 11c) 'Remarks by the President upon Arrival at Barksdale Air Force Base', Barksdale Air Force Base, Louisiana (Available from: http://georgewbush-whitehouse.archives.gov/news/releases/2001/09/20010911-1.html).

Bush, G. W. (2001, September 12) 'Remarks by the President in Photo Opportunity with the National Security Team', The Cabinet Room, The White House, Washington, DC (Available from: http://georgewbush-whitehouse.archives.gov/news/releases/2001/09/20010912-4.html).

Bush, G. W. (2001, September 13) 'National Day of Prayer and Remembrance for the Victims of the Terrorist Attacks on September 11, 2001', A Proclamation by the President of the United States of America (Available from: http://georgewbush-whitehouse.archives.gov/news/releases/2001/09/20010913-7.html).

Bush, G. W. (2001, September 14) 'President's Remarks at National Day of Prayer and Remembrance', The National Cathedral, Washington, DC (Available from: http://georgewbush-whitehouse.archives.gov/news/releases/2001/09/20010914-2.html).

Bush, G. W. (2001, September 16) 'Remarks by the President upon Arrival', South Lawn, The White House (Available from: http://georgewbush-whitehouse.archives.gov/news/releases/2001/09/20010916-2.html).

Selected bibliography 199

Bush, G. W. (2001, September 17) 'Guard and Reserves "Define Spirit of America"', The Pentagon (Available from: http://georgewbush-whitehouse.archives.gov/news/releases/2001/09/20010917-3.html).

Bush, G. W. (2001, September 20) 'Address to a Joint Session of Congress and the American People', United States Capitol Building, Washington, DC (Available from: http://georgewbush-whitehouse.archives.gov/news/releases/2001/09/20010920-8.html).

Bush, G. W. (2001, October 7) 'Presidential Address to the Nation', The Treaty Room, The White House, Washington, DC (Available from: http://georgewbush-whitehouse.archives.gov/news/releases/2001/10/20011007-8.html).

Bush, G. W. (2001, October 14) 'CNN Late Edition with Wolf Blitzer', South Lawn, The White House (Available from: http://transcripts.cnn.com/TRANSCRIPTS/0110/14/le.00.html).

Bush, G. W. (2001, October 24) 'President Discusses Stronger Economy and Homeland Defense', Dixie Printing Company, Glen Burnie, Maryland (Available from: http://georgewbush-whitehouse.archives.gov/news/releases/2001/10/20011024-2.html).

Bush, G. W. (2001, November 6) 'President Bush: "No Nation Can Be Neutral in This Conflict"', Warsaw Conference on Combatting Terrorism (Available from: http://georgewbush-whitehouse.archives.gov/news/releases/2001/11/20011106-2.html).

Bush, G. W. (2001, November 8) 'President Discusses War on Terrorism', Address to the Nation, World Congress Center, Atlanta, Georgia. (Available from: http://georgewbush-whitehouse.archives.gov/news/releases/2001/11/20011108-13.html).

Bush, G. W. (2001, November 10) 'President Bush Speaks to United Nations', United Nations General Assembly, U.N. Headquarters, New York (Available from: http://georgewbush-whitehouse.archives.gov/news/releases/2001/11/20011110-3.html).

Bush, G. W. (2001, November 13) 'Joint Statement by President George W. Bush and President Vladimir V. Putin on Afghanistan' (Available from: http://georgewbush-whitehouse.archives.gov/news/releases/2001/11/20011113-9.html).

Bush, G. W. (2001, November 19) 'President Discusses War, Humanitarian Efforts', The Cabinet Room, The White House (Available from: http://georgewbush-whitehouse.archives.gov/news/releases/2001/11/20011119-12.html).

Bush, G. W. (2001, December 11) 'President Speaks on War Effort to Citadel Cadets', The Citadel, Charleston, South Carolina (Available from: http://georgewbush-whitehouse.archives.gov/news/releases/2001/12/20011211-6.html).

Bush, G. W. (2002, January 29) 'President Delivers State of the Union Address', The United States Capitol Building, Washington, DC (Available from: http://georgewbush-whitehouse.archives.gov/news/releases/2002/01/20020129-11.html).

Bush, G. W. (2002, March 11) 'President Thanks World Coalition for Anti-Terrorism Efforts', South Lawn, The White House (Available from: http://georgewbush-whitehouse.archives.gov/news/releases/2002/03/20020311-1.html).

Bush, G. W. (2002, March 13) 'President Bush Holds Press Conference', The James S. Brady Briefing Room, The White House (Available from: http://georgewbush-whitehouse.archives.gov/news/releases/2002/03/20020313-8.html).

Bush, G. W. (2002, March 22) 'President Outlines U.S. Plan to Help World's Poor', United Nations Financing for Development Conference, Cintermex Convention Center, Monterrey, Mexico (Available from: http://georgewbush-whitehouse.archives.gov/news/releases/2002/03/20020322-1.html).

Bush, G. W. (2002, April 17) 'President Outlines War Effort', Remarks by the President to the George C. Marshall ROTC Award Seminar on National Security, Cameron Hall,

Virginia Military Institute, Lexington, Virginia (Available from: http://georgewbush-whitehouse.archives.gov/news/releases/2002/04/20020417-1.html).

Bush, G. W. (2002, June 1) 'President Bush Delivers Graduation Speech at West Point', United States Military Academy, West Point, New York (Available from: http://georgewbush-whitehouse.archives.gov/news/releases/2002/06/20020601-3.html).

Bush, G. W. (2002, June 8) 'President Bush Meets with Egyptian President Mubarak', Camp David, Maryland (Available from: http://georgewbush-whitehouse.archives.gov/news/releases/2002/06/20020608-4.html).

Bush, G. W. (2002, June 24) 'President Bush Calls for New Palestinian Leadership', The Rose Garden; The White House (Available from: http://georgewbush-whitehouse.archives.gov/news/releases/2002/06/20020624-3.html).

Bush, G. W. (2002, September 12) 'President's Remarks at the United Nations General Assembly', United Nations General Assembly, New York (Available from: http://georgewbush-whitehouse.archives.gov/news/releases/2002/09/20020912-1.html).

Bush, G. W. (2002, October 7) 'President Bush Outlines Iraqi Threat', Cincinnati Museum Center – Cincinnati Union Terminal, Cincinnati, Ohio (Available from: http://georgewbush-whitehouse.archives.gov/news/releases/2002/10/20021007-8.html).

Bush, G. W. (2003, January 28) 'President Delivers "State of the Union"', US Capitol Building, Washington, DC (Available from: http://georgewbush-whitehouse.archives.gov/news/releases/2003/01/20030128-19.html).

Bush, G. W. (2003, February 26) 'President Discusses the Future of Iraq', American Enterprise Institute Dinner, Washington Hilton Hotel, Washington, DC (Available from: http://georgewbush-whitehouse.archives.gov/news/releases/2003/02/20030226-11.html).

Bush, G. W. (2003, May 9) 'President Bush Presses for Peace in the Middle East', Remarks by the President in Commencement Address at the University of South Carolina, Columbia, South Carolina (Available from: http://georgewbush-whitehouse.archives.gov/news/releases/2003/05/20030509-11.html).

Bush, G. W. (2003, November 6) 'President Bush Discusses Freedom in Iraq and Middle East', Remarks by the President at the 20th Anniversary of the National Endowment for Democracy, United States Chamber of Commerce, Washington, DC (Available from: http://georgewbush-whitehouse.archives.gov/news/releases/2003/11/20031106-2.html).

Bush, G. W. (2003, December 14) 'President Bush Addresses Nation on the Capture of Saddam Hussein', The Cabinet Room, Washington, DC (Available from: http://georgewbush-whitehouse.archives.gov/news/releases/2003/12/20031214-3.html).

Bush, G. W. (2004, August 6) 'Newshour with Jim Lehrer', UNITY 2004 Conference in Washington, DC (Available from: http://www.pbs.org/newshour/bb/politics/july-dec04/snapshot_8-6.html).

Bush, G. W. (2004, January 20) 'State of the Union', United States Capitol, Washington, DC (Available from: http://georgewbush-whitehouse.archives.gov/news/releases/2004/01/20040120-7.html).

Bush, G. W. (2005, January 20) 'Inauguration – President Sworn into Second Term' (Available from: http://georgewbush-whitehouse.archives.gov/news/releases/2005/01/20050120-1.html).

Bush, G. W. (2005, March 8) 'President Discusses War on Terror', National Defense University, Fort Lesley J. McNair (Available from: http://georgewbush-whitehouse.archives.gov/news/releases/2005/03/20050308-3.html).

Bush, G. W. (2006, July 28) 'President Bush & Prime Minister Blair of the United Kingdom Participate in Press Availability', The East Room, The White House,

Washington, DC (Available from: http://georgewbush-whitehouse.archives.gov/news/releases/2006/07/20060728-1.html).

Bush, G. W. (2006, August 7) 'President Bush and Secretary of State Rice Discuss the Middle East Crisis', The White House, Washington, DC (Available from: http://georgewbush-whitehouse.archives.gov/news/releases/2006/08/20060807.html).

Bush, G. W. (2006, August 31) 'President Bush Addresses American Legion National Convention', Salt Palace Convention Center, Salt Lake City, Utah (Available from: http://georgewbush-whitehouse.archives.gov/news/releases/2006/08/20060831-1.html).

Bush, G. W. (2006, October 6) 'President Discusses War on Terror at National Endowment for Democracy', Ronald Reagan Building and International Trade Center, Washington, DC (Available from: http://georgewbush-whitehouse.archives.gov/news/releases/2005/10/20051006-3.html).

Bush, G. W. (2008, January 28) 'President Bush Delivers State of the Union Address', Chamber of the United States House of Representatives, United States Capitol (Available from: http://georgewbush-whitehouse.archives.gov/news/releases/2008/01/20080128-13.html).

Bush, G. W. (2010) *Decision Points*. 1st edn. New York: Crown Publishers.

Bush, G. W. (2011, May 23) 'The Wave of Freedom: Early Lessons from the Middle East' (Available from: http://www.bushcenter.com/human-freedom/wave-of-freedom).

Buzan, B. (2004) *The United States and the Great Powers: World Politics in the Twenty-First Century*. Cambridge: Polity.

Byman, D. (2007) 'US Counter-Terrorism Options, A Taxonomy', *Survival* 49 (3): 121–50.

Call, S. (2007) *Danger Close: Tactical Air Controllers in Afghanistan and Iraq*. 1st edn. College Station: Texas A&M University Press.

Callinicos, A. (1995) *Theories and Narratives: Reflections on the Philosophy of History*. Durham, NC: Duke University Press.

Campbell, D. (1998) *Writing Security: United States Foreign Policy and the Politics of Identity*. Rev. edn. Minneapolis: University of Minnesota Press.

Campbell, J. L. and Pedersen, O. K. (2001) *The Rise of Neoliberalism and Institutional Analysis*. Princeton, NJ: Princeton University Press.

Carothers, T. and Ottaway, M. (2005) 'The New Democracy Imperative'. In Carothers, T. and Ottaway, M. (eds.), *Uncharted Journey: Promoting Democracy in the Middle East*. Washington, DC: Carnegie Endowment for International Peace, pp. 3–12.

Carothers, T. (2004) 'Promoting Democracy and Fighting Terror (2003)'. In Carothers, T. (ed.), *Critical Mission: Essays on Democracy Promotion*. Washington, DC: Carnegie Endowment for International Peace, pp. 63–74.

Carothers, T. (2005) 'Choosing a Strategy'. In Carothers, T. and Ottaway, M. (eds.), *Uncharted Journey: Promoting Democracy in the Middle East*. Washington, DC: Carnegie Endowment for International Peace, pp. 193–208.

Carothers, T. (2006) 'The Backlash against Democracy Promotion', *Foreign Affairs* 85 (2): 55–68.

Carothers, T. (2007a) *U.S. Democracy Promotion during and after Bush*. Washington, DC: Carnegie Endowment for International Peace.

Carothers, T. (2007b) 'The "Sequencing" Fallacy', *Journal of Democracy* 18 (1): 12–27.

Carothers, T. (2012) *Democracy Policy under Obama: Revitalization or Retreat?* Washington, DC: Carnegie Endowment for International Peace.

Carpenter, J. S. (2008) 'Bush's Freedom Agenda: Alive but Not Kicking', PolicyWatch # 1332, Washington Institute of Near East Affairs, January 24.

Selected bibliography

CFR (Council on Foreign Relations) (2006) *National Security Consequences of U.S. Oil Dependency*. Washington, DC: Council on Foreign Relations.

Chafetz, G. R., Spirtas, M. and Frankel, B. (eds.) (1999) *The Origins of National Interests, Cass Series on Security Studies*. London: F. Cass.

Chamberlin, J. (2004) *Comparisons of U.S. and Foreign Military Spending: Data from Selected Public Sources*. CRS Report for Congress: Order Code RL32209; Updated January 28.

Cheney, D. (2002, January 27) 'The Vice President Appears on ABC's *This Week*', ABC's *This Week* (Available from: http://georgewbush-whitehouse.archives.gov/vicepresident/news-speeches/speeches/vp20020127.html).

Chollet, D. H. and Goldgeier, J. M. (2008) *America between the Wars: From 11/9 to 9/11: The Misunderstood Years between the Fall of the Berlin Wall and the Start of the War on Terror*. 1st edn. New York: BBS PublicAffairs.

Clarke, R. A. (2004) *Against All Enemies: Inside America's War on Terror*. 1st trade paperback edn. New York: Free Press.

Clinton, H. R. (2009, January 13) 'Statement of Senator Hillary Rodham Clinton Nominee for Secretary of State', Senate Foreign Relations Committee (Available from: http://foreign.senate.gov/testimony/2009/ClintonTestimony090113a.pdf).

Clinton, H. R. (2009, April 22) 'Transcript Taken from the BBC – Clinton Warns of Iran Sanctions', House Foreign Relations Committee (Available from: http://news.bbc.co.uk/1/hi/world/americas/8012921.stm).

Clinton, H. R. (2009, July 10) 'Town Hall on the Quadrennial Diplomacy and Development Review at the Department of State', Secretary of State, Dean Acheson Auditorium, Washington, DC (Available from: http://www.state.gov/secretary/rm/2009a/july/125949.htm).

Clinton, H. R. (2009, November 3) 'Remarks at the Forum for the Future', Marrakech, Morocco (Available from: http://www.state.gov/secretary/rm/2009a/11/131236.htm).

Clinton, H. R. (2011, January 25) 'Remarks with Spanish Foreign Minister Trinidad Jimenez after Their Meeting', Treaty Room, Washington, DC (Available from: http://www.state.gov/secretary/rm/2011/01/155280.htm).

Clinton, H. R. (2011, November 7) 'Keynote Address at the National Democratic Institute's 2011 Democracy Awards Dinner', Andrew W. Mellon Auditorium, Washington, DC (Available from: http://www.state.gov/secretary/rm/2011/11/176750.htm).

Clinton, W. J. (1995) *Presidential Decision Directive 39* (Available from: http://www.fas.org/irp/offdocs/pdd39.htm).

Cobley, P. (2001) *Narrative, the New Critical Idiom*. London: Routledge.

Cohen, E. A. (2001) 'Iraq Can't Resist Us', *Wall Street Journal (Eastern edition)*, December 18: A.16.

Cohen, J. (2008, November 24) 'State's Glassman on Alliance for Youth Movement Summit: U.S. partners with private sector for youth summit in New York December 3–5', US Department of State, Washington, DC (Available from: http://iipdigital.usembassy.gov/st/english/texttrans/2008/11/20081124173327eaifas0.8017237.html#ixzz1MuJsimoZ).

Cohen, J. (2010, September 7) 'Interview between Christina Larson and Jared Cohen: State Department Innovator Goes to Google', Foreign Policy (Available from: http://www.foreignpolicy.com/articles/2010/09/07/jared_cohen).

Cohen, M. J. (1997) *Fighting World War Three from the Middle East: Allied Contingency Plans, 1945–1954*. London: Frank Cass.

Cook, S. A., Albright, M. K. and Weber, V. (2005) *In Support of Arab Democracy: Why and How*. Independent Task Force Report No. 54

Cooper, H. (2009) 'Talking Softly about Democracy Promotion', *New York Times*, January 29 (Available from: http://www.nytimes.com/2009/01/30/us/politics/30web-cooper.html).
Cooper, H. and Sanger, D. E. (2006) 'U.S. Plan Seeks to Wedge Syria Away from Iran', *New York Times* (Available from: http://www.nytimes.com/2006/07/23/washington/23diplo.html?scp=15&sq=Rafik+Hariri&st=nyt).
Cordesman, A. H. (2008) 'Iran and the United States: The Nuclear Issue', *Middle East Policy* 15 (1): 19–29.
Cox, M. (1995) *US Foreign Policy after the Cold War: Superpower without a Mission?* London: Pinter.
Cox, M. (2000) 'Wilsonianism Resurgent? The Clinton Administration and the Promotion of Democracy'. In Cox, M., Ikenberry, G. J. and Inoguchi, T. (eds.), *American Democracy Promotion: Impulses, Strategies, and Impacts*. Oxford: Oxford University Press, pp. 218–39.
Crampton, T. (2003) 'Iraq Official Warns on Fast Economic Shift', *New York Times*, October 14 (Available from: http://www.nytimes.com/2003/10/14/business/worldbusiness/14iht-trade_ed3_.html).
Croft, S. (2006) *Culture, Crisis and America's War on Terror*. Cambridge: Cambridge University Press.
Daalder, I. H. and Lindsay, J. M. (2003) *America Unbound: The Bush Revolution in Foreign Policy*. Washington, DC: Brookings Institution.
Dalacoura, K. (2005) 'US Democracy Promotion in the Arab Middle East since September 11, 2001: A Critique', *International Affairs* 81 (5): 963–79.
Dalacoura, K. (2006) 'Islamist Terrorism and the Middle East Democratic Deficit: Political Exclusion, Repression and the Causes of Extremism', *Democratization* 13 (3): 508–25.
Dalacoura, K. (2011) *Islamist Terrorism and Democracy in the Middle East*. Cambridge: Cambridge University Press.
Deeb, M.-J. (2008) Personal interview with Chief of African and Middle Eastern Division, Library of Congress, Washington, DC, May 4.
Der Derian, J. (2002) 'In Terrorem: Before and after 9/11'. In Booth, K. and Dunne, T. (eds.), *Worlds in Collision: Terror and the Future of Global Order*. New York: Palgrave Macmillan, pp. 101–17.
Deudney, D. and Meiser, J. (2008) 'American Exceptionalism'. In Cox, M. and Stokes, D. (eds.), *US Foreign Policy*. Oxford: Oxford University Press, pp. 24–42.
Diamond, L. (2005) *Squandered Victory: The American Occupation and the Bungled Effort to bring Democracy to Iraq*. New York: Times Books.
Diamond, L. and McFaul, M. (2006) 'Seeding Liberal Democracy'. In Marshall, W. (ed.), *With All Our Might: A Progressive Strategy for Defeating Jihadism and Defending Liberty*. Oxford: Rowman and Littlefield, pp. 49–67.
Diehl, J. (2007) 'A Lasting Freedom Agenda', *Washington Post*, April 30, A15.
Dienstag, J. F. (1997) *'Dancing in Chains': Narrative and Memory in Political Theory*. Stanford, CA: Stanford University Press.
Dijk, T. A. van. (1998) *Ideology: A Multidisciplinary Approach*. London: Sage Publications.
Dinmore, G. (2006) 'US and UK Develop Democracy Strategy for Iran', *Financial Times*, April 21 (Available from: http://www.ft.com/cms/s/0/4546fed8-d158-11da-a38b-0000779e2340.html?nclick_check=1).
Dobbins, J. (2008a) 'Does Nation-Building Have a Future? Lessons from Afghanistan', New America Foundation, 1630 Connecticut Avenue, Washington, DC, August 21 (Available from: http://www.youtube.com/watch?v=ZF2SB1qrhN0).

Dobbins, J. (2008b) *After the Taliban: Nation-Building in Afghanistan*. Washington, DC: Potomac Books.

Dobriansky, P. J. (2001, December 21) 'The Diplomatic Front of the War on Terrorism: Can the Promotion of Democracy and Human Rights Tip the Scales?', Heritage Lecture No. 724 (Available from: http://www.heritage.org/research/homelandsecurity/hl724.cfm).

DOS (United States Department of State) (2004) 'BMENA', US Department of State (Available from: http://bmena.state.gov/).

DOS (2006a) 'Inaugural Meeting of the Secretary's Advisory Committee on Democracy Promotion', Washington, DC (Available from: http://2001-2009.state.gov/r/pa/prs/ps/2006/75525.htm).

DOS (2006b) 'Iran Democracy Program Announcement', Department of State, Washington, DC (Available from: http://2002-2009-mepi.state.gov/62704.htm).

DOS (2008) 'Institutionalizing the Freedom Agenda: President Bush Calls on Future Presidents and Congresses to Continue Leading the Cause of Freedom Worldwide', Washington, DC (Available from: http://2001-2009.state.gov/r/pa/prs/ps/2008/oct/110871.htm).

DOS (2009) Foundation for the Future (Available from: http://foundationforfuture.org/en/).

Du Gay, P., Evans, J. and Redman, P. (2000) *Identity: A Reader*. London: Sage Publications.

Dumbrell, J. (1997) *American Foreign Policy: Carter to Clinton*. London: Palgrave Macmillan.

Dunn, D. H. (2005) 'Bush, 11 September and the Conflicting Strategies of the "War on Terrorism"', *Irish Studies in International Affairs* 16 (Nov.): 11–33.

Dunn, D. H. and Hassan, O. (2010) 'Strategic Confusion: America's Conflicting Strategies and the War on Terrorism'. In Siniver, A. (ed.), *International Terrorism post-9/11: Comparative Dynamics and Responses*. London: Routledge, pp. 57–82.

Dunne, M. (2005) 'Integrating Democracy into the U.S. Policy Agenda'. In Carothers, T. and Ottaway, M. (eds.), *Uncharted Journey: Promoting Democracy in the Middle East*. Washington, DC: Carnegie Endowment for International Peace, pp. 209–27.

Eagleton, T. (1991) *Ideology: An Introduction*. London: Verso.

Eagleton, T. (2003) *Sweet Violence: The Idea of the Tragic*. Malden: Blackwell.

Egan, R. D. (2002) 'Anthrax'. In Collins, J. M. and Glover, R. (eds.), *Collateral Language: A User's Guide to America's New War*. London: New York University Press, pp. 15–26.

Eisenhower, D. D. (1957) 'Special Message to the Congress on the Middle East Situation', January 5. Online by Gerhard Peters and John T. Woolley, The American Presidency Project (Available from: http://www.presidency.ucsb.edu/ws/?pid=11007).

Eisenman, S. (2007) *The Abu Ghraib Effect*. London: Reaktion Books.

Elbayar, K. (2005) 'NGO Laws in Selected Arab States', *International Journal of Not-for-Profit Law* 7 (4): 3–27.

Epstein, J. (2003) 'Leviathan', *New York Review of Books* 50 (7): 13–14.

Epstein, S. B., Serafino, N. M. and Miko, F. T. (2007) *Democracy Promotion: Cornerstone of US Foreign Policy?*, CRS Report for Congress: Order Code RL34296; Updated December 26.

Esposito, J. L. and Voll, J. O. (1996) *Islam and Democracy*. New York: Oxford University Press.

Fairclough, N. (1992) *Discourse and Social Change*. Cambridge, UK: Polity Press.

Fairclough, N. (1995) *Critical Discourse Analysis: The Critical Study of Language*. London: Longman.

Fairclough, N. (2003) *Analysing Discourse: Textual Analysis for Social Research*. London: Routledge.

Falk, R. (2002) 'A Just Response: September 19, 2001'. In Heuvel, K. V. (ed.), *A Just Response: The Nation on Terrorism, Democracy and September 11, 2001*. New York: Thunder's Mouth Press, pp. 210, 246, 266.

Falk, R. A. (2003) *The Great Terror War*. New York: Olive Branch Press.

Fattah, H. M. (2006) 'Democracy in the Arab World, a U.S. Goal, Falters', *New York Times*, April 10.

Fay, B. (1996) *Contemporary Philosophy of Social Science: A Multicultural Approach*. Oxford, UK: Blackwell.

Feldman, N. (2004) *After Jihad: America and the Struggle for Islamic Democracy*. 1st paperback edn. New York: Farrar, Straus and Giroux.

FFF (Foundation for the Future) (2008) 'Foundation for the Future' (Available from: http://www.foundationforfuture.org//?q=en/).

FFF (2009) *Foundation for the Future: Annual Report 2008*. Amman, Jordan

Fielding, Nick (2005) 'MI6 Chief Told PM: Americans "Fixed" Case for War', *Sunday Times Online*, March 20 (Available from: http://www.timesonline.co.uk/tol/news/uk/article432626.ece).

Finkel, D. (2005) 'U.S. Ideals Meet Reality in Yemen', *Washington Post*, December 18, A01 (Available from: http://www.washingtonpost.com/wp-dyn/content/article/2005/12/17/AR2005121701237_pf.html).

Finnemore, M. (1996a) 'Norms, Culture, and World Politics: Insights from Sociology's Institutionalism', *International Organization* 50 (2): 325–47.

Finnemore, M. (1996b) *National Interests in International Society*. Ithaca, NY: Cornell University Press.

Fleischer, A. (2001, September 12) 'Press Briefing by Ari Fleischer', The James S. Brady Briefing Room, The White House, Washington, DC (Available from: http://georgewbush-whitehouse.archives.gov/news/releases/2001/09/20010912-8.html).

Fleischer, A. (2001, September 13) 'Press Briefing by Ari Fleischer', Office of the Press Secretary (Available from: http://georgewbush-whitehouse.archives.gov/news/releases/2001/09/20010913-12.html).

Foner, E. (1998) *The Story of American Freedom*. New York: W. W. Norton.

Foner, E. (2003) *The Idea of Freedom in the American Century, Lawrence F. Brewster Lecture in History*. Greenville, NC: Dept. of History, Thomas Harriot College of Arts and Sciences, East Carolina University.

Foucault, M. (2002) *Archaeology of Knowledge*. London; New York: Routledge.

Foucault, M. and Gordon, C. (1980) *Power/Knowledge: Selected Interviews and Other Writings, 1972–1977*. 1st American edn. New York: Pantheon Books.

Freedman, L. (2008) *A Choice of Enemies: America Confronts the Middle East*. 1st edn. New York: Public Affairs.

Freeman, M. (2008) 'Democracy, Al Qaeda, and the Causes of Terrorism: A Strategic Analysis of U.S. Policy', *Studies in Conflict & Terrorism* 31 (1): 40–59.

Friedman, M. (1958 [1995]) *Foreign Economic Aid: Means and Objectives, Essays in Public Policy No. 60*. Stanford, CA: Hoover Institution Classics.

Friedman, M. (1962 [2002]) *Capitalism and Freedom*. 40th anniversary edn. London: University of Chicago Press.

Friedman, T. L. (2003) *Longitudes and Attitudes: The World in the Age of Terrorism*. New York: Anchor Books.

206 Selected bibliography

Friedman, T. L. (2005) 'What Were They Thinking?', *New York Times* op-ed, October 7 (Available from: http://select.nytimes.com/2005/10/07/opinion/07friedman.html?_r=1).

Frum, D. (2003) *The Right Man: The Surprise Presidency of George W. Bush*. 1st edn. New York: Random House.

Fukuyama, F. (1989) 'The End of History?', *The National Interest*, Summer.

Fukuyama, F. (2004) *State-Building: Governance and World Order in the 21st Century*. Ithaca, NY: Cornell University Press.

Fukuyama, F. (2005) 'Do We Really Know How to Promote Democracy?', Foreign Policy Association Lecture, New York, May 24 (Available from: http://www.fpa.org/calendar_url2420/calendar_url_show.htm?doc_id=273305).

Fukuyama, F. (2006a) 'Identity, Immigration, and Liberal Democracy', *Journal of Democracy* 17 (2): 5–20.

Fukuyama, F. (2006b) *After the Neocons: America at the Crossroads*. London: Profile.

Fukuyama, F. (2007) *America at the Crossroads: Democracy, Power, and the Neoconservative Legacy*. New Haven, CT: Yale University Press.

Fukuyama, F. (2010) 'What Became of the "Freedom Agenda"?', *Wall Street Journal Online* (Available from: http://online.wsj.com/article/SB10001424052748703630404575053710666766720.html).

Fukuyama, F. and McFaul, M. (2007) 'Should Democracy Be Promoted or Demoted?', *Washington Quarterly* 31 (1): 23–45.

G8–BMENA. (2006) 'The G8 & the Broader Middle East and North Africa' (Available from: http://g8bmena.org/).

Gadamer, H.-G. (1994) 'Preface'. In Grondin, J. (ed.), *Introduction to Philosophical Hermeneutics*. New Haven: Yale University Press, pp. xiii–xv.

Gadamer, H.-G. (2004) *Truth and Method*, translated by Weinsheimer, J. and Marshall, D. G. 2nd rev. edn. London: Continuum.

Gaddis, J. L. (1982) *Strategies of Containment: A Critical Appraisal of Postwar American National Security Policy*. Oxford: Oxford University Press.

Gaddis, J. L. (1997) *We Now Know: Rethinking Cold War History*. Oxford: Clarendon Press.

Gaddis, J. L. (2004) *Surprise, Security, and the American Experience*. London: Harvard University Press.

Gallup. (2009) 'George W. Bush Presidential Job Approval' (Available from: http://www.gallup.com/poll/116500/Presidential-Approval-Ratings-George-Bush.aspx).

Ganji, A. (2006) 'Money Can't Buy Us Democracy', *New York Times*, August 1 (Available from: http://www.nytimes.com/2006/08/01/opinion/01ganji.html).

Gardels, N. (2005) 'The Rise and Fall of America's Soft Power', *New Perspectives Quarterly* 22 (1): 6–19.

Gause, G. F. III (2005) 'Can Democracy Stop Terrorism?', *Foreign Affairs* 84 (5):62–76.

Gerecht, R. M. (2005) The Islamic Paradox: Religion and Democracy in the Middle East. Paper presented to the Pew Forum on Religion and Public Life, Florida, May 24.

Ghattas, K. (2011) 'How Does the US View Tunisia's Revolt?', BBC, Washington, DC (Available from: http://www.bbc.co.uk/news/world-us-canada-12200851).

Giddens, A. (1976) *New Rules of Sociological Method: A Positive Critique of Interpretative Sociologies*. London: Hutchinson.

Giddens, A. (1979) *Central Problems in Social Theory: Action, Structure, and Contradiction in Social Analysis*. Berkeley: University of California Press.

Giddens, A. (1984) *The Constitution of Society: Outline of the Theory of Structuration*. Berkeley: University of California Press.

Gills, B. K. (2000) 'American Power, Neo-liberal Economic Globalisation, and Low-Intensity Democracy: An Unstable Trinity'. In Cox, M., Ikenberry, J. G. and Inoguchi, T. (eds.), *American Democracy Promotion: Impulses, Strategies, and Impacts*. Oxford: Oxford University Press, pp. 326–44.

Gills, B. K., Rocamora, Joel and Wilson, Richard (1993) *Low Intensity Democracy: Political Power in the New World Order*. London: Pluto Press.

Glassman, James K. (2008, November 24) 'State's Glassman on Alliance for Youth Movement Summit: U. S. Partners with Private Sector for Youth Summit in New York December 3–5', US Department of State, Washington, DC (Available from: http://iipdigital.usembassy.gov/st/english/texttrans/2008/11/20081124173327eaifas0.8017237.html#ixzz1MuJsimoZ).

Goldgeier, James (2008) Personal interview at Council for Foreign Relations, Washington, DC, June 18.

Goldstein, Judith and Keohane, Robert O. (1993) *Ideas and Foreign Policy: Beliefs, Institutions, and Political Change*. Ithaca: Cornell University Press.

Gould, Harry D. (1998) 'What Is at Stake in the Agent-Structure Debate?' In Kubálková, V., Onuf, N. and Kowert, P. (eds.), *International Relations in a Constructed World*. London: M. E. Sharpe, pp. 79–98

Grey, Stephen (2004) 'America's Gulag', *The New Statesman*, May 17.

Greenway, H. D. S. (2007) 'Once Again, U. S. Policy Lies in Shambles', *New York Times*, June 19 (Available from: http://www.nytimes.com/2007/06/19/opinion/19iht-edgreenway.1.6210440.html?_r=1).

Grossberg, Lawrence (1992) *We Gotta Get Out of This Place: Popular Conservatism and Postmodern Culture*. New York: Routledge.

Grugel, Jean (2002) *Democratization: A Critical Introduction*. Hampshire: Palgrave Macmillan.

Gurtov, Melvin (2006) *Superpower on Crusade: The Bush Doctrine in US Foreign Policy*. Boulder: Lynne Rienner Publishers.

Haass, Richard (1997) *The Reluctant Sheriff: The United States after the Cold War*. New York, NY: Council on Foreign Relations Press.

Haass, Richard (2001, December 6) 'The Political Future of Afghanistan', printed for the use of the Committee on Foreign Relations: 77–065 DTP.

Haass, Richard (2009) *War of Necessity; War of Choice: A Memoir of Two Iraq Wars*. New York, NY: Simon & Schuster.

Habermas, Jürgen (1975) *Legitimation Crisis*. London: Heinemann.

Hahn, Peter, L. (2005) *Crisis and Crossfire: The United States and the Middle East since 1945, Issues in the History of American Foreign Relations*. Washington, DC: Potomac Books.

Hall, Peter, A. (1993) 'Policy Paradigms, Social Learning, and the State: The Case of Economic Policy Making in Britain', *Comparative Politics* 25 (3): 275–96.

Hall, Peter, A. and Rosemary, C. R. Taylor (1996) 'Political Science and the Three New Institutionalisms', *Political Studies* 46 (5): 958–62.

Hall, Stuart (1996) 'The West and the Rest: Discourse and Power'. In Hall, S., Held, D., Hubert, D., and Thompson, K. (eds.), *Modernity: An Introduction to Modern Societies*. Cambridge, UK: Blackwell, pp. 184–227.

Hall, Stuart (2000) "Who Needs 'Identity?'". In Du Gay, P., Evans, J. and Redman, P. (eds.), *Identity: A Reader*. London: Sage Publications, pp. 15–30

Hall, Stuart (2001) 'Foucault: Power, Knowledge and Discourse'. In Wetherell, M., Yates, S. and Taylor, S. (eds.), *Discourse Theory and Practice: A Reader*. London: Sage, pp. 72–81.

Hall, Stuart and Grossberg, Lawrence (1996) 'On Postmodernism and Articulation: An Interview with Stuart Hall'. In Hall, S., Morley, D and Chen, K.-H. (eds.), *Stuart Hall: Critical Dialogues in Cultural Studies*. London: Routledge, pp. 131–50.

Halliday, Fred (2005) *The Middle East in International Relations: Power, Politics and Ideology*. Cambridge: Cambridge University Press.

Harding, James, Wolffe, Richard and Blitz, James (2002) 'U. S. Will Rebuild Iraq As Democracy, Says Rice', *Financial Times*, London.

Hariman, Robert (2003) 'Speaking of Evil', *Rhetoric and Public Affairs* 6 (3): 511–17.

Harvey, David. (2005) *A Brief History of Neoliberalism*. Oxford: Oxford University Press.

Hassan, Oz (2008) Bush's Freedom Agenda: Ideology and the Democratization of the Middle East. *Democracy and Security* 4 (3): 268–89.

Hassan, Oz (2009) George W. Bush, September 11th and the Rise of the Freedom Agenda in US-Middle East Relations: A Constructivist Institutionalist Approach. PhD thesis, Political Science and International Studies, University of Birmingham, Birmingham, UK (Available from: http://etheses.bham.ac.uk/399/).

Hassan, Oz (2011a) Ethnographic research interviewing protesters involved in Tahrir Square Uprisings, June–October, Egypt.

Hassan, Oz (2011b) Interviews with anonymous MEPI funding recipients in Egypt, June–October.

Hassan, Oz and Hammond, Andrew (2011) 'The Rise and Fall of America's Freedom Agenda in Afghanistan: Counter-Terrorism, Nation-Building and Democracy', *International Journal of Human Rights* 15 (4): 532–551.

Hawthorne, Amy (2003a) 'Can the United States Promote Democracy in the Middle East?', *Current History* (Jan): 21–6.

Hawthorne, Amy (2003b) 'The Middle East Partnership Initiative: Questions Abound', *Arab Reform Bulletin*, Carnegie Endowment (September) (Available from: http://www.carnegieendowment.org/sada/index.cfm?fa=show&article=21581&solr_hilite=).

Hawthorne, Amy (2005) Statement of Amy Hawthorne Independent Middle East Democracy Promotion Specialist. Hearing on Redefining Boundaries: Political Liberalization in the Arab World, April 21.

Hay, Colin (1996a) *Re-stating Social and Political Change, Sociology and Social Change*. Buckingham, UK: Open University Press.

Hay, Colin (1996b) 'Narrating Crisis: The Discursive Construction of the "Winter of Discontent"', *Sociology* 30 (2): 253–77.

Hay, Colin (2001) 'The "crisis" of Keynesianism and the rise of Neoliberalism in Britain: An ideational institutionalist approach'. In Campbell, J. L. and Pedersen, O. K. (eds.), *The Rise of Neoliberalism and Institutional Analysis*. Oxford: Princeton University Press, pp. 193–218.

Hay, Colin (2002) *Political Analysis*. Basingstoke, UK: Houndmills.

Hay, Colin (2006) 'Constructivist Institutionalism'. In Rhodes, R. A. W., Binder, S. A. and Rockman B. A. (eds.) *The Oxford Handbook of Political Institutions*. Oxford: Oxford University Press, pp. 56–74.

Hay, Colin and Rosamond, Ben (2002) 'Globalization, European Integration and the Discursive Construction of Economic Imperatives', *Journal of European Public Policy* 9 (2): 147–67.

Hayek, Friedrich A. von (1944) *The Road to Serfdom*. London: G. Routledge & sons.

Heidegger, Martin (1967) *Being and Time*. Oxford: Blackwell.

Heiss, Mary Ann (2006) 'Oil, Allies, Anti-Communism, and Nationalism: U. S. Interests in the Middle East since 1945'. In Petersen, T. T. (ed.) *Controlling the Uncontrollable?: The Great Powers in the Middle East*. Trondheim: Tapir Academic Press, pp. 77–95.

Hobson, Christopher (2005) 'A Forward Strategy of Freedom in the Middle East: US Democracy Promotion and the "War on Terror"', *Australian Journal of International Affairs* 59 (1): 39–53.

Hollis, Martin and Smith, Steve (1991) *Explaining and Understanding International Relations*. Oxford: Oxford University Press.

HCFA (House Committee on Foreign Affairs) (2007) Joint Hearing Before the Subcommittee on International Organisations, Human Rights, and Oversight and the Subcommittee on Europe of the Committee on Foreign Affairs House of Representatives. Extraordinary Rendition in U. S. Counterterrorism Policy: The Impact on Transatlantic Relations, First Session, April 17.

Howard, Peter (2004) 'Why Not Invade North Korea? Threats, Language Games, and US Foreign Policy', *International Studies Quarterly* 48 (4): 805–828.

Hudson, Michael C. (2005) 'The United States in the Middle East'. In Fawcett, L. (ed.) *International Relations of the Middle East*. Oxford: Oxford University Press, pp. 283–305.

Hudson, Valerie M. (2007) *Foreign Policy Analysis: Classic and Contemporary Theory*. Lanham: Rowman & Littlefield Pub.

Hughes, Richard T. (2004) *Myths America Lives By*. Urbana: University of Illinois Press.

Huntington, Samuel P. (1968) *Political Order in Changing Societies*. New Haven: Yale University Press.

Huntington, Samuel P. (2005) *Who Are We?: America's Great Debate*. New York: Free Press.

Hurst, Steven (2005) 'Myths of Neoconservatism: George W. Bush's "Neoconservative" Foreign Policy', *International Politics* 42 (1): 75–96.

Ibrahim, Saad Eddin (2006) 'The "New Middle East" Bush is Resisting', *Washington Post*, August 23; A15.

IISS (The International Institute for Strategic Studies) (2007) 'Hamas Coup in Gaza', *International Institute for Strategic Studies* 13 (5): 1–2.

Ikenberry, John G. (2008) 'The Rise of China and the Future of the West', *Foreign Affairs* 87 (1): 23–37.

Indyk, Martin. (2002) 'Back to the Bazaar', *Foreign Affairs* 81 (1):75–88.

Ingram, Edward (2007) 'Pairing off Empires: The United States as Great Britain in the Middle East'. In Petersen, T. T. (ed.) *Controlling the Uncontrollable? The Great Powers in the Middle East*. Troudheim: Norway Tapir Academic Press, pp. 1–21.

IQ2 (2007) 'Motion: Spreading Democracy in the Middle East is a Bad Idea' (Available from: http://www.youtube.com/watch?v=b_dFFuq4tH8&feature= PlayList&p=7CAC 1BB5CE8F2887&index=0).

Jackson, Richard (2005) *Writing the War on Terrorism: Language, Politics and Counter-Terrorism*. Manchester: Manchester University Press.

Jaffe, Amy Myers and Lewis, Steven W. (2002) 'Beijing's Oil Diplomacy', *Survival* 44 (1): 115–34.

Jepperson, Ronald L., Wendt, Alexander and Katzenstein, Peter (1996) 'Norms, Identity and Culture in National Security'. In Katzenstein, P. (ed.) *The Culture of National Security: Norms and Identity in World Politics*. New York: Columbia University Press, pp. 33–75.

Jervis, Robert (2003) 'Understanding the Bush Doctrine', *Political Science Quarterly* 118 (3): 365–88.

Jessop, Bob (1990) *State Theory: Putting the Capitalist State in Its Place*. Cambridge, UK: Polity Press.

Selected bibliography

Jessop, Bob (2005) 'Critical Realism and the Strategic-Relational Approach', *New Formations* 56: 40–53.

JSP (Joint Strategic Plan) (2006) *Strategic Plan: Fiscal Years 2007–2012*, The US Department of State and the US Agency for International Development.

Juhasz, Antonia (2006) *The Bush Agenda: Invading the World, One Economy at a Time*. London: Duckworth.

Kagan, Robert (2009) 'Obama's Iran Realism', *The Guardian Online*, June 17 (Available from: http://www.guardian.co.uk/commentisfree/cifamerica/2009/jun/17/obama-iran-realism-diplomacy).

Kant, Immanuel (1999 [1797]) *Metaphysical Elements of Justice: Part I of The Metaphysics of Morals*, edited by Ladd, J. 2nd edn. Indianapolis: Hackett Pub. Co.

Kapstein, Ethan B. (1990) *The Insecure Alliance: Energy Crises and Western Politics since 1944*. New York: Oxford University Press.

Katzenstein, Peter J. (1996) *The Culture of National Security: Norms and Identity in World Politics, New Directions in World Politics*. New York: Columbia University Press.

Katzenstein, Peter, Keohane, Robert and Krasner, Stephen (1998) 'International Organizations and the Study of World Politics', *International Organization* 52 (4): 645–85.

Katzman, Kenneth (2003) *Iraq: US Efforts to Change the Regime*. CRS Report for Congress: Order Code RL31339; Updated December 10.

Katzman, Kenneth (2005) *Afghanistan: Post-War Governance, Security, and US Policy*. CRS Report for Congress: Order Code RL30588; Updated February 17.

Kaye, Dalia Dassa, Wehrey, Frederic, Grant, Audra K. and Stahl, Dale (2008) *More Freedom, Less Terror?: Liberalization and Political Violence in the Arab World*. Santa Monica: RAND Corporation.

Kennedy, Paul M. (1987) *The Rise and Fall of the Great Powers: Economic Change and Military Conflict from 1500 to 2000*. 1st edn. New York, NY: Random House.

Keynes, John Maynard (1936) *The General Theory of Employment, Interest and Money*. London: Macmillan and co. ltd.

Khalilzad, Zalmay and Wolfowitz, Paul (1997) 'Overthrow Him', *Weekly Standard*, December 1.

Kilmeade, Brian (2011) 'Credit Bush's Freedom Agenda for Egypt Uprising?', February 15 at 05:46 (Available from: http://video.foxnews.com/v/4539751/credit-bushs-freedom-agenda-for-egypt-uprising/).

Kinzer, Stephen (2003) *All the Shah's Men: An American Coup and the Roots of Middle East Terror*. New Jersey: John Wiley & Son.

Kirkpatrick, David D. (2012) 'Struggling, Egypt Seeks Loan From I. M. F.', *New York Times*, January 16 (Available from: http://www.nytimes.com/2012/01/17/world/middleeast/egypt-seeks-3-2-billion-loan-from-imf.html?ref=opinion).

Kissinger, Henry (1994) *Diplomacy*. New York: Simon & Schuster.

Klein, Naomi (2007) *The Shock Doctrine: The Rise of Disaster Capitalism*. 1st edn. New York: Metropolitan Books/Henry Holt.

Klotz, Audie and Lynch, Cecelia (2007) *Strategies for Research in Constructivist International Relations*. Armonk, NY: M. E. Sharpe.

Krasner, Stephen (1984) 'Approaches to the State: Alternative Conceptions and Historical Dynamics', *Comparative Politics* 16 (2): 223–46.

Krauthammer, Charles (2001) 'The Bush Doctrine: A. B. M., Kyoto, and the New American Unilateralism', *Weekly Standard*, June 4.

Krauthammer, Charles (2004a) 'In Defense of Democratic Realism', *The National Interest* 77: 15–25.

Krauthammer, Charles (2004b) 'Democratic Realism: An American Foreign Policy for a Unipolar World', Irving Kristol Lecture at AEI Annual Dinner; Washington, DC (Available from: http://www.aei.org/publications/pubID.19912,filter.all/pub_detail. asp).

Krauthammer, Charles (2005) 'Three Cheers for the Bush Doctrine', *Time Magazine*, March 7 (Available from: http://www.time.com/time/columnist/krauthammer/article/0,9565,1035052,00.html).

Krauthammer, Charles (2011a) 'From Freedom Agenda to Freedom Doctrine', *Washington Post*, February 10 (Available from: http://www.washingtonpost.com/wp-dyn/content/article/2011/02/10/AR2011021005339.html).

Krauthammer, Charles (2011b) 'From Baghdad to Benghazi', *Washington Post*, March 3 (Available from: http://www.washingtonpost.com/opinions/from-baghdad-to-benghazi/2011/03/03/ABstsYN_story.html).

Krugman, Paul (2001) 'Reckonings; Guns and Bitterness', *New York Times*, February 4 (Available from: http://www.nytimes.com/2001/02/04/opinion/reckonings-guns-and-bitterness.html).

Krugman, Paul (2004a) 'Battlefield of Dreams', *New York Times*, May 4 (Available from: http://www.nytimes.com/2004/05/04/opinion/battlefield-of-dreams.html).

Krugman, Paul (2004b) 'Who Lost Iraq?', *New York Times*, June 29 (Available from: http://www.nytimes.com/2004/06/29/opinion/who-lost-iraq.html).

Kubba, Laith (2008) Personal interview, National Endowment for Democracy, Washington, DC, July 18.

Kuhn, Thomas S. (1996) *The Structure of Scientific Revolutions*. 3rd ed. Chicago, IL: University of Chicago Press.

Kurth, James (2006) 'America's Democratization Projects Abroad', *The American Spectator*, November 14 (Available from: http://spectator.org/archives/2006/11/14/americas-democratization-proje).

Laclau, Ernesto and Mouffe, Chantal (2001) *Hegemony and Socialist Strategy: Towards A Radical Democratic Politics*. 2nd ed. London: Verso.

LaFeber, Walter. (1994) *The American Age: United States Foreign Policy at Home and Abroad since 1750*. 2nd ed. (2 vols). New York: Norton.

Laffey, Mark and Weldes, Jutta (1997) 'Beyond Belief: Ideas and Symbolic Technologies in the Study of International Relations', *European Journal of International Relations* 3 (2): 193–237.

Lander, Mark (2009) 'Obama Sends Special Envoy to Mideast', *New York Times*, January 27 (Available from: http://www.nytimes.com/2009/01/27/washington/27diplo. html?fta=y).

Lantos, Tom (2005) Introduction of the ADVANCE Democracy Act of 2005 – Hon. Tom Lantos (Extension of Remarks March 3, 2005). Congressional Record; 109th Congress, Thomas E349, Washington, DC.

Lawler, Peter (2002) 'The 'Good War" after September 11', *Government and Opposition* 32 (2): 151–72.

Lawrence, Robert Z. (2006a) *A U. S.–Middle East Trade Agreement: A Circle of Opportunity?* Policy Analyses in International Economics 81. Washington, DC: Peterson Institute for International Economics.

Lawrence, Robert Z. (2006b) *Recent U. S. Free Trade Initiatives in the Middle East: Opportunities but No Guarantees*. Boston: John F. Kennedy School of Government, Harvard University, Faculty Research Working Paper Series.

Selected bibliography

Layder, Derek (1998) 'The Reality of Social Domains: Implications for Theory and Method'. In May, T. and Williams, M. (eds.), *Knowing the Social World*. Buckingham: Open University Press, pp. 86–102.

Legro, Jeffrey (2005) *Rethinking the World: Great Power Strategies and International Order, Cornell Studies in Security Affairs*. Ithaca, NY: Cornell University Press.

Lemann, Nicholas (2004) 'Remember the Alamo: How George W. Bush Reinvented Himself', *The New Yorker*, October 18: 148–61.

Leverett, Flynt and Bader, Jeffrey (2005) 'Managing China–U. S. Energy Competition in the Middle East' *Washington Quarterly* 29 (1): 187–201.

Levy, Jack (1988) Domestic Politics and War: The Origin and Prevention of Major Wars. *Journal of Interdisciplinary History* 18 (4): 653–73.

Lieven, Anatol and Hulsman, John (2006) *Ethical Realism: A Vision for America's Role in the World*. New York: Vintage Books.

Lincoln, Abraham (2003) *Quotations of Abraham Lincoln*. Massachusetts: Applewood Books.

Lincoln, Bruce (1989) *Discourse and the Construction of Society: Comparative Studies of Myth, Ritual, and Classification*. New York: Oxford University Press.

Lind, Michael (2003) 'The Weird Men behind George Bush's War', *The New Statesmen*, April 7: 10–13.

Lipset, Seymour Martin (1996) *American Exceptionalism: A Double-Edged Sword*. London: W. W. Norton.

LiteracyHub (2008) 'About the Literacy Hub' (Available from: http://www.literacyhub. org/English/about.php).

Little, Douglas (2004) *American Orientalism: The United States and the Middle East since 1945*. Chapel Hill: University of North Carolina Press.

Lizza, Ryan (2011) 'The Consequentialist: How the Arab Spring remade Obama's Foreign Policy', *The New Yorker*, May 2.

Lockman, Zachary (2004) *Contending Visions of the Middle East: The History and Politics of Orientalism*, The Contemporary Middle East; 3. Cambridge: Cambridge University Press.

Looney, Robert (2003) 'The Neoliberal Model's Planned Role in Iraq's Economic Transition', *Middle East Journal* 57 (4): 568–86.

Lowenstein, Roger (2001) 'Don't Let Patriotism Dull the Market's Edge', *Wall Street Journal (Eastern edition)*, September 19: A.20.

Lynch, Timothy J. and Singh, Robert (2008) *After Bush: The Case for Continuity in American Foreign Policy*. Cambridge: Cambridge University Press.

MacAskill, Ewen (2009) 'Barack Obama Sticks to Cautious Approach Despite Iran Upheaval: Republicans Unhappy as US President Resists Temptation to Respond to Jibes from Iranian Leaders', *The Guardian*, June 21 (Available from: http://www. guardian.co.uk/world/2009/jun/21/barack-obama-iran-protests).

MacFarquhar, Neil (2005) 'Unexpected Whiff of Freedom Proves Bracing for the Mideast', *New York Times*, March 6.

Macherey, Pierre (1978) *A Theory of Literary Production*. London: Routledge & Kegan Paul.

Mackie, J. L. (1977) *Ethics: Inventing Right and Wrong*. Harmondsworth, NY: Penguin.

Magnusson, Paul (2003) 'A Man of Many Missions: Trade Honcho Bob Zoellick Has a Strong Diplomatic Agenda', *Business Week*, 3826, 94.

Mani, Rama (2003) 'In Pursuit of an Antidote: The Response to September 11 and the Rule of Law', *Conflict, Security and Development* 3 (1): 97–108.

Mann, James. (2004) *Rise of the Vulcans: The History of Bush's War Cabinet*. London: Penguin Books.

Mann, Sean. (2007) 'A Look at the ADVANCE Democracy Act of 2007', Project on Middle East Democracy, Washington, DC (Available from: http://pomed.org/publications/newsletter/december-2007-newsletter/).

Mansfield, Edward D. and Snyder, Jack L. (2005) *Electing to Fight: Why Emerging Democracies go to War*. London: MIT Press.

Mark, Clyde R. (2006) 'Israel: U. S. Foreign Assistance'. In Lang, J. E. (ed.), *The Israeli-United States Relationship*. New York: Nova Science Publishers.

Mathews, Jessica (2005) 'Foreword'. In Carothers, T. and Ottaway, M. (eds.), *Uncharted Journey: Promoting Democracy in the Middle East*. Washington, DC: Carnegie Endowment for International Peace, pp. vii-viii.

Mazarr, Michael J. (2003) 'George W. Bush, Idealist', *International Affairs* 79 (3): 503–522.

McCarthy, Erin (2002) 'Justice'. In Collins, J. M. and Glove, R. (eds.), *Collateral Language: A User's Guide to America's New War*. London: New York University Press, pp. 125–37.

McCartney, Paul T. (2004) 'American Nationalism and US Foreign Policy from September 11 to the Iraq War', *Political Science Quarterly* 119 (3): 399–423.

McClellan, Scott (2008) *What Happened: Inside the Bush White House and Washington's Culture of Deception*. New York: Public Affairs.

McDowell, John (1978) 'Are Moral Requirements Hypothetical Imperatives?', *Proceedings of the Aristotelian Society* 52: 13–29.

McInerney, Stephen (2008) 'The President's Budget Request for Fiscal Year 2009', *Democracy, Governance, and Human Rights in the Middle East*. Washington, DC: Project on Middle East Democracy.

McInerney, Stephen. (2010) 'The Federal Budget and Appropriations for Fiscal Year 2011', *Democracy, Governance, and Human Rights in the Middle East*. Washington, DC: Project on Middle East Democracy.

McInerney, Stephen. (2011) 'The Federal Budget and Appropriations for Fiscal Year 2012', *Democracy, Governance, and Human Rights in the Middle East*. Washington, DC: Project on Middle East Democracy.

Mcmanus, Doyle (2005) 'Bush Pulls 'Neocons' Out of the Shadows' *Los Angeles Times*, January 2 (Available from: http://articles.latimes.com/2005/jan/22/nation/na-neocons22).

McNaughton, David (1988) *Moral Vision: An Introduction to Ethics*. Oxford, UK: B. Blackwell.

McNerney, Michael J. (2005) 'Stabilization and Reconstruction in Afghanistan: Are PRTs a Model or a Muddle?', *Parameters* (Winter 2005–6): 32–46.

Mead, Walter Russell (2001) *Special Providence: American Foreign Policy and How It Changed the World*. New York: Knopf.

Mead, Walter Russell (2005) *Power, Terror, Peace, and War: America's Grand Strategy in a World at Risk*. New York: Vintage Books.

Mearsheimer, John J. and Walt, Stephen M. (2007) *The Israel Lobby and U. S. Foreign Policy*. St Ives: Allen Lane.

MEPI (The Middle East Partnership Initiative) (2011) 'Where we work' (Available from: http://mepi.state.gov/where-we-work.html).

Michelfelder, Diane P. and Palmer, Richard E. (1989) *Dialogue and Deconstruction: The Gadamer-Derrida Encounter*. Albany: State University of New York Press.

Selected bibliography

Milbank, Dana (2007) 'Closed-Door Openness at Foggy Bottom', *Washington Post*, April 17, A02.

Milliken, Jennifer (1999) 'The Study of Discourse in International Relations: A Critique of Research Methods', *European Journal of International Relations* 5 (2): 225–54.

Milliken, Jennifer (2001) *The Social Construction of the Korean War: Conflict and its Possibilities, New Approaches to Conflict Analysis*. Manchester: Manchester University Press.

Milton-Edwards, Beverley (2006) *Contemporary Politics in the Middle East*. 2nd ed. Cambridge: Polity.

Mohamedi, Fareed and Sadowski, Yahya (2001) 'The Decline (but Not Fall) of US Hegemony in the Middle East', *Middle East Report* 220 (31): 12–22.

Monten, J. (2005) 'The Roots of the Bush Doctrine: Power, Nationalism, and Democracy Promotion in US Strategy', *International Security* 29 (4): 112–56.

Murden, Simon (2002) *Islam, the Middle East, and the New Global Hegemony, The Middle East in the International System*. Boulder, CL: Lynne Rienner Publishers.

Murphy, Dan (2007) 'Israel, US, and Egypt back Fatah's fight against Hamas', *The Christian Science Monitor*, May 25 (Available from: http://www.csmonitor.com/2007/0525/p07s02-wome.html).

Musharraf, Pervez (2006) *In the Line of Fire: A Memoir*. London: Simon & Schuster.

NCTAUS (National Commission on Terrorist Attacks upon the United States) (2004) *The 9/11 Commission Report: Final Report of the National Commission on Terrorist Attacks upon the United States*. New York: Norton.

NDS (National Defense Strategy) (2005) *The National Defense Strategy of the United States of America*. Washington, DC: Department of Defense.

Neep, Daniel (2004) 'Dilemmas of Democratization in the Middle East: The "Forward Strategy of Freedom"', *Middle East Policy* 11 (3): 73–84.

Nietzsche, Friedrich Wilhelm (2008 [1886]) *The Birth of Tragedy and Other Writings*. Edited by Geuss, R. and Speirs, R. Cambridge: Cambridge University Press.

NMS (National Military Strategy) (2004) *The National Military Strategy of the United States of America: A Strategy for Today; A Vision for Tomorrow*. Washington, DC: Office of the Chairman, The Joint Chiefs of Staff.

Noland, Marcus and Pack, Howard (2007) *The Arab Economies in a Changing World*. Washington, DC: Peterson Institute for International Economics.

NSC (National Security Council) (2002) 'The National Security Strategy of the United States of America' (Available from http://www.whitehouse.gov/nsc/nss.html).

NSC (2006) 'The National Security Strategy of the United States of America' (Available from http://www.strategicstudiesinstitute.army.mil/pdffiles/nss.pdf).

NSCT (National Stratgey for Combating Terrorism) (2006) 'National Strategy for Combating Terrorism', National Security Council, September (Available from: http://georgewbush-whitehouse.archives.gov/nsc/nsct/2006/index.html).

Nye, Joseph S. (2004) 'Can America Regain Its Soft Power after Abu Ghraib?', *Yale Global Online* (Available from: http://yaleglobal.yale.edu/display.article?id=4302).

Nye, Joseph S. (2007) *Understanding International Conflicts: An Introduction to Theory and History*. 6th ed. New York: Pearson/Longman.

NYT (*New York Times*) (2006) 'World Briefing | Middle East: Egypt: Mubarak's Son Meets Bush And Cheney', *New York Times*, May 16 (Available from: http://query.nytimes.com/gst/fullpage.html?res=9D0DE3D9153EF935A25756C0A9609C8B63&scp=4&sq=Mubarakper cent20Egyptper cent20oppositionper cent20crackdown&st=cse).

NYT (2012) 'Egypt's Economic Crisis', *New York Times*, January 20 (Available from: http://www.nytimes.com/2012/01/21/opinion/egypts-economic-crisis.html?_r=1).

Selected bibliography 215

Obama, Barack (2007) 'Strengthening our Common Security by Investing in our Common Humanity: Obama for America' (Available from: http://www.cgdev.org/doc/blog/obama_strengthen_security.pdf).

Obama, Barack (2008, March 2) 'Q & A: Obama on Foreign Policy', *Washington Post* (Available from: http://www.washingtonpost.com/wp-dyn/content/article/2008/03/02/AR2008030201982.html).

Obama, Barack (2009, January 20) 'President Barack Obama's Inaugural Address' (Available from: http://www.whitehouse.gov/the-press-office/president-barack-obamas-inaugural-address).

Obama, Barack (2009, January 26) 'Interview with President Obama', *Al Arabiya* (Available from: http://www.alarabiya.net/articles/2009/01/27/65087.html).

Obama, Barack (2009, June 4) 'Remarks by the President on a New Beginning', June 4. The University of Cairo, Egypt (Available from: http://www.whitehouse.gov/the_press_office/Remarks-by-the-President-at-Cairo-University-6-04-09/).

Obama, Barack (2010, September 23) 'Remarks by the President to the United Nations General Assembly', United Nations Building, New York (Available from: http://www.whitehouse.gov/the-press-office/2010/09/23/remarks-president-united-nations-general-assembly).

Obama, Barack (2011, February 1) 'Remarks by the President on the Situation in Egypt', Grand Foyer, the White House (Available from: http://www.whitehouse.gov/the-press-office/2011/02/01/remarks-president-situation-egypt).

Obama, Barack (2011, February 10) 'Statement of President Barack Obama on Egypt' (Available from: http://www.whitehouse.gov/the-press-office/2011/02/10/statement-president-barack-obama-egypt).

Obama, Barack (2011, May 19) 'Remarks by the President on the Middle East and North Africa', State Department, Washington, DC (Available from: http://www.whitehouse.gov/the-press-office/2011/05/19/remarks-president-middle-east-and-north-africa).

Onuf, Nicholas (1997) 'A Constructivist Manifesto'. In Burch, K. and Denemark, R. A. (eds.), *Constituting International Political Economy, Vol. 10*. London: Lynne Rienner, pp. 7–20.

Onuf, Nicholas (1998) 'Constructivism: A User's Manual'. In Kubálková, V., Onuf, N. and Kowert, P (eds.), *International Relations in a Constructed World*. London: M. E. Sharpe, pp. 58–78.

Onuf, Nicholas (2001) 'The Politics of Constructivism'. In Fierke, K. M. and Jørgensen, K. E. (eds.), *Constructing International Relations: The Next Generation*. Armonk, NY: M. E. Sharpe, pp. 236–54

Oren, Michael B. (2007) *Power, Faith, and Fantasy: America in the Middle East – 1776 to the Present*. New York: W. W. Norton & Co.

Orme, William (2002) 'U. N. May Broaden Peace Mission: Council Hears of Appeals for Security Outside Kabul', *Los Angeles Times*, February 7.

Ottaway, Marina (2005) 'The Problem of Credibility'. In Carothers, T. and Ottaway, M. (eds.), *Uncharted Journey: Promoting Democracy in the Middle East*. Washington, DC: Carnegie Endowment for International Peace, pp. 173–192.

Ottaway, Marina (2011) Interview with author at Carnegie Endowment, Washington, DC, November 8.

Overbye, Dennis and Glanz, James (2001) 'A Nation Challenged: Nuclear Fears; Pakistani Atomic Expert, Arrested Last Week, Had Strong Pro-Taliban Views', *New York Times*, November 2 (Available from: http://www.nytimes.com/2001/11/02/world/nation-challenged-nuclear-fears-pakistani-atomic-expert-arrested-last-week-had.html?sec=&spon=&pagewanted=all).

216 Selected bibliography

Owen, John M. IV. (2005) 'Iraq and the Democratic Peace', *Foreign Affairs* 84 (6): 122–7.
Packenham, Robert A. (1973) *Liberal America and the Third World: Political Development Ideas in Foreign Aid and Social Science*. New Jersey: Princeton University Press.
Palmer, Mark (2003) *Breaking The Real Axis of Evil: How to Oust the World's Last Dictators by 2025*. Lanham: Rowman & Littlefield Publishers.
Patterson, Eric (2012) 'Obama and Sustainable Democracy Promotion', *International Studies Perspectives* 13 (1): 26–42.
Peters, B. Guy (2005) *Institutional Theory in Political Science: The 'New Institutionalism'*. 2nd ed. London: Continuum.
Plato (1997) *Plato Complete Works*, edited by J. M. Cooper. Cambridge: Hackett Publishing Company.
Plesch, Dan (2005) 'The Neo-Cons: Neo-Conservative Thinking since the Onset of the Iraq War'. In Danchev, A. and Macmillan, J. (eds.) *The Iraq War and Democratic Politics*. London: Routledge, pp. 47–58.
PNAC (Project for a New American Century) (1998) 'Project for a New American Century: Letter to President Clinton on Iraq' (Available from: http://www.newamericancentury.org/lettersstatements.htm).
Pollack, Kenneth M. (2003) 'Securing the Gulf', *Foreign Affairs* 82 (4): 2–16.
Pollack, Kenneth M. (2004) *The Persian Puzzle: The Conflict between Iran and America*. 1st ed. New York: Random House.
Pollack, Kenneth M. (2006) 'Grand Strategy: Why America Should Promote a New Liberal Order in the Middle East', *Blueprint Magazine*; The Brookings Institute, July 22.
Polletta, Francesca (2006) *It Was Like a Fever: Storytelling in Protest and Politics*. Chicago: University of Chicago Press.
Posch, Walter (2006) 'Staying the Course: Permanent U. S. Bases in Iraq?', *Middle East Policy* XIII (3): 101–20.
Powell, Colin (2001, February 23) 'Secretary of State Colin L. Powell Press Briefing Aboard Aircraft En Route to Cairo, Egypt', aircraft en route to Cairo, Egypt (Available from: http://www.fas.org/news/iraq/2001/02/iraq-010224zsb.htm).
Powell, Colin (2002, December 12) 'Transcript: The U. S. Middle East Partnership Initiative', The Heritage Foundation, Washington, DC (Available from: http://www.heritage.org/research/middleeast/wm180.cfm)
Powell, Colin (2004) 'A Strategy of Partnerships', *Foreign Affairs* 82 (1): 22–34.
Prado, C. G. (2006) *Searle and Foucault on Truth*. Cambridge: Cambridge University Press.
Pressman, Jeremy (2009) 'Power without Influence: The Bush Administration's Foreign Policy Failure in the Middle East', *International Security* 33 (4): 149–79.
Purdum, Todd S. (2005) 'For Bush, a Taste of Vindication in the Mideast', *New York Times*, March 9.
Purvis, Trevor and Hunt, Alan (1993) 'Discourse, Ideology, Discourse, Ideology, Discourse, Ideology . . .', *British Journal of Sociology* 44 (3): 473–99.
QDDR. (2010) *Quadrennial Diplomacy and Development Review*. Washington, DC: Department of State and USAID.
Quandt, William B. (2003) 'Algeria's Uneasy Peace'. In Diamond, L., Plattner, M. F. and Brumberg, D. (eds.), *Islam and Democracy in the Middle East*. London: John Hopkins University Press, pp. 58–66.
Quandt, William B. (2005) *Peace Process: American Diplomacy and the Arab–Israeli Conflict since 1967*. 3rd ed. Washington, DC: Brookings Institution Press; University of California Press.

Rashed, Waleed (2011) Personal interview with co-founder of the April 6th Movement, Tahrir Square, Cairo, July 29.
Rauch, Jonathan (2003) 'After Iraq, the Left has a New Agenda: Contain America First', *National Journal* May 26: 1607–8.
Reid, Tim (2002) 'Senate Shows Emphatic Support for Use of Force', *The Times*, October 12, p. 20.
Reporters Sans Frontières (2003) *Israel/Palestine: The Black Book*. London: Pluto Press in association with Reporters Without Borders.
Reus-Smit, Christian (2004) *American Power and World Order, Themes for the 21st century*. Cambridge: Polity Press.
Reus-Smit, Christian (2005) 'Constructivism'. In Burchill, S., Linklater, A., Devetak, R., Donnelly, J., Paterson, M., Reus-Smit, C. and True, J. (eds.), *Theories of International Relations*. Hampshire: Palgrave Macmillan, pp. 188–212.
Rice, Condoleezza (2000) 'Campaign 2000: Promoting the National Interest', *Foreign Affairs* 79 (1): 45–62.
Rice, Condoleezza (2002, September 8) 'CNN Late Edition with Wolf Blitzer', CNN International (Available from: http://transcripts.cnn.com/TRANSCRIPTS/0209/08/le.00.html).
Rice, Condoleezza (2005, December 12) 'Foundation for the Future', Manama, Bahrain (Available from: http://bmena.state.gov/c16716.htm).
Rice, Condoleezza. (2006, July 13) 'Press Briefing by Secretary of State Condoleezza Rice and National Security Advisor Steve Hadley', Kempinski Grand Hotel, Heiligendamm, Germany (Available from: http://georgewbush-whitehouse.archives.gov/news/releases/2006/07/20060713-8.html).
Rice, Condoleezza (2006, November 6) 'Inaugural Meeting of Members of the Advisory Committee on Democracy Promotion', Washington, DC (Available from: http://2001-2009.state.gov/secretary/rm/2006/75578.htm).
Rice, Condoleezza (2009, January 15) 'Ceremony to Commemorate Foreign Policy Achievements (2001–2009)', Benjamin Franklin Room, Department of State, Washington, DC (Available from: http://2001-2009.state.gov/secretary/rm/2009/01/114092.htm).
Rice, Condoleezza (2011) *No Higher Honour: A Memoir of My Years in Washington*. New York: Simon & Schuster.
Rice, Susan and Graff, Corinne (2009) 'Can "Freedom Only" Secure Our Future?', *Mcgill International Review* Fall: 44–51.
Richardson, J. L. (1994) *Crisis Diplomacy: The Great Powers since the Mid-Nineteenth Century*, Cambridge Studies in International Relations; 35. Cambridge: Cambridge University Press.
Ricks, Thomas E. (2006) *Fiasco: The American Military Adventure in Iraq*. New York: Penguin Press.
Ricoeur, Paul (1984) *Time and Narrative Vol. 1*. Chicago: University of Chicago Press.
Robertson, Geoffrey (2006) *Crimes against Humanity: The Struggle for Global Justice*. 3rd ed. New York: New Press.
Roe, Emery (1994) *Narrative Policy Analysis: Theory and Practice*. Durham, NC: Duke University Press.
Rose, David (2008) 'The Gaza Bombshell', *Vanity Fair*, April (Available from: http://www.vanityfair.com/politics/features/2008/04/gaza200804).
Rosen, Stanley (2003) *Hermeneutics as Politics*. 2nd edn. New Haven, CT: Yale University Press.

218 Selected bibliography

Rostow, W. W. (1960) *The Stages of Economic Growth, a Non-Communist Manifesto*. Cambridge: University Press.

Rozen, Laura (2008) 'Freedom Fighters: The State of the Bush Administration's Democracy-Promotion Push', *Mother Jones*, January 11 (Available from: http://www.motherjones.com/politics/2008/01/freedom-fighters-state-bush-administrations-democracy-promotion-push).

Rubin, Barry M. and Rubin, Judith Colp (2003) *Yasir Arafat: A Political Biography*. New York: Oxford University Press.

Rubin, Barry. (1999) 'China's Middle East Strategy', *Middle East Review of International Affairs* 3 (1): 46–54.

Ruggie, John Gerard (1998a) *Constructing the World Polity: Essays on International Institutionalization, The New International Relations*. London: Routledge.

Ruggie, John Gerard (1998b) 'What Makes the World Hang Together? Neo-Utilitarianism and the Social Constructivist Challenge'. In Ruggie, J. G. (ed.), *Constructing the World Polity: Essays on International Institutionalisation*. London: Routledge, pp. 1–39.

Rumsfeld, Donald (2001, December 11) 'Ceremony for Remembrance', the Pentagon, Washington, DC, with General Richard Myers, Chairman, Joint Chiefs of Staff (Available from: http://www.defenselink.mil/speeches/speech.aspx?speechid=503).

Rumsfeld, Donald (2001, November 21) 'Address to the Men and Women of Fort Bragg/Pope AFB', Fort Bragg, North Carolina (Available from: http://www.defenselink.mil/speeches/speech.aspx?speechid=499).

Rumsfeld, Donald (2001, October 9) 'Department of Defense News Briefing – Secretary Rumsfeld and Gen. Myers', Washington, DC (Available from: http://www.defence.gov/transcripts/transcript.aspx?transcriptid=2034).

Rumsfeld, Donald (2001, October 11) 'Memorial Service in Remembrance of Those Lost on September 11th', the Pentagon, Arlington, VA (Available from: http://www.defenselink.mil/speeches/speech.aspx?speechid=448).

Rumsfeld, Donald (2001, October 12) 'Secretary Rumsfeld Interview with the New York Times', interview with Tom Shanker, *New York Times* (Available from: http://www.defence.gov/transcripts/transcript.aspx?transcriptid=2097).

Rumsfeld, Donald (2001, September 14) 'Cabinet Meeting Prayer on the National Day of Prayer and Remembrance', no location specified (Available from: http://www.defenselink.mil/speeches/speech.aspx?speechid=437).

Rumsfeld, Donald (2001, September 18) 'DoD News Briefing – Secretary Rumsfeld', the Pentagon (Available from: http://www.defenselink.mil/transcripts/transcript.aspx?transcriptid=1893).

Rumsfeld, Donald (2002, May 9) 'Secretary of Defense Donald H. Rumsfeld speaking at Tribute to Milton Friedman', the White House (Available from: http://www.defenselink.mil/speeches/speech.aspx?speechid=216).

Rumsfeld, Donald (2006, December 7) 'Interview with Secretary Donald Rumsfeld and Cal Thomas of Fox News Watch', location undisclosed (Available from: http://www.defenselink.mil/transcripts/transcript.aspx?transcriptid=3824).

Rumsfeld, Donald (2006, July 6) 'Secretary of Defense Donald Rumsfeld Interviews with Mr. Bob Woodward', location undisclosed, released by DOD on October 2, 2006 (Available from: http://www.defenselink.mil/Transcripts/Transcript.aspx?TranscriptID=3744).

Rumsfeld, Donald (2011) *Known and Unknown: A Memoir*. New York: Sentinel.

Rycroft, Matthew (2005) 'The Secret Downing Street Memo', *Sunday Times Online*, May 1 (Available from: http://www.timesonline.co.uk/tol/news/politics/election2005/article387390.ece).

Sadiki, Larabi (2010) 'Tunisia: The Battle of Sidi Bouzid' (Available from: http://english. aljazeera.net/indepth/opinion/2010/12/20101227142811755739.html).
Said, Edward W. ([1978] 2003) *Orientalism*. St Ives: Penguin Books.
Salameh, Mamdouh G. (2003) 'Quest for Middle East Oil: the US versus the Asia-Pacific Region', *Energy Policy* 33 (11): 1085–91.
Schmidt, Donald E. (2005) *The Folly of War: American Foreign Policy, 1898–2005*. New York: Algora Pub.
Schmidt, Vivien (2000) 'Democracy and Discourse in an Integrating Europe and a Globalizing World', *European Law Journal* 6 (3): 277–300.
Schmidt, Vivien (2006) 'Institutionalism'. In Hay, C., Lister, M. and Marsh, D. (eds.), *The State: Theories and Issues*. Basingstoke: Palgrave Macmillan, pp. 98–117.
Searle, John R. (1995) *The Construction of Social Reality*. New York: Free Press.
Searle, John R. (2004) *Mind: A Brief Introduction*. Oxford: Oxford University Press.
Searle, John R. (2005 [1969]) *Speech Acts: An Essay in the Philosophy of Language*. London: Cambridge University Press.
Searle, John R. (2007) *Freedom and Neurobiology: Reflections on Free Will, Language, and Political Power, Columbia Themes in Philosophy*. New York: Columbia University Press.
Senior State Department Official A. (2011) Personal interview between the author and Senior State Department Official in Washington, DC, November.
Senior State Department Official B. (2011) Personal interview between the author and Senior State Department Official in Washington, DC, November.
Shahine, Gihan (2006) 'Two to Go', *Al-Ahram Weekly*, June 15–21, Issue No. 799 (Available from: http://weekly.ahram.org.eg/2006/799/eg22.htm).
Sharp, Jeremy M. (2005a) *The Middle East Partnership Initiative: An Overview*. CRS Report for Congress: Order Code RS21457; Updated February 8.
Sharp, Jeremy M. (2005b) *The Broader Middle East and North Africa Initiative: An Overview*. CRS Report for Congress: Order Code RS22053.
Sharp, Jeremy M. (2006) *US Democracy Promotion Policy in the Middle East: The Islamist Dilemma*. CRS Report for Congress: Order Code RL33486; Updated June 15.
Sharp, Jeremy M. (2007) *Egypt: Background and U. S. Relations*. CRS Report for Congress: Order Code RL33003; Updated March 29.
Sharp, Jeremy M. (2009) *Syria: Background and US Relations*. CRS Report for Congress: Order Code RL33487; Updated March 11.
Sharp, Jeremy M. (2011) US Foreign Assistance to the Middle East: Historical Background, Recent Trends, and the FY2011 Request. CRS Report for Congress: Order Code RL32260; Updated June 15.
Sharpcott, Richard (1994) 'Conversation and Coexistence: Gadamer and the Interpretation of International Society', *Millennium* 23 (1): 57–83.
Sick, Gary, Parsi, Trita, Takeyh, Ray and Slavin, Barbara (2008) 'Iran's Strategic Concerns and US Interests', *Middle East Policy* 15 (1): 1–18.
Silberstein, Sandra (2002) *War of Words: Language, Politics and 9/11*. London: Routledge.
Singer, Peter (2004) *The President of Good and Evil: Taking G. W. Bush Seriously*. London: Granta Books.
Skinner, Quentin (2006) 'A Third Conception of Liberty'. In Miller, D. (ed.) *The Liberty Reader*. Boulder, CL: Paradigm Publishers, pp. 243–265.
Slack, Jennifer Daryl (1996) 'The Theory and Method of Articulation in Cultural Studies'. In Hall, S., Morley, D and Chen, K.-H. (eds.), *Stuart Hall: Critical Dialogues in Cultural Studies*. London: Routledge, pp. 112–27.

Selected bibliography

Slackman, Michael (2007) 'Rice Speaks Softly in Egypt, Avoiding Democracy Push', *New York Times*, January 16.

Sluglett, Peter (2005) 'The Cold War in the Middle East'. In Fawcett, L. (ed.), *International Relations of the Middle East*. Oxford: Oxford University Press, pp. 41–58.

Smith, Steve (2002) 'US Democracy Promotion: Critical Questions' In Cox, M., Ikenberry, G. J. and Inoguchi, T. (eds.), *American Democracy Promotion: Impulses, Strategies, and Impacts*. New York: Oxford University Press, pp. 63–82.

Smith, Tony (1994) *America's Mission: The United States and the Worldwide Struggle for Democracy in the Twentieth Century*. Princeton: Princeton University Press.

Smith, Tony (2000) 'National Security Liberalism and American Foreign Policy' In Cox, M., Ikenberry, G. J. and Inoguchi, T. (eds.), *American Democracy Promotion: Impulses, Strategies, and Impacts*. New York: Oxford University Press, pp. 85–102.

Smith, Tony (2007) *A Pact with the Devil: Washington's bid for World Supremacy and the betrayal of the American Promise*. New York: Routledge.

State Department Official A. (2011) Personal interview between the author and Senior State Department Official in Washington, DC, November.

State Department Official B. (2011) Personal interview between the author and Senior State Department Official in Washington, DC, November.

State Department Official C. (2011) Personal interview between the author and Senior State Department Official in Washington, DC, November.

Steger, Manfred B. (2005) 'From Market Globalism to Imperial Globalism: Ideology and American Power after 9/11', *Globalizations* 2 (1): 31–46.

Steinmo, Sven, Thelen, Kathleen Ann and Longstreth, Frank (1992) *Structuring Politics: Historical Institutionalism in Comparative Analysis*, Cambridge Studies in Comparative Politics. Cambridge: Cambridge University Press.

Stolberg, Sheryl G. (2011) 'Still Crusading, but Now on the Inside', *New York Times*, March 29 (Available from: http://www.nytimes.com/2011/03/30/world/30power.html?_r=1).

Struck, Doug (2001) 'Fleeing Taliban Left Pakistanis in Mazar-e-Sharif' *Washington Post*, November 12 (Available from: http://community.seattletimes.nwsource.com/archive/?date=20011112&slug=insidemazar12).

Suskind, Ron (2004) *The Price of Loyalty: George W. Bush, The White House, and the Education of Paul O'Neill*. London: Simon & Schuster.

Suskind, Ron (2006) *The One Percent Doctrine: Deep Inside America's Pursuit of its Enemies Since 9/11*. New York: Simon & Schuster.

Sztompka, Piotr (1994) *The Sociology of Social Change*. Oxford, UK: Blackwell.

Talbott, Strobe (2008) 'Foreword'. In Wittes, T. C. (ed.) *Freedom's Unsteady March*. Washington, DC: Brookings Institution Press, pp. ix-xi.

Taylor, Alan R. (1991) *The Superpowers and the Middle East*. New York: Syracuse University Press.

Taylor, William B. (2011) Personal interview with the Special Coordinator for Transitions, Ambassador William B. Taylor, The State Department, Washington, DC, November.

Teimourian, Hazhir (2001) 'West "Provoked" into Bombings', BBC News, February 16 (Available from: http://news.bbc.co.uk/1/hi/world/middle_east/1174684.stm).

Thomas, Caroline (2005) 'Globalization and Development in the South'. In Ravenhill, J. (ed.) *Global Political Economy*. Oxford: Oxford University Press, pp. 317–43.

Thompson, John B. (1984) *Studies in the Theory of Ideology*. Cambridge, UK: Polity Press.

Thucydides (1972) *History of the Peloponnesian War*, edited by Warner, R. and Finley, M. I. Harmondsworth, NY: Penguin Books.

Tocqueville, Alexis De (2002 [1835]) *Democracy in America*. London: The Folio Society.
Traub, James (2008) *The Freedom Agenda: Why America Must Spread Democracy [Just Not The Way George Bush Did]*. New York: Farrar, Straus and Giroux.
Truman, Harry S. (1956) *The Memoirs of Harry S. Truman, Volume Two: Years of Hope and Trial 1946–1953*. New York: Hodder and Stoughton.
Tully, James (2008) *Public Philosophy in a New Key: Imperialism and Civic Freedom*. Cambridge: Cambridge University Press.
Turner, Mandy (2006) 'Building Democracy in Palestine: Liberal Peace Theory and the Election of Hamas', *Democratization* 13 (5): 739–55.
USAID (2005) *U.S.A.I.D. History* (Available from: http://www.usaid.gov/who-we-are/usaid-history).
USAID (2011) 'US Overseas Loans and Grants: Obligations and Loan Authorisations' (Available from: http://gbk.eads.usaidallnet.gov/docs/).
Usborne, David (2001) 'Bush Asks Arafat to Give Sharon a Chance', *The Independent Online*, February 10 (Available from: http://www.independent.co.uk/news/world/middle-east/bush-asks-arafat-to-give-sharon-a-chance-691155.html).
USDS–BNEA (2003) *The Middle East Partnership Initiative: Promoting Economic Growth* (Available from: http://2001-2009.state.gov/p/nea/rls/22250.htm).
Virilio, Paul (1991) *The Aesthetics of Disappearance*. 1st English ed. New York: Semiotext(e).
Vulliamy, Ed (2002) 'New Evidence Hints at Hijack Link to Anthrax Attacks Terrorism Crisis – Observer Special', *Observer*, March 24 (Available from: http://www.guardian.co.uk/world/2002/mar/24/terrorism.anthrax).
Wallace, Jennifer (2007) *The Cambridge Introduction to Tragedy*. Cambridge: Cambridge University Press.
Waltz, Kenneth N. (1986) 'Reflections on Theory of International Politics: A Response to My Critics'. In Keohane, R. (ed.) *Neorealism and its Critics*. New York: Columbia University Press, pp. 322–45.
Walzer, Michael (2006) *Just and Unjust Wars: A Moral Argument with Historical Illustrations*. 4th ed. New York: Basic Books.
Weisman, Steven R. (2005) 'Rice Urges Egyptians and Saudis to Democratise', *New York Times*, June 21 (Available from: http://query.nytimes.com/gst/fullpage.html?res=980DE1D9133BF932A15755C0A9639C8B63&pagewanted=all).
Weisman, Steven R. (2006a) 'Bush Defends His Goal of Spreading Democracy to the Mideast', *New York Times*, January 27.
Weisman, Steven R. (2006b) 'Democracy Push by Bush Attracts Doubters in Party', *New York Times*, March 17.
Weisman. (2006c) 'U. S. Program Is Directed at Altering Iran's Politics', *New York Times*, January 27 (Available from: http://www.nytimes.com/2006/04/15/washington/15diplo.html).
Weldes, Jutta (1996) 'Constructing National Interests', *European Journal of International Relations* 2 (3): 275–318.
Weldes, Jutta (1998) 'Bureaucratic Politics: A Critical Constructivist Assessment', *Mershon International Studies Review* 42 (2): 216–25.
Weldes, Jutta (1999a) *Constructing National Interests: The United States and the Cuban Missile Crisis*. Minneapolis, MN: University of Minnesota Press.
Weldes, Jutta (1999b) 'The Cultural Production of Crises: US Identity and Missiles in Cuba'. In Weldes, J., Laffey, M., Gusterson, H. and Duvall, R. (eds.), *Cultures of Insecurity: States, Communities, and the Production of Danger*. Minnesota: University of Minnesota Press, pp. 35–62.

222 Selected bibliography

Wendt, Alexander (1999) *Social Theory of International Politics*, Cambridge Studies in International Relations; 67. Cambridge, UK: Cambridge University Press.

Whitehead, Laurence (2003) *Democratization: Theory and Experience*. Oxford: Oxford University Press.

Wiarda, Howard J. (1997) *Cracks in the Consensus: Debating the Democracy Agenda in U. S. Foreign Policy*, The Washington Papers, vol. 172. Westport, CN: Praeger.

Williams, Kristian (2006) *American Methods: Torture and the Logic of Domination*. Cambridge, MA: South End Press.

Williamson, John (2004) 'A Short History of the Washington Consensus'. In Serra, N. and Stiglitz, J. E. (eds.), *From the Washington Consensus Towards a New Global Governance*. Barcelona: Fundación CIDOB, pp. 14–30.

Willis, Michael (1999) *The Islamist Challenge in Algeria: A Political History*. New York: New York University Press.

Wittes, Tamara Cofman and Yerkes, Sarah E. (2006) *What Price Freedom? Assessing the Bush Administration's Freedom Agenda*. Washington, DC: The Saban Centre for Middle East Policy at the Brookings Institute.

Wittes, Tamara Cofman (2008a) *Freedom's Unsteady March: America's Role in Building Arab Democracy*. Washington, DC: Brookings Institution Press.

Wittes, Tamara Cofman (2008b) Personal interview, Brookings Institute, Washington, DC, July 1.

Wittes, Tamara Cofman (2011) Personal interview with the Deputy Assistant Secretary for Near Eastern Affairs, The State Department, Washington, DC, November 10.

Wittkopf, Eugene R., Kegley, Charles W., Scott, James M. and Kegley, Charles W. (2002) *American Foreign Policy: Pattern and Process*. 6th ed. Belmont, CA: Wadsworth/ Thomson Learning.

Wolfowitz, Paul (1997) 'The United States and Iraq'. In Calabrese, J. (ed.) *The Future of Iraq*. Washington, DC: Middle East Institute, pp. 107–13

Wolfowitz, Paul (2001, December 6) 'Deputy Secretary Wolfowitz Interview with Middle East Broadcasting Centre', interview with Thabet El-Bardicy, Middle East Broadcasting Centre (Available from: http://www.defence.gov/transcripts/transcript.aspx?transcriptid=2625).

Wolfowitz, Paul (2002, October 4) 'Prepared Testimony: "Building a Military for the 21st Century"', To the Senate Armed Services Committee (Available from: http://armed-services.senate.gov/statemnt/2001/011004wolf.pdf).

Wolfowitz, Paul (2011, February 11) 'BBC Newsnight Interview about Removal of Hosni Mubarak in Egypt', aired on UK television, BBC 2, 22.30–23.10 (GMT).

Wolfowitz, Paul (2011) 'Is Mubarak's Fall in Egypt a Vindication of Bush's "Freedom Agenda"?' (Available from: http://www.foxnews.com/on-air/journal-editorial-report/transcript/mubaraks-fall-egypt-vindication-bushs-freedom-agenda).

Wolman, David (2008) 'Cairo Activists Use Facebook to Rattle Regime', *Wired* 16 (11): October 20.

Woodward, Bob (2002) *Bush at War*. London: Simon and Schuster.

Woodward, Bob (2004) *Plan of Attack*. London: Pocket Books.

Woodward, Bob (2006) *State of Denial*. New York: Simon & Schuster.

Xu, Xiaojie (2000) 'China and the Middle East: Cross-Investment in the Energy Sector', *Middle East Policy* 7 (3): 122–36.

Yaqub, Salim (2004) *Containing Arab Nationalism: The Eisenhower Doctrine and the Middle East*. Chapel Hill: University of North Carolina Press.

Yergin, Daniel (1991) *The Prize: The Epic Quest for Oil, Money, and Power*. New York: Simon & Schuster.

Yergin, Daniel (1993) 'The Prize: Empires of Oil', BBC, UK (Available from: http://video.google.com/videoplay?docid=-2875384919976618602).

Young, John W. and Kent, John (2004) *International Relations since 1945: A Global History*. Oxford: Oxford University Press.

Zakaria, Fareed (2004) *The Future of Freedom: Illiberal Democracy at Home and Abroad*. New York: W. W. Norton & Co.

Zakaria, Fareed (2009) 'The Post-Imperial Presidency', *Newsweek*, December 5 (Available from: http://www.newsweek.com/id/225824).

Zehfuss, Maja (2002) *Constructivism in International Relations: The Politics of Reality*, Cambridge Studies in International Relations; 83. Cambridge: Cambridge University Press.

Zehfuss, Maja (2003) Forget September 11. *Third World Quarterly* 24 (3): 523–28.

Zoellick, Robert B. (2001, September 20) 'Countering Terror with Trade', *Washington Post*, A35.

Zoellick, Robert B. (2003, June 23) 'Global Trade and the Middle East', World Economic Forum, Dead Sea, Jordan (Available from: http://www.ustr.gov/Document_Library/USTR_Speeches/2003/Global_Trade_the_Middle_East.html).

Zoubir, Yahia H. (2009) 'The US and Tunisia: Model of Stable Relations'. In Looney, E. R. (ed.) *Handbook of US–Middle East Relations: Formative Factors and Regional Perspectives*. London: Routledge, pp. 249–61.

Zunes, Stephen (2003) *Tinderbox: U. S. Foreign Policy and the Roots of Terrorism*. London: Zed Books.

Index

Abbas, Mahmoud 135
Abu Dhabi 168
Abu Ghraib prison 24–5, 154
Afghanistan 8, 89–107, 109, 112, 117, 120, 122, 124, 126, 130, 134–5, 157, 159, 161, 183, 191–2; Basra 115; Bonn agreement 98–9, 108, 192; Kabul 99, 104–5, 108–10, 115; Mazar-e-Sharif 104
Africa, Sub-Sahara 131
agency–structure 7, 32–37, 41, 182, 187–8
Ahmadinejad, Mahmoud 161
Ajami, Fouad 128, 192
Al-Arabiya 161
al-Assad, Bashar 175
al-Qaeda 6, 19, 22–3, 93, 98–9, 104, 120, 180
Albright, Madeline 27–8
Algeria 2, 20, 193
Allawi, Ali Abdul-Amir 146
Althusser, Louis 48–9
American Enterprise Institute 125, 192
Annapolis Peace Conference 133
anthrax 110–12
appeasement 85–6
April 6th Movement 25, 166
Arab Human Development Report (2002) 128
Arafat, Yasir 69, 118; death of 135
Armitage, Richard 95, 186
articulation 45–8
Ashcroft, John 72, 74
assistance: democracy 25, 29, 126, 130, 132–3, 148, 176, 179; foreign military and economic 13–15, 18, 29, 164, 186
authoritarian/autocratic regimes 2–3, 9, 13, 21–2, 24–5, 29, 130, 137, 139–40, 144, 149–53, 172–4, 176, 183

Bahrain 2, 22, 132, 133, 175–6, 193
ballistic missiles 17, 62, 109–10
banking 133, 150
behaviouralism 47, 187, 188, 189
Ben Ali, Zine El Abidine 1–2, 171
Bentham, Jeremy 66
Berlin, Isaiah 153–4, 185, 194
BlackBerry Messenger 1
Blair, Tony 4, 27, 109, 182, 183
Bletchley II meeting 8, 112, 116, 124, 138, 183, 192, 193
bloggers 1, 141
Broader Middle East and North Africa agreement (BMENA) 12, 126, 132–4, 148–9, 193, 194
Bolton, John 186
Bosnia, avoid another 98
Bouazizi, Mohammed 1, 172, 178
Brahimi, Lakhdar 98–9
Bremer, Paul 145–7
Britain 11, 13, 15, 152, 186
Bush, George H.W.
Bush, George W.: administration 3–9, 11–13, 15, 18–19, 21, 23–30, 56–156, 157–67, 169–70, 172, 176–8, 180, 181–5; Bush Doctrine 4, 9, 21, 27, 78, 140; Harvard Business School 66–7; Presidential candidacy 56–68, 70, 94, 189, 193; religion 81; War Cabinet 113

caliphate 23
capitalism 63–67, 145, 149, 188
CAQDAS (computer-assisted qualitative data analysis software) 53–5
Carothers, Thomas 25, 28, 58–9, 144, 150, 159, 174–5
Carpenter, J. Scott 139, 141–2, 184, 194
Carter, Jimmy 14

Index

Chalabi, Ahmed 70
Cheney, Elizabeth (Liz) 25, 127–9, 142, 193
Cheney, Richard (Dick) 27, 69, 70, 83, 96, 109, 113, 115, 146, 192, 193
China 17, 57, 63, 66, 70, 189, 194; Chinese workers in Iraq 70
Clinton, Hillary 159, 161, 163, 164, 166, 167, 173–4, 180
Clinton, William Jefferson (Bill) 26, 27, 59–60, 68–71, 95, 115, 150, 190, 191, 193
coalition against terror 99, 105
Coalition Provisional Authority 142, 145–6
Cohen, Eliot A. 95
Cohen, Jared 162, 165–7
Cold War 13–17, 57, 65, 115, 163; post-Cold War 7, 15, 56–62, 68, 97, 105, 115, 123, 155, 182, 192
conflict of interests problem 6, 19, 117, 127, 130, 136–9, 171, 174, 178, 180, 184, 185
Congress US 14, 27, 53, 68, 74, 102, 128, 138–9, 141, 160, 162, 186, 193
conservative pragmatism 9, 157–60, 185
conservative radicalism 9, 126–7, 140–5, 159–60, 181, 184
constructivism 5, 7, 31–7, 44—50, 54, 56, 71–2, 78, 83, 100, 116, 152, 181
containment 13, 26, 56, 60, 122
crisis 6–8, 30, 39–43, 47–52, 71, 82–4
Cyprus 193

Dasein 34–5, 43, 45, 77, 187, 188
Dearlove, Sir Richard 109
decline 7, 13, 57, 60, 159
decoupling 115, 182
Defense, US Department of 53, 91, 96, 108, 112, 129, 130, 142, 184
democratisation 6, 19–22, 29, 63–4, 98–100, 106, 114, 117, 127–8, 132, 138, 141, 143–4, 149, 153, 154, 156, 164, 171, 178, 184, 191, 192
demographics 149, 171, 176
DeMuth, Christopher 113, 192
Denmark 134
deontic power 44, 61, 106, 158
Derrida 188
de-structuring 43, 188
development 9, 11, 15, 64, 102, 119, 128, 133, 147, 149, 153, 159, 163–4, 169, 171, 175, 177
dialogue 10, 30, 49, 161, 168, 170, 185
digital/digitisation 9, 165–70, 185
Dionysian 73, 76, 83

Dobbins, James F. 97–9
Dobriansky, Paula J. 101–2, 186, 193
domination 9, 44–5, 127, 151, 154, 156, 164, 184–5
domino theory 8, 108, 115, 116, 118, 124, 146, 183, 192
dystopia 111, 114

education 65, 119, 128, 133, 148, 149, 159, 175
Egypt 2, 15, 18, 21, 22, 25, 95, 113, 116, 117, 130, 133, 135, 136, 137, 140, 141, 143, 155, 166, 168, 169, 171–9, 181, 190, 193; Cairo 2, 3, 140, 141
Eisenhower Doctrine 11, 14
elections 1, 20, 21, 37, 134–6, 140–2, 150, 161–5, 172, 175, 178
embassies, U.S. 25, 52, 137, 168, 169, 191
En-Nahda 172
Europe 4, 16, 24, 57, 106, 123, 130, 133, 134, 151, 174, 177, 179, 186, 193
evil 75–81, 84, 86–91, 99, 101, 105, 111–12, 121, 190, 191, 192; Axis of Evil 138, 142
exceptionalism, American 8, 33, 81, 87, 88
exemplarism 29, 114–5, 133, 146, 158–9, 161
existentialism 34
extraordinary rendition 24, 95–6, 139–40, 158
extremism 30, 101, 121–3, 127, 148, 164–6

fabula 72
Facebook 1, 2, 4, 166, 169, 194
FARC 166
fascism 86, 113, 121
Fatah 69, 14
Fatah al-Islam 130
Fleischer, Ari 72, 78,
Foucault, Michel 44
Foundation for the Future 133
France 11, 18, 172, 186, 189
Friedman, Milton 14, 65–6, 145
Friedman, Thomas 155
Forward Strategy of Freedom 12, 63, 123, 193
free trade 9, 63, 65, 67–8, 102, 127, 131–2, 145–7, 149–54, 163–4
Fukuyama, Francis 23–4, 57, 62, 101, 116, 186

Gadamer, Hans-Georg 34, 188
Gaddafi, Colonel Muammar 2, 167, 171, 174

Geneva Conventions 96
Georgia 166
Germany 86, 98, 134, 189
Gershman, Carl 193
Gerson, Michael 122
Ghannouchi, Mohammed 1
Ghoneim, Wael 2
Gingrich, Newt 146
Glassman, James K. 165-6
globalisation 65, 155, 163
God 63, 75-7, 80, 82, 87, 90, 100, 118, 123, 127, 136, 163, 192
Goldwater, Barry 66
Google 2, 166
Gore, Al 7, 59, 60, 150
Gore-Mubarak Commission 150
Greater Middle East Initiative 132, 193
Greece 13, 14, 29, 134
Group of Eight (G8) 132-3, 177
Guantanamo Bay 25, 96, 140, 158, 161
Gulf Cooperation Council 174
Gulf of Tonkin Resolution 27
Gulf War 1991 26, 81, 96

Haass, Richard 57, 62, 100, 107, 144
habeas corpus 95-6, 158
Habermas, Jurgen 40
Hamas 20, 136, 140, 142-3, 162, 183
Hariri, Rafik 136
Hayek, Friedrich A. 65-6
Hegel, Georg Wilhelm Friedrich 57, 147
hegemonic stability theory 7, 60-1, 124, 182
Heidegger, Martin 34, 187, 188
hermeneutics 30, 40, 47, 51, 72, 188, 189
Hezbollah 21, 136
Hussein, Saddam 24, 26, 68-70, 113-16, 120, 142
Husserl, Edmund 30, 45
Hyde, Henry 137

Ibrahim, Saad Eddin 117
idealism 11, 30, 57-9, 88, 101, 127, 134
ideological-discursive formation 5-9, 44-5, 50-1, 54, 56, 59, 66, 68, 77, 88-9, 97, 99, 105-6, 116, 124-5, 132, 136-7, 142, 145, 149, 152, 158, 177, 181-5
imperial right 9, 151-2, 164, 170, 177
interpellation 45-51, 73-5, 84, 86, 110, 118, 188
International Monetary Fund 64, 177
Intifada 68, 118, 190
Iran 2, 4, 9, 13-5, 17, 20, 62, 94, 99, 113, 142-3, 159-62, 174, 176, 178, 193

Iraq 2, 8, 12-7, 21, 24-8, 61, 68-71, 96, 103, 106-9, 112-16, 119-124, 126, 134-6, 139, 142-8, 152, 154, 157-9, 167, 182-3, 192, 193; Ba'ath Party 24, 127; Baghdad 114, 115, 192; banks 145; insurgency 21, 119-21, 136, 143, 145, 183
International Republican Institute 129, 141
International Security Assistance Force (ISAF) 99
Israel 6, 16, 18-21, 24, 68-9, 71, 115, 118, 125, 132, 133, 136, 139, 141, 150, 161, 171, 178-9, 193
Italy 13

jihad 23, 120-1
Jordan 2, 14-5, 95, 102, 131-5, 137, 143, 150, 193
justice 8, 63, 82, 84, 89—97, 99-103

Kant, Immanuel 151, 191
Karzai, Hamid 99-100
Kuhn, Thomas 37-8
Kuwait 2, 83, 135, 143, 193

Lebanon 2, 14, 21, 122, 135-6, 141, 157, 161, 193; Beirut Spring 136; Cedar Revolution 135
Leverett, Flynt 19, 23
liberalism 12, 28, 57-8, 63-4, 71, 88, 97, 113, 115, 123-4, 132, 154, 176, 188, 192; liberalisation 29, 63-4, 127, 132, 143, 150-3, 156, 178
liberty (positive and negative) 9, 30, 153-5, 170, 185
Libya 2, 22, 171, 174-6, 181, 193; Benghazi 174; Tobruk 174
literacy 133, 149

McCain, John 159, 193
Mediterranean Sea 18, 71
MEFTA (Middle East Free Trade Area) 12, 126, 131-4, 145, 14-150, 177
MEPI (Middle East Partnership Initiative) 12, 119, 126-34, 137, 141-4, 148-9, 160, 168-9, 172, 178, 193, 194; MEPI alumni 175
microfinance 133
modernisation thesis 7, 9, 23, 63-8, 124, 127, 145-6, 149, 153, 163-4, 171-2, 177, 182, 184
moral crusade 8, 78, 86-7, 89-93, 97-101, 106, 110, 112, 114, 117-18, 120, 122, 124, 159, 191

morality 8, 24, 36, 75–7, 81–3, 86–7, 134, 154, 185, 193; moral absolutism 87; moral realism 8, 77–8, 89, 91, 124
Morocco 2, 95, 130, 132, 133, 135, 143, 167, 175, 193
Mossadegh, Mohammed 14
movements.org 166
MTV 166
Mubarak, Gamal 141
Mubarak, Hosni 2–3, 53, 117, 130, 141, 155, 166–67, 171, 173–5, 178
multilateralism 62, 132–3, 138, 149
Musharraf, Pervez 95

narratives 32, 42–3, 48–52, 72, 125, 183, 188
National Defense Strategy 17
National Democratic Institute 129, 141
National Security Presidential Directive 58 (NSPD58) 157, 194
National Security Strategy (NSS) 61, 117, 147, 157
NATO (North Atlantic Treaty Organisation) 2, 94, 174–5
NED (National Endowment for Democracy) 53, 129, 158, 193
neoconservatism 3, 25–8, 57, 187
neoliberalism 7, 9, 27–8, 65–7, 102, 124, 127, 145–6, 149–55, 162, 164, 170, 177–8, 182–5
Nietzsche, Friedrich 73, 76
NVivo 53–4, 79

Obama, Barack 4, 6, 9, 53, 157–181, 185; Cairo speech 157, 165, 168; candidacy 158, 163
oil 5, 6, 15–9, 67, 70–1, 144, 186
Oman 2, 132, 193
One Percent Doctrine 109
Onuf, Nicolas 31, 34, 45, 47, 75, 187
OPEC 177
Operation Enduring Freedom 89, 92–97, 106
Operation Iraqi Freedom 107, 116
Orientalism 45

Pacific Ocean 17
Pakistan 2, 95, 109, 122, 159, 161
Palestinian Territories 20, 22, 24, 68–71, 115, 118, 122, 125, 132–3, 135–9, 142, 150, 161, 193
Palmer, Mark 138, 192, 193
Pentagon, the 23, 60, 71, 79, 83, 102, 104, 106, 112
Persian Gulf 16, 18, 19, 27, 71

Philippines 154
Plato 93, 95
Poland 166
postmodernism 31
poverty 15, 19, 22–3, 63, 117–8, 131, 133, 144, 148–9, 163
Powell, Colin 70, 95, 106, 119, 127, 149
power: deontic 44, 61, 106, 158; human spirit 62, 144
primacy 7, 59, 60–1, 94, 99, 106, 110, 124, 142, 151–6, 182
proliferation 6, 18, 110, 112, 124, 159,
protectionism 152, 176
punctuated evolution 7, 37–42, 124

Qatar 193
Quadrennial Diplomacy and Development Review 163–4, 168
Qualified Industrial Zones 150

Reagan, Ronald 14, 58, 61, 63, 65–6, 87, 181, 189, 193
realism 27, 30, 58–9, 61–2, 77–8, 89, 134—7, 159–60
rendition 24, 95–6, 139–40, 158
Republican Party 56–9, 137, 187, 190,
Rice, Condoleezza 3, 24, 69, 78, 111, 113–4, 128, 133–7, 141–3, 157, 160, 165, 192, 193
Rice, Susan 163
Roosevelt, Franklin 74
Rumsfeld, Donald 3, 27, 70, 72, 76, 79, 80, 84, 89, 91, 94, 97, 104, 108, 112–3, 119, 121, 145, 186, 191, 192
Russia 13, 189

Said, Edward 45,
Said, Khaled 2
sanctions 26, 70, 108, 136, 146, 152, 161
Saudi Arabia 1–2, 6, 14, 16–18, 113, 135, 137, 143–4, 175–6, 193
SCAF 174
Searle, John R. 37, 40, 44, 61, 188–9
securitisation 48, 52
Serbia 166
Sharia law 23
Sharon, Ariel 69,
Shia 21, 120, 136
Slaughter, Anne-Marie 160, 193
Spain 131, 134
structuralism 33–5
Sunni 120
Switzerland 134
Syria 2, 9, 14–15, 22, 94–5, 135–6, 142–3, 160–1, 167, 175–6, 193; banks 136

Tahrir Square 2, 5, 25, 53, 155, 173, 178, 181
Taiwan 63
Taliban 90–4, 97–99, 104–106
Tantawi, Mohamed Hussein 174
Tanzim fighters 69
teleological 57, 62–4, 115–17, 124, 147, 153, 165
torture 24, 95–6, 106, 140, 154, 158, 172, 191
tragedy 8, 72–7, 80–6, 100, 124, 190
transatlantic 16
transcendental 63, 67, 77, 118–9, 123–4
Truman Doctrine 13–14
Tunisia 1–2, 22, 171–7, 181, 193
Turkey 13–14, 17, 134
Twitter 1–2, 4, 161–2, 169, 194

Ukraine 166
unilateralism 62, 93, 124
United Arab Emirates 193
United Kingdom 134, 189
United Nations 2, 62, 69, 77, 98, 163,
UNSCR 1378 98
UNSCR 1386 99
UNSCR 1937 174

uranium 109, 161–2
USAID 64, 126, 128, 137, 139, 144, 148, 168, 178, 193
utopia 7, 10, 67, 87–8, 101, 114, 117–19, 147, 156, 170, 185

Vietnam War 15, 27, 105
vindicationalism 8, 29, 135, 158,

warlords 99
Wikileaks 166
Wilson, Woodrow 13, 101
Wittes, Tamara Cofman 19, 28, 130, 148, 160, 168, 175
WMD 108–14
Wolfowitz, Paul 3, 26, 70, 78, 98, 111—15, 130, 166, 186, 192
World Bank 151, 177

Yemen 2, 22, 133, 137, 139, 143, 175–6, 181, 193
youth 1–5, 69, 165–6
YouTube 166

Zakaria, Fareed 21, 159, 192
Zoellick, Robert B. 102, 131, 145, 152, 187

Printed in Great Britain
by Amazon.co.uk, Ltd.,
Marston Gate.